DICTIONARY OF CONCEPTS IN CULTURAL ANTHROPOLOGY

DICTIONARY OF CONCEPTS IN CULTURAL ANTHROPOLOGY

Robert H. Winthrop

Reference Sources for the Social Sciences and Humanities, Number 11
Raymond G. McInnis, Series Editor

Greenwood Press
New York • Westport, Connecticut • London

Library of Congress Cataloging-in-Publication Data

Winthrop, Robert H.
 Dictionary of concepts in cultural anthropology / Robert H.
Winthrop.
  p. cm.—(Reference sources for the social sciences and
humanities, ISSN 0730–3335 ; no. 11)
 Includes bibliographical references and index.
 ISBN 0–313–24280–1
 1. Ethnology–Dictionaries. I. Title. II. Series.
GN307.W56 1991
306'.03—dc20   91–6283

British Library Cataloguing in Publication Data is available.

Library of Congress Catalog Card Number: 91–6283
ISBN: 0–313–24280–1
ISSN: 0730–3335

First published in 1991

Greenwood Press, 88 Post Road West, Westport, CT 06881
An imprint of Greenwood Publishing Group, Inc.

Printed in the United States of America

The paper used in this book complies with the
Permanent Paper Standard issued by the National
Information Standards Organization (Z39.48–1984).

10 9 8 7 6 5 4 3 2 1

Contents

Series Foreword

In all disciplines, scholars seek to understand and explain the subject matter in their area of specialization. The object of their activity is to produce a body of knowledge about specific fields of inquiry. As they achieve an understanding of their subject, scholars publish the results of their interpretations (that is, their research findings) in the form of explanations.

Explanation, then, can be said to organize and communicate understanding. When reduced to agreed-upon theoretical principles, the explanations that emerge from this process of organizing understanding are called concepts.

Concepts serve many functions. They help us identify topics we think about, help classify these topics into related sets, relate them to specific times and places, and provide us with definitions. Without concepts, someone has said, "man could hardly be said to think."

Like knowledge itself, the meanings of concepts are fluid. From the moment an authority introduces a concept into a discipline's vocabulary, where it is given a specific meaning, that concept has the potential to acquire a variety of meanings. As new understandings develop in the discipline, inevitably the meanings of concepts are revised.

Although this pattern in the formation of the meaning of concepts is widely recognized, few dictionaries—certainly none in a consistent manner—trace the path a concept takes as it becomes embedded in a research topic's literature.

Dictionaries in this series uniformly present brief, substantive discussions of the etymological development and contemporary use of the significant concepts in a discipline or subdiscipline. Another feature that distinguishes these dictionaries from others in the field is their emphasis upon bibliographic information.

Volumes contain about 100 entries. Consistently, entries comprise four parts. In the first part, brief statements give the current meaning of a concept. Next, discursive paragraphs trace a concept's historical origins and connotative development. In part three, sources mentioned in part two are cited, and where appropriate, additional notes briefly highlight other aspects of individual references. Finally, in part four, sources of additional information (that is, extensive reviews, encyclopedia articles, and so forth) are indicated.

Thus with these volumes, whatever the level of their need, students can explore the range of meanings of a discipline's concepts.

For some, it is the most fundamental need. What is the current meaning of Concept X? Of Concept Y? For others with more intensive needs, entries are departure points for more detailed investigation.

These concept dictionaries, then, fill a long-standing need. They make more accessible the extensive, often scattered literature necessary to knowing a discipline. To have helped in their development and production is very rewarding.

Raymond G. McInnis

Preface

Cultural anthropology describes and interprets the culturally patterned thought and behavior of contemporary and near-contemporary societies. It is inherently pluralistic, seeking a framework in which the distinctive perspectives of each cultural world can be appreciated. This work is an effort to describe the major concepts that have shaped the discipline, treated historically and theoretically.

As an academic enterprise, anthropology dates only to the late nineteenth century. As an intellectual tradition, however, it is far older. The discipline of anthropology is the product of the European confrontation with the cultural other, an encounter spanning several centuries of exploration, trade, conquest, and colonization. The goal of this work is to set modern, theoretically explicit anthropology in its proper context, within its broader intellectual tradition. Aristotle and Rousseau, Hobbes and Marx, Turgot and Herder were all contributors to this enterprise, as much as were the acknowledged anthropologists of the past century.

As the anthropologist Cora DuBois observed, "Legitimate problems go out of fashion, not because they are resolved but simply because of what might be called the quest for generational autonomy. By the third professional generation, old questions are raised once more, but with no awareness that they had earlier and valuable formulations" (DuBois 1967:34–35). Aristotle offered (in my view) a more sophisticated concept of community than did the modern theorists of community studies such as Robert Redfield or Conrad Arensberg. Similarly, the concept of mode of production offered by Karl Marx was analytically more powerful than the parallel notions created by twentieth-century scholars such as Julian Steward, in an era that had forgotten Marx or found it convenient not to acknowledge him. This professional amnesia takes its toll. In however cursory a fashion, I have tried to demonstrate the depth of anthropology's intellectual development.

There are, however, some significant limitations to the scope of this work. The point of view is that of the English-speaking world, and the principal protagonists are American and British anthropologists, with occasional consideration of other European scholars. There is some justification for this. Britain and the United States have been crucial in the development of anthropological theory. Furthermore, anthropology remains an imperfectly internationalized discipline, with a number of national traditions embodying rather different intellectual assumptions and historical experience. Ultimately, I have had to write about that which I know. A French, Russian, Japanese, or Indian anthropologist would make a different selection of terms (screened through the filter of a different language) and would interpret them somewhat differently.

This is a dictionary of *concepts*, a compilation of key ideas. It is not a technical lexicon, defining the minutiae of kinship terminologies or subsistence techniques. Nonetheless, I have included technical terms where appropriate. Thus MARRIAGE includes definitions of exogamy, endogamy, hypergamy, and the like. DESCENT explains the (often shifting) usage of gens, sib, clan, phratry, moiety, and lineage. Such technical terms as are defined, and those concepts not meriting their own entries, are listed in the index. Throughout, references to other entries are printed in SMALL CAPS.

Above all I have tried to make the work useful not only for students, but also for colleagues, especially colleagues in other disciplines who need a guide through the anthropological labyrinth. Nonetheless, I have written primarily for students, not professors, giving the sort of information that I wish I had had on hand during my studies. Because I would like the reader to be able to move easily to the works cited, to examine key arguments in their original form, I have limited the references almost entirely to those available in any adequate college library. I have tried to let authors speak for themselves, quoting from primary sources as much as possible.

Works cited are listed in the first bibliography (References) of each article, while additional readings are offered in a second bibliography (Sources). To clarify historical developments, I have whenever possible listed references in terms of the original date of publication, with the date of the edition consulted given in brackets. Thus: Franz Boas. 1896 [1940]. "The Limitations of the Comparative Method of Anthropology." Occasional references in the text to the postwar period refer somewhat ingenuously to that era following the Second World War. A few abbreviations that are used in the references are defined in a list following the acknowledgments. Occasional references to classical authors are merely cited in the text, with standard abbreviations: thus Aristotle, *Pol.* [= *Politics*] 1253a.

The selection of terms is inevitably somewhat arbitrary. The work contains eighty entries. This was reduced from what was originally a much longer list, consolidating a number of entries made for clearer exposition. Thus the entry on INEQUALITY treats class, slavery, pluralism, rank, and stratification, as well as caste and ethnicity (which have their own entries). Incest is treated within the entry on FAMILY. Reflecting the orientation of the volume, some entries are primarily of historical significance (for example ANIMISM and SURVIVAL), while others describe quite recent developments (such as INTERPRETATION and SOCIO-BIOLOGY). The reader seeking some initial orientation might consult the entries on ANTHROPOLOGY, CULTURE and SOCIAL STRUCTURE.

In *A History of Western Philosophy*, Bertrand Russell acknowledged the enormous scope of his subject, and apologized to those many scholars more knowledgeable than he in most of the topics considered. Yet, he noted, if "this were considered a sufficient reason for respectful silence, it would follow that no man should undertake to treat of more than some narrow strip of history" (Russell 1945:x). In an era of hyperspecialization there is an urgent need to cultivate more than another narrow strip of the anthropological field. I hope the limitations of a single author are more than balanced by the advantages of a common point of view and an effective coordination of the various topics. In any case, no reader is likely to be more aware than I of the limitations and imperfections of this work, or the scope of the task undertaken.

References

DuBois, Cora. 1967. "The Curriculum in Cultural Anthropology." David G. Mandelbaum et al., eds., *The Teaching of Anthropology*. Abr. ed. Berkeley and Los Angeles: University of California Press.

Russell, Bertrand. 1945. *A History of Western Philosophy*. New York: Simon and Schuster.

List of Concepts

Acculturation
Adaptation
Animism
Anthropology
Applied Anthropology
Association
Band
Caste
Chiefdom
Civilization
Communication
Community
Comparative Method
Cultural Ecology
Culture
Culture Area
Culture Change
Curing
Custom
Descent
Development
Diffusion
Economy
Emic/Etic
Ethnicity
Ethnography
Ethnology
Ethnoscience
Evolution

Family
Folk Culture
Folklore
Functionalism
Gender
Historicism
Inequality
Interpretation
Kinship
Language
Law
Magic
Mana
Marriage
Materialism
Migration
Mode of Production
Myth
Nature
Network
Pattern
Peasantry
Personality
Primitive
Psychic Unity
Race
Rationality
Relativism
Religion

Acknowledgments

I have benefited from discussions with and encouragement from numerous friends and colleagues, including Dennis Gray, Leon Swartzberg, Bill Lyon, Keith Chambers, Anne Chambers, Ruth Heinze, Barry Hewlett, Jim Rock, Bill Ashworth, Jeff LaLande, Erland Anderson, Susan Anderson, John Kaiser, and Quentin Faulkner. Two of my teachers, Robert Spencer and Yi-Fu Tuan, deserve special thanks for showing me the possibility of serious, humanistically informed scholarship within the social sciences. I owe a debt of gratitude to Bill Simmons for introducing me to the field of anthropology.

James Sabin of Greenwood Press, and a series of editors, Mary Sive, Loomis Mayer, Mildred Vasan, and Lynn Flint, have shown considerable patience and enthusiasm. My great thanks to them. Ray McInnis, series editor, deserves special appreciation for his editorial judgment in pioneering this series, for his much-tried patience, and his strong support. I owe particular thanks to Marlyss Schwengels, the volume's copy editor, for valor above and beyond the call of duty in rescuing the manuscript from a burning building. My appreciation also goes to the staff of the Southern Oregon State College Library for their assistance.

My family (both nuclear and extended) has given me great support and shown remarkable forbearance in this project. My wife (and colleague) read and critiqued each entry, which certainly improved the result. My children encouraged me through a shrewd combination of bribes and threats. To three generations of family, Kate, Rebecca, Anna, my mother, Lee Gordon, Dick Rice and Eve Rice, my love and appreciation.

Abbreviations

AA	*American Anthropologist* (new series, unless otherwise noted)
ARA	*Annual Review of Anthropology*
CA	*Current Anthropology*
DHI	*Dictionary of the History of Ideas*, 5 vols. (1973)
DSS	Carl Darling Buck, *A Dictionary of Selected Synonyms in the Principal Indo-European Languages*, Chicago: University of Chicago Press (1949)
ERE	James Hastings, ed., *Encyclopedia of Religion and Ethics,* 13 vols. (1908–1926)
ESS	*Encyclopedia of the Social Sciences*, 15 vols. (1930–1935)
GEC	Ake Hultkrantz, *General Ethnological Concepts*, Copenhagen: Rosenkilde & Bagger (1960)
GEL	H. G. Liddell and Robert Scott, *A Greek-English Lexicon,* rev. ed., Oxford: Clarendon Press (1966)
IESS	*International Encyclopedia of the Social Sciences*, 17 vols. (1968)
JAFL	*Journal of American Folklore*
NCE	*New Catholic Encyclopedia*, 15 vols. (1967)
OED	*Oxford English Dictionary*

THE DICTIONARY

A

ACCULTURATION. Culture change under conditions of direct contact between the members of two societies.

Acculturation describes the process of cultural transformation resulting from the contact of societies. Generally, though not exclusively, this occurs under conditions of significant inequality in the scale, power, or technological complexity of the societies involved.

The term originated in anthropological writings of the late nineteenth century where, however, it was used in a far broader sense. John Wesley Powell stated in 1881 that "The great boon to the savage tribes of this country . . . has been the presence of civilization, which, under the laws of acculturation, has irresistibly improved their culture by substituting new and civilized for old and savage arts, new for old customs—in short, transforming savages into civilized life" (in De Laguna 1960:787–88). Otis Mason (in 1895) paraphrased Powell's usage in these terms: "The peoples of the earth have intermarried, traded, taught one another, lent, borrowed, and improved upon each other's activities. To this general transfer Powell gives the name acculturation" (in De Laguna 1960:788).

W. J. McGee, writing in 1898, used the term in much the same way, but added a distinction between piratical and amicable forms of acculturation. Piratical acculturation, characteristic of "savagery and barbarism," was mechanical and narrowly imitative; amicable acculturation, occurring in "civilization and enlightenment," involved a more rational and consistent integration of new technique. As an example of piratical acculturation, McGee noted that the Seri Indians "have learned to collect flotsam, and to use tattered sailcloth in lieu of pelican-skin blankets, cask staves in lieu of shells as paddles for their balsas . . . and iron spikes in lieu of bone harpoons" (McGee 1898:244). The acceptance of discrete culture traits, described by Powell, Mason, and McGee as acculturation, would today be termed DIFFUSION.

Acculturation in Boasian Anthropology

The modern CULTURE concept (as elaborated in American ANTHROPOLOGY by Franz Boas and his followers) developed originally as a response to the perceived inadequacies of nineteenth century evolutionary theory (see EVOLUTION). Emphasis was placed not on grouping societies into a few broad evolutionary grades, but on understanding each culture in its distinctiveness, diffusion providing the primary explanatory mechanism. In this view each culture consisted of a historically conditioned array of traits (domestication of dogs, ritual use of tobacco, presence of female shamans, etc.), in terms of which a given society could be compared with its neighbors.

Such a research program was inherently self-limiting. By 1920 even proponents such as Alfred Kroeber admitted the "comparative sterility" of a narrowly diffusionist ETHNOLOGY (Kroeber 1920:381). In contrast to the trait list approach, a new perception of culture was emerging that dominated the next three decades of research: "the vision of culture as built upon more or less integrated patterns or configurations of concepts and values, a 'subjective world' relative to each people" (De Laguna 1960:792).

Franz Boas's survey article "The Methods of Ethnology," also appearing in 1920, set out three new areas for investigation: the manner in which cultural behavior is patterned (i.e., organized through certain underlying premises: see PATTERN); the psychological or subjective aspect of cultural behavior; and the process of acculturation. Boas spoke of those

> who are no longer satisfied with the systematic enumeration of standardized beliefs and customs of a tribe, but who begin to be interested in the question of the way in which the individual reacts to his whole social environment. . . . Each cultural group has its own unique history, dependent partly upon the peculiar inner development of the social group, *and partly upon the foreign influences to which it has been subjected.* (Boas 1920:316–17, emphasis added)

From this perspective, the impact of one society upon another (e.g., the impact of Euro-American CIVILIZATION upon a Native American TRIBE) could not be understood merely as the addition or subtraction of discrete culture traits (as with Powell), but as a potentially major transformation of behavior, values, and mode of ADAPTATION. Acculturation was used to describe the process and the consequences of such encounters. The conditions under which culture contact occurred—the power relations holding between the two societies, the responses by the dominated culture, and the underlying cultural premises that served to explain what transpired—these became the major concerns of acculturation studies.

By the mid-1930s, the Social Science Research Council was prompted to prepare a "Memorandum for the Study of Acculturation" to clarify the concept and to encourage comparable research. Acculturation was defined as "those phenomena which result when groups of individuals having different cultures come into continuous, first-hand contact, with subsequent changes in the original culture patterns of either or both groups" (Redfield et al. 1936:149).

The Development of Acculturation Studies

A large proportion of acculturation studies concerned changes in North American Indian cultures (e.g., Linton 1940). However, such research soon extended far beyond the United States. Beginning in the late 1920s Robert Redfield began an ambitious, comparative study of four Yucatecan (Mexican) communities, chosen to represent varying degrees of acculturation (Redfield 1934; see also FOLK CULTURE). By 1940 it was possible to hold a symposium that included research reports on acculturation in the United States, the Philippines, West Africa, India, and Central America (Herskovits 1941). British anthropologists, though operating from a distinct theoretical position, and generally preferring the term culture contact to acculturation, also contributed extensively to this literature (e.g., Wilson and Wilson 1945).

Many acculturation studies of the thirties and forties had a strongly psychological orientation, examining how the acculturation process influenced modal PERSONALITY, or conversely, how traditional cultural values affected the outcome of the acculturation process (see Gillin 1942; Hallowell 1945). Other research emphasized cultural responses to disruption and acculturation, such as the development of millenarian religious movements, for example, the Ghost Dance in Native North America and the cargo cult in Melanesia (Nash 1937; Burridge 1960). Since the 1960s the concept of acculturation has been largely superseded by more theoretically complex approaches to CULTURE CHANGE (see DEVELOP MENT; SOCIAL MOVEMENT).

References

Boas, Franz. 1920. "The Methods of Ethnology." *AA* 22:311–21.
Burridge, Kenelm. 1960 [1970]. *Mambu: A Study of Melanesian Cargo Movements and Their Ideological Backgrounds*. New York: Harper & Row. An examination of the Melanesian response to acculturation through millenarianism.
De Laguna, Frederica. 1960. "[Introduction to Section VII] Method and Theory of Ethnology." F. De Laguna, ed., *Selected Papers from the American Anthropologist, 1888–1920*. Washington, D.C.: American Anthropological Association. An important source for understanding early American anthropology.
Gillin, John. 1942. "Acquired Drives in Culture Contact." *AA* 44:545–54. A psychologically oriented examination of the acculturation process.
Hallowell, A. Irving. 1945 [1967]. "Sociopsychological Aspects of Acculturation." A. I. Hallowell, *Culture and Experience*. New York: Schocken.
Herskovits, Melville J. 1941. "Some Comments on the Study of Cultural Contact." *AA* 43:1–10. A report on a symposium on acculturation studies worldwide.
Kroeber, Alfred. 1920. "Review of Robert H. Lowie, *Primitive Society*." *AA* 22:377–81. Kroeber was critical of the limited insights produced by diffusionist studies.

Linton, Ralph, ed. 1940 [1963]. *Acculturation in Seven American Indian Tribes*. Glouces-
      ter, Mass.: Peter Smith. Includes a useful synthesis on the acculturation process.
McGee, W. J. 1898. "Piratical Acculturation." *AA* [o.s.] 11:243–49. Reflects an earlier
      usage.
Nash, Phileo. 1937 [1955]. "The Place of Religious Revivalism in the Formation of the
      Intercultural Community on Klamath Reservation." Fred Eggan, ed., *Social An-
      thropology of North American Tribes*. Enl. ed. Chicago: University of Chicago
      Press.
Redfield, Robert. 1934. "Culture Change in Yucatan." *AA* 36:57–69. An early report
      of Redfield's studies.
Redfield, Robert, et al. 1936. "Memorandum for the Study of Acculturation." *AA* 38:149–
      52. Provided a common reference point for later acculturation research.
Wilson, Godfrey, and Monica Wilson. 1945 [1968]. *The Analysis of Social Change,
      Based on Observations in Central Africa*. Cambridge: Cambridge University Press.
      Exemplified a British understanding of acculturation.

Sources of Additional Information

An overview of the acculturation concept is presented in Melville Herskovits, *Cultural
Dynamics*, New York: Knopf, 1964, ch. 10. The survey article by Ralph Beals, "Acculturation," Sol Tax, ed., *Anthropology Today: Selections*, Chicago: University of
Chicago Press, 1953 [1962], is still useful, and has an ample bibliography. An excellent
account of developments in American anthropology from 1920 through 1945, the key
period for acculturation studies, is provided by George Stocking, "Ideas and Institutions
in American Anthropology: Thoughts Toward a History of the Interwar Years," G.
Stocking, ed., *Selected Papers from the American Anthropologist, 1921–1945*, Washington, D.C.: American Anthropological Association, 1976. An American case study is
provided by Margaret A. Gibson, *Accommodation Without Assimilation: Sikh Immigrants
in an American High School*, Ithaca, N.Y.: Cornell University Press, 1988.

ADAPTATION. The process of mutual adjustment between CULTURE and environment, enhancing the survival and stability of a social system.

In its broad biological sense adaptation implies that organisms undergo modification of both form and behavior to increase opportunities for survival within
a particular environment. In the context of ANTHROPOLOGY, adaptation signifies
that any culture is shaped by the interaction between environmental constraints
and subsistence strategies, that is, the particular combinations of resources,
technology, ECONOMY, and SOCIAL STRUCTURE which ensure survival within a
habitat.

While the adaptationist perspective includes a variety of theories, all assign
priority to material causes in explaining culture patterns. According to Yehudi
Cohen, "Adaptation in man is the process by which he makes effective use for
productive ends of the energy potential in his habitat. . . . Every culture can be
conceptualized as a strategy of adaptation, and each represents a unique social
design for extracting energy from the habitat" (Cohen 1968:41–42). This view
implies that the culture of a given population is profoundly structured, though
not completely determined, by the subsistence strategy it pursues. This per-

spective has been summarized by Karl Heider who contends that "there is an interrelationship between environment, subsistence, and society; that this interrelationship is systematic; and that research strategy should be directed towards describing specific systems and towards discovering the regularities or general principles of these systems" (Heider 1972:208).

Although there are numerous ways of describing and differentiating adaptive systems, a common approach is to classify them in terms of a predominant subsistence strategy. At the most general level, at least five such subsistence forms can be identified:

> **Hunting and Gathering (and/or Fishing).** Subsistence is based upon available plant and animal resources, typically involving small groups organized as migratory BANDS with a low level of economic surplus.
>
> **Pastoralism.** Subsistence is dependent upon domesticated herd animals, with the social order based on transhumant (migratory) TRIBES.
>
> **Horticulture.** The environment is transformed through plant domestication, cultivated with relatively simple technology, and supporting sedentary tribes or CHIEFDOMS.
>
> **Agriculture.** Cultivation through animal traction and complex irrigation systems yields a high level of surplus, supporting large populations organized as STATES.
>
> **Industrialism.** The economy is based on complex technological processes, with manufacturing dominant over agriculture, supporting states with very large, primarily urban populations (see URBANISM).

In each case important correlations exist between subsistence form, level of surplus, population size and density, and extent of social stratification (see Cohen 1968:48–52; see also INEQUALITY).

Intellectual Background

Interest in the relationship between culture and environment has a long history. Until the last century, however, this took the form of a geographic or climatic determinism, the assumption that environmental conditions directly mold PERSONALITY and WORLD VIEW. In this way Sir John Chardin reported on his travels in Persia (1720): "The hot climates enervate the Mind as well as the Body, lay [i.e., suppress] the quickness of the Fancy, necessary for the invention and improvement of Arts" (in Glacken 1967:553). Similarly, the German historian and philosopher Johann Gottfried von Herder (1744–1803) expounded at length on the relation between "national genius and the environment." Herder observed that "all sensual people, fashioned to their country, are so much attached to the soil, and so inseparable from it. The constitution of their body, their way of life, the pleasures and occupations to which they have been accustomed from their infancy, and the whole circle of their ideas, are climatic" (Herder 1791:10).

The idea of adaptation took on scientific significance with the advent of Darwinian evolutionary theory. The problem of explaining the variation and adaptation of species motivated much of Charles Darwin's research. Thus in visiting the Galápagos Islands, he noted that thirteen closely related species of finches had evolved, each differing in beak shape and body size, reflecting adaptations to varying diets and habitats (Lack 1953). In *The Origin of Species* Darwin was concerned with showing "how the innumerable species inhabiting this world have been modified, so as to acquire that perfection of structure and coadaptation which justly excites our admiration" (Darwin 1859:6). His solution to the problem was the theory of natural selection.

In parallel fashion, cultural EVOLUTION became the dominant paradigm of nineteenth century social science. Nonetheless, a serious examination of the interrelation (to use Heider's phrase) of environment, subsistence, and society was slow to develop. Several reasons can be suggested.

Until the advent of a more relativistic anthropology in this century (see REL-ATIVISM), Western thought presumed the superiority of civilized as opposed to so-called PRIMITIVE societies. RACE was widely assumed to determine the level of cultural achievement, and thus in the perspective of an earlier anthropology, "racial differences often sufficed to account for differences in social institutions and beliefs between savages [*sic*] and civilized men" (Forde 1970:16). Furthermore, the strongly idealist bias of Victorian anthropology discouraged the explanation of cultural difference in terms of material conditions or environmental constraints (Forde 1970:16). Finally, Europeans were presumed to transform NATURE, while non-Europeans (i.e., tribal peoples) existed within its sway. Given these assumptions, the adaptationist concern to understand the mutual influence of culture and environment was an irrelevancy.

Emergence of the Adaptationist Perspective

A concern with adaptation, seen most prominently in American anthropology, emerged as the result of several distinct developments in method and theory. These include environmental possibilism, ethnological preoccupation with CUL-TURE AREA studies, and the search for general and comparative principles underlying the diversity of cultural forms.

What has been termed environmental possibilism involves a weak form of correlation between geography and culture, holding that environmental factors establish limits on the development of cultural forms. An early example appeared in Franz Boas's study of the Central Eskimo: "The migrations or the accessibility of the game compel the natives to move their habitations from time to time, and hence the distribution of the villages depends, to a great extent, upon that of the animals which supply them with food," a point he documented in detail (Boas 1888:11). Betty Meggers's analysis of the relation between social complexity and environment offers a more recent example: "The level to which a culture can develop is dependent upon the agricultural potentiality of the environment it occupies" (Meggers 1954:815). The possibilist approach has continued to guide much research, in broad evolutionary comparisons as well as detailed ETHNOGRAPHY (see Ellen 1982: ch. 2).

The use of the culture area concept in ETHNOLOGY, common in the first several decades of this century, also encouraged the juxtaposition of environmental and cultural factors. In seeking to demarcate the major aboriginal culture regions, for example in North America, data on climate, resources, subsistence strategy, social organization, and CUSTOM were to some degree synthesized (e.g., Kroeber 1939). Although ultimately unsatisfactory, the culture area approach provided a foundation for more rigorous adaptationist theories, notably that of CULTURAL ECOLOGY.

Finally, a concern with the interrelations between the material and non-material aspects of social life emerged in American anthropology in reaction to the overly cautious ethnological reconstructions of Boasian HISTORICISM. "The solution," Elvin Hatch has argued, "was to penetrate behind custom and locate a substratum which is immune to the vicissitudes of history and which could be conceived as the foundation of the more superficial and variable features of the cultural whole" (Hatch 1973:223). Beginning in the 1930s, American anthropologists increasingly sought this substratum in issues of subsistence, economy, and environment.

In postwar anthropological theory the concept of adaptation has attained a major, and perhaps even dominant, role. The entire spectrum of cultural data has been interpreted in terms of adaptation. SYMBOLISM, RITUAL, and TABOO are now as commonly explained in materialist terms as is economy or social organization. What has been termed the adaptationist perspective currently comprises not one but a series of theoretical persuasions, differing in the degree of adherence to biological and ecological models, to evolutionary theory, to materialist philosophy, and to Marxist dialectic. See CULTURAL ECOLOGY; EVOLUTION; MATERIALISM; MODE OF PRODUCTION; SOCIOBIOLOGY.

References

Boas, Franz. 1888 [1964]. *The Central Eskimo*. Lincoln: University of Nebraska Press. An early study, heavily influenced by Boas's geographic training.

Cohen, Yehudi A. 1968. "Culture as Adaptation." Y. Cohen, ed., *Man in Adaptation: The Cultural Present*. Chicago: Aldine.

Darwin, Charles. 1859 [1952]. *The Origin of Species by Means of Natural Selection*. Great Books of the Western World, vol. 49, Darwin. Chicago: Encyclopaedia Britannica.

Ellen, Roy. 1982. *Environment, Subsistence and System: The Ecology of Small-Scale Social Formations*. Cambridge: Cambridge University Press. A modern synthesis of the ecological viewpoint in anthropology.

Forde, C. Daryll. 1970. "Ecology and Social Structure." Royal Anthropological Institute, *Proceedings*, 1970, pp. 15–29. A discussion of adaptationist theory from a British perspective.

Glacken, Clarence J. 1967. *Traces on the Rhodian Shore: Nature and Culture in Western Thought from Ancient Times to the End of the Eighteenth Century*. Berkeley and Los Angeles: University of California Press. A geographer's history of ideas bearing on European perceptions of the environment.

Hatch, Elvin. 1973. "The Growth of Economic, Subsistence, and Ecological Studies in American Anthropology." *Journal of Anthropological Research* 29:221–43.

Heider, Karl G. 1972. "Environment, Subsistence, and Society." *ARA* 1:207–26. A useful review article.

Herder, Johann Gottfried von. 1791 [1968]. *Reflections on the Philosophy of the History of Mankind*. Abr. Frank Manuel, ed. Chicago: University of Chicago Press.

Kroeber, A. L. 1939. "Cultural and Natural Areas of Native North America." *University of California Publications in American Archaeology and Ethnology* 38:1–242. A major example of the culture-area literature.

Lack, David. 1953. "Darwin's Finches." *Scientific American* 188 (4): 66–72.

Meggers, Betty J. 1954. "Environmental Limitation on the Development of Culture." *AA* 56:801–24. A comparative study on adaptation and cultural evolution, in the possibilist tradition.

Sources of Additional Information

One of the earliest texts illustrating the adaptationist view in anthropology was C. Daryll Forde's *Habitat, Economy and Society*, London: Methuen, 1934 [1963]; it provides a useful contrast with later works such as Ellen 1982 (see References). For a general discussion of anthropological theories oriented toward issues of adaptation and evolution, see Marvin Harris, *The Rise of Anthropological Theory*, New York: Crowell, 1968, chs. 22, 23. A more technical treatment of the adaptation concept is provided in Alexander Alland, Jr., "Adaptation," *ARA* 4:59–74, 1974.

A useful set of readings is provided in two volumes edited by Yehudi A. Cohen: *Man in Adaptation: The Cultural Present*, Chicago: Aldine, 1968, and *Man in Adaptation: The Institutional Framework*, Chicago: Aldine, 1971. Two somewhat more specialized collections of papers concerning cultural adaptation are Emilio F. Moran, ed., *The Ecosystem Concept in Anthropology*, Boulder, Colo.: Westview Press, 1984; and Donald J. Ortner, ed., *How Humans Adapt: A Biocultural Odyssey*, Washington, D.C.: Smithsonian Institution, 1983.

ALLIANCE. See MARRIAGE.

ANIMISM. A religious or RITUAL practice based on a belief in the existence of spirit beings.

The term animism was introduced into ANTHROPOLOGY by Edward Tylor (1832–1917), who appropriated the term (from the Latin *anima*, soul) to describe a culture PATTERN centering on a belief in spirits, often associated with ritual involving propitiation or worship. As conceived by Tylor, the animist perspective assumes that elements of the material world possess souls or spirits and that the souls of the dead persist as ghosts (Tylor 1871:2: chs. 11, 12). Such spirit beings could take wildly varied forms, inhabiting trees, streams, rocks, or fire; they could be guardians of an individual or household, or the embodiment of hunted animals.

The theory of animism is characteristic of most nineteenth century speculations on RELIGION, in two respects. First, primary emphasis was placed on the problem of origins—how did religion begin? Second, the explanation was couched in intellectualist terms. The key problem for Victorian anthropologists (who were seldom well disposed to any religious tradition) was to determine by what thought processes such mistaken notions could have come about (see Stocking 1987:188–97). In Tylor's view, "thinking men, as yet at a low level of culture, were deeply impressed by two groups of biological problems. In the first place, what is it that makes a difference between a living body and a dead one; what causes waking, sleep, trance, disease, death? In the second place, what are those human shapes which appear in dreams and visions?'' (Tylor 1871:2:12). Through such cogitations (Tylor held), the belief in spirit beings emerged.

For Tylor and his adherents, animism, "the belief in Spiritual Beings," constituted "a minimum definition of Religion" (Tylor 1871:2:8). Thus the doctrine of animism involves not only a theory of religion, but an argument as to the scope of religious phenomena. In particular, Tylor was concerned to refute arguments that there existed PRIMITIVE peoples lacking religion, rightly criticizing numerous authors for failing "to have recognized anything short of the organized and established theology of the higher races as being religion at all" (Tylor 1871:2:4; see also RELATIVISM). By arguing for the universality of the animist perspective, Tylor (1871:2:10) could strengthen the argument for cultural EVOLUTION, which sought to demonstrate a continuity in the development of social institutions from so-called primitive to civilized societies.

The Critique of Animism

Although widely accepted in the Victorian period, the theory of animism did not lack for critics. Andrew Lang (1844–1912), and after him Wilhelm Schmidt, argued that a belief in gods could not have developed from prior notions of souls and spirits (as Tylor maintained), for such "high-god" beliefs occur in a number of culturally simple societies (see Evans-Pritchard 1965:31–2). In the view of R. R. Marett, emotional experience rather than intellectual deduction offered the key to the origins of religion. In *The Threshold of Religion* (1914), Marett sought to supplement animist theory by postulating an earlier stage of religious experience, which he termed animatism, involving the experience of an undifferentiated supernatural force or power (see MANA). Emile Durkheim (1858–1917), stressing the public and social character of religion, rejected animism as the original stratum of religious experience in favor of the ritual celebration of social bonds through the mediating identity of a sacred plant or animal, termed TOTEMISM (Durkheim 1915: ch. 2).

The notion of animism as defining a distinct stage in the evolution of religion has not been sustained by modern ETHNOGRAPHY. Rather, in tribal societies a belief in spirits is normally combined with other religious patterns. For example, the Shasta of aboriginal California assumed the existence of numerous spirits, termed *axeki*. Such spirits were not conceived as an independent cultural complex; instead, both as sources of affliction and as familiars, they played an essential role in Shasta SHAMANISM (Dixon 1907:471–89).

The concept of animism retains utility as a category of ETHNOLOGY, describing a religious pattern involving a belief in spiritual beings without the elaborated theological doctrine characteristic of a literate religious TRADITION, such as Christianity or Islam. Animism is in this sense a manifestation of FOLK CULTURE and can exist side by side with more complex cult and doctrine. Melford Spiro's ethnography of animist cult and belief in rural Burma, and their coexistence with

Theravada Buddhism, provides an excellent illustration of one such complex cultural system (Spiro 1967: ch. 1).

References

Dixon, Roland P. 1907. *The Shasta.* American Museum of Natural History, *Bulletin* 17: pt. 5:381–498.
Durkheim, Emile. 1915 [1965]. *The Elementary Forms of the Religious Life.* Joseph Swain, trans. New York: Free Press. A classic work in the anthropology of religion.
Evans-Pritchard, E. E. 1965. *Theories of Primitive Religion.* Oxford: Clarendon Press. An excellent introduction.
Marett, R. R. 1914. *The Threshold of Religion.* 2d ed. New York: Macmillan. A classic discussion of taboo, magic, and animism.
Spiro, Melford. 1967. *Burmese Supernaturalism.* Englewood Cliffs, N.J.: Prentice-Hall. A sophisticated study of animist belief and its integration within a complex religious system.
Stocking, George W., Jr. 1987. *Victorian Anthropology.* New York: Free Press.
Tylor, Edward. 1871 [1958]. *Primitive Culture.* 2 vols. New York: Harper & Brothers (Harper Torchbook). The classic work in the theory of animism.

Sources of Additional Information

A sympathetic overview of Tylor's theory of religion is provided by Robert Lowie, *Primitive Religion*, 2d ed., New York: Liveright, 1948, ch. 5.

ANTHROPOLOGY. An integrated complex of disciplines that examines the development, unity, and diversity of the human species, considered from both biological and cultural perspectives.

Anthropology is uniquely ambitious among the scholarly disciplines in encompassing within its field of study the entire history of the human species: its origins, prehistoric development, and cultural and linguistic expression within living societies. Predicated on the adaptive interaction of biology and culture, the discipline of anthropology shares perspectives with the natural sciences, social sciences, and humanities, without being reducible to any one of these.

The intellectual roots of anthropology date to antiquity. A number of classical writers—Herodotus (ca. 484–425 B.C.) most notably—chronicled the distinctive lifeways of alien peoples. The expansion of exploration beginning in the Renaissance dramatically increased the European interest in such societies, an interest manifested by the antiquarian collections of exotic artifacts and the compilations of remarkable customs so common in the sixteenth and seventeenth centuries (Hodgen 1964; see ETHNOLOGY). This interest in the exotic characterized the Enlightenment writers of the eighteenth century as well, for whom such reports had a dual function, providing a sense of the diversity that human societies could exhibit and, more importantly, suggesting within this diversity the common, underlying imprint of human NATURE (see also PSYCHIC UNITY). This quintessentially anthropological concern was expressed by Jean-Jacques

Rousseau (1712–1778): "To study *men*, one must look close at hand; but to study *man*, one must learn to look into the distance; one must first observe the differences in order to discern the [common] properties" (in Lévi-Strauss 1963:11; emphasis added).

The term anthropology derives from the Greek *anthropos* (the generically human) + *logos* (discourse), though Greek usage (by Aristotle) had a quite restricted sense: the study of human nature, specifically the mutual relation of body and soul, physiology and psychology. It occurred in English from the sixteenth century, but until the nineteenth was largely confined to the realm of anatomy or natural philosophy (*OED*).

The discipline as presently understood took institutional form between roughly 1850 and 1880. In Britain, for example, James Hunt (in 1863) advocated "anthropology" to describe a new discipline, "the science of the whole nature of man" (in Stocking 1987:247), in contrast with an earlier ETHNOLOGY that had been concerned more narrowly with the origin and MIGRATION of peoples. While Hunt's Anthropological Society of London in fact provided an institutional base for a racist and antievolutionary perspective (see RACE), by the 1870s the term anthropology had been established as a comprehensive term for a nonracialist, evolutionary science of humankind (Stocking 1987:254–57; see also Brinton 1892).

The Subdisciplines of Anthropology

In the United States, at least, anthropology is conventionally divided into four fields of study:

(1) Biological anthropology, earlier termed physical anthropology, is concerned with both the development of the human species and its contemporary biological expression. It thus encompasses the study of human EVOLUTION (paleoanthropology), the form and behavior of the primate order (primatology), within which *Homo sapiens* forms one lineage, and the physical diversity of the human species (human variation).

(2) Archaeology examines human cultural expression as reflected in the artifactual record, in particular through the excavation of the remains of human settlements. It seeks to document both the specific cultural PATTERNS of past human groups and the broad shifts in the scale, complexity, and ADAPTATION of human societies manifested over the entire archaeological record (cultural evolution). Although concerned primarily with human societies preceding written records (prehistory), the study of the material remains of later societies (historic archaeology) can provide information impossible to obtain through historical documents.

(3) Linguistic anthropology, while having close ties to the field of linguistics proper, can be distinguished by a concern with the use of LANGUAGE in its social context (rather than as an abstract code) and with the interplay of cultural values and lingustic expression (see also COMMUNICATION).

(4) Cultural anthropology documents the socially established patterns of thought and behavior of contemporary or near-contemporary societies. It can be

distinguished from other social sciences by an insistence on research through open-ended participation (see ETHNOGRAPHY), by a holistic frame of reference in which any element of belief or behavior must be understood in its total social context, and by a theoretical concern with the mediation of behavior and experience by CULTURE. In both France and Britain the concept of SOCIAL STRUCTURE is given analytic priority, and in those countries the field is more commonly referred to as social anthropology.

This characterization of the subfields of anthropology needs qualification in two respects. First, the organization of anthropology varies considerably from country to country, in part reflecting national traditions regarding the respective roles of universities, museums, and governmental research, and in part differing attitudes regarding the appropriate relation of the natural sciences, social sciences and humanities. Second, to an increasing extent significant anthropological problems cut across this fourfold division. Thus paleoanthropology is concerned with the mutual influence of emerging biological capacities and cultural expression in the early stages of human evolution (Tanner 1981). Ethnoarchaeology involves ethnographic research in support of archaeological goals, examining, for example, tool making and artifact dispersion in hunter-gatherer camps (Kramer 1979). SOCIOBIOLOGY seeks to determine in what ways culturally patterned behavior is guided by the evolutionary constraints of natural selection.

Cultural Anthropology: New Directions

Far more than the other subfields, cultural anthropology has been uniquely affected by political and philosophical changes in the postwar period. However universal the intended scope of cultural anthropology may have been, in practice it has meant predominantly the study of people of color by whites, the study of BANDS and TRIBES by scholars from powerful STATES, and the study of non-Western cultures by those working within a European intellectual TRADITION. A number of scholars have documented the association of anthropology with colonial administration (Asad 1973; cf. Ogan 1975); others have criticized the supposedly conservative assumptions of much anthropological theory and research.

The transformation of so-called PRIMITIVE cultures in the later twentieth century has altered permanently the character of anthropological inquiry. Those who associate anthropology exclusively with the study of technologically simple societies, unaffected by wider forces of CULTURE CHANGE, are left with a pessimistic view of the discipline's prospects (Lévi-Strauss 1978). Others consider the intellectual task of anthropology as one of universal relevance, equally applicable to industrialized nations (see URBANISM) and to the peasant-dominated societies of the Third World (see DEVELOPMENT).

Considered in historical perspective, anthropology assumes a dual character. In principle, by investigating human experience in all societies, it should offer a broader standard against which the adequacy of one's own institutions can be better assessed. In reality, the discipline emerged as a consequence of that worldwide cultural and political dominance by the West which began in the late

Renaissance—an era that is now ending. Whether anthropology can be transformed into a discipline of global rather than merely Western significance, fostering the encounter of cultures as a dialogue among equals, remains to be seen (see Diamond 1974; Pandian 1985).

References

Asad, Talal, ed. 1973. *Anthropology and the Colonial Encounter*. London: Ithaca Press. Documents the complex relations between British anthropology and colonial rule.
Brinton, Daniel G. 1892. "The Nomenclature and Teaching of Anthropology." *AA* [o.s.] 5:263–71.
Diamond, Stanley. 1974. *In Search of the Primitive: A Critique of Civilization*. New Brunswick, N.J.: Transaction Books.
Hodgen, Margaret T. 1964. *Early Anthropology in the Sixteenth and Seventeenth Centuries*. Philadelphia: University of Pennsylvania Press.
Kramer, Carol, ed. 1979. *Ethnoarchaeology: Implications of Ethnography for Archaeology*. New York: Columbia University Press.
Lévi-Strauss, Claude. 1963. "Rousseau: Father of Anthropology." *Unesco Courier* 16:3:10–14.
———. 1978. *Tristes Tropiques*. John and Doreen Weightman, trans. New York: Atheneum. An eloquent meditation on the nature of anthropology and its prospects.
Ogan, Eugene. 1975. "Decolonising Anthropology." *Meanjin Quarterly* (Melbourne) 34 (3): 328–36. Discusses the moral and intellectual ambiguities surrounding the call for an indigenous rather than a "colonial" discipline.
Pandian, Jacob. 1985. *Anthropology and the Western Tradition*. Prospect Heights, Ill.: Waveland Press. Argues for the value of anthropology as a humanistic discipline.
Stocking, George W., Jr. 1987. *Victorian Anthropology*. New York: Free Press. An excellent history of the formation of anthropology in Britain.
Tanner, Nancy M. 1981. *On Becoming Human*. Cambridge: Cambridge University Press.

Sources of Additional Information

Two works offering well-organized (if somewhat dated) guides to the discipline, emphasizing training and careers, are Charles Frantz, *The Student Anthropologist's Handbook: A Guide to Research, Training, and Career*, Cambridge, Mass.: Schenkman, 1972; and Morton H. Fried, *The Study of Anthropology*, New York: Crowell, 1972.

Stanley Diamond, *Anthropology: Ancestors and Heirs*, The Hague: Mouton, 1980, discusses anthropological traditions, national traditions, and the development of a "critical" anthropology. In brief compass, Eric Wolf's *Anthropology*, New York: Norton, 1974, sets the discipline in its broader intellectual context.

A number of volumes offer historical orientations to the other subdisciplines. The development of biological anthropology is treated in Frank Spencer, ed., *A History of American Physical Anthropology, 1930–1980*, New York: Academic Press, 1982; and George W. Stocking, Jr., ed., *Bones, Bodies, Behavior: Essays on Biological Anthropology*, Madison: University of Wisconsin Press, 1988. On linguistic anthropology see Floyd G. Lounsbury, "One Hundred Years of Anthropological Linguistics," J. O. Brew, ed., *One Hundred Years of Anthropology*, Cambridge, Mass.: Harvard University Press, 1968; and Dell Hymes, *Essays in the History of Linguistic Anthropology*, Amsterdam and Philadelphia: John Benjamins, 1983. Regarding archaeology see Glyn Daniel, *A*

Hundred and Fifty Years of Archaeology, Cambridge, Mass.: Harvard University Press, 1976.

APPLIED ANTHROPOLOGY. The utilization of anthropological theory and methods, especially those of social-cultural anthropology, to achieve practical ends.

The notion of an applied ANTHROPOLOGY is at first glance straightforward. Nonetheless, the aims, the activities, and even the legitimacy of such a field have been widely debated. The activities aided by applied anthropology have included the administration of overseas territories, the pacification, settlement, and assistance of Native American peoples, war and counterinsurgency (the Second World War and the Vietnam War, in particular), agronomy, economic and community development, education, and a wide range of health and social welfare programs.

Applied anthropology has been variously defined. According to George Foster, applied anthropology involves research intended "to ameliorate contemporary social, economic, and technological problems" (Foster 1969:54). For Erve Chambers, "applied anthropologists use the knowledge, skills, and perspective of their discipline to help solve human problems and facilitate change" (Chambers 1985:8). An institutional definition of sorts is provided by the Society for Applied Anthropology (established in 1941): Its members are involved chiefly in social-cultural anthropology, in particular in planned social change, organizational management, and the improvement of perceived social problems. Yet while applied anthropology suggests the practical application of cultural anthropology, all subfields have their applied spheres. Examples include planned language change (for linguistics), cultural resource management (for archaeology), and forensic and engineering applications (for biological anthropology).

Emergence of a Discipline

The application of anthropology (or ETHNOLOGY) to colonial administration appears to have been first pursued in Britain. According to B. C. Brodie (writing in 1856), ethnology was "of great practical importance, especially in this country [Britain], whose numerous colonies and extensive commerce bring it into contact with so many varieties of the human species differing in their physical and moral qualities" (in Foster 1969:182). In 1904 Sir Richard Temple advocated that a school of applied anthropology be established at Cambridge to train colonial administrators, though this plan was not implemented. Shortly thereafter, however, anthropological appointments of an applied character began within the colonies and dominions: in Nigeria (1908), Anglo-Egyptian Sudan (1909), the Gold Coast (1920), New Guinea (1921), and the Union of South Africa (1925) (Foster 1969:186–89).

Much of this work concerned indigenous political systems, particularly as these were influenced by the British policy of Indirect Rule. There is in fact a striking congruence in this period between the colonialist concern for smoothly administered native dependencies, governed in an ostensibly traditional manner, and the British anthropologists' efforts to analyze tribal societies as social isolates existing in equilibrium (see FUNCTIONALISM). Nonetheless, most British anthropologists appear to have been uninterested in actively assisting colonial rule. Raymond Firth's statement (in 1936) was characteristic:

> Social anthropology should be concerned with understanding how human beings behave in social groups, not with trying to make them behave in any particular way by assisting an administrative policy. . . . Missionary, government officer and mine manager are free to use anthropological methods and results in their own interests, but they have no right to demand as a service that anthropology should become their handmaid. (in James 1973:47).

The scope of applied anthropology in the United States, at least through the 1930s, was largely defined by the problems of SURVIVAL and ADAPTATION of the American Indians. The Bureau of American Ethnology (BAE), organized in 1879 under the direction of John Wesley Powell, became the first government agency to undertake sustained ethnographic studies. Yet while Powell had urged that a scientific ethnology was essential for any humane resolution of the "Indian problem," in practice the BAE functioned largely to produce descriptive ETHNOGRAPHY. Even research that could have had significant policy applications, such as Charles Royce's analysis of federal/Indian treaty relations (published in 1899), or James Mooney's study of the 1890 Ghost Dance (Mooney 1896), were disseminated by the bureau in ways designed to minimize their political visibility and their practical effect (see Hinsley 1979).

In the 1930s, as ACCULTURATION and CULTURE CHANGE became dominant theoretical issues, anthropological research had more to offer in the domain of application. An Applied Anthropology Unit was formed within the Bureau of Indian Affairs, concerned largely with implementation of the Indian Reorganization Act (McNickle 1979). Industrial research also influenced the development of an applied anthropology, notably through Elton Mayo's multidisciplinary studies of industrial productivity at Western Electric's Hawthorne plant. Numerous anthropologists were involved in such research, utilizing not the CULTURE theory of Boasian anthropology, but the functionalist perspective of a factory as a social system, derived in particular from the work of A. R. Radcliffe-Brown (see Spicer 1977:120–23; FUNCTIONALISM). The Second World War forced policy-directed research concerning overseas cultures on a grand scale, in support of military intelligence, psychological warfare, and subsequently, administration and reconstruction. Beginning in the late 1940s, the U.S. government initiated programs of economic assistance and community DEVELOPMENT in many parts of the world, with extensive participation by anthropologists (see Goodenough 1963; Spicer 1977:130–36).

The Transformation of Applied Anthropology

Despite this history, the position of applied anthropology in the postwar period has been equivocal (see Goldschmidt 1979). In part this has reflected a polarization between academic and nonacademic perspectives, but there have been more substantive issues involved as well.

Applied anthropology has involved a strongly meliorist stance: In the name of social improvement, foreign or domestic, anthropological knowledge has been placed at the disposal of government policy. Yet if there is, to quote Lucien Lévy-Bruhl, "no science of ends, only a science of means" (in Bastide 1974:4), who is to determine desirable ends, or the social good? A perspective based on putatively universal values (modernization, progress, etc.) is potentially in contradiction with one which takes cultural RELATIVISM as a methodological assumption. In social terms, should an applied anthropology support the cultural autonomy of subordinate groups, or the policies of a dominant STATE?

Applied anthropology in the 1980s is far more diverse in aims, in methods, and in its clientele (see van Willigen 1986). To an increasing extent, target groups are not seen merely as the passive recipients of social inquiry or directed change, but as participants in guiding programs or establishing policy (see Schensul 1973). In the words of Roger Bastide, applied anthropology is to be understood "less as a rational art which is to be added to an objective science, than as a science creating itself in the action of groups and their efforts at modelling and remodelling themselves" (Bastide 1974:8).

References

Bastide, Roger. 1974. *Applied Anthropology*. Alice Morton, trans. New York: Harper & Row. Bastide stresses the dialectic of theory and practice; the clash of relativism and universal values.

Chambers, Erve. 1985. *Applied Anthropology: A Practical Guide*. Englewood Cliffs, N.J.: Prentice-Hall. A good survey, with extensive bibliography.

Foster, George. 1969. *Applied Anthropology*. Boston: Little, Brown. An overview, dated but valuable.

Goldschmidt, Walter. 1979. "On the Interdependence Between Utility and Theory." Walter Goldschmidt, ed., *The Uses of Anthropology*. Washington, D.C.: American Anthropological Association. Goldschmidt criticizes postwar anthropology for losing the productive link between theory and practice.

Goodenough, Ward H. 1963. *Cooperation in Change*. New York: Russell Sage Foundation. A major text on overseas community development.

Hinsley, Curtis M., Jr. 1979. "Anthropology as Science and Politics: The Dilemmas of the Bureau of American Ethnology, 1879 to 1904." Walter Goldschmidt, ed., *The Uses of Anthropology*. Washington, D.C.: American Anthropological Association.

James, Wendy. 1973. "The Anthropologist as Reluctant Imperialist." Talal Asad, ed., *Anthropology and the Colonial Encounter*. London: Ithaca Press. The volume focuses on British anthropology.

McNickle, D'Arcy. 1979. "Anthropology and the Indian Reorganization Act." Walter Goldschmidt, ed., *The Uses of Anthropology*. Washington, D.C.: American Anthropological Association. Describes the involvement of anthropologists in the Bureau of Indian Affairs in the Collier era.

Mooney, James. 1896 [1965]. *The Ghost-Dance Religion and the Sioux Outbreak of*

1890. Abr. ed., A. F. C. Wallace, ed. Chicago: University of Chicago Press. A classic study of a millenarian movement.

Schensul, Stephen L. 1973. "Action Research: The Applied Anthropologist in a Community Mental Health Program." Alden Redfield, ed., *Anthropology Beyond the University*. Southern Anthropological Society, *Proceedings*, 7.

Spicer, Edward H. 1977. "Early Applications of Anthropology in North America." A. F. C. Wallace et al., eds., *Perspectives on Anthropology, 1976*. Washington, D.C.: American Anthropological Association. A useful survey.

van Willigen, John. 1986. *Applied Anthropology: An Introduction*. South Hadley, Mass.: Bergin & Garvey, 1986. A recent textbook, illustrating the wide range of research now undertaken in applied anthropology.

Sources of Additional Information

Regarding anthropology's potential contribution to formulating (rather than merely implementing) government policy, see Walter Goldschmidt, ed., *Anthropology and Public Policy: A Dialogue*, Special Publication, 21, Washington, D.C.: American Anthropological Association, 1986. Current information on applied anthropology can be found in the journal *Human Organization* and the newsletter *Practicing Anthropology*, both publications of the Society for Applied Anthropology. The National Association for the Practice of Anthropology (a unit of the American Anthropological Association, Washington, D.C.) has a useful *Bulletin* series.

ASSOCIATION. 1. A group formed for a specific purpose, usually with voluntary recruitment. 2. In an ethnographic context, a group organized on a basis other than KINSHIP or territory.

Association is derived from the Latin *associare*, to join together, the root term being *socius*, united, allied, from which society is also derived. In general usage, an association is "a body of persons who have combined to execute a common purpose or advance a common cause" (*OED*). Examples in Western societies are abundant. Observing the United States in the 1830s, Alexis de Tocqueville commented that "associations are established to promote the public safety, commerce, industry, morality, and religion. There is no end which the human will despairs of attaining through the combined power of individuals united into a society" (de Tocqueville 1840:1:199). In common usage an association is a formal social group based on voluntary recruitment, with an explicit, culturally recognized function. In ANTHROPOLOGY the concept has been used somewhat more broadly, to denote any group recruited on a basis other than kinship or territory (Ember and Ember 1985:352).

The concept of association has been strongly influenced by theories of cultural EVOLUTION. From this perspective, PRIMITIVE society was organized through kinship, to the exclusion of other principles of group formation. Thus Lewis Henry Morgan argued that unilineal DESCENT systems (e.g., clans) "furnished the nearly universal plan of government of ancient society" (Morgan 1877:61). The legal research of Henry Maine supported this view, contrasting so-called primitive and modern societies in terms of the derivation of status and the character of social bonds. From early forms of society, "in which all the relations of Persons are summed up in the relations of Family," there has been an evolutionary progression to "a phase of social order in which all these relations arise from the free agreement of Individuals" (Maine 1861:99). A similar contrast, though with an opposite moral, is seen in the work of Ferdinand Tönnies: the bonds forged of common kinship and residence characteristic of rural FOLK CULTURE are contrasted favorably with the supposedly fragile and pragmatic links of association (Gesellschaft) found in urban life (Tönnies 1887; see also COMMUNITY; URBANISM).

Association as an Analytic Category

The place of associations in BAND and tribal societies was examined by Heinrich Schurtz in 1902 (see Lowie 1920:297–323) and by Hutton Webster in 1908 (Webster 1932). In 1920 Robert Lowie presented a modern treatment of the topic in *Primitive Society*, where he attacked the evolutionists' overemphasis on descent organization:

> If Morgan were right, individuals in lower cultures would differ from one another socially only as members of this or that sib [i.e., clan]. . . . [However] primitive tribes are stratified by age distinctions, by differences of sex and of matrimonial status, and affiliations with one of the resulting groups may affect the individual's life far more powerfully than his sib membership. (Lowie 1920:257)

Lowie proposed "association" to describe all "social units not based on the kinship factor" (Lowie 1920:257), though it would appear he would equally have excluded territorial units such as TRIBES.

In this fashion, association becomes purely a residual category, signifying all groups formed on a principle other than kinship or territory. This casts the net rather wide. Among traditional bands and tribes such groups would include age-sets, fraternities formed by age cohorts (see Ritter 1980; Bernardi 1985); secret societies, normally unisex associations based on rigorous initiation (see RITES OF PASSAGE), esoteric RITUAL, and supernatural powers (Little 1949); military orders, providing personnel not only for warfare, but often for police duties as well, a form of association common among many of the North American Plains tribes (Provinse 1955); unisex clubs (usually for males), open to initiates of all ages, a common Melanesian culture PATTERN (Webster 1932: ch. 1); and youth dormitories, involving both sexes under a specified age cohabiting in a pattern of sexual communism, as among the Muria of central India (Elwin 1968).

Although such forms of association are characteristic of small-scale societies with subsistence economies, other, quite different forms of association occur in urban contexts, and more generally, in STATE-level societies. It seems useful, therefore, to distinguish three patterns of association: first, as a principle of SOCIAL STRUCTURE; second, as a mechanism of urban life; and third, as a model of COMMUNITY.

1. In the examples given above, band and tribal associations structure social relations across an entire society, cross-cutting patterns of solidarity established

through kinship or territory. As Alfred Kroeber noted regarding Zuni society, "The clans, the fraternities, the priesthoods, the kivas, in a measure the gaming parties . . . cause segmentations which produce an almost marvellous complexity, but can never break the national entity apart" (Kroeber 1917:185).

2. The urbanization and industrialization of what were formerly tribally organized societies create the same pressures of anonymity and political and cultural isolation that are familiar to the urban West. In these settings membership in voluntary associations provides a basis for mutual aid, political influence, and the perpetuation of a cultural identity, yielding groups at least superficially similar to those long documented in Euro-American societies (see Little 1957; Ross 1976).

3. Through a combination of ideological distinctiveness and social withdrawal, the principle of voluntary association underlies numerous attempts to recreate community within the structure of the modern state, as witnessed by such varied forms as kibbutzim, communes, and monasteries (see Bennett 1977).

References

Bennett, John W. 1977. "The Hutterian Colony: A Traditional Voluntary Agrarian Commune with Large Economic Scale." Peter Dorner, ed., *Cooperative and Commune*. Madison: University of Wisconsin Press. Bennett describes one of the most successful communitarian societies.

Bernardi, Bernardo. 1985. *Age Class Systems: Social Institutions and Polities Based on Age*. David I. Kertzer, trans. Cambridge: Cambridge University Press.

de Tocqueville, Alexis. 1840 [1945]. *Democracy in America*. 2 vols. Phillips Bradley, trans. and ed. New York: Vintage Books. A classic ethnography of the United States.

Elwin, Verrier. 1968. *The Kingdom of the Young*. London: Oxford University Press. On the Indian youth dormitory.

Ember, Carol R., and Melvin Ember. 1985. *Anthropology*. 4th ed. Englewood Cliffs, N.J.: Prentice-Hall.

Kroeber, A. L. 1917 [1952]. "Zuni Kin and Clan." A. L. Kroeber, *The Nature of Culture*. Chicago: University of Chicago Press.

Little, Kenneth. 1949. "The Role of the Secret Society in Cultural Specialization." *AA* 51:199–212. Little describes secret societies in West Africa.

———. 1957 [1982]. "The Role of Voluntary Associations in West African Urbanization." Johnnetta B. Cole, ed., *Anthropology for the Eighties: Introductory Readings*. New York: Free Press.

Lowie, Robert H. 1920 [1961]. *Primitive Society*. New York: Harper & Brothers. One of the first comprehensive texts on social organization.

Maine, Henry. 1861 [1972]. *Ancient Law*. New York: Dutton.

Morgan, Lewis Henry. 1877. *Ancient Society*. Chicago: Charles H. Kerr. A major work of Victorian evolutionary theory.

Provinse, John H. 1955 [1972]. "The Underlying Sanctions of Plains Indian Culture." Fred Eggan, ed., *Social Anthropology of North American Tribes*. Enl. ed. Chicago: University of Chicago Press.

Ritter, Madeline. 1980. "The Conditions Favoring Age-Set Organization." *Journal of Anthropological Research* 36:87–104.

Ross, Jack C. 1976. *An Assembly of Good Fellows: Voluntary Associations in History.*
    Westport, Conn.: Greenwood Press. A broad study, with a sociological slant.
Tönnies, Ferdinand. 1887 [1963]. *Community and Society.* Charles Loomis, trans. New
    York: Harper & Row. A romantic critique of industrial society.
Webster, Hutton. 1932. *Primitive Secret Societies: A Study in Early Politics and Religion.*
    2d ed. New York: Macmillan.

Sources of Additional Information

A broad consideration of the cultural significance of associations is provided by Robert
T. Anderson, "Voluntary Associations in History," *AA* 73:209–222, 1971.

B

BAND. A relatively small and self-sufficient group, with subsistence based on some combination of hunting, gathering, and fishing, characterized by near equality of wealth, extensive reciprocity, and informal leadership.

From an evolutionary perspective, a band is the simplest and longest enduring form of human society and can be contrasted with the larger but still egalitarian TRIBE, the ranked CHIEFDOM, and the highly stratified STATE. Bands are characterized by a foraging ADAPTATION, in which a range of naturally occurring resources is sought through some combination of hunting, gathering, and fishing. A foraging adaptation contrasts with the transformation of the environment involved in food production (generally characteristic of tribes, chiefdoms, and states), whether this be through pastoralism or agriculture. In most settings— with the exception of certain unusually rich environments such as the North American Northwest Coast—foraging techniques offer only a relatively low surplus, that is, yields above that needed for immediate consumption. Wealth differences in bands are therefore minimal. Furthermore, the movement entailed in foraging makes extensive possessions impractical, hence the technical and material simplicity characterizing most band societies.

Images of Band Society

Missionaries, travelers, and colonial administrators long remarked about the material simplicity and informal political organization of band societies. From the European perspective these characteristics marked such groups as mentally and often morally inferior. Thus the Jesuit Pedro Chirino wrote in 1604, regarding the Negritos of the Philippines, that "they neither plant nor reap, and seek their livelihood only by roaming like beasts, half naked, through the mountains with their wives and children" (in Rosaldo 1982:312).

Much the same opinion was expressed by Charles Darwin, in describing the

Yahgan of Tierra del Fuego. The value placed on sharing food and possessions was held as a mark of inferiority: "The perfect equality among the individuals composing the Fuegian tribes must for a long time retard their civilization. . . . Even a piece of cloth given to one is torn into shreds and distributed" (Darwin 1832:47). From an early date this image (or better, caricature) of foraging bands was utilized as the baseline of human development, the initial or near-initial stage of cultural EVOLUTION, for example in the work of the French philosopher Condorcet (1743–1794), or the American anthropologist Lewis Henry Morgan (1818–1881) (Slotkin 1965:364–65; Morgan 1877:10; see PRIMITIVE).

Models of Band Organization

The SOCIAL STRUCTURE of band societies has been the subject of much research. In 1906 Marcel Mauss and Henri Beuchat produced an influential study of the seasonal variation in Inuit (Eskimo) band structure, depicting the transformation between summer and winter in matters of settlement PATTERN, LAW, RITUAL, and ideology (Mauss and Beuchat 1906). In the 1930s Julian Steward incorporated the analysis of band organization into his influential studies of hunter-gatherer CULTURAL ECOLOGY, drawing on earlier research by A. R. Radcliffe-Brown (1931). Steward argued that exogamous patrilineal bands—outmarrying groups organized through the principle of common male DESCENT—occurred widely among hunter-gatherers as an adaptation to the hunting of dispersed, small herds of game (Steward 1955:124 [orig. 1936]). He also described alternative patterns, notably the composite bands, involving larger, nonexogamous groups adapted to hunting large herds, with unrelated families integrated "on the basis of constant association and cooperation rather than of actual or alleged kinship" (Steward 1955:143). Steward considered Bushmen, Pygmies, and Australian aborigines as examples of the patrilineal pattern; and the Algonkian and Athabaskan peoples of the subarctic examples of the composite pattern. Elman Service has suggested the phrase patrilocal band to describe Steward's patrilineal band model, wishing to emphasize the role of common residence rather than common descent in structuring such groups (Service 1966:32–35; see FAMILY).

The model of the patrilineal/patrilocal band has been widely criticized. Later research has emphasized the structural flexibility of bands: "The fluid organization of recent hunters has certain adaptive advantages, including the adjustment of group size to resources, the leveling out of demographic variance, and the resolution of conflict by fission" (Lee and DeVore 1968:8). In light of more recent studies, Steward's composite band appears far more characteristic of foraging societies than any based on patrilineal organization (see Barnard 1983:195–97).

Later Research

Since the 1970s, research on band societies has taken several novel directions.

1. In contrast to an earlier assumption that a foraging adaptation is highly inefficient, and thus that band societies commonly existed in a situation of bare survival, more recent studies suggest that subsistence through foraging requires

on the average far less labor than food production (Sahlins 1972; cf. Hawkes and O'Connell 1981). This has significant implications for theories of cultural EVOLUTION. By this evidence, the neolithic transition from hunting and gathering to food production can no longer be viewed as merely a rational and self-evident response to dietary insufficiency, but rather must reflect a complex series of social and ecological transformations.

2. Considerable research on bands has been guided by Marxist theory (see MATERIALISM), seeking to clarify band-based foraging as a distinct MODE OF PRODUCTION, involving generalized reciprocity, de-emphasis of accumulation, and collective ownership of land and resources. Eleanor Leacock and Richard Lee suggest a complex of cultural patterns common to band-based foragers, including "egalitarian patterns of sharing; strong antiauthoritarianism; an emphasis on the importance of cooperation in conjunction with great respect for individuality; [and] marked flexibility in band membership and in living arrangements generally" (Leacock and Lee 1982:7–8).

3. Under the rubric of optimal foraging theory, a number of studies have investigated the effects of ecological conditions on band composition and foraging strategies, moving beyond a traditional cultural ecology in the use of detailed predictive models involving calculations of hunter-gatherer energy expenditure, task scheduling, and risk (Winterhalder and Smith 1981; see also SOCIOBIOLOGY).

References

Barnard, Alan. 1983. "Contemporary Hunter-Gatherers: Current Theoretical Issues in Ecology and Social Organization." *ARA* 12:193–214. A good overview.

Darwin, Charles. 1832 [1968]. "The Tierra del Fuegians." Alan Dundes, ed., *Every Man His Way: Readings in Cultural Anthropology*. Englewood Cliffs, N.J.: Prentice-Hall.

Hawkes, Kristen, and James F. O'Connell. 1981. "Affluent Hunters? Some Comments in Light of the Alyawara Case." *AA* 83:622–26. A critique of Sahlins's thesis regarding relative "affluence" in band societies.

Leacock, Eleanor, and Richard Lee. 1982. "Introduction." Eleanor Leacock and Richard Lee., eds., *Politics and History in Band Societies*. Cambridge: Cambridge University Press. Strongly recommended.

Lee, Richard, and Irven DeVore. 1968. "Problems in the Study of Hunters and Gatherers." R. Lee and I. DeVore, eds., *Man the Hunter*. Chicago: Aldine. A theoretically important (if somewhat dated) collection of papers.

Mauss, Marcel, and Henri Beuchat. 1906 [1979]. *Seasonal Variations of the Eskimo: A Study in Social Morphology*. London: Routledge & Kegan Paul. A pioneering study of band organization.

Morgan, Lewis Henry. 1877. *Ancient Society*. Chicago: Charles H. Kerr.

Radcliffe-Brown, A. R. 1931 [1977]. "The Social Organization of Australian Tribes." Adam Kuper, ed., *The Social Anthropology of Radcliffe-Brown*. London: Routledge & Kegan Paul. Presents the patrilineal band model.

Rosaldo, Renato. 1982. "Utter Savages of Scientific Value." Eleanor Leacock and

Richard Lee., eds., *Politics and History in Band Societies*. Cambridge: Cambridge University Press.

Sahlins, Marshall. 1972. "The Original Affluent Society." M. Sahlins, *Stone Age Economics*. Chicago: Aldine. An influential essay on the leisure of foraging societies.

Service, Elman R. 1966. *The Hunters*. Englewood Cliffs, N.J.: Prentice-Hall.

Slotkin, J. S., ed. 1965. *Readings in Early Anthropology*. Chicago: Aldine.

Steward, Julian H. 1955. "The Patrilineal Band" and "The Composite Hunting Band." Julian H. Steward, *Theory of Culture Change*. Urbana: University of Illinois Press. These are an expansion of a classic 1936 paper on band organization.

Winterhalder, Bruce, and Eric A. Smith, eds. 1981. *Hunter-Gatherer Foraging Strategies: Ethnographic and Archaeological Analyses*. Chicago: University of Chicago Press. Papers applying optimal foraging theory to model the adaptations and structures of band societies.

Sources of Additional Information

Richard B. Lee and Irven DeVore, eds., *Kalahari Hunter-Gatherers: Studies of the !Kung San and Their Neighbors*, Cambridge: Harvard University Press, 1976, is an excellent collection of papers illustrating the broad range of research now undertaken in band societies. Another perspective is provided by Tim Ingold et al., eds., *Hunters and Gatherers, 2: Property, Power and Ideology*, Oxford: Berg, 1988. A range of studies regarding resource use in band societies is provided by Nancy M. Williams and Eugene S. Hunn, eds., *Resource Managers: American and Australian Hunter-Gatherers*, Boulder, Colo.: Westview Press, 1982.

BELIEF. See RATIONALITY.

C

CASTE. 1. An explicitly hierarchical social system based on hereditary, endogamous groups, in which each is characterized by a specific status, occupation, mode of life, and pattern of customary interactions with other such groups. 2. One of the endogamous units of such a system.

Caste is one of a number of terms (cf. order, estate, class) denoting a ranked segment of society. Although caste is used primarily with reference to India, it is a European term, applied (at least originally) by Europeans to the analysis of Hindu life.

The English "caste" derives from the Spanish and Portuguese *casta*, signifying race, lineage, or breed. In colonizing the Americas, the Spanish applied the term to what today would be called a clan or lineage (see DESCENT). The Portuguese, in contrast, who reached India in 1498, used *casta* to describe the numerous endogamous (in-marrying), hereditary social groups that they found to be the essential components of Indian society (Pitt-Rivers 1971). The latter sense of the term appeared in English in the early seventeenth century. Caste subsequently took on the more abstract sense of a social system composed of such endogamous, hereditary units. The following analysis will consider caste primarily as an Indian phenomenon, with some attention also given to the relevance of caste as a cross-cultural category.

In the Hindu perspective, society is of necessity highly differentiated; there is a PATTERN of behavior appropriate to each caste and stage of life. In the words of A. L. Basham, "This thoroughgoing recognition that men are not the same, and that there is a hierarchy of classes [i.e., castes] each with its separate duties and distinctive way of life, is one of the most striking features of ancient Indian sociology" (Basham 1959:137). In this respect the Hindu WORLD VIEW differs fundamentally from the egalitarian assumptions of modern European social thought, a fact that may account for much of the conceptual difficulty surrounding the caste notion in Western social science (see Dumont 1970:1–20).

Caste in India

In principle, castes are hereditary and endogamous. The major exception to this principle is found in hypergamous MARRIAGE, where wives of slightly lower caste rank marry husbands of slightly higher status. In daily life castes are separated from one another by numerous exclusionary practices predicated on ideas of purity and pollution relative to caste rank. Behavior involving contact through touch, or through the sharing of food or personal articles, is thus an indicator of relatively equal status. In principle, each caste group has a distinctive occupation (e.g., farming, leather tanning, carpentry), or in Celestin Bouglé's phrase, an obligatory monopoly, with which caste status is intimately connected (Bouglé 1908:8). Finally, this array of caste groups is ordered in an explicit hierarchy, arranged in terms of the degree of ritual purity possessed by each group.

Each of these elements by itself—endogamy, hierarchy, separation, and hereditary occupation—can be found in other social contexts. As a system, however, caste is distinctive in the way in which these principles combine to create groups that are on the one hand isolated symbolically through differences in RITUAL status, and on the other interrelated economically through a hereditary division of labor. According to Bouglé, "The spirit of caste unites these three tendencies, repulsion, hierarchy and hereditary specialization, and all three must be borne in mind if one wishes to give a complete definition of the caste system" (Bouglé 1908:9).

The specific social units to which caste refers is a matter of complexity. The earlier literature on India referred to caste in terms of four major divisions, each with a distinct role. These were, as J. A. Dubois observed, "for Brahmins, priesthood and its various duties; for Kshatriyas, military service in all its branches; for Vaisyas, agriculture, trade, and cattle-breeding; and for Sudras, general servitude" (Dubois 1816:14). These four divisions (known as *varnas*) constitute a hierarchy, from the highest ranked group (being the most ritually pure), the Brahmans, to the lowest group, the Sudras. Yet the *varnas* do not describe functioning caste groups, but rather provide an ideological template, a set of broad categories, through which a ranking of the actual endogamous caste units (known as *jātis*) can be justified (see Fox 1969).

Between the broad *varna* categories and the endogamous, geographically localized *jātis* there exist both regional caste associations and what David Mandelbaum has termed *jati-clusters*, "a set of separate jatis, classed together under one name, whose members are treated by others as having the same general status" (Mandelbaum 1970:19). In short, caste organization is highly segmented, and social identity is relative to the hierarchical distance separating the individuals involved. As André Béteille has noted, "People view themselves as belonging to units of different orders [varna, jati-cluster, jati, etc.] in different contexts" (Béteille 1969:150; see also Bailey 1963; Mandelbaum 1970).

Theories of Caste

Anthropological debate regarding the caste concept has been dominated by two related questions: (1) What principles determine caste ranking? and (2) Is caste a cross-cultural phenomenon, or is it limited to the South Asian CULTURE AREA?

At least in the Indian context, there are both collective and individual factors determining one's ranking in the hierarchy of purity and status. One's hereditary caste affiliation carries with it a certain standing, at least in part justified in terms of the traditional occupation and customary practices of the group. However, deliberate or inadvertent actions that violate caste principles can temporarily lower an individual's status below that of his reference group, hence the extreme importance placed on regulating the interaction between caste groups (see Mayer 1960; Dumont 1970). Yet it is difficult to move from these generalizations to a set of rules that would predict a group's position in the caste hierarchy on the basis of occupation, patterns of behavior, wealth, and other relevant factors, for as H. N. Stevenson has noted, caste involves "many different principles of status evaluation . . . intricately interwoven to form the pattern of Hindu life (Stevenson 1960:974).

An essentially homologous structure of social relations based on different symbolic principles can be seen in Swat (Pakistan), where ideas of honor and shame replace those of purity and pollution. Barth (1971) among others would argue that this is a form of caste system. Yet Swat remains at the borders of Indian civilization: whether caste phenomena can be found entirely outside the South Asian culture sphere remains a fundamental point of controversy (see Barnett et al. 1976; Berreman 1968; see also INEQUALITY).

References

Bailey, F. G. 1963. "Closed Social Stratification in India." *Archives européenes de sociologie* 4:107–24. An analysis of the multiple referents of caste in India.

Barnett, Steve, et al. 1976. "Hierarchy Purified: Notes on Dumont and His Critics." *Journal of Asian Studies* 35:627–46. A defense of Louis Dumont's structuralist-inspired approach to the phenomenon of caste in India.

Barth, Fredrik. 1971. "The System of Social Stratification in Swat, North Pakistan." E. R. Leach, ed., *Aspects of Caste in South India, Ceylon and North-West Pakistan.* Cambridge: Cambridge University Press.

Basham, A. L. 1959. *The Wonder That Was India.* New York: Grove Press. An authoritative survey of ancient India.

Berreman, Gerald. 1968. "Caste: Concept of Caste." *IESS* 2:333–39. Caste is presented as a comparative concept describing extreme social stratification.

Béteille, André. 1969. *Castes, Old and New: Essays in Social Structure and Social Stratification.* Bombay: Asia Publishing House. Emphasizes the relations between caste, economy, and politics.

Bouglé, Celestin. 1908 [1971]. *Essays on the Caste System.* D. F. Pocock, trans. Cambridge: Cambridge University Press. An early yet theoretically sophisticated statement.

Dubois, J. A. 1816 [1906]. *Hindu Manners, Customs and Ceremonies.* 3d ed. Henry K.

Beauchamp, trans. Oxford: Clarendon Press. Reprinted 1972. An ethnographic classic of South Asia.

Dumont, Louis. 1970. *Homo Hierarchicus: The Caste System and Its Implications*. Mark Sainsbury, trans. Chicago: University of Chicago Press. An essential text; the best introduction to caste in India.

Fox, Richard G. 1969. "*Varna* Schemes and Ideological Integration in Indian Society." *Comparative Studies in Society and History* 11:27–45.

Mandelbaum, David. 1970. *Society in India*. 2 vols. Berkeley and Los Angeles: University of California Press. Provides an exhaustive survey of Indian social organization, including family, caste, and kinship, with full bibliography.

Mayer, Adrian C. 1960. *Caste and Kinship in Central India: A Village and Its Region*. Berkeley and Los Angeles: University of California Press. An excellent, detailed ethnographic study of caste organization in a rural community.

Pitt-Rivers, Julian. 1971. "On the Word 'Caste'." T. O. Beidelman, ed., *The Translation of Culture: Essays to E. E. Evans-Pritchard*. London: Tavistock.

Stevenson, H. N. C. 1960. "Caste." *Encyclopaedia Britannica* 4:973–82.

Sources of Additional Information

Stephen A. Tyler, *India: An Anthropological Perspective,* Pacific Palisades, Calif.: Goodyear, 1973, gives a brief introduction to the ethnology of South Asia. M. N. Srinivas, *Social Change in Modern India*, Berkeley and Los Angeles: University of California Press, 1966, gives an interesting overview of culture change in matters of caste and religion in modern India. A range of perspectives on caste is provided in Dennis B. McGilvray, ed., *Caste Ideology and Interaction*, Cambridge: Cambridge University Press, 1982. An overview and theory of the emergence of the caste system is detailed in Morton Klass, *Caste: The Emergence of the South Asian Social System*, Philadelphia: ISHI, 1980.

CHANGE. See CULTURE CHANGE.

CHIEFDOM. A political system involving organized INEQUALITY of rank, based upon distinctions of KINSHIP and DESCENT.

A chiefdom is a kin-based society, like the more egalitarian TRIBE. It contrasts with the tribe in having a relatively permanent structure of political inequality centering on chiefly office without, however, possessing the autonomous political institutions of the STATE. Such societies are based on rank, with leaders and followers differentiated in status yet ultimately linked by kinship, a situation that contrasts with stratification based on CASTE or class (see INEQUALITY). Thus the concept of chiefdom describes "social complexity in stateless societies" (Earle 1987:279). Although some authors consider the chiefdom as one structural variant of the tribe (Sahlins 1968:20), more commonly the two terms are contrasted (Creamer and Haas 1985), as in the usage followed here.

Chief derives from the Latin *caput*, head. From the thirteenth century, chief was used figuratively to describe the leader of a group, the highest authority; from the sixteenth century it had a specifically ethnological sense as "the head man or ruler of a clan, tribe, or small uncivilized community" (*OED*), from which derives chiefdom in its present sense. Thus Spanish and English explorers of the Northwest Coast in the late eighteenth century commented extensively on the power and wealth of chiefs and the deference accorded them by their people. Jacinto Caamano, exploring ca. 1792 the coast of what is now British Columbia, described his reception by the (Tsimshian?) Indians. He was brought by bearers to a chief's house, some thirty-five by fifty-five feet in size "with walls and roofs of well-fitted planking," where he was received by the leaders of two villages assembled with their followers, entertained with ceremonial dances, presented with a gift of a nutria skin, and carried ceremoniously back to his ship (in Gunther 1972:106–9).

As this account suggests, chiefdoms are characterized by economic surplus, realized as distinctions of wealth between chiefs and commoners. In addition to the subsistence production of the local household or village, characteristic of tribes, the chiefdom creates a redistributive ECONOMY through which surplus flows as gift or tribute to its leaders. This in turn permits "clearly defined social hierarchies exhibiting significant differences in status" (Creamer and Haas 1985:740). The chiefdom serves to integrate a number of communities or local economies, often with considerable ecological diversity. In general, the chiefdom involves a system of leadership, "a hierarchy of major and minor authorities holding forth over major and minor subdivisions" of territory (Sahlins 1968:26).

Ethnology of Chiefdoms

Chiefdoms have been documented in numerous areas, with widely differing modes of ADAPTATION. The economy of the Northwest Coast, while also utilizing gathering and hunting, rested in particular on the rich fishing of the region, one of the rare examples of a ranked society with a foraging subsistence base (Boas 1920). However, because the Northwest Coast communities appear to have lacked extensive regional integration, some scholars have questioned whether societies of this CULTURE AREA should be considered chiefdoms (Earle 1987:284). In Oceania both Polynesia and Micronesia had chiefdoms based primarily on horticulture and fishing (Mason 1963). The numerous chiefdoms of sub-Saharan Africa varied in adaptation, many relying primarily on horticulture, others on a mixture of horticulture and herding (Richards 1940). In the Middle East pastoralism provided a basis for numerous ranked societies (Barth 1974). Finally, the existence of chiefdoms in a number of other regions has been inferred through the archaeological record, for example in neolithic Europe (Renfrew 1973) and Central America (Creamer and Haas 1985).

Leadership and Social Structure

The political role of the chief should be distinguished from the more transient and informal leadership occurring in BANDS and tribes. In Melanesia, for example, the latter pattern is generally referred to as big-man leadership. In the big-man polity there is no permanent office, but a constant striving for influence, achieved through the redistribution of wealth and the creation of alliances. As Marshall Sahlins (1963:164) has said of the Melanesian pattern, "Little or no authority is given by social ascription: leadership is a creation . . . of followership." The chief, in contrast, succeeds to office, frequently by inheritance. Regarding the position of the *khan* or chief among the pastoralist Basseri of Iran, Fredrik Barth has commented that "he is traditionally granted a vast and not clearly delimited field of privilege and command, and power is conceived as emanating *from* him, rather than delegated *to* him by his subjects" (Barth 1974:387).

In the chiefdom the organization of authority and succession to office are generally guided by principles of kinship. As Paul Kirchhoff recognized in 1935, such societies are most commonly based on a ranked and segmented kin group termed the conical clan. In such systems lineage segments are graded in terms of their kinship distance from the ancestral founder as, at a higher level, clans themselves are graded (Fried 1957:4–6; Sahlins 1968:49–50). In this fashion the senior individual (usually male) of the highest ranked lineage within a clan succeeds to the role of clan chief, the same principle applying at higher and lower levels of organization (see Richards 1940:99–103; Kiste 1974:51–53). Such groups are often recruited through a principle of unilineal descent. However, in many societies (notably in Polynesia), membership in such groups is ambilineal, obtained through either father or mother, depending on which is most advantageous. This type of descent group is often termed a ramage (see Firth 1957:198; on kin groups see DESCENT).

Most postwar research on chiefdoms has derived from studies of CULTURAL ECOLOGY or EVOLUTION. Both cultural anthropologists and archaeologists have sought the forces responsible for the emergence of the chiefdom from a less differentiated and smaller scale tribal base. Among the causes suggested are the need to manage production and redistribution in ecologically complex regions, the necessity of organizing effectively for warfare, and the incremental advantages accruing to an incipient elite by controlling critical resources (see Earle 1987:291–98). Other research has involved the ideological basis of ranked societies. The political control of chiefdoms is frequently mediated by religious sanctions and SYMBOLISM (see also MANA and TABOO), often expressed through a monumental architecture, complex RITUAL, or the sacred character of chiefly office (Renfrew 1973; Webster 1976).

References

Barth, Fredrik. 1974. "Chieftainship." Yehudi Cohen, ed., *Man in Adaptation: The Cultural Present*. 2d ed. Chicago: Aldine. On the pastoralist Basseri of Iran.
Boas, Franz. 1920 [1940]. "The Social Organization of the Kwakiutl." F. Boas, *Race, Language and Culture*. New York: Free Press. A ranked society of the Northwest Coast.
Creamer, Winifred, and Jonathan Haas. 1985. "Tribe versus Chiefdom in Lower Central America." *American Antiquity* 50:738–54.
Earle, Timothy K. 1987. "Chiefdoms in Archaeological and Ethnohistorical Perspective." *ARA* 16:279–308. A very useful review article.
Firth, Raymond. 1957 [1971]. "A Note on Descent Groups in Polynesia." Nelson

Graburn, ed., *Readings in Kinship and Social Structure*. New York: Harper & Row.

Fried, Morton H. 1957. "The Classification of Corporate Unilineal Descent Groups." *Journal of the Royal Anthropological Institute* 87:1–29.

Gunther, Erna. 1972. *Indian Life of the Northwest Coast of North America as Seen by the Early Explorers and Fur Traders During the Last Decades of the Eighteenth Century*. Chicago: University of Chicago Press.

Kiste, Robert C. 1974. *The Bikinians: A Study in Forced Migration*. Menlo Park, Calif.: Cummings. An excellent study in chiefly politics and social change.

Mason, Leonard. 1963. "Suprafamilial Authority and Economic Process in Micronesian Atolls." Andrew P. Vayda, ed., *Peoples and Cultures of the Pacific*. Garden City, N.Y.: Natural History Press.

Renfrew, Colin. 1973. "Monument, Mobilization and Social Organization in Neolithic Wessex." C. Renfrew, ed., *The Explanation of Culture Change*. London: Duckworth.

Richards, Audrey I. 1940. "The Political System of the Bemba Tribe—North-eastern Rhodesia." Meyer Fortes and E. E. Evans-Pritchard, eds., *African Political Systems*. London: Oxford University Press.

Sahlins, Marshall D. 1963 [1968]. "Poor Man, Rich Man, Big Man, Chief: Political Types in Melanesia and Polynesia." Andrew P. Vayda, ed., *Peoples and Cultures of the Pacific*. Garden City, N.Y.: Natural History Press.

———. 1968. *Tribesmen*. Englewood Cliffs, N.J.: Prentice-Hall. A useful introductory text.

Webster, David L. 1976. "On Theocracies." *AA* 78:812–28.

Sources of Additional Information

Elman R. Service, *Primitive Social Organization*, 2d ed., New York: Random House, 1971, ch. 5, gives a useful introduction, though the evolutionary processes he postulates for the emergence of chiefdoms have been significantly supplemented by later research.

CIVILIZATION. 1. The cumulative, world-wide development of scientific knowledge and technique, originating with the emergence of STATE-level societies. 2. That group of world cultures associated with state-level societies, characterized by social stratification, urbanism, literacy, codified TRADITIONS, and extensive trade.

Civilization derives from the Latin *civilitas*, meaning in its primary sense the art of civil government, or politics; and secondarily, courteousness, politeness (see *OED*). *Civilitas* thus referred to the world of the citizen (*civis*) as opposed to that of the tribesman or "barbarian." Like its latter-day equivalent "civilization," *civilitas* suggested both a particular type of social order (the state as opposed to the TRIBE) and a value judgment (the moral superiority of the complex, urban society).

The word civilization entered English usage in the late eighteenth century, originally as a synonym for civility. Adam Ferguson, discussing the "History of Rude Nations," noted ironically, "We are ourselves the supposed standards of politeness and civilization; and where our own features do not appear, we apprehend, that there is nothing which deserves to be known" (Ferguson 1767:75). In reference to a particular type or stage of society, the term appeared somewhat later. Thus the historian Henry Buckle (in 1857), referred to Egypt as "a civilization . . . which forms a striking contrast to the barbarism of the other nations of Africa" (in *OED*).

As a concept, civilization thus stands in contrast (and implicit superiority) to so-called PRIMITIVE society, a form of ethnocentrism which has limited the concept's usefulness in ANTHROPOLOGY. Perhaps for this reason, the anthropological usage has varied. Three senses can be distinguished: (1) least usefully, civilization has been treated as equivalent to CULTURE; (2) civilization has been treated as an aspect of culture, specifically the more technical and scientific, particularly those cultures stemming from complex societies; and (3) civilizations (used in the plural) have been treated as a subclass of world cultures, those characterized by complex systems of social INEQUALITY and state-level politics.

Civilization as Culture

Many anthropologists have used civilization and culture synonymously. Edward Tylor's classic definition of culture began with these words: "Culture or Civilization . . . is that complex whole which includes knowledge, belief, art, morals, law, custom, and any other capabilities and habits acquired by man as a member of society" (Tylor 1871:1:1). Alfred Kroeber described the Yurok of California as "surrounded by peoples speaking diverse languages but following the same remarkable civilization" (Kroeber 1925:1). However, this use of civilization to describe societies of all levels of complexity and scale is today rare.

Civilization as Science and Technique

A second usage sees civilization as the sum of all scientific knowledge and its technical application. In this sense civilization is unitary and worldwide in scope, contrasting with culture as the specific complex of belief and CUSTOM characteristic of a particular society. In the words of Edward Sapir, "Civilization, as a whole, moves on; culture comes and goes" (Sapir 1924:317). This distinction between civilization and culture was elaborated by the sociologist Alfred Weber (see Weber 1935). In a more modern statement (1972), Colin Renfrew defined civilization as "the self-made environment of man, which he has fashioned to insulate himself from the primeval environment of nature alone" (in Griffeth and Thomas 1981:182).

Civilization as a Stage of Evolution

The most common use of the term civilization, and also the most problematic, is as a type of society. It is not difficult to identify likely candidates for the title: China, India, Europe, ancient Egypt, ancient Greece, all are frequently described as civilizations. What precisely that designation signifies is more difficult to answer.

Many nineteenth century studies, focusing on the EVOLUTION of culture, viewed civilization as the last and highest of a series of discrete stages in the development of human societies. Thus Lewis Henry Morgan, in *Ancient Society*, posited seven stages of cultural evolution, each characterized by certain technological innovations. Beginning with lower, middle, and upper savagery, Morgan's scheme proceeded through lower barbarism (characterized by the use of pottery), middle barbarism (animal domestication and irrigation agriculture), and upper barbarism (the use of iron), culminating with civilization, characterized by "the use of a phonetic alphabet and the production of literary records" (Morgan 1877:10–12).

The anthropological study of civilizations was eclipsed in the first several decades of this century by criticisms of the methods and assumptions of evolutionary studies such as Morgan's, by an ethnographic focus on tribal societies, and by a pervasive concern with cultural RELATIVISM, in light of which "civilization" appeared an invidious concept. However, since the Second World War anthropologists have again shown serious interest in this type of society. Considerable research, combining archaeology, history, and cultural anthropology, has been devoted to explaining both the origins of civilizations (see Flannery 1972) and their significant characteristics as cultural SYSTEMS.

Characteristics of Civilizations

Civilizations have been characterized in various ways. Etymologically, a civilization may be defined simply as the cultural complex associated with a state-level society; this is the usage adopted by Kent Flannery (1972:400). Others have suggested certain diagnostic traits, for example, writing (Morgan and others); a combination of writing, cities, and trade (Herbert Kuhn); or yet more complex criteria, such as V. Gordon Childe's ten traits, which add to the above three such characteristics as taxation, monumental building, incipient science, and full-time craft specialization (see Wolf 1967:446–48). All of these approaches assume that civilizations involve highly differentiated social orders and economies based on surplus rather than subsistence.

Delimiting the boundaries of civilizations has proved to be complex. At times, a civilization has been equated with the ambit of a state (China, India, etc.). A somewhat different approach begins by acknowledging that civilizations transcend the boundaries of discrete societies, and that within a civilization core states may exist in complex interaction with less stratified societies on their periphery (see Wolf 1967). Furthermore, a civilization may include numerous ethnic groups or particular cultures. South Asia provides an example, with its congeries of tribes, states, LANGUAGES, and regional cultures. It is in this sense that Louis Dumont and David Pocock argued that "India is one. The very existence, and influence, of the traditional higher, sanskritic, civilisation demonstrates without question the unity of India" (Dumont and Pocock 1957:9). Kroeber (in later writings) used an even larger aggregate, the *oikumene* or "inhabited world," which Wolf has defined as "a sphere of inter-influencing civilizations, with secondary effects on the isolated cultures in the interstices and along the margins" (Wolf 1967:451; see also Kroeber 1946). In this sense, as Robert Redfield noted, the Asiatic, Middle Eastern, and European civilizations have formed an oikumene, as did the Andean and Mesoamerican civilizations of the New World (Redfield 1960:406).

Finally, civilizations constitute a distinctive type of cultural system. As a class they are characterized by certain distinctive modes in the organization and transmission of cultural knowledge and in the tempo and character of CULTURE CHANGE. Specialists (e.g., priests, scholars) both codify and criticize tradition, while the existence of extensive stratification and occupational specialization ensure that PATTERNS of value and WORLD VIEW may vary significantly within any given civilization. As Redfield noted, "A civilization is a great culture; it is also a compound culture; rural people and townspeople are apart, different, and traditionally interconnected" (Redfield 1960:404; see FOLK CULTURE; PEASANTRY; URBANISM).

The task of making this complexity intelligible in ethnographic terms has been daunting. The COMMUNITY study has provided one approach. Certain anthropologists, such as Kroeber, looked to the concepts of style and pattern as keys to an underlying cultural unity within civilizations. Scholars more oriented to cultural MATERIALISM have emphasized the concept of MODE OF PRODUCTION in their analyses. In any case, civilizations differ from BANDS and tribes (more traditional objects of anthropological study) not only by greater social complexity, but by a difference in scale of several orders of magnitude. For this reason the ethnographic study of a civilization poses special problems and necessitates new, and often interdisciplinary, techniques (see Hsu 1970; Singer 1972; Ames 1976).

References

Ames, Michael. 1976. "Detribalized Anthropology and the Study of Asian Civilizations." *Pacific Affairs* 49:313–24. Evaluates Milton Singer's approach to the study of Indian civilization.

Dumont, Louis, and David Pocock. 1957. "For a Sociology of India." *Contributions to Indian Sociology* 1:7–22. Discusses the interdependence of ethnographic and textual approaches in the study of Indian civilization.

Ferguson, Adam. 1767 [1966]. *An Essay on the History of Civil Society*. Edinburgh: Edinburgh University Press. An early comparative study of social institutions; a work of the Scottish Enlightenment.

Flannery, Kent. 1972. "The Cultural Evolution of Civilizations." *Annual Review of Ecology and Systematics* 3:399–426. Flannery summarizes the major theories regarding the emergence of civilizations.

Griffeth, Robert, and Carol G. Thomas, eds. 1981. *The City-State in Five Cultures*. Santa Barbara, Calif.: ABC-Clio.

Hsu, Francis L. K. 1970. "Methodology in the Study of Literate Civilizations." Raoul Naroll and Ronald Cohen, eds., *A Handbook of Method in Cultural Anthropology*. New York: Columbia University Press.

Kroeber, A. L. 1925 [1976]. *Handbook of the Indians of California*. New York: Dover.
———. 1946 [1952]. "The Ancient Oikumene as a Historic Culture Aggregate." A. L. Kroeber, *The Nature of Culture*. Chicago: University of Chicago Press. Many essays in this collection concern the study of civilizations.

Morgan, Lewis Henry. 1877 [1963]. *Ancient Society*. Eleanor Leacock, ed. New York: World Publishing.

Redfield, Robert. 1960 [1962]. "Civilization." R. Redfield, *Human Nature and the Study of Society*. Collected Papers, vol. 1. Chicago: University of Chicago Press.

Sapir, Edward. 1924 [1949]. "Culture, Genuine and Spurious." David G. Mandelbaum, ed., *Selected Writings of Edward Sapir in Language, Culture and Personality*. Berkeley and Los Angeles: University of California Press. Notable for its contrast of civilization and culture.

Singer, Milton. 1972. *When a Great Tradition Modernizes: An Anthropological Approach to Indian Civilization*. London: Pall Mall Press.

Tylor, Edward. 1871 [1958]. *Primitive Culture*. 2 vols. New York: Harper & Brothers (Harper Torchbook). A classic of early anthropology.

Weber, Alfred. 1935 [1961]. "Fundamentals of Culture-Sociology." Talcott Parsons et al., eds., *Theories of Society*. New York: Free Press. Weber developed a systematic contrast of civilization and culture.

Wolf, Eric. 1967. "Understanding Civilizations: A Review Article." *Comparative Studies in Society and History* 9:446–65. Wolf reviews various approaches to defining civilization and explaining its evolution.

Sources of Additional Information

The relationship between the concepts of culture and civilization is reviewed by Alfred Kroeber and Clyde Kluckhohn in *Culture: A Critical Review of Concepts and Definitions*, New York: Random House (Vintage), orig. ed. 1952, pp. 15–30. Frederick Barnard's "Culture and Civilization in Modern Times," *DHI* 1:613–21, discusses the varying views of civilization held by European writers, philosophers, and historians. Andrew Bard Smookler, *The Parable of the Tribes: The Problem of Power in Social Evolution*, Berkeley and Los Angeles: University of California Press, 1984, seeks "a general theory of civilization's evolution."

CLASS. See INEQUALITY.

COMMUNICATION. The transmission of information through LANGUAGE or other semiotic means.

Communication is derived from the same root as is COMMUNITY, namely, that which is common or shared. In the abstract, communication occurs when any change in one phenomenon results in some change in another. Communication can involve any two (or more) entities: a switch and lightbulb, two computers, two honey bees, or two persons at a cocktail party. Through the process of communication, two isolated elements are brought into relationship. More elaborately, through communication elements are assimilated into a larger SYSTEM, and their relationship may be said to exhibit structure. This process, which can be formalized and quantified, is the concern of mathematical communication theory (see Cherry 1966).

Communication and organization are thus closely linked. Furthermore, communication is essential to the existence of any society, whether human or non-human. ANTHROPOLOGY is concerned with the nature and modes of human communication, understood as a culturally constituted process (see CULTURE).

Historically the study of communication has been dominated by the field of linguistics, the study of language (see Lyons 1968). Through the first several decades of this century, anthropology was closely allied with linguistics, through common involvement in the task of recording and analyzing languages in the field context. For anthropologists this meant the study of non-written languages, particularly those of tribal groups (see Hymes 1983). As linguistics became increasingly formal, emphasizing the study of language as a pure, isolated system, anthropological and linguistic studies of language and communication diverged.

Four directions of research have served to distinguish recent anthropological studies of communication. These include (1) the relation of language to other modes of communication (paralanguage, kinesics, and artifactual systems); (2) communicative praxis, the study of language and other forms of communication in their context of use; (3) the place of human communication in ethological and evolutionary perspective; and (4) the mutual influence of language and culture as symbolic systems within a given society. The first three topics are discussed below; the last topic is treated under LANGUAGE. For further information see also ETHNOSCIENCE, SEMIOTICS, and SYMBOLISM.

Modes of Communication

Edward Sapir has defined language as "a system of phonetic symbols for the expression of communicable thought and feeling" (Sapir 1933:7). In a fundamental sense, language has primacy in human communication. Although linguistics has long dominated the analysis of human communication, insights from such fields as ETHNOGRAPHY, ethology (animal behavior studies), and psychiatry have suggested that other modes of communication accompany, amplify, and modify the process of human speech.

Paralanguage encompasses the nonverbal, meaningful vocal utterances that accompany speech (see Trager 1964). Paralanguage includes both voice qualities (pitch and articulation) and vocalizations (cries, sighs, etc.). Kinesics involves communication by body posture, movement, and spacing (see Birdwhistell 1970; La Barre 1972). Kissing, bowing, crossing the legs, queuing in lines, as well as more subtle movements of the head, trunk, and limbs—all are examples of kinesic communication. Finally, much communication involves reference to or manipulation of artifacts; obvious examples include clothing and architecture, as well as explicitly symbolic forms (flags, crosses, etc.). All of these communicative modes converge in RITUAL (see Rappaport 1979).

The Ethnography of Speaking

The field of linguistics has commonly analyzed language as a code, abstracted from its social and cultural context. Linguistic theory has emphasized the rules of language rather than the acts of speech, as seen in Ferdinand de Saussure's concern with "langue" (language) over "parole" (speech), or Noam Chomsky's concern with "competence" over "performance" (Lyons 1968:51–52). In contrast, a major thrust of postwar anthropological studies has been to examine the communication process (in particular, the speech process) as a cultural activity, in the full sense of that term. One aspect, known commonly as sociolinguistics, has been described as "the study of verbal behavior in terms of the social characteristics of speakers, their cultural background, and the ecological properties of the environment in which they interact" (Gumperz 1974:250; see also Rubin 1973). Dialectical contrasts (in phonology or grammar), code switching, and specialized lexicons are all manifestations of sociolinguistic variation.

The idea of an ethnography of speaking, developed in particular by Dell Hymes, extends this approach (see Hymes 1964). It recognizes a cultural REL-ATIVISM in both the aims and the norms of communication. The deliberately elusive discourse of Zen instruction or the paralinguistic utterances of shamanic performance are examples of culturally patterned communication that find no clear counterpart in Euro-American speech communities. As Hymes has noted: "We need to build a theory of language that starts from what we can see to be actually the case in the world, man's polymorphous (and to the ethnologist, perhaps perverse) capacity to communicate in codes other than language, to use more languages than one, to make shifting choices as to codes and communication over time" (Hymes 1967:42).

Evolutionary Perspectives

Language has frequently been described as a uniquely human attribute. However, from a bioevolutionary perspective, it is difficult to explain the development of such a complex and crucial mode of communication in humans without the existence of similar capacities in closely related primate species. Since the 1960s long-term field studies have expanded our understanding of communication among the higher primates. Systematic experiments in teaching nonvocal language systems to apes (via signing and other techniques) have produced startling if contested results (Hill 1978; see also EVOLUTION; SOCIOBIOLOGY).

References

Birdwhistell, Ray L. 1970. *Kinesics and Context: Essays on Body Motion Communication*. Philadelphia: University of Pennsylvania Press.
Cherry, Colin. 1966. *On Human Communication: A Review, a Survey, and a Criticism*. 2d ed. Cambridge, Mass.: MIT Press. An advanced introduction to mathematical communication theory and related topics.
Gumperz, John J. 1974. "Linguistic and Social Interaction in Two Communities." Ben G. Blount, ed., *Language, Culture and Society: A Book of Readings*. Cambridge, Mass.: Winthrop Publishers. A sociolinguistic study comparing speech patterns in Indian and Norwegian communities.
Hill, Jane H. 1978. "Apes and Language." *ARA* 7:89–112. A major review of research.
Hymes, Dell. 1964 [1974]. "Toward Ethnographies of Communication." Dell Hymes, *Foundations in Sociolinguistics: An Ethnographic Approach*. Philadelphia: University of Pennsylvania Press. The volume contains pioneering essays in modern linguistic anthropology.
———. 1967. "Linguistic Problems in Defining the Concept of 'Tribe'." June Helm,

ed., *Essays on the Problem of Tribe*. Proceedings of the American Ethnological
    Society, 1967. Hymes explores the relation between social boundaries and lan-
    guage boundaries in tribal societies.
————. 1983. "The Americanist Tradition in Linguistics." Dell Hymes, *Essays in the
    History of Linguistic Anthropology*. Amsterdam and Philadelphia: John Benjamins.
La Barre, Weston. 1972. "Paralinguistics, Kinesics, and Cultural Anthropology."
    Thomas Sebeok et al., eds., *Approaches to Semiotics: Cultural Anthropology,
    Education, Linguistics, Psychiatry, Psychology*. The Hague: Mouton. La Barre
    emphasizes the variety of kinesic data to be found cross-culturally.
Lyons, John. 1968. *Introduction to Theoretical Linguistics*. Cambridge: Cambridge Uni-
    versity Press. A demanding introductory text.
Rappaport, Roy A. 1979. "The Obvious Aspects of Ritual." Roy A. Rappaport, *Ecology,
    Meaning, and Religion*. Richmond, Calif.: North Atlantic Books. Rappaport ex-
    plores the communicative dimension of ritual.
Rubin, Joan. 1973. "Sociolinguistics." John J. Honigmann, ed., *Handbook of Social
    and Cultural Anthropology*. Chicago: Rand McNally. A comprehensive overview.
Sapir, Edward. 1933 [1949]. "Language." David G. Mandelbaum, ed., *Selected Writings
    of Edward Sapir in Language, Culture and Personality*. Berkeley and Los Angeles:
    University of California Press. Strongly recommended.
Trager, George L. 1964. "Paralanguage: A First Approximation." Dell Hymes, ed.,
    Language in Culture and Society. New York: Harper & Row.

Sources of Additional Information

Edward Hall's *The Hidden Dimension*, Garden City, N.Y.: Anchor, 1969, provides
an excellent, nontechnical introduction to kinesics. Gregory Bateson's *Steps to an Ecology
of Mind*, New York: Ballantine Books, 1972, is challenging and highly recommended.
For a synthesis of anthropological and psychiatric perspectives, see Jurgen Ruesch and
Gregory Bateson, *Communication: The Social Matrix of Psychiatry*, New York: Norton,
1951. A broad review of nonverbal communications is offered in Fernando Poyatos, ed.,
New Perspectives in Nonverbal Communications, New York: Pergamon Press, 1983.

COMMUNITY. A geographically localized population distinguished by exten-
    sive social interaction, relative self-sufficiency, and a common CULTURE or
    identity.

The word community is derived from the Latin *communis*, that which is shared,
common, public. In its medieval Latin form the term acquired a concrete sense,
as a distinct body of individuals sharing certain qualities, for example, fellow
town dwellers (*OED*). Thus community can refer either to a quality of social
life or to a specific group—a significant ambiguity.

Community (*koinonia*) was a significant concept for the Greeks. Aristotle's
ideal of community, namely a group of individuals known to one another and
linked by a bond of good will, manifested through acts of reciprocity in a
framework of economic autarchy, can still serve as a useful model (see *Nic.
Eth.* 1132b; *Pol.* 1252b, 1256b, 1326b). Community has also held a central
place in Christian TRADITION. The biblical ideal of community (Ps. 133:1; Acts
4:32–35) provided a powerful example to later generations, reflected in both

Catholic monasticism and many Protestant sects (Bonhoeffer 1954). In the secular sphere, this ideal inspired an enormous utopian literature (and many utopian experiments), aimed at fostering civic virtue and social harmony, through a rationally conceived plan for the organization of small, self-sufficient societies (Kanter 1972).

Community has thus had an immense role in the history of Western social thought (see Nisbet 1953; Friedrich 1959). The ideal of community has served both as social criticism and social aspiration. It reflects a tension between what is perceived as the fellowship, equality, and autarchy of a past era or golden age, and the alienation, hierarchy, and dependence inherent in an existing society. In this sense community is not a value-free construct but an ideological symbol (see Geertz 1964:62–63), functioning not to approximate objective, disinterested knowledge, but to provide "authoritative concepts" that form the basis of political thought and action. Much of the social scientific literature on community, as in the work of Ferdinand Tönnies, has been heavily influenced by this tradition (Tönnies 1887; see also FOLK CULTURE).

Community as an Anthropological Concept

One can distinguish theoretically weak and strong senses of community in the anthropological literature. In the former sense, community is understood simply as the context in which ETHNOGRAPHY is undertaken—any localized population forming the effective unit of participant-observation research (e.g., Gmelch 1980). In the latter, more significant sense, community is understood as a specific type of social group, characterized (at a minimum) by a relatively small population with close social ties, enduring over several generations. This is, in Conrad Arensberg's phrase, "a structured social field of interindividual relationships unfolding through time" (Arensberg 1961:250).

Somewhat more precisely, Robert Redfield defined community (the "little community") in terms of four characteristics: distinctiveness, smallness, homogeneity, and self-sufficiency. A community must possess distinct boundaries, and its members a distinctive identity; it must be small enough to be personally observable; its members must be similar in cultural perspective; and it must be self-sufficient not only economically but socially, encompassing the full range of the life cycle (Redfield 1955:4). This last requirement, that a community constitute a socially complete, self-reproducing unit, led Arensberg to argue that "a monastery, whatever its spirit, cannot be a community . . . .[neither can] a mining camp, an old age home, a children's village, an army" (Arensberg 1961:254). Not all anthropologists have accepted this restriction.

Several types of criteria have been used to define the nature of community. These include affective criteria, which stress the existence of solidarity among the members of a group (Kanter 1972); structural criteria, which emphasize the functional interdependence of roles and institutions, collectively yielding a stable and self-sufficient social order (Redfield 1955: ch. 3; see FUNCTIONALISM); and cultural criteria, which posit a common tradition as indispensable to community life (Tönnies 1887; cf. Cole 1977:358–65).

Later Research

With the shift of anthropological concern, beginning in the 1930s, from TRIBES to STATES, ethnographic technique was applied to a much more complex social field. What came to be known as "community studies" (see Arensberg 1961) were attempts to understand the cultures and institutions of state societies (in particular, agrarian states such as India, Morocco, or Mexico) through a relatively traditional ethnographic focus on localized communities. However, the idea that an isolated community can serve as an ethnographic representation of a national reality has been widely criticized and no longer attracts serious support. Conversely, numerous studies analyzed CULTURE CHANGE in peasant communities (see PEASANTRY) without considering the significance of economic and political constraints exerted at the regional or national level. Yet as McKim Marriott (1955) has demonstrated in the case of South Asia, rural communities are not isolates. More recent studies of peasantries have utilized comparative, historical, and regional approaches to overcome the ethnographic fiction of the autonomous, isolated community (see Cohen 1977; Cole 1977; Schwartz 1978; Chambers and Young 1979).

The concept of community inherited from European tradition has been revised in other ways as well. Communities need not be fundamentally harmonious and consensual: what Bernard Siegel and Alan Beals (1960) have described as "pervasive factionalism" appears to be compatible with the long-term stability of community organization. Korsi Dogbe's research in sub-Saharan Africa has suggested a WORLD VIEW in which community has a cosmological significance, and the relation between individual and group is understood very differently than it is in the Western (and ultimately Aristotelian) model (Dogbe 1980). Perhaps the anthropological concept of community is more culture-bound than has generally been recognized. Finally, considerable attention has been given to community as an intentional (if temporary) social form. In this sense, community may entail both the momentary abolition of formal SOCIAL STRUCTURE—what Victor Turner has called *communitas*—and the deliberate creation of communitarian societies (see Turner 1969: ch. 4; Bennett 1975).

References

Arensberg, Conrad M. 1961. "The Community as Object and as Sample." *AA* 63:241–64. A useful if dated overview.
Bennett, John W. 1975. "Communes and Communitarianism." *Theory and Society* 2:63–94. An anthropological perspective on community and communitarian experiments.
Bonhoeffer, Dietrich. 1954. *Life Together*. London: SCM Press. A Protestant reflection on community life.
Chambers, Erve, and Philip Young. 1979. "Mesoamerican Community Studies: The Past Decade." *ARA* 8:45–69. A review with extensive bibliography.
Cohen, Erik. 1977. "Recent Anthropological Studies of Middle Eastern Communities and Ethnic Groups." *ARA* 6:315–47.

Cole, John W. 1977. "Anthropology Comes Part-Way Home: Community Studies in Europe." *ARA* 6:349–78.

Dogbe, Korsi. 1980. "Concept of Community and Community Support Systems in Africa." *Anthropos* 75:781–98. Examines the idea of community within African tradition.

Friedrich, Carl J. 1959. "The Concept of Community in the History of Political and Legal Philosophy." C. J. Friedrich, ed., *Nomos II: Community*. New York: Liberal Arts Press. Community from Aristotle to Rousseau.

Geertz, Clifford. 1964. "Ideology as a Cultural System." David E. Apter, ed., *Ideology and Discontent*. New York: Free Press.

Gmelch, George. 1980. "Urban Fieldwork: Anthropologists in Cities." George Gmelch and Walter P. Zenner, eds., *Urban Life*. New York: St. Martin's Press.

Kanter, Rosabeth Moss. 1972. *Commitment and Community: Communes and Utopias in Sociological Perspective*. Cambridge, Mass.: Harvard University Press. A highly readable overview of communitarian experiments.

Marriott, McKim. 1955. "Little Communities in an Indigenous Civilization." McKim Marriott, ed., *Village India: Studies in the Village Community*. Chicago: University of Chicago Press. Emphasizes the dependence of a South Asian village upon a regional power structure.

Nisbet, Robert. 1953 [1962]. *Community and Power*. New York: Oxford University Press. A study of the place of community in Western thought.

Redfield, Robert. 1955. *The Little Community*. Chicago: University of Chicago Press. An important—if dated—model for understanding peasant communities.

Schwartz, Norman B. 1978. "Community Development and Culture Change in Latin America." *ARA* 7:235–61. Reviews anthropological studies of community development.

Siegel, Bernard J., and Alan R. Beals. 1960. "Pervasive Factionalism." *AA* 62:394–417. Argues that factionalism and community stability are compatible.

Tönnies, Ferdinand. 1887 [1963]. *Community and Society*. Charles Loomis, trans. New York: Harper & Row. A romantic interpretation of community and tradition.

Turner, Victor. 1969 [1977]. *The Ritual Process: Structure and Anti-Structure*. Ithaca, N.Y.: Cornell University Press. Considers "communitas" as the temporary abolition of formal social roles.

Sources of Additional Information

An excellent example of the community study genre is provided by Oscar Lewis, *Life in a Mexican Village: Tepoztlan Restudied*, n.p.: University of Illinois Press, 1951. A more recent study of the ideological aspects of community is offered in Carol J. Greenhouse, *Praying for Justice: Faith, Order, and Community in an American Town*, Ithaca, N.Y.: Cornell University Press, 1986. A range of studies, emphasizing peasant communities, is presented in Owen M. Lynch, ed., *Culture and Community in Europe: Essays in Honor of Conrad M. Arensberg*, Delhi: Hindustan, 1984.

COMPARATIVE METHOD. The search for comparable culture PATTERNS in multiple societies; in particular, the comparison of traits isolated from their cultural context.

The problem of comparison has been a significant issue for ANTHROPOLOGY for well over a century. There has been an enduring tension between the anthropological axiom of holism, the need to evaluate any element of belief or behavior in its broader cultural context, and the goals of abstraction, comparison, and generalization. The history of the so-called comparative method in anthropology can be considered under three phases: (1) the wide-ranging use of apparent ethnographic parallels by nineteenth century evolutionary anthropologists (this can be considered the era of the comparative method in the strict sense); (2) the critique of this approach, notably by American anthropologists of the Boas school; and (3) the development of more systematic efforts at cultural comparison, particularly since the 1940s.

Comparison in Evolutionary Anthropology

The prominent place accorded the comparative method by nineteenth century anthropology is the result of several influences. In part, the evolutionists inherited from Enlightenment writers such as Jacques Turgot (1727–1781) a concern for the nature of social progress and the stages leading to CIVILIZATION that was implicitly comparative (Stocking 1987:14–15). Additionally, the field of comparative anatomy, one of the most prestigious of the sciences in the nineteenth century, established comparison as a key method of scientific research (Ackerknecht 1954:118–22).

Victorian anthropology sought to identify the major stages of cultural EVOLUTION so as to reconstruct the history of particular institutions (e.g., MARRIAGE, LAW, or RELIGION). Given the assumption that all societies must pass through comparable stages in the course of their DEVELOPMENT, it followed that a study of the beliefs and CUSTOMS of contemporary PRIMITIVE societies (so-called) would reveal the early practices of what was now civilization. John McLennan, in his study *Primitive Marriage*, emphasized the evolutionary relevance of ethnological data from tribal Central Africa, North America, India, and Oceania, for "these facts of today are, in a sense, the most ancient history. . . . that is most archaic which lies nearest to the beginning of human progress" (McLennan 1865:6). The discovery of parallels in belief and custom in diverse and supposedly unrelated societies was taken as evidence of the accuracy of evolutionary reconstructions and a confirmation of PSYCHIC UNITY. Furthermore, through the doctrine of SURVIVALS, evolutionary writers felt free to utilize sayings and practices of civilized societies that appeared to reflect the endurance of earlier customs in an attentuated, symbolic form.

Thus James Frazer, in arguing for the institution of RITUAL sacrifice of kings in primitive societies, cited reports regarding kingly suicide from Ethiopia, Central Africa, Prussia, Sweden, and south India, and tales of regicide from Arthurian legend. He also bolstered his thesis by citing supposed survivals of this practice, as seen in the custom of temporary, mock kingship in Thailand, Samarkand, Morocco, Cornwall, and Nigeria; various folk customs of mock execution from Mummers' Plays in Bavaria, Saxony, and Bohemia; and customs involving the burial or immolation of pasteboard effigies at Carnival season in Latium and the Abruzzi, Malta, Provence, Normandy, and Brittany (Frazer 1890:223–60).

The Boasian Critique

The evolutionists' goal of reconstructing the development of specific institutions, rather than understanding a whole way of life, encouraged the arbitrary comparison of traits stripped of any cultural context. While the comparativist position relied primarily on the ethnographic data from contemporary BANDS and TRIBES to reconstruct human prehistory, the doctrine of survivals also ensured that, when the argument necessitated, STATE-level societies could be ransacked for examples. With this rather ambidextrous logic, almost any thesis could be substantiated.

The American anthropologist Franz Boas—who apparently coined the term "comparative method" (*GEC*, p. 49)—offered an influential critique both of this method and of the rigid and dogmatic use of evolutionary theory then common. "The comparative method," Boas argued, " . . . has been remarkably barren of definite results, and I believe it will not become fruitful until we renounce the vain endeavor to construct a uniform systematic history of the evolution of culture" (Boas 1896:280). Boas emphasized the importance of DIFFUSION as an explanatory principle and, in place of wide ranging comparisons, advocated a more ethnographic approach, examining "customs in their relation to the total culture of the tribe practicing them" (Boas 1896:276; see HISTORICISM). This critique set the tone for much of American anthropology for the next forty years. In Britain the rise of FUNCTIONALISM, which placed almost exclusive emphasis on the analysis of bounded, small-scale societies, similarly discouraged comparativist approaches.

Cultural Comparison: Later Approaches

Since the late nineteenth century two quite different approaches have been used to place the comparative method on a more rigorous footing.

(1) What has come to be known as the cross-cultural or hologeistic ("whole-world") method continues the emphasis of evolutionist anthropology on the comparison of discrete culture traits, but utilizes statistical techniques operating on systematic samples of world cultures to test propositions. The approach is thus positivist and largely inductive. Pioneered by Edward Tylor in a study of the relation of DESCENT, residence, and KINSHIP behavior (Tylor 1889), cross-cultural methods were explored by a number of Dutch anthropologists, beginning with S. R. Steinmetz, and developed most extensively in the United States through the Human Relations Area Files (Köbben 1952; Murdock 1957).

(2) Since the 1940s the importance of cultural comparison has been recognized by anthropologists of a variety of perspectives, not—as with the advocates of cross-cultural survey—as a separate enterprise, but (more productively) as a necessary outgrowth of theory and research. Thus Fred Eggan advocated an emphasis on limited or "controlled" comparison, combining the perspectives of British structural-functionalism and American ETHNOLOGY (Eggan 1954). In

the field of CULTURAL ECOLOGY, Julian Steward among others sought cross-cultural regularities in the evolution of societies by examining patterns of ADAPTATION to the environment (Steward 1949). In ETHNOSCIENCE, Ward Goodenough has stressed the complementarity of culture-dependent (emic) and culture-independent (etic) categories in the formulation of cultural comparisons (Goodenough 1970: ch. 4; see EMIC/ETIC).

References

Ackerknecht, Erwin H. 1954. "On the Comparative Method in Anthropology." Robert F. Spencer, ed., *Method and Perspective in Anthropology*. Minneapolis: University of Minnesota Press.

Boas, Franz. 1896 [1940]. "The Limitations of the Comparative Method of Anthropology." F. Boas, *Race, Language and Culture*. New York: Free Press. The basic critique.

Eggan, Fred. 1954. "Social Anthropology and the Method of Controlled Comparison." *AA* 56:743–63.

Frazer, James G. 1890 [1959]. *The New Golden Bough*. 1 vol., abr. Theodor H. Gaster, ed. New York: Criterion Books. Frazer's classic work is a catalog of arbitrary and ill-founded, cross-cultural comparisons.

Goodenough, Ward. 1970. *Description and Comparison in Cultural Anthropology*. Chicago: Aldine.

Köbben, Andre J. 1952 [1961]. "New Ways of Presenting an Old Idea: The Statistical Method in Social Anthropology." Frank W. Moore, ed., *Readings in Cross-Cultural Methodology*. New Haven, Conn.: HRAF Press. Has a useful history of cross-cultural studies.

McLennan, John F. 1865 [1970]. *Primitive Marriage: An Inquiry into the Origin of the Form of Capture in Marriage Ceremonies*. Peter Rivière, ed. Chicago: University of Chicago Press. Arguably the first study to systematically use the comparative method.

Murdock, George Peter. 1957. "World Ethnographic Sample." *AA* 59:664–87.

Steward, Julian. 1949. "Cultural Causality and Law: A Trial Formulation of the Development of Early Civilizations." *AA* 51:1–27.

Stocking, George W., Jr. 1987. *Victorian Anthropology*. New York: Free Press.

Tylor, Edward B. 1889 [1961]. "On a Method of Investigating the Development of Institutions; Applied to Laws of Marriage and Descent." Frank W. Moore, ed., *Readings in Cross-Cultural Methodology*. New Haven, Conn.: HRAF Press. This work initiated statistical treatment of cross-cultural data.

Sources of Additional Information

Contrasting views on the value of cross-cultural studies in contemporary anthropology can be found in Marvin Harris, *The Rise of Anthropological Theory*, New York: Crowell, 1968, chs. 6 and 21; and Edmund Leach, "The Comparative Method in Anthropology," *IESS* 1:339–45, 1968. For a useful bibliography, see Oscar Lewis, "Comparisons in Cultural Anthropology," Frank W. Moore, ed., *Readings in Cross-Cultural Methodology*, New Haven, Conn.: HRAF Press, 1961. A variety of technical issues are treated in Raoul Naroll and Ronald Cohen, eds., *A Handbook of Method in Cultural Anthropology*, New York: Columbia University Press, 1970, pts. 5–7. Concerning the limits and possibilities of anthropological comparison, see Ladislav Holy, ed., *Comparative Anthropology*, Oxford: Blackwell, 1987.

CULTURAL ECOLOGY. The study of the ADAPTATION of human societies or populations to their environments, emphasizing the specific arrangements of technique, ECONOMY, and social organization through which CULTURE mediates the experience of the natural world.

Ecology is derived from the Greek *oikos*, the household (cf. ECONOMY). The term was advanced by Ernst Haeckel in 1870, in his classification of the subfields of zoology: "By ecology, we understand the study of the economy, of the household, of animal organisms . . . the relationships of animals with both the inorganic and the organic environments, above all the beneficial and inimical relations with other animals and plants" (in Bates 1962:222). An ecological approach is therefore contextual, situating its subjects in a network of mutually conditioning relationships. The field of cultural ecology, a phrase coined by Julian Steward, examines "the processes by which a society adapts to its environment" (Steward 1968:43), emphasizing the specific forms through which culture mediates the human experience of NATURE (see CULTURE AREA).

The Initial Paradigm

In the period 1930–1940 a number of works examined systematically the relation of environmental conditions and cultural expression. C. Daryll Forde's *Habitat, Economy and Society* was a broad, comparative text on this theme (Forde 1934). E. E. Evans-Pritchard's *The Nuer* analyzed with great sophistication the connection between seasonal subsistence strategies, social organization, and patterns of thought in a Nilotic pastoralist TRIBE (Evans-Pritchard 1940). However, it was the work of Julian Steward that first provided a truly ecological theory of culture, considering (1) the interrelation of SOCIAL STRUCTURE, subsistence technique, and environment (the problem of adaptation), and (2) the relation between growth in the scale, complexity, and stratification of societies and change in their patterns of adaptation (the problem of EVOLUTION). Marvin Harris has described Steward's 1936 essay "The Economic and Social Basis of Primitive Bands," in which the first elements of this theory were proposed, as "among the most important achievements of modern anthropology" (Harris 1968:666; see Steward 1955: chs. 7, 8).

Steward made two analytic distinctions that have proved of permanent value. First, he rejected the then widely accepted view of culture as an undifferentiated phenomenon, in which all elements are interrelated and equally significant in patterning a society. Arguing that different components of culture are differentially responsive to adaptive processes, Steward put forward the idea of a culture core, "the constellation of features which are most closely related to subsistence activities and economic arrangements" (Steward 1955:37). Second, Steward also rejected the idea that much of the same processes of adaptation could apply to societies of different scale and political complexity, in short, of differing levels of sociocultural integration. Thus a patrilineal hunting BAND and an industrial STATE differ fundamentally not only in the nature and variety of significant resources, but in the ways these resources are controlled, distributed, and transformed in the process of adaptation (see Steward 1968:50–53). To a striking extent, these concepts anticipated the program of later Marxist anthropology, particularly in the key notion of MODE OF PRODUCTION (see also MATERIALISM).

Although a concept of unilinear evolution had provided nineteenth-century anthropologists with a comparative and generalizable body of theory through which the complexity of cultural data could be interpreted, the inaccuracy and ethnocentrism of this approach led to its eclipse in favor of detailed, descriptive ETHNOGRAPHY and studies of culture history emphasizing DIFFUSION. Yet by 1930 this atheoretical HISTORICISM appeared largely unproductive. Steward was in large measure responsible for reintroducing the issue of evolution to culture theory.

For example, culture-historical accounts of the emergence of irrigation-based agricultural societies in the American Southwest had stressed the crucial role of the diffusion of food crops from Mesoamerica. Yet Steward emphasized that the discovery of patterns of diffusion cannot replace the identification of evolutionary processes. He argued that "the development of Pueblo sociocultural patterns are comprehensible only in terms of the processes of population growth, extension of biological families into lineages, eventual consolidation of lineages into larger settlements, and the appearance of many village institutions that cut across kinship groups" (Steward 1968:46).

Later Research

In the postwar period, research in ecological anthropology (as it is now more commonly known) has taken several directions, reflecting a greater awareness of the methods and findings of geography, general ecology, nutrition, biological anthropology, and systems theory. (See Ellen 1982 for an overview of more recent research.) These include research in biocultural adaptation, growth of an emic perspective in ecological studies, and emergence of a systems approach to modeling the interrelation of environment and culture.

(1) Studies of the interdependence of biological and cultural adaptation within particular ecological systems suggest a returning interest in a holistic ANTHROPOLOGY. A notable example is found in the superior fitness conferred by sickle-cell anemia in a malarial environment, a pattern of adaptation associated with the propagation of root horticulture in tropical Africa (see Wiesenfeld 1969).

(2) In mediating the human experience of nature, each culture creates a model of its environment, mapping through names, categories, and other symbols the topography, climatic conditions, flora, and fauna relevant for a given mode of life. It is in terms of this model that members of a culture act in regard to their environment. No study of ecological anthropology can be complete if it ignores this subjective or emic dimension (see EMIC/ETIC). Harold Conklin's study of Hanunoo (Philippines) cultural categories regarding shifting horticulture was an

early example of what has become a major research focus in ecological anthropology (see Conklin 1954; see also ETHNOSCIENCE).

(3) The concept of SYSTEM has become an important element of modern ecological research. This perspective, embodying the principles of structure, hierarchy, and circular causation, has facilitated the task of modeling complex interactions between culture and environment. One result has been a willingness to consider the interaction of nonmaterial processes (e.g., RITUAL and SYMBOLISM) with more conventionally "ecological" phenomena such as nutrition, climate, and subsistence technique. Roy Rappaport's study of warfare, ritual, and nutrition in Highland New Guinea has been an influential example (Rappaport 1968).

References

Bates, Marston. 1962. "Human Ecology." Sol Tax, ed., *Anthropology Today: Selections*. Chicago: University of Chicago Press. A useful survey of the concept.

Conklin, Harold C. 1954 [1969]. "An Ethnoecological Approach to Shifting Agriculture." Andrew P. Vayda, ed., *Environment and Cultural Behavior*. Garden City, N.Y.: Natural History Press.

Ellen, Roy. 1982. *Environment, Subsistence, and System: The Ecology of Small-Scale Social Formations*. Cambridge: Cambridge University Press. Highly recommended as an introduction to modern ecological anthropology.

Evans-Pritchard, E. E. 1940. *The Nuer: A Description of the Modes of Livelihood and Political Institutions of a Nilotic People*. Oxford: Oxford University Press. An important, early study.

Forde, C. Daryll. 1934 [1963]. *Habitat, Economy and Society: A Geographical Introduction to Ethnology*. London: Methuen.

Harris, Marvin. 1968. *The Rise of Anthropological Theory*. New York: Crowell. A history of culture theory, with a strong materialist bias.

Rappaport, Roy A. 1968. *Pigs for the Ancestors: Ritual in the Ecology of a New Guinea People*. New Haven, Conn.: Yale University Press. An influential study combining ecological and symbolic perspectives.

Steward, Julian. 1955. *Theory of Culture Change: The Methodology of Multilinear Evolution*. Urbana: University of Illinois Press. These essays provided much of the foundation of cultural ecology.

————. 1968 [1977]. "The Concept and Method of Cultural Ecology." *Evolution and Ecology: Essays on Social Transformation*. Jane C. Steward and Robert F. Murphy, eds. Urbana: University of Illinois Press.

Wiesenfeld, Stephen L. 1969. "Sickle-Cell Trait in Human Biological and Cultural Evolution." Andrew P. Vayda, ed., *Environment and Cultural Behavior*. Garden City, N.Y.: Natural History Press.

Sources of Additional Information

An extensive bibliography is presented in James N. Anderson, "Ecological Anthropology and Anthropological Ecology," John J. Honigmann, ed., *Handbook of Social and Cultural Anthropology*, Chicago: Rand McNally, 1973. Julian Steward's *Basin-Plateau Aboriginal Sociopolitical Groups*, Bureau of American Ethnology, *Bulletin* 120, 1938, exemplifying the approach of cultural ecology, is an ethnographic classic. The emergence of cultural ecology is treated in Fred W. Voget, *A History of Ethnology*, New York: Holt, Rinehart and Winston, 1975, ch. 17. Tim Ingold, *The Appropriation of Nature: Essays on Human Ecology and Social Relations*, Iowa City: University of Iowa Press, 1987, discusses major issues in the anthropological study of adaptation, environment, and culture.

CULTURAL RELATIVISM. See RELATIVISM.

CULTURE. (1) That set of capacities which distinguishes *Homo sapiens* as a species and which is fundamental to its mode of ADAPTATION. (2) The learned, cumulative product of all social life. (3) The distinctive patterns of thought, action, and value that characterize the members of a society or social group. (4) A series of mutually incompatible concepts, developing after the Second World War: (a) in social ANTHROPOLOGY, the arrangements of belief and CUSTOM through which social relations are expressed; (b) in materialist studies, the patterned knowledge, technique, and behavior through which humans adapt to the natural world; (c) in ETHNOSCIENCE, a set of standards for behavior considered authoritative within a society; (d) in symbolic studies, a system of meanings through which social life is interpreted.

The aim of anthropology is the controlled and value-free investigation of both the unity and the diversity of the human species. It seeks to explain, on the one hand, the uniqueness of the human species within the biological world and, on the other, the astonishing variety of ways in which this humanness is manifested. The anthropologist struggles with the task of understanding human beings in naturalistic terms while respecting those attributes that appear to make *Homo sapiens* radically dissimilar from any other species. The concept of culture has been central to this endeavor.

In the ideal, culture should provide a unifying concept for the discipline, marking off a certain range of phenomena for investigation and, from the varying perspectives of biological, archaeological, cultural, and linguistic anthropology, articulating observations by means of theory. (On these subfields, see ANTHROPOLOGY.) In reality, anthropology has lacked a single broadly accepted and theoretically productive definition of culture. The ambiguities and multiple interpretations of the culture concept follow from the tasks imposed upon it: to reconcile human uniqueness with human diversity; to order the immensely heterogeneous data of human belief and custom; and to provide a point of common understanding for each of the anthropological subdisciplines, which in general have widely differing theoretical concerns.

It is useful to distinguish four stages in the development of the culture concept. "Culture" is not a term created by the science of anthropology, a field scarcely a century old. The first episode in the history of the culture concept was its development as a general category of Western thought. The second, from roughly the mid-nineteenth century to perhaps 1900, involved the emergence of a distinctively anthropological sense of culture, heavily influenced by the evolutionary assumptions of that period. The third, lasting at least in America until shortly after the Second World War, was in many ways a reaction to the evolutionary orientation of the preceding period. The term took on a strongly pluralistic and ostensibly value-free character. Cultures (in the plural) were seen as essentially autonomous worlds of value and meaning. The fourth, beginning in approximately the 1950s, involved the development of a series of competing perspectives within cultural anthropology. Each of these entailed a theory of culture, and thus what had been (in any given period) a fairly consistently defined concept now became refracted into a wide range of interpretations.

Culture and Cultivation

Anthropologists have taken considerable pains to distinguish their understanding of culture, closely linked to the ideas of CUSTOM and society, from an earlier, more general sense of culture as cultivation. But it would be truer to say that in making culture the keystone of the anthropological vocabulary, much was owed to the term's prescientific usage.

The sense of culture as cultivation rests upon an ancient and powerful agrarian metaphor. The English word culture, like its French, Spanish, and German cognates, derives from the Latin *colo*, to cultivate, meaning not only to cultivate the soil, but by extension to take care of or tend to anything, to foster or cultivate any particular study, to honor or worship any deity. Classical authors extended the metaphor to the realm of personal development. For Cicero, philosophy was cultivation of the soul: as a field is unproductive without cultivation, so is the soul without teaching (*Tusc. Disput.* 2.5.13). Similar images can be found in writings of the Renaissance and Enlightenment periods.

The classical metaphor of cultivation implied a distinction between the natural and the cultural, between the human essence or potential and its outward realization as guided by learning in society (see NATURE). For writers of the nineteenth century this dichotomy remained fundamental. The *Oxford English Dictionary*, that late Victorian monument to English usage, defined culture in these terms: "Worship . . . the action or practice of cultivating the soil . . . the training, development, and refinement of mind, tastes, and manners . . . the intellectual side of civilization."

In the nineteenth century the notion of culture as cultivation was extended to become an abstraction and an absolute, that set of ideals capable of guiding social life (Williams 1958). The writings of the English critic Matthew Arnold (1822–1888) offer a case in point. To the common Victorian argument for the reform of society through the revision of institutions, Arnold counterposed, in *Culture and Anarchy*, the need for the development and propagation of culture, which he defined as "an ideal of human perfection . . . increased sweetness, increased light, increased life, increased sympathy" (Arnold 1869:64).

Such views represented a reaction to drastic and all-encompassing social change. The Victorian culture concept, Raymond Williams has argued, developed as an effort at "a total qualitative assessment" of society, with the aim of revitalization and reconstruction (Williams 1958:295). With the emergence of culture as an abstraction and a holistic concept, attempting to characterize an entire way of life, Victorian usage prepared the ground for the subsequent anthropological interpretation of culture.

Evolution

As an investigation of human nature, human physical variation, and the variety of human institutions, the science of anthropology is not new. Classical authors such as Herodotus and Tacitus made serious attempts to describe the customs of the foreign peoples they encountered, and these writers had their counterparts in other literate civilizations. In Europe, from at least the thirteenth century, there was a growing fascination with the ways of life of non-European peoples, as seen in the writings of explorers, antiquarians, and philosophers alike (see ETHNOLOGY). In a more profound sense, however, the discipline of anthropology dates from the formation of an explicit, technical concept of culture, in the nineteenth century.

In the English-speaking world, Edward Tylor's *Primitive Culture* (1871) first presented the term in an anthropological context. Tylor began *Primitive Culture* with the following statement:

> Culture or civilization, taken in its wide ethnographic sense, is that complex whole which includes knowledge, belief, art, morals, law, custom, and any other capabilities and habits acquired by man as a member of society. The condition of culture among the various societies of mankind, insofar as it is capable of being investigated on general principles, is a subject apt for the study of laws of human thought and action. (Tylor 1871:1:1)

Culture for Tylor was a unity, the collective possession and achievement of humankind. At the same time, it admitted to degrees or stages: A society may have a higher or lower, a more or less developed form of culture. Tylor, like Lewis Henry Morgan in *Ancient Society* (1877), postulated a threefold sequence in culture history, an evolution from savagery through barbarism to CIVILIZATION, the latter equated with contemporary European society (see PRIMITIVE).

Two points made Tylor's definition both distinctive and significant. First, he considered culture to be panhuman. The idea that all human beings were carriers of culture (albeit, in Tylor's view, to different degrees) was still a contested doctrine, as the then-contemporary dichotomy of *Naturvölker* and *Kulturvölker*, natural and cultural beings, suggests. Second, in searching for culture he cast his net wide, recognizing (and here he is very modern) the significance of number systems, stone tools, house forms, MYTHS, divinatory practices, games, cookery—in short, all capabilities and habits that humans acquire as members of a society.

George Stocking has argued that Tylor drew much from the contemporary humanistic debate in Britain (exemplified by the writings of Matthew Arnold) regarding the idea of culture (Stocking 1968:69–90). More definitely, he was influenced by his wide reading of the German ethnographers and ethnologists, whose use of the term culture in some respects anticipated his own. As Joan Leopold has demonstrated, "the works of the Humboldts and Humboldtians, possibly also of Adelung and Vater, gave Tylor a general acquaintance and those of Klemm a more technical, ethnographic familiarity with the word 'culture' " (Leopold 1980:89).

Anthropology embodies a tension between Enlightenment and Romantic assumptions. The first seeks to analyze the development of human societies in terms of certain progressive tendencies or universal principles (frequently centering on an idea of ever-increasing RATIONALITY); the second, to understand the characteristic genius, the distinctive configurations of meaning and value of particular societies. This is, in short, the contrast between a Voltaire and a Herder. The doctrine of cultural EVOLUTION, upheld by Tylor as well as by his contemporaries Lewis Henry Morgan (b. 1818), Henry Maine (b. 1822), John McLennan (b. 1827), and John Lubbock (b. 1834), typified the optimism and rationalism of the Enlightenment. What Tylor valued in the study of culture was its regularities, not its outward variety: "One set of savages is like another," he quoted Dr. Johnson approvingly, adding, "How true a generalization this really is, any Ethnological Museum may show" (Tylor 1871:1:6).

The Boasian Era

In the century since the publication of *Primitive Culture*, both the theory and practice of anthropology have been transformed, and the anthropological understanding of culture has changed accordingly. During the first decades of the twentieth century, particularly in the United States, the rallying cry for this refashioning of anthropology was the critique of evolutionism. With it came a rejection of the monistic and value-laden understanding of culture championed by evolutionary writers. This theoretical redirection coincided with and was encouraged by the initiation of methodical, firsthand research among various aboriginal peoples of the Americas, Africa, Asia, and Oceania.

In 1896, in a justly famous critique of the COMPARATIVE METHOD, Franz Boas argued for "a detailed study of customs in their relation to the total culture of the tribe practicing them, in connection with an investigation of their geographical distribution among neighboring tribes" (Boas 1896:276). The emphasis now was on the DIFFUSION (rather than evolution) of discrete culture traits, and this orientation—Boas's so-called historical method—had the merit of encouraging sustained and detailed ethnographic study of particular tribal communities (see ETHNOGRAPHY). By 1930 the development of the culture concept had proceeded to what might be termed its classical stage. The concept was now pluralistic, each culture localized in a discrete society. As Boas then defined it, "Culture embraces all the manifestations of social habits of a community, the reactions of the individual as affected by the habits of the group in which he lives, and the products of human activities as determined by these habits" (Boas 1930:79).

This interpretation, which Zygmunt Bauman has termed the "differential" concept of culture, can be distinguished from earlier views by three key elements:

It is historicist, holistic, and determinative of behavior (Bauman 1973:17–38; cf. Stocking 1968:200). The historicist view assumed that each society reflected an essentially autonomous world of value and meaning. HISTORICISM and its correlate cultural RELATIVISM were popularized in particular by Ruth Benedict's comparative study *Patterns of Culture* (Benedict 1934).

The sense of holism dictated that each culture be examined as a totality and each trait understood in its context. In part, this approach reflected the constraints of prolonged field research, but it followed equally from the idea of historicism— each culture being a reality sui generis, the whole greater than the sum of its parts.

Finally, this view of culture was deterministic: culture shaped behavior. The Boasian culture concept had a dual character, concerned not only with artifacts and behaviors, but also with motivations and values, the latter given explanatory priority. In part this reflected a reaction to the then-common doctrine of the biological or racial determination of behavior (see RACE; SUPERORGANIC). In part, also, it stemmed from a recognition of the seemingly obligatory character of TRADITION which ethnographers encountered in their research. However circular their reasoning, anthropologists in this era came to view culture as itself a cause underlying the distinctive customs of a society.

The theoretical concerns of anthropologists in the 1920s through 1940s centered on certain problems implicit in the differential model of culture. Chief among these was the issue of cultural integration: how to reconcile the multiplicity of culture traits (the raw data of ethnography) with the supposed unity and singularity of any given culture considered as a whole. This issue derived from the Boasian sense that culture and society were directly correlated: each society was assumed to have a distinctive culture. This view was encouraged by the overwhelming predominance of tribal societies in the ethnographic research of this period, and by a rather static and consensual view of the nature of tribal social life (see TRIBE). As John Bennett has argued, "Culture thus was identified with a holistic tribal unity, and finally this unity was assumed to be present in every human grouping, in all societies" (Bennett 1954:172).

At least until mid-century, three solutions to the problem of cultural integration were in contention. One approach, stressing the autonomy of the cultural sphere, was concerned with delineating the phenomenon of PATTERN in culture, regularities in form, style, and significance—a view championed by Alfred Kroeber (1952:104). Another solution was to postulate a close (or even causal) relation between PERSONALITY and culture, with the unifying character of a culture to be found in supposedly distinctive patterns of personality formation. This led to a concern with child rearing practices and the process of cultural learning (enculturation), a subject widely known through the work of Margaret Mead (1930). Finally, under the inspiration of Emile Durkheim and A. R. Radcliffe-Brown, British anthropologists in particular sought the unity of culture in the contribution of each custom to the maintenance of a total SOCIAL STRUCTURE, an orientation termed FUNCTIONALISM.

Post-War Anthropology

The Second World War represents a watershed in the development of the culture concept. Until this time "culture" had been used with reasonable consistency, as a relatively fixed and distinctive configuration of norms and values determining the way of life of a society. However, the findings of ethnographic research became increasingly difficult to reconcile with this view. Earlier studies had grappled with the problem of CULTURE CHANGE, at first in terms of the DIFFUSION or innovation of distinct culture elements, and later as a process of ACCULTURATION under conditions of culture contact. Yet in either view change remained something anomalous in an otherwise stable system. The ubiquitousness of culture change, the variability of cultural knowledge within a society, and the flexibility with which social norms are interpreted and heeded—all these facts conspired to prompt a reinterpretation of the idea of culture.

A number of competing perspectives appeared from the late 1950s through the early 1970s, each entailing a distinctive theory and concept of culture. Aside from the evident inadequacy of earlier formulations, several factors were responsible for this change. Anthropologists became more sophisticated in matters theoretical, more aware of the need for rigor and explicitness in formulating scientific arguments. The settings of anthropological research became far more varied, as did the problems studied; not only the tribal outback but equally the peasant village, the urban tenement, and the industrial workplace became normal settings for ethnography. Perhaps most important, there was a gradual recognition that the ideas of other disciplines could be directly relevant to anthropological issues. In this fashion the influence of anthropology's more traditional partners psychology and sociology was eclipsed by the doctrines (and perhaps also the chic) of ecology, linguistics, neuroscience, historiography, economics, and philosophy.

If there has been a common denominator to these divergent trends in postwar anthropological theory, it is the rejection of culture as prime mover, and the corresponding search for other explanatory principles through which to interpret the data of ethnography. Broadly speaking, this challenge has been met in three ways: by eliminating culture altogether as a theoretically significant concept; by retaining a broad interpretation of culture, but harnessing it to a materialist framework of explanation; and by narrowing the meaning of culture to provide the focus of one of a number of anthropological perspectives loosely falling within an idealist tradition.

Alternatives to culture. A number of anthropologists would eliminate the concept of culture altogether in favor of other conceptual schemes. The British tradition of social anthropology has to a large extent done this all along, emphasizing social structure rather than culture, a preference that may reflect the different conditions holding in tribal communities under British as opposed to American control. As W. J. M. Mackenzie has written, "The Americans had to work principally with languages, artifacts, individual survivors; the British could sit and watch quietly, in the midst of social systems which were super-ficially untouched by British rule'' (in Bauman 1973:1).

Others have rejected the concept of culture out of an adherence to positivism. As George Murdock commented (in 1972),

> It now seems to me distressingly obvious that culture, social system, and all com-parable supra-individual concepts, such as collective representation, group mind, and social organism, are illusory conceptual abstractions inferred from observations of the very real phenomena of individuals interacting with one another and with their natural environments. (in Sahlins 1976:95)

Instead, writers such as Murdock and Fredrik Barth turned to principles such as utilitarian advantage to explain social life. In this view the patterns recognized (or reified) as culture are better understood as the reflection of a continuous series of goal-seeking transactions between individuals, operating under the con-straints of scarce time and resources (Barth 1966; see also SOCIAL STRUCTURE).

Materialist theories of culture. Another approach has been to retain for culture a broad sweep, but to tie the concept to a specific explanatory argument, generally of a materialist persuasion. Most commonly such approaches have centered on the problem of adaptation to the material constraints of the environment, as in the definition given by Yehudi Cohen: "A culture is made up of the energy systems, the objective and specific artifacts, the organizations of social and political relations, the modes of thought, the ideologies, and the total range of customary behaviors that are transmitted from one generation to another by a social group and that enable it to maintain life in a particular habitat" (Cohen 1974:1) The approach of Marxist anthropology, in contrast, has stressed the role of culture in mediating the contradictions inherent in a society's relations of production, thus linking culture to the notion of ideology (see MATERIALISM; MODE OF PRODUCTION).

Idealist theories. Within an idealist tradition a number of anthropologists have chosen to narrow the domain of the culture concept in an effort to impart a degree of rigor to what was perceived to be a vague and distended category. Despite many differences, all such approaches reject the notion of culture as something concrete, whether this be artifacts or behavior; all assume that cultures should be understood as systems of thought. Here, however, the similarities end.

Proponents of ethnoscience, such as Ward Goodenough, equate culture with cognition, providing systems of classification that structure our understanding of the social and natural worlds. The task of the ethnographer in this view is to formulate "a set of standards that, taken as a guide for acting and interpreting the acts of others, leads to behavior the community's members perceive as in accord with their expectations of one another." More briefly, culture is "a set of standards that seems to be authoritative" (Goodenough 1970:101, 103). In large measure, ethnoscience presumes LANGUAGE as a model for culture. As Roger Keesing has commented, "so reconceived, cultures are epistemologically in the same realm as language (Saussure's *langue* or Chomsky's competence), as inferred ideational codes lying behind the realm of observable events'' (Keesing 1974:77).

From the perspective of STRUCTURALISM, culture is manifested as systems of contrasting signs, expressed in diverse domains (language, myth, KINSHIP, etc.), yet all reflecting underlying structures of the human mind (see also SEMIOTICS). This approach has been developed in particular through the writings of Claude Lévi-Strauss (see Lévi-Strauss 1963). In the structuralist vision, culture does not figure as a pluralistic concept, distinguishing one society from another, as was true in the Boasian era. Instead, culture is ultimately a single, global ensemble of signs, within which each society manifests variations. In Keesing's phrase, "the mind imposes culturally patterned order, a logic of binary contrast, of relations and transformations, on a continuously changing and often random world" (Keesing 1974:78–79). For Lévi-Strauss the fundamental contrast is not drawn between societies, but between the universe of culture and that of nature, which the former orders and transcends.

A third approach is taken through the analysis of SYMBOLISM (the domain of symbolic anthropology), represented by the work of Clifford Geertz. For Geertz, culture exists (and thus can be studied) only in the meaningful interaction of social life. Emphasizing—as did Boas—the plurality of cultural worlds, Geertz seeks to avoid both the reduction of culture to an individual's knowledge of rules and typologies (as with ethnoscience) and its elevation to an autonomous system independent of human action (as with structuralism). Symbolic anthropology views all acts and events as potentially meaningful, but also intrinsically ambiguous. Culture, Geertz has argued, is not a cause to which events or institutions may be attributed, but a context within which they may be made intelligible (Geertz 1973:14). Thus in Geertz's view the inherently fallible process of INTERPRETATION is fundamental to the experience of culture, for native and ethnographer alike.

Culture Theory: The 1980s

The salient characteristic of anthropology in the 1980s was intellectual fission: an ever-greater diversity of theoretical influences, matched by an increasing fragmentation of research specialties. As Eric Wolf aptly commented, "What was once a secular church of believers in the primacy of Culture has now become a holding company of diverse interests" (Wolf 1980). Some anthropologists, notably proponents of the extreme bioevolutionist perspective termed SOCIO-BIOLOGY, would dispense with a concept of culture altogether. Aside from such efforts at reductionism, two trends have had particular importance in culture theory. One has involved a radically relativistic perspective of cultural knowledge, often termed "postmodernism"; the other, an effort to develop a theory of cultural process that can account for both individual action and collective constraint, examining the creation and reproduction of culture through "practice."

Postmodernism. The phrase postmodernism describes an eclectic movement, originating in aesthetics, architecture, and philosophy, espousing a systematic scepticism not only of particular inherited styles and traditions, but even of the possibility of a securely grounded theoretical perspective. Postmodernism entails what Jean-Francois Lyotard has termed "incredulity towards metanarratives" (in Marcus and Fischer 1986:8), whether this involves the notions of progress and development inherent in modern capitalism, of sexuality and repression in Freudian theory, or of class and revolution in Marxism. It offers "an ongoing critique of the West's most confident, characteristic discourses" (Clifford 1986:10).

Applied to anthropology, this view implies a stance of extreme scepticism regarding the possibility of reliable and objectifiable knowledge of culture. This is in effect the logical extension of an anthropological axiom, the contingency of cultural knowledge, but now applied as much to the ethnographer as to the informant. As James Clifford has summarized a recent collection of essays on postmodernist ethnography,

> they see culture as composed of seriously contested codes and representations. . . .
> Their focus on text making and rhetoric serves to highlight the constructed, artificial
> nature of cultural accounts. It undermines overly transparent modes of authority,
> and it draws attention to the historical predicament of ethnography, the fact that it
> is always caught up in the invention, not the representation, of cultures. (Clifford
> 1986:2)

The effect has been to turn attention from the society observed to the anthropologist observing.

Both the explicitly postmodernist genre of ethnography, and the wider field of symbolic anthropology of which it is an outgrowth, have been criticized for fostering a self-indulgent subjectivity, and for exaggerating the esoteric and unique aspects of a culture at the expense of more prosaic but significant questions (for example, issues of power and INEQUALITY) that encourage comparison and theoretical synthesis. Roger Keesing has noted the irony that "the presently ascendant symbolist/interpretive anthropological modes require radical alterity [Otherness] more than ever, in a world where such boundaries as there ever were are dissolving by the day" (Keesing 1989; see also Keesing 1987; Sangren 1988).

The reproduction of cultural forms: practice. The adequacy of modern culture theory has been called into question by its inability to reconcile a series of ostensibly compatible principles, among these being the contrasts of continuity and change, freedom and structure, individual and society. Beginning in the mid–1970s, a number of writers sought to resolve these antinomies by focusing on the power of individuals to generate cultural forms in the conduct of everyday life, a concern with what may be termed—following Pierre Bourdieu—practice (see Ortner 1984:144–60). As Sherry Ortner has characterized this, a theory of practice seeks to explain "the genesis, reproduction, and change of form and meaning of a given social/cultural whole" (Ortner 1984:149).

There has been a convention in anthropology that cultural (or social) change is problematic, necessitating explanation, while cultural stability is not. Practice theory challenges this view. Culture is understood as constantly created and renewed; it is more accurately viewed as a process than as an entity. As Roy Wagner has observed, "The contexts of culture are perpetuated and carried forth by acts of objectification, by being invented out of each other and through each other. This means that we cannot appeal to the force of something called 'tradition,' or 'education,' or spiritual guidance to account for cultural continuity, or for that matter cultural change" (Wagner 1981:50). Furthermore, the ease of communication in the late twentieth century has meant that cultural forms need no longer have a definitive social context: Principles of Gandhian nonviolence informed the American civil rights movement, while American television programs are disseminated throughout Asia. Increasingly, cultural practice involves the creative recombination of forms originating in radically different societies (see Appadurai 1990).

The writings of Pierre Bourdieu represent an ambitious effort to explain the reproduction and transformation of cultural forms. Bourdieu insists that most cultural knowledge is not theoretical or explicit, but tacit, learned through practice. Particular life-environments produce structures of tacit dispositions (which he terms *habitus*) through which culturally appropriate practices and representations are generated. This structured, tacit, cultural knowledge is lived rather than formally learned, literally embodied through characteristic postures, movements, and actions. The *habitus* involves "an infinite capacity for generating products—thoughts, perceptions, expressions and actions—whose limits are set by the historically and socially situated conditions of its production" (Bourdieu 1990:55). Bourdieu offers a theory of learning that seeks to account for both the consistency and creativity inherent in cultural practice, one which avoids reducing practice to either the "mechanical reproduction" of an existing cultural form, or the wholly free activity of an autonomous actor devoid of social or cultural constraints (Bourdieu 1990:52–56).

References

Appadurai, Arjun. 1990. "Disjuncture and Difference in Global Cultural Economy." *Public Culture* 2 (2): 1–24.
Arnold, Matthew. 1869 [1950]. *Culture and Anarchy*. J. D. Wilson, ed. Cambridge: Cambridge University Press. A highly influential statement of the preanthropological understanding of culture.
Barth, Fredrik. 1966 [1981]. "Models of Social Organization (I–III)." F. Barth, *Process and Form in Social Life*. London: Routledge & Kegan Paul.
Bauman, Zygmunt. 1973. *Culture as Praxis*. London and Boston: Routledge and Kegan Paul. A challenging discussion of culture drawing on Marxism, semiotics, and a broad humanistic scholarship.
Benedict, Ruth. 1934. *Patterns of Culture*. Boston: Houghton Mifflin. A representative (and highly influential) statement of the differential concept of culture.
Bennett, John W. 1954. "Interdisciplinary Research and the Concept of Culture." *AA* 56:169–179. A strong argument against the use of culture as an explanatory concept.

Boas, Franz. 1896 [1940]. "The Limitations of the Comparative Method of Anthro-
    pology." F. Boas, *Race, Language and Culture*. New York: Free Press. A major
    critique of evolutionary anthropology.
———. 1930. "Anthropology." *ESS* 2:73–110.
Bourdieu, Pierre. 1990. The *Logic of Practice*. Richard Nice, trans. Stanford, Calif.:
    Stanford University Press.
Clifford, James. 1986. "Introduction: Partial Truths." James Clifford and George E.
    Marcus, eds., *Writing Culture: The Poetics and Politics of Ethnography*. Berkeley
    and Los Angeles: University of California Press.
Cohen, Yehudi, ed. 1974. *Man in Adaptation: The Cultural Present*. 2d ed. Chicago:
    Aldine. A useful anthology emphasizing the adaptationist perspective.
Geertz, Clifford. 1973. *The Interpretation of Cultures*. New York: Basic Books. Presents
    a symbolic/interpretive perspective.
Goodenough, Ward H. 1970. *Description and Comparison in Cultural Anthropology*.
    Chicago: Aldine. An exposition of the ethnoscientific or cognitive approach.
Keesing, Roger. 1974. "Theories of Culture." *ARA* 3:73–97. A good overview and
    critique of postwar theories.
———. 1987. "Anthropology as Interpretive Quest." *CA* 28:161–76.
———. 1989. "Theories of Culture Revisited." Paper presented at the American An-
    thropological Association Annual Meeting, Washington, D.C.
Kroeber, Alfred. 1952. *The Nature of Culture*. Chicago: University of Chicago Press. A
    selection of papers, strongly historicist and anti-positivist.
Leopold, Joan. 1980. *Culture in Comparative and Evolutionary Perspective: E. B. Tylor
    and the Making of* Primitive Culture. Berlin: Dietrich Reimer Verlag.
Lévi-Strauss, Claude. 1963. *Structural Anthropology*. Claire Jacobson and Brooke
    Schoepf, trans. New York: Basic Books.
Marcus, George E., and Michael M. J. Fischer. 1986. *Anthropology as Cultural Critique*.
    Chicago: University of Chicago Press. A good introduction to the postmodernist
    viewpoint in ethnography.
Mead, Margaret. 1930. *Growing Up in New Guinea*. New York: Mentor.
Morgan, Lewis Henry. 1877. *Ancient Society*. Chicago: Charles H. Kerr.
Ortner, Sherry B. 1984. "Theory in Anthropology since the Sixties." *Comparative
    Studies in Society and History* 26 (1): 126–66. An excellent overview.
Sahlins, Marshall. 1976. *Culture and Practical Reason*. Chicago: University of Chicago
    Press.
Sangren, P. Steven. 1988. "Rhetoric and the Authority of Ethnography: 'Postmodernism'
    and the Social Reproduction of Texts." *CA* 29:405–35.
Stocking, George W., Jr. 1968. *Race, Culture, and Evolution: Essays in the History of
    Anthropology*. New York: Free Press.
Tylor, Edward B. 1871 [1958]. *Primitive Culture*. 2 vols. New York: Harper. An essential
    text in the development of an anthropological culture concept.
Wagner, Roy. 1981. *The Invention of Culture*. Rev. ed. Chicago: University of Chicago
    Press.
Williams, Raymond. 1958. *Culture and Society, 1780–1950*. New York: Harper and
    Row.
Wolf, Eric. 1980. "They Divide and Subdivide, and Call It Anthropology." *The New
    York Times*, Nov. 30, 1980, Sec. 4:9.

Sources of Additional Information

In *Culture: A Critical Review of Concepts and Definitions*, New York: Random House, Vintage Books, 1963 (orig. 1952), Alfred Kroeber and Clyde Kluckhohn provide an exhaustive review of definitions of culture as of mid-century, a work that reveals clearly the eclectic (in fact, muddled) state of culture theory in that period. Diane J. Austin-Broos, ed., *Creating Culture: Profiles in the Study of Culture*, Sydney: Allen & Unwin, 1987, provides an interesting series of essays on major culture theorists, including not only anthropological standard bearers (e.g., Boas, Lévi-Strauss), but also more recent writers both within and outside the discipline of anthropology, such as Geertz, Bourdieu, Habermas, Foucault, and E. P. Thompson.

A number of histories of anthropology exist. See Marvin Harris, *The Rise of Anthropological Theory: A History of Theories of Culture*, New York: Thomas Y. Crowell, 1968; and Murray Leaf, *Man, Mind, and Science: A History of Anthropology*, New York: Columbia University Press, 1979. For the nineteenth century, see George W. Stocking, Jr., *Victorian Anthropology*, New York: Free Press, 1987.

Introductory readers offering theoretically oriented excerpts from the past century of anthropological writing include Frederick Gamst and Edward Norbeck, eds., *Ideas of Culture: Sources and Uses*, New York: Holt, Rinehart and Winston, 1976; and Herbert Applebaum, ed., *Perspectives in Cultural Anthropology*, Albany: State University of New York Press, 1987. Two anthologies concerned with the significance of the culture concept for the anthropology of the 1990s are Morris Freilich, ed., *The Relevance of Culture*, New York: Bergin & Garvey, 1989; and Robert H. Winthrop, ed., *Culture and the Anthropological Tradition*, Lanham, Md.: University Press of America, 1990.

CULTURE AREA. A region of relative environmental and cultural uniformity, characterized by societies with significant similarities in mode of ADAPTATION and SOCIAL STRUCTURE.

Culture area is a heuristic concept, providing a geographic ordering of societies on the basis of shared environmental and cultural features. For example, the Northwest Coast may be distinguished from other areas of aboriginal North America by an adaptation based on anadromous fishing, an ECONOMY of high surplus, and a ranked polity involving ceremonial wealth displays.

The idea of culture area resulted from the conjunction of geographic and ethnological studies, beginning in the later nineteenth century, notably in Germany and the United States. Adolf Bastian (1826–1905) devised systems of culture area classification in preparing collections at the Museum für Völkerkunde in Berlin. He proposed in 1868, for example, five culture areas for North America: Athapaskan-Algonkian, Oregon, Dakota, Florida, and Mexican (Koepping 1983:134). In the 1880s and 1890s, Friedrich Ratzel (1844–1904) and his pupil Leo Frobenius examined the DIFFUSION of culture traits (e.g., the form and construction of the bow in West Africa) as a basis for demarcating areas of common cultural influence. This approach was elaborated on by the later *Kulturkreislehre* or "Culture-Circle" School (Schmidt 1939:25–27; Penniman 1974:177–78). The concept was apparently first utilized in American ANTHRO-

POLOGY by Otis Mason in 1895 (revised 1907), in his classification of the aboriginal Americas (Kroeber 1939:7). Mason's approach was almost entirely environmental: he characterized the arctic area, for instance, mainly in terms of cold, ice and snow, bear, fox, and aquatic mammals (Mason 1907:427).

Diffusionist Studies

The major use of the culture area concept, however, occurred in historical, diffusionist ETHNOLOGY, encouraged both in North America and in Europe, in the first several decades of this century, by a strong opposition to evolutionary theory (see EVOLUTION; HISTORICISM). In the United States, Clark Wissler sought to reconcile the influences of environment and diffusion in the patterning of aboriginal CULTURE. He argued that (1) culture traits (e.g., the tipi, the sun dance) diffuse essentially uniformly from an original center, implying that the center of a trait distribution is also its earliest occurrence (the age-area hypothesis); and (2) ecological zones and culture areas are broadly congruent, implying a mild environmental determinism (Wissler 1926:197, 216).

German-speaking ethnologists, led by Fritz Gräbner and Wilhelm Schmidt, developed a more elaborate and systematic treatment of diffusion, which differed from the American approach principally in assuming the transmission of whole culture complexes or culture circles (*Kulturkreise*) on a global basis, rather than the movement of discrete traits over limited areas. These supposed complexes (e.g., the Melanesian totemistic culture circle, the matrilineal agrarian culture circle) are thus ethnological reconstructions, broadly independent of particular environments, and not strictly comparable to culture areas (see Schmidt 1939:181–90, 222).

Critique of the Concept

The utility of the culture area concept lies primarily in describing broad patterns of cultural diffusion. For example, it is the diffusion of CASTE organization and Sanskritic TRADITION that defines the South Asian culture area. In other respects, the concept is now of minor theoretical significance. From an ecological perspective, Roy Ellen has argued that most culture areas are "too gross spatially. . . . Cultural and environmental diversity within such [a subcontinental] area defies its systematic examination" (Ellen 1982:9). The culture area is also historically heterogeneous, for typically, as Sapir noted, "the various culture elements that serve to define it are of very different ages" (Sapir 1916:425–26).

The underlying problem is the inconsistent criteria by which classifications are constructed, with predictably incommensurate results. The boundaries of the aboriginal California culture area, for example, were sketched quite differently by Otis Mason, Clark Wissler, and Alfred Kroeber (Kroeber 1939:53). As Julian Steward noted, "Disagreement is inevitable because . . . there is no objective means for weighing the importance of local differences and for deciding which categories of elements shall be ascribed greatest importance" (Steward 1955:82). Since the Second World War, renewed interest in cultural evolution, the development of CULTURAL ECOLOGY, and a concern to develop more rigorously comparative and generalizable propositions in anthropological theory (see COMPARATIVE METHOD) have severely limited the application of the culture area concept.

References

Ellen, Roy. 1982. *Environment, Subsistence and System: The Ecology of Small-Scale Social Formations*. Cambridge: Cambridge University Press. A useful introduction.

Koepping, Klaus-Peter. 1983. *Adolf Bastian and the Psychic Unity of Mankind*. St. Lucia, Australia: University of Queensland Press.

Kroeber, A. L. 1939. "Cultural and Natural Areas of Native North America." *University of California Publications in American Archaeology and Ethnology* 38:1–242. The culmination of the culture area approach in North American ethnology.

Mason, Otis. 1907. "Environment." Frederick W. Hodge, ed., *Handbook of American Indians North of Mexico*. 2 vols. Bureau of American Ethnology, *Bulletin* 30 (pt. 1): 427–30.

Penniman, T. K. 1974. *A Hundred Years of Anthropology*. New York: Morrow.

Sapir, Edward. 1916 [1949]. "Time Perspective in Aboriginal American Culture: A Study in Method." David G. Mandelbaum, ed., *Selected Writings of Edward Sapir in Language, Culture and Personality*. Berkeley and Los Angeles: University of California Press. A major work in Boasian ethnology.

Schmidt, Wilhelm. 1939. *The Culture Historical Method of Ethnology*. S. A. Sieber, trans. New York: Fortuny's. A good introduction to the *Kulturkreislehre* perspective.

Steward, Julian. 1955. "Culture Area and Culture Type in Aboriginal America: Methodological Considerations." J. Steward, *Theory of Culture Change: The Methodology of Multilinear Evolution*. Urbana: University of Illinois Press. A critique of the culture area concept.

Wissler, Clark. 1926 [1971]. *The Relation of Nature to Man in Aboriginal America*. New York: AMS Press. An early effort at a cultural-environmental synthesis.

Sources of Additional Information

A general discussion of diffusionist research and the culture area concept is found in Marvin Harris, *The Rise of Anthropological Theory*, New York: Crowell, 1968, ch. 14. See also *GEC*, s.v. "culture area." German diffusionist studies are treated in Robert Lowie, *The History of Ethnological Theory*, New York: Rinehart, 1937, ch. 11. Harold E. Driver, "The Contribution of A. L. Kroeber to Culture Area Theory and Practice," *Indiana University Publications in Anthropology and Linguistics, Memoir* 18, 1962, provides a history of culture area research in North American ethnology. For a useful North American case study, see William Y. Adams and Sharon Mitchell, "The Yuman Anomaly," Robert H. Winthrop, ed., *Culture and the Anthropological Tradition*, Lanham, Md.: University Press of America, 1990.

CULTURE CHANGE. Any shared, relatively enduring transformation of culturally patterned belief or behavior.

Considered historically any given society reveals a record of transformation, a mingling of continuity and change. Understanding the various modes of culture change—their causes, processes, and consequences—remains a major challenge for ANTHROPOLOGY. Related concepts include DIFFUSION, ACCULTURATION, EVOLUTION, and DEVELOPMENT.

Culture change embraces any shared, relatively enduring transformation of culturally patterned belief or behavior (see Barnett 1953). Social change is a near synonym, though more common in British usage, and often implies the study of change in institutions, for example, KINSHIP or ECONOMY (Wilson and Wilson 1945). Diffusion describes culture change occurring through the communication of discrete traits or techniques (e.g., the alphabet or gunpowder). Acculturation, in contrast, involves change brought about through direct contact, a confrontation of competing cultural systems, generally with significant inequality in the scale, power, or technological complexity of the societies involved.

Diffusion also contrasts with invention, the development of qualitatively new cultural forms. The question of the respective roles of diffusion and invention in culture change has been a matter of controversy since the Victorian era. Independent invention provided the primary mechanism for change in theories of cultural evolution; historically oriented ETHNOLOGY, in contrast, proposed diffusion as the exclusive or near-exclusive basis of culture change.

This debate reflects a more basic disagreement regarding the limits of creativity in human societies. Proponents of diffusion assume that innovation is unusual and that change in a given society is predominantly the result of imitation. Advocates of the pervasive character of invention take the opposite perspective (see Mason 1895; Barnett 1953; for an archaeological perspective see Renfrew 1979).

While concepts such as diffusion and invention interpret change as a succession of particular, contingent events, the notions of evolution and development belong to a different realm of discourse, the generalizing domain of social theory or the natural sciences. Both terms envision change as a directional process and a systematic transformation. They differ in their scope and in their philosophical or ideological background.

In its broadest sense evolution describes a cumulative (and generally irreversible) process involving an increase in variety, complexity, and quantity, whether in reference to galaxies, species, or cultures (Goudge 1973:174). In anthropology, theories of cultural evolution have provided a means of explaining change and diversity on a large scale, as seen in the emergence of successive patterns of ADAPTATION or SOCIAL STRUCTURE (see BAND; TRIBE; CHIEFDOM; STATE). DEVELOPMENT, in contrast, has far narrower connotations, referring chiefly to the twentieth century transformation of predominantly rural and agrarian societies of the Third World (see PEASANTRY), typically through industrial production, an expanded market economy, and URBANISM. In the implicit preference accorded Western economic and social forms, the concept of development reflects some strongly ethnocentric assumptions (see RELATIVISM).

Change and Progress

The Western interpretation of change has been strongly influenced by what Robert Nisbet has termed the metaphor of growth, the analogy of society with a biological organism, a perspective dating to the ancient Greeks. As each organism has a distinctive cycle of growth, so too have societies. Thus change is seen as intrinsic to a society, rather than being caused by external events; it is also directional, cumulative, and essentially irreversible (see Nisbet 1969:3–11).

One manifestation is the cyclical understanding of history, in which each society undergoes an inevitable trajectory from inchoate beginnings, through ascent to a harmonious and creative cultural maximum, to a culminating decadence or disintegration (see Spengler 1918; Kroeber 1944). An alternative interpretation is the doctrine of progress, envisioning history as a gradual, linear, and unlimited physical and moral improvement—a dominant element of European thought since the eighteenth century. According to the French economist Jacques Turgot (1727–1781), over the long term "manners are softened, the human mind enlightened . . . and the total mass of human kind . . . advances ever, though slowly, towards greater perfection" (in Teggart 1949:242). With some changes in style, the same sentiment could have been uttered by a Victorian evolutionist.

Change and Culture Theory

The speculative ethnology of the Renaissance and Enlightenment recognized MIGRATION and diffusion as major mechanisms for culture change and diversity. Victorian anthropology, in contrast, came to emphasize a unilineal cultural evolution, postulating savagery, barbarism, and CIVILIZATION as necessary stages successively attained by each society in the course of its development. However, evolutionary anthropologists were not concerned with describing the transformation of particular societies, but merely with constructing a hypothetical history of institutions.

The reaction to evolutionary anthropology, beginning about 1900, de-emphasized the study of culture change: in Boasian HISTORICISM because of an emphasis on the reconstruction of precontact aboriginal cultures, in British FUNCTIONALISM because of a concern with demonstrating how the interrelation of institutions yielded social stability. The recognition of culture change as an essential anthropological problem, beginning with studies of acculturation in the late 1920s, did not so much transform the concept of CULTURE as add another topic for research. Fredrik Barth has aptly criticized the "comfortable convention in social anthropology . . . of treating 'social change' as if it were a topic of anthropological investigation like 'religion' or 'domestic organization'" (Barth 1967:661).

This perspective altered considerably in the 1970s and 1980s, as an increasing concern with process rather than PATTERN—for example in culture theory centering on the concept of practice—made change appear a normal element of all social life. Furthermore, the rapid transformation of both tribal and agrarian peasant societies, which occurred in the aftermath of the Second World War, stimulated new approaches to the study of culture change in anthropology—generally under the rubric of modernization or development—studies that have been particularly important in APPLIED ANTHROPOLOGY.

References

Barnett, Homer G. 1953. *Innovation: The Basis of Culture Change*. New York: McGraw-
    Hill. A broad overview.
Barth, Fredrik. 1967. "On the Study of Social Change." *AA* 69:661–69.
Goudge, Thomas A. 1973. "Evolutionism." *DHI* 2:174–89. Reviews the intellectual
    history of the concept.
Kroeber, Alfred. 1944. *Configurations of Culture Growth*. Berkeley and Los Angeles:
    University of California Press. Kroeber argues for the existence of culture cycles
    in history.
Mason, Otis T. 1895. [1966]. *The Origins of Invention: A Study of Industry among
    Primitive Peoples*. Cambridge, Mass.: MIT Press.
Nisbet, Robert A. 1969. *Social Change and History: Aspects of the Western Theory of
    Development*. New York: Oxford University Press.
Renfrew, Colin. 1979. "Colonialism and Megalithismus." C. Renfrew, *Problems in
    European Prehistory*. Cambridge: Cambridge University Press.
Spengler, Oswald. 1918 [1966]. *The Decline of the West*. 2 vols. Charles Atkinson,
    trans. New York: Knopf.
Teggart, Frederick J., ed. 1949. *The Idea of Progress: A Collection of Readings*. Rev.
    by George Hildebrand. Berkeley and Los Angeles: University of California Press.
    An excellent anthology, strong on classical and medieval sources.
Wilson, Godfrey, and Monica Wilson. 1945 [1968]. *The Analysis of Social Change,
    Based on Observations in Central Africa*. Cambridge: Cambridge University Press.
    The perspective of British social anthropology.

Sources of Additional Information

A classic study of culture change is Wilson D. Wallis, *Culture and Progress*, New York: McGraw-Hill, 1930. In *Cultural Dynamics*, New York: Knopf, 1966, Melville J. Herskovits reviews the major mechanisms and concepts of culture change, from a traditional ethnological perspective. An excellent anthology, combining theory and case studies, is Ivan A. Brady and Barry L. Isaac, eds., *A Reader in Culture Change*, 2 vols., New York: John Wiley/Halstead Press, 1975.

CURING. The culturally defined process of diagnosis and treatment through which physical, mental, or spiritual impairment is corrected and health restored.

The fact of illness confronts humans with their own vulnerability. Curing represents an effort to reestablish human control by interpreting misfortune and intervening appropriately to alleviate suffering. Each act of diagnosis and treatment involves an attempt to transform NATURE through the understandings of CULTURE. The study of curing in its cultural context has gradually been formalized as a distinct specialty, medical anthropology. This field is inherently interdisciplinary, for "medical anthropology acts at a vital intersection of body, mind, and community. It thus embraces a range of anthropological concerns, biological and ecological, cultural and symbolic, personal and social" (Hahn and Kleinman 1983:321).

Early ETHNOGRAPHY commonly included reference to belief and CUSTOM concerned with illness and its cure, generally interpreted through the concepts of ANIMISM, MAGIC, SHAMANISM, TABOO, or WITCHCRAFT. Such practices were frequently offered as evidence of a prescientific mentality, rather than examined as medical systems in their own right (e.g., Tylor 1871: ch. 14; see also PRIMITIVE). Adolph Bandelier's study of trephination (cranial incisions) in aboriginal Bolivia, in contrast, was an early example of a new genre, ethnographic studies on specifically medical or surgical topics (Bandelier 1904). In 1932 Forrest Clements offered a synthesis of so-called primitive medical systems, based on the DIFFUSION of key explanatory principles (sorcery, object intrusion, spirit possession, soul loss, and breach of taboo), seeking "their relative antiquity, probable origin, and historical connections" (Clements 1932:185).

Curing and Culture

In contrast to a concern with discrete medical beliefs or practices, the emergence of a modern medical anthropology was marked by the recognition of curing as an integrated SYSTEM of ideas and practices. In this vein, W. H. R. Rivers (1864–1922) insisted that native medical practices "are not a medley of disconnected and meaningless customs . . . [but rather] are inspired by definite ideas concerning the causation of disease." Arguing that WORLD VIEW determines the cultural interpretation of disease, Rivers stressed that native practices and ideas jointly constitute a "social institution" (in Wellin 1977:49; see also Rivers 1924).

This perspective was exemplified in E. E. Evans-Pritchard's study *Witchcraft, Oracles and Magic among the Azande* (Evans-Pritchard 1937). His achievement lay in demonstrating the coherence of Zande beliefs, the manner in which divination, magic, and accusations of witchcraft interact to provide a consistent means of explaining illness and other misfortune (see RATIONALITY). Later ethnographic studies such as Victor Turner's *Drums of Affliction* have stressed the social character of illness and curing in kin-based societies (see TRIBE), as well as the complex SYMBOLISM of the curing process. For the Ndembu, the cause of illness is found principally in social conflict or transgression rather than individual pathology. Diagnosis and cure (as with RITUAL generally) serve to adjust "the individual to the traditional social order into which he is born" (Turner 1968:22). Cognitive theory has also been influential, as in Charles Frake's study of the classification of illness by the Subanum of Mindanao (Frake 1961; see ETHNOSCIENCE).

Biological and Ecological Approaches

Through the early 1950s, medical anthropology remained essentially ethnological in scope. Erwin Ackerknecht, for example, had argued in 1942 that non-Western medicine was magical in character and that such belief systems could not be explained in terms of biological or environmental conditions (in Wellin 1977:52). This perspective altered considerably in the late 1950s because of changes within both ANTHROPOLOGY and the biological sciences. First, with the growth of APPLIED ANTHROPOLOGY, research was directed to the interrelation of cultural and environmental constraints, for example, in adapting public health programs to foreign cultural settings (Paul 1958). Greater interest in CULTURAL ECOLOGY and ADAPTATION also encouraged this trend. Second, the emergence of population genetics likewise favored an integrated biocultural approach in medical anthropology. Thus Frank Livingstone (1958) explained the distribution of sickle-cell anemia in West African populations in terms of the greater fitness the trait conferred in a malarial environment, which in turn was associated with the diffusion of slash-and-burn horticulture within the tropical rainforest.

The Critique of Biomedicine

Research, which today would be defined as medical anthropology, was originally "fragmented among a variety of already established 'anthropologies,'" including psychological, biological, and applied anthropology, and the anthropology of religion (Greenwood et al. 1988:1). By the 1970s a distinctive scholarship had emerged, reflected in new institutional arrangements. In the United States, for example, a Society for Medical Anthropology was established in 1971 (Todd and Ruffini 1979:7). Numerous journals, symposia, and conferences also attest to its institutional success. In part, these changes reflect both the extensive support available for all aspects of medical research in the postwar period and a growing acceptance of anthropologists in Western clinical settings (Young 1982:257–58).

This has meant, however, that as medical anthropology has gained coherence, it has been increasingly influenced by Western medical theory and practice ("biomedicine"). The biomedical model reflects a strongly reductionist perspective, and it differs in this regard from most non-Western systems of curing: "The central concern of Biomedicine is not general well-being, nor individual persons, nor simply their bodies, but their bodies in disease. . . . While patients suffer 'illness' (the patient's construal of affliction), physicians treat 'disease' (their reduction of problems in the patient's life world to disordered physiology)" (Hahn and Kleinman 1983:312). In the prominent influence exerted by biomedicine, the development of medical anthropology parallels that of several other subfields in which both subject and methods were largely defined (at least initially) by mature, autonomous, Western-oriented disciplines. The relationship of legal anthropology to LAW, and of economic anthropology to economics (see ECONOMY), provide obvious examples.

Recent research within medical anthropology has been structured to a significant extent by debate over the biomedical model of curing. Davydd Greenwood et al. noted "concern that the discipline of late has tended to become the handmaiden of biomedicine and that not enough attention is paid to the culture of biomedical theory and practice" (Greenwood et al. 1988:1). This debate reflects fundamental disagreement regarding the validity of non-Western medical systems and the degree to which insights and methods of research developed in studying non-Western systems should be applied to Western biomedicine.

As Gretchen Lang has written in her study of Dakota interpretations of diabetes, the distinction between illness and disease "recognizes that illness is strongly influenced by culture, and is part of a social system of shared meanings and rules for behavior." Furthermore, such cultural perspectives shape "ways in which illness is presented, how care is evaluated by the patient, and how one cares for oneself" (Lang 1990:286). Other anthropologists have argued that culture-specific assumptions shape not only the patient's experience of illness and treatment, but the theory and methods of biomedicine itself. As Byron Good has commented, illness "is fundamentally semantic or meaningful and . . . all clinical practice is inherently interpretive" (in Young 1982:262). Daniel Moerman has suggested that biomedicine in fact relies heavily on symbolism and metaphor for the effectiveness of its curing, despite assumptions to the contrary by its practitioners (Moerman 1979).

Medical anthropology has come to encompass not only the serious examination of non-Western medical systems, but a critical interpretation of Western biomedicine. Rather than forming merely a narrow specialty, curing in anthropological perspective offers a domain of research that rigorously explores the interface of culture and biology, "providing opportunities to grasp major topics in general anthropology and to examine them in highly specific contexts" (Greenwood et al. 1988:2). Such research is not only intrinsically important, but could provide a model for the effective integration of theory in a unified anthropology.

References

Bandelier, A. 1904. "Aboriginal Trephining in Bolivia." *AA* 6:440–47. An early study.
Clements, Forrest E. 1932. "Primitive Concepts of Disease." *University of California Publications in American Archaeology and Ethnology* 32:185–252. A comparative analysis of the diffusion of culture traits.
Evans-Pritchard, E. E. 1937. *Witchcraft, Oracles, and Magic among the Azande*. Oxford: Clarendon Press. A classic study in ritual, world view, and rationality.
Frake, Charles. 1961. "The Diagnosis of Disease Among the Subanum of Mindanao." *AA* 63:113–32. An ethnoscientific approach.
Greenwood, Davydd, et al., eds. 1988. "Introduction" [to "Theme Issue: Medical Anthropology."] *American Ethnologist* 15:1–3.
Hahn, Robert A., and Arthur Kleinman. 1983. "Biomedical Practice and Anthropological Theory: Frameworks and Directions." *ARA* 12:305–33. A critical review of biomedicine from an anthropological viewpoint, with extensive bibliography.
Lang, Gretchen C. 1990. "Talking About a New Illness with the Dakota: Reflections on Diabetes, Food, and Culture." Robert H. Winthrop, ed., *Culture and the Anthropological Tradition*. Lanham, Md.: University Press of America.
Livingstone, Frank B. 1958. "Anthropological Implications of Sickle-Cell Gene Distribution in West Africa." *AA* 60:533–62. A classic study in the interrelation of culture, biology, and environment.
Moerman, Daniel E. 1979. "Anthropology of Symbolic Healing." *CA* 20:59–80.
Paul, Benjamin D. 1958 [1977]. "The Role of Beliefs and Customs in Sanitation Programs." David Landy, ed., *Culture, Disease, and Healing: Studies in Medical Anthropology*. New York: Macmillan.

Rivers, W. H. R. 1924. *Medicine, Magic, and Religion*. New York: Harcourt, Brace.
    An important early study arguing for the coherence of non-Western medical beliefs.
Todd, Harry F., Jr., and Julio L. Ruffini. 1979. "Introduction." H. Todd and J. Ruffini,
    eds., *Teaching Medical Anthropology: Model Courses for Graduate and Under-
    graduate Instruction*. Society for Medical Anthropology, Special Publication, 1.
    Extensive bibliographies.
Turner, Victor W. 1968. *The Drums of Affliction: A Study of Religious Processes among
    the Ndembu of Zambia*. Oxford: Clarendon Press. A study of curing from a
    symbolic perspective.
Tylor, Edward B. 1871 [1958]. *Primitive Culture*. 2 vols. New York: Harper & Brothers.
Wellin, Edward. 1977. "Theoretical Orientations in Medical Anthropology: Continuity
    and Change over the Past Half-Century." David Landy, ed., *Culture, Disease,
    and Healing: Studies in Medical Anthropology*. New York: Macmillan. Provides
    an excellent historical overview.
Young, Allan. 1982. "The Anthropology of Illness and Sickness." *ARA* 11:257–85. A
    good review with extensive bibliography.

Sources of Additional Information

A useful collection of readings is provided in Peter Morley and Roy Wallis, eds., *Culture and Curing*, Pittsburgh: University of Pittsburgh Press, 1979. A somewhat broader selection is provided in Michael Logan and Edward Hunt, Jr., eds., *Health and the Human Condition: Perspectives on Medical Anthropology*, North Scituate, Mass.: Duxbury Press, 1978. An introductory text providing a broad review of the field is given in Ann McElroy and Patricia K. Townsend, *Medical Anthropology in Ecological Perspective*, Boulder, Colo.: Westview Press, 1985. Ronald C. Simons and Charles C. Hughes, eds., *The Culture-Bound Syndromes: Folk Illnesses of Psychiatric and Anthropological Interest*, Dordrecht, the Netherlands: D. Reidel, 1985, provide a good compilation of papers on this interdisciplinary topic.

CUSTOM. A practice characteristic of a society or social group.

The word custom derives from the Latin *suescere*, to be accustomed, to be used to. The Greek equivalent is *ethos*, while from the same root comes *ethnos*, a group of people accustomed to live together, a nation (cf. ETHNOGRAPHY; ETHNOLOGY; ETHNICITY). In short, custom is the outward manifestation of group identity and the bonds of common CULTURE.

At least in the anthropological context, custom is primarily an observer's category. In attempting to describe an alien society, it provides a convenient means of encapsulating the most dramatic differences between the cultures of the observer and the observed. Custom carries with it for this reason an element of ethnocentrism. As Edward Sapir commented, "One uses it more easily to refer to geographically remote, to primitive or to bygone societies than to one's own" (Sapir 1931:658).

Early Ethnography

The description of alien customs has a long pedigree. Both Herodotus (d. 425 B.C.) and Tacitus (d. ca. A.D. 120) were notable observers of tribal peoples and their customs. The medieval writer Isidore of Seville (d. A.D. 636) commented more abstractly on the relation between formal LAW (*lex*) and custom (*consuetudo*), arguing that the latter "is a sort of [law] established by *mores*; which is taken instead of *lex* when *lex* fails.... And *consuetudo* is so-called because it is in common use" (in Slotkin 1965:21).

In any significant sense, however, an ethnological awareness of the diversity of custom began with the Renaissance, as trade and exploration transformed the medieval world picture. Many collections of alien customs were published in the sixteenth century. One of the earliest was Johann Boemus's *Omnium gentium mores, leges, & ritus* (The Customs, Rites, and Laws of All Nations), published in 1520. According to Margaret Hodgen: "With the clear intention of isolating the major social institutions for inspection, and with some degree of orderliness, Boemus placed special emphasis on divergences in marriage and the family, divergences in social organization, in religions, funeral rites, weapons, warfare, justice, diet, and apparel" (Hodgen 1964:138). For certain writers of this period, such as Montaigne (d. 1592), this wealth of data produced a scepticism toward European institutions, in effect an early expression of cultural RELATIVISM. Montaigne wrote, "There is nothing in which the world varies so much as in customs and laws. Many a thing is abominable here that is commended elsewhere" (in Slotkin 1965:55).

The notion of custom held a conspicuous place in the emerging ethnographic literature. Thus a seventeenth century account of eastern India described the practice of widow immolation (suttee) as "that Diabolicall Custome," and commented regarding the treatment of mendicant monks, "wherever they come, the inhabitants of the Countrey are forced, by their Antient Custome (now not easily to be broken) to give them rice, butter, tobacco, Oyle, or what else they demand" (Bowrey 1680:14, 20). John Davies's history of Christian missions in Tahiti commented charitably that the Tahitians "are more mild generous and hospitable, and have fewer horrid customs" than peoples of adjoining islands (Davies 1830:31). Edward Lane's *Manners and Customs of the Modern Egyptians* offered numerous examples. Thus: "It is a very common custom in Cairo to hang an aloe-plant over the door of a house . . . and this is regarded as a charm to insure long and flourishing lives to the inmates, and long continuance to the house itself" (Lane 1836:263).

Custom and Culture

The concept of custom as sketched above is incompatible with current ethnographic assumptions in several respects. First, customs are patterns of behavior abstracted from their larger cultural context, that is, from the strategies of ADAPTATION, the organization of KINSHIP and politics, and the SYSTEMS of belief through which social life unfolds. Second, they are commonly depicted as invariable practices, which individuals have no choice (or desire) but to follow. Custom thus suggests an arbitrary or simply irrational action (see RATIONALITY), followed through the force of social habit.

In summary, the idea of custom carries an ethnocentric bias ("horrid customs'') and has had a significant role in the anthropological rhetoric regarding so-called PRIMITIVE societies. As E. S. Hartland wrote in *Primitive Law*,

> The savage is far from being the free and unfettered creature of Rousseau's imagination. On the contrary, he is hemmed in on every side by the customs of his people, he is bound in the chains of immemorial tradition not merely in his social relations, but in his religion, his medicine, his industry, his art: in short, every aspect of his life. (Hartland 1924:138)

With the advent of serious ethnography based on participant observation, this caricature of social life was gradually superseded by a more realistic understanding. As R. R. Marett commented (in 1912), ''The immobility of custom, I believe, is largely the effect of distance'' (in Kuper 1973:31). The work of Bronislaw Malinowski was definitive in replacing the image of custom-bound ''primitives'' with that of rational human beings operating within coherent (if to us, alien) systems of belief and value, in the pursuit of their own ends. He condemned ''the piecemeal items of information, of customs, beliefs, and rules of conduct floating in the air, or rather leading a flat existence on paper with the third-dimension, that of life, completely lacking.'' Instead, for Malinowski (and for later generations of anthropologists), ''the true problem is not to study how human life submits to rules—it simply does not; the real problem is how the rules become adapted to life'' (Malinowski 1926:126, 127).

Custom thus marks an episode in the development of ethnographic method. The aim of providing a detailed description of social life remains essential to ANTHROPOLOGY, but in seeking an adequate understanding of these data, the notion of custom has been replaced by the concept of CULTURE. The study of custom for its own sake today characterizes not anthropology, but FOLKLORE.

References

Bowrey, Thomas. 1680 [1967]. *A Geographical Account of Countries Round the Bay of Bengal, 1669–1679.* Richard C. Temple, ed. Hakluyt Society, 2d ser., no. 12. Nendeln, Liechtenstein: Kraus Reprint. Bowrey was a sea captain, and within limits he provided a remarkably observant record of Indian geography and social life.

Davies, John. 1830 [1961]. *The History of the Tahitian Mission, 1799–1830.* C. W. Newbury, ed. Hakluyt Society, 2d ser., no. 116. Cambridge: Cambridge University Press. This work is thin ethnographically; its principal interest is as a record of culture contact.

Hartland, E. Sidney. 1924 [1969]. *Primitive Law.* New York: Harper & Row.

Hodgen, Margaret T. 1964. *Early Anthropology in the Sixteenth and Seventeenth Centuries.* Philadelphia: University of Pennsylvania Press. An excellent history of Renaissance ethnology.

Kuper, Adam. 1973. *Anthropologists and Anthropology: The British School, 1922–1972.* New York: Pica Press.

Lane, Edward William. 1836 [1966]. *Manners and Customs of the Modern Egyptians.* New York: Dutton. Lane's work is a detailed and relatively unprejudiced account, based on long residence.

Malinowski, Bronislaw. 1926. *Crime and Custom in Savage Society*. London: Routledge & Kegan Paul. A landmark study challenging then-dominant ideas regarding the role of custom in shaping behavior.

Sapir, Edward. 1931. "Custom." *ESS* 4:658–62.

Slotkin, J. S. 1965. *Readings in Early Anthropology*. Viking Fund Publications in Anthropology, 40. Chicago: Aldine.

Sources of Additional Information

James Frazer's *Golden Bough* (1890) is a classic example of the Victorian evolutionist approach to custom; though obsolete theoretically, it provides an immense compilation of customs bearing on the cross-cultural study of magic and religion. The abridged, one-volume edition is most useful: *The New Golden Bough*, Theodor H. Gaster, ed. New York: Criterion Books, 1959.

D

DESCENT. The cultural principles by which group membership, with its rights and obligations, is determined by relationship to a specified ancestor, putative or real.

A major issue of ANTHROPOLOGY concerns the basis for social order in societies lacking distinct political institutions, a situation characteristic of both BANDS and TRIBES. The cultural postulate of descent and, concretely, the groups such as clans or lineages that are formed on this basis, provide a major mechanism of social organization in kin-based societies.

The notion of descent centers on a principle of membership: An individual is affiliated with others through a common ancestor. On this basis, persons become members of groups, receive rights, particularly rights in real and personal property, and incur obligations, such as the RITUAL requirements of ancestor worship. This genealogical connection is commonly reckoned through ancestors of a single sex (unilineal descent). If the connection runs through females this is termed matrilineal descent; if through males, patrilineal descent. The unilineal descent principle yields unambiguous membership status and nonoverlapping groups, features that permit a group to exert effective social control in a range of contexts, as in the ownership of property.

Other variants exist. In some societies both matrilineal and patrilineal principles are employed in different contexts to create groups that differ in their rights and obligations, for example, the control of property in contrast to the performance of ritual. This is termed dual or double descent. In contrast a system is ambilineal or cognatic when genealogical links may be traced through either male or female kin to establish descent from a given ancestor. Both systems contrast with bilateral KINSHIP, in which an individual traces genealogical ties outward through both male and female relatives rather than downward from a specified ancestor. The result is a grouping of indefinite size reckoned from a given individual, termed a kindred.

The principle of descent should be distinguished from that of transmission, as W. H. R. Rivers noted in 1914. In transmission, a right must be relinquished by one individual before being taken up by another, as in inheritance of property or succession to office; in descent, an individual takes on a status shared by others, and thus joins in their rights and obligations (Scheffler 1986:340). Descent forms an essential aspect of the study of kinship.

Evolutionist Descent Theory

The study of descent groups and the principles by which they are formed has been an enduring topic of anthropological interest since the early nineteenth century. However, as Ward Goodenough has argued, the development of descent theory in anthropology was distorted by the Victorian assumption of a clear evolutionary progression in family organization, ideas of procreation, and rules of kin group membership (Goodenough 1970:39–41).

Specifically (it was argued), in the earliest PRIMITIVE societies physical paternity was unknown. The result was matriarchy, with the FAMILY unit based on the bond of a mother to her children, and kin groups formed through matrilineal descent. The dawning recognition of paternity, together with technological changes enhancing the power of men (such as warfare), resulted in the emergence of patriarchy, with polygynous MARRIAGE providing the basis of family organization, accompanied by patrilineal descent. Finally, the patriarchal stage was in turn superseded by the recognition of kin ties through both parents (bilateral kinship), resulting in a more egalitarian relation between men and women, and a monogamous family unit (see EVOLUTION; GENDER).

This evolutionary reconstruction of the development of family, descent, and society was widely advocated, for example in 1861 by the historian J. J. Bachofen (see Bachofen [1967]) and later through the detailed research of Lewis Henry Morgan (1877:62). The analytic importance of descent and descent groups was reinforced by the legal research of Henry Maine: ''The unit of an ancient society was the Family, of a modern society the Individual'' (Maine 1861:74). Maine's recognition of the predominance of kin group over individual, of the corporate and enduring character of the patriarchal group, and of status as opposed to contract as the key determinant of social relations in tribal societies, provided later anthropologists with a conceptual tool kit with which to analyze their detailed studies of descent and kinship (see Maine 1861: ch. 5).

In retrospect, the nineteenth century foundations of descent theory are open to criticism on several fronts. First, and most obviously, the construct of ''primitive matriarchy'' and the supposedly universal evolutionary sequence of matrilineal/patrilineal/bilateral descent was specious, and soon disproven (see e.g., Swanton 1905). Second, it was erroneous to transform a principle of group formation into a master key to tribal social life (see TRIBE), conflating descent with the recognition of kinship, or the determination of political succession and inheritance. Although Rivers had, by 1910, distinguished descent and kinship (see Schneider 1984:102–3), long after the demise of evolutionist assumptions "whole societies were still classified as matrilineal, patrilineal, or bilateral" (Goodenough 1970:41; cf. Murdock 1949: ch. 8). Third, due at least in part to the intellectualist bias of evolutionary anthropology (matrilineality as a consequence of "ignorance" of paternity, etc.), and the legalistic emphasis imparted by Maine, principles of descent have frequently been considered social facts sui generis, rather than outcomes of complex economic and ecological factors—a perspective now widely criticized.

Terminological Confusions

The analysis of kinship and descent patterns has thrown up a cloud of terminology. Morgan's preferred term for the unilineal descent group was the Latin *gens* (plural *gentes*): a named, exogamous (outmarrying) group, with totemic associations (Morgan 1877:65, 170; see also TOTEMISM). Robert Lowie, complaining of the "hopeless confusion of nomenclature," suggested the Anglo-Saxon sib as the generic term for a unilineal descent group, reserving the term *gens* for a patrilineal group, and the Gaelic clan for a matrilineal one (Lowie 1920:111). If this were not bad enough, British usage employs clan as the generic term (matrilineal or patrilineal), a practice that is now generally followed, sib and *gens* being obsolete (see Murdock 1949:67). The term tribe, which today refers to a particular form of kin-based society, has also figured as the equivalent of clan or sib, exemplified by the biblical "twelve tribes" of Israel (Gen. 49:28)—a usage now also obsolete. Where higher-order groups occur, combining two or more clans, the term phratry is commonly used. Where a tribe is composed of two, complementary sets of clans, each is termed a moiety, from the French *moitié*, or "one half".

At the opposite end of the scale, the term lineage was used on occasion as the equivalent of clan (e.g., Gifford 1926:392), but through the writings of British anthropologists it has come to denote a clan segment. In this usage, now widely followed, the members of a lineage are linked by exact, known genealogical ties; the members of a clan (composed of multiple lineages), in contrast, claim a common ancestor, though this focal ancestor may be mythological, or the links joining the clan members putative rather than genealogically precise (Evans-Pritchard 1940:192–93; Murdock 1949:46). Finally, the principle of ambilineal descent yields what is variously termed a cognatic descent group, a nonunilinear descent group, a ramage, or a sept (see Goodenough 1955; Firth 1957).

Functionalism and the Lineage Model

In the 1930s and 1940s British anthropologists, under the theoretical impetus of FUNCTIONALISM, made the lineage concept the centerpiece of their ethnographic studies, notably in sub-Saharan Africa. In this perspective the lineage principle became the foundation of tribal African SOCIAL STRUCTURE, governing both the control of territory and the formation of groups (Kuper 1982:78–86). As Meyer Fortes wrote regarding the Tallensi of West Africa, "Tale society is built up round the lineage system. . . . It is the skeleton of their social structure, the bony framework which shapes their body politic; it guides their economic life and moulds their ritual ideas and values" (Fortes 1945:30).

This approach was particularly influential in the description of so-called segmentary lineage systems, notably portrayed in E. E. Evans-Pritchard's study of the Nilotic Nuer (1940). For the Nuer, lineage identity was not fixed, but rather segmentary and relative, individuals recognizing wider or narrower agnatic (patrilineal) affiliations based on deeper or shallower ancestral ties, as the situation demanded. Lineages, while not in themselves political, territorial entities, provided an idiom for territorial organization. When confronted by a common enemy, for example, political segments that might otherwise act in opposition to one another could combine on the basis of a genealogically more distant agnatic tie, a process termed complementary opposition.

The segmentary lineage principle has been posited as the political basis for many societies lacking STATE institutions. In describing the Nuer, Evans-Pritchard wrote that "in the absence of political institutions providing central administration in a tribe and co-ordinating its segments, it is the system of lineages of its dominant clan which gives it structural distinctness and unity by the association of lineage values, within a common agnatic structure, with the segments of a territorial system" (Evans-Pritchard 1940:236).

Later Critiques

The body of structural-functionalist theory that coalesced around the concept of the unilineal descent group (see Fortes 1953) has received severe criticism in the postwar period. First, the adequacy and even the basic ethnographic accuracy of the classic models of African unilineal descent systems have been widely questioned. In Adam Kuper's acerbic comment, "Even the Nuer are not like *The Nuer*" (Kuper 1982:84; see also Karp and Maynard 1983). Second, the relevance of unilineal descent models for other CULTURE AREAS has been criticized, as in the case of Melanesia (see Barnes 1962); such critiques have often invoked the alternative model of ambilineal descent, notably in Polynesia (see Firth 1957; see also Goodenough 1970: ch. 2). Third, functionalist theory presumes that it is the fact of descent which structures group relations within tribal societies. This idea, too, has been challenged by those who see alliances between groups, engendered through patterned marital exchange (see MARRIAGE), as fundamental to tribal order, a perspective encouraged by the tenets of STRUCTURALISM (see Leach 1961:121–23). Finally, descent theory has been criticized more fundamentally as giving explanatory priority to the domain of kinship, as broadly construed, over ecological, economic, and political factors, and as imposing a set of constructs that lack emic (indigenous cultural) reality (see Schneider 1984; EMIC/ETIC). Most of these issues remain controversial.

References

Bachofen, J. J. [1967]. *Myth, Religion, and Mother Right: Selected Writings of Johann Jakob Bachofen*. Ralph Manheim, trans. Princeton, N.J.: Princeton University

Press. Bachofen was an early advocate of the theory of primitive matriarchy. Includes portions of *Das Mutterrecht* (1861).

Barnes, J. A. 1962. "African Models in the New Guinea Highlands." *Man* 52:5–9. An influential critique of descent theory.

Evans-Pritchard, E. E. 1940 [1969]. *The Nuer: A Description of the Modes of Livelihood and Political Institutions of a Nilotic People*. Oxford: Oxford University Press. One of the classic works of British functionalist ethnography.

Firth, Raymond. 1957 [1968]. "A Note on Descent Groups in Polynesia." Paul Bohannon and John Middleton, eds., *Kinship and Social Organization*. Garden City, N.Y.: Natural History Press. Firth discusses ambilineal descent systems.

Fortes, Meyer. 1945. *The Dynamics of Clanship Among the Tallensi*. London: Oxford University Press.

———. 1953. "The Structure of Unilineal Descent Groups." *AA* 55:17–41. A major synopsis of functionalist studies.

Gifford, Edward W. 1926. "Miwok Lineages and the Political Unit in Aboriginal California." *AA* 28:389–401.

Goodenough, Ward. 1955. "A Problem in Malayo-Polynesian Social Organization." *AA* 57:71–83.

———. 1970. *Description and Comparison in Cultural Anthropology*. Chicago: Aldine. An influential critique influenced by ethnoscience.

Karp, Ivan, and Kent Maynard. 1983. "Reading *The Nuer*." *CA* 24:481–503.

Kuper, Adam. 1982. "Lineage Theory: A Critical Retrospect." *ARA* 11:71–95. A major review.

Leach, Edmund. 1961. "Aspects of Bridewealth and Marriage Stability among the Kachin and Lakher." E. Leach, *Rethinking Anthropology*. London: Athlone Press. An argument for marital exchange as a complement to descent as a structuring principle of kin-based societies.

Lowie, Robert. 1920 [1961]. *Primitive Society*. New York: Harper & Brothers. An early text on social organization.

Maine, Henry. 1861 [1972]. *Ancient Law*. New York: Dutton.

Morgan, Lewis Henry. 1877. *Ancient Society*. Chicago: Charles H. Kerr. An important work of evolutionist anthropology.

Murdock, George Peter. 1949. *Social Structure*. New York: Macmillan.

Scheffler, Harold. 1986. "The Descent of Rights and the Descent of Persons." *AA* 88:339–50.

Schneider, David M. 1984. *A Critique of the Study of Kinship*. Ann Arbor: University of Michigan Press. An argument against classical descent theory, from the perspective of a symbolically oriented cultural anthropology.

Swanton, John R. 1905. "The Social Organization of American Tribes." *AA* 7:663–73. Swanton's study discredited claims for the evolutionary priority of matrilineality.

Sources of Additional Information

In "The Classification of Corporate Unilineal Descent Groups," *Journal of the Royal Anthropological Institute* 87: 1–29, 1957, Morton H. Fried examines the nature and function of descent group organization in a range of societies, from egalitarian to highly stratified. A brief review of forms of descent groups (territorial clan, dispersed clan, etc.) is provided in Marshall Sahlins, *Tribesmen*, Englewood Cliffs, N.J.: Prentice-Hall, 1968, ch. 4.

DEVELOPMENT. A process of social change yielding greater complexity; specifically, the transformation of agrarian societies toward greater wealth, URBANISM, industrialization, and INEQUALITY.

Development involves transformation with direction: "gradual advancement through progressive stages, growth from within" (*OED*). For the Western social sciences, particularly since the Second World War, the concept of development has subsumed a variety of theories and policies concerned with the economic, social, and political transformation of agrarian societies (the so-called Third World), those states characterized by relatively simple technologies, low capital accumulation, and a rural sector dominated by PEASANTRY. The changes typically envisioned in development scenarios include a growth of industrialization, urbanism, and—rather more vaguely—the introduction of Western institutions and bodies of knowledge.

The notion of development rests on both a fact and a value. It recognizes the fact of the extreme disparity of wealth, patterns of production, and modes of life between the industrialized and non-industrialized worlds (see INEQUALITY). It also affirms a particularly Western value, that of progress, embodying a sense of history as a gradual moral and physical improvement, and of change as inevitably tending toward greater social complexity and economic RATIONALITY (see CULTURE CHANGE). Much, though not all, of the development literature appears to suggest an eventual global convergence on essentially Western patterns of FAMILY, KINSHIP, politics, and ECONOMY.

Development and Modernization

The dominant approach in development policy—commonly termed modernization theory—has equated development with Westernization. Like the nineteenth century proponents of a unilineal cultural EVOLUTION, modernization theorists have taken the experience of the Western industrial states as the norm for all development. As W. E. Moore has baldly stated, "Because so many aspects of the social order in the underdeveloped areas of the world do not conform with the models set by the advanced countries, there is room for improvement in practically any direction one looks" (Moore 1963:89–90). The process of development, in this view, involves a convergence upon Western patterns in all phases of life, a transformation," "from primitive, subsistence economies to technology-intensive, industrialized economies; from subject to participant political cultures; from closed, ascriptive status systems to open, achievement-oriented systems; from extended to nuclear kinship units; from religious to secular ideologies" (Tipps 1973:204).

This perspective reflects an uneasy amalgamation of several intellectual and ideological influences. Most versions of modernization theory are dualistic, reducing a wide range of social, economic, political, and religious differences to two all-embracing ideal types. The contrast of "developed" and "underdeveloped" worlds implicit in modernization theory echoes a long tradition in Western social thought, seen for example in Henry Maine's distinction of societies organized by status as opposed to contract, or Ferdinand Tönnies's contrast of COMMUNITY and ASSOCIATION (see Tipps 1973:204–8). Within anthropology, Robert Redfield was an influential exponent of this approach with his research, beginning in the 1920s, on the contrasting patterns of FOLK CULTURE and CIVILIZATION (see also PRIMITIVE).

The fields of economic history and development economics have provided a second, and more focused, influence on modernization theory. Such studies of the stages and underlying causes of economic growth and change reflect a history of research dating to the mid-nineteenth century (see Hoselitz 1960). One effect has been to emphasize economic variables in explaining growth and in establishing development policy, often to the neglect of noneconomic factors (e.g., RELIGION or SOCIAL STRUCTURE). A second has been to confound economic growth with culture change, equating an increase in productivity and consumption with a more general Westernization. However, as Harold Schneider has noted, much recent research in economic ANTHROPOLOGY has demonstrated "the possibility of development divergent from Europeanization" (Schneider 1975:273–74; see ECONOMY).

Finally, modernization theory and development policy have to a large extent been shaped by the political exigencies of the Cold War (De Gregori and Pi-Sunyer 1969: ch. 1). Development policy is largely a creation of the postwar period, when Eastern and Western blocs vied for influence over nonaligned (and often recently independent) nations. As one critic has argued, " 'Development' and 'modernization' came to be viewed as long-range solutions to the threats of instability and Communism in the Third World" (Tipps 1973:210; see also APPLIED ANTHROPOLOGY).

Alternative Views of Development

Within the anthropological domain, at least, critical responses to development theory and policy have taken two main forms.

(1) The supposed opposition between TRADITION and development assumed by modernization theorists has been widely questioned. The patterns of transformation occurring in the postwar period are not converging upon a Western cultural model but are instead complexly conditioned by the history and the traditions of each society. As M. N. Srinivas has shown in the case of India, the increased opportunities for social mobility that have occurred through industrialization have not resulted in a repudiation of the CASTE system, but have instead yielded an increasing imitation of high-caste practices by lower groups hoping to improve their standing, a phenomenon he has termed "Sanskritization" (Srinivas 1966).

(2) From a more radical perspective, the concept of development has been heavily criticized for serving to obscure the actual economic and political relationship that has existed between the industrial and agrarian worlds. Thus dependency theory has stressed the role of colonial (and neocolonial) states in creating the very conditions of "underdevelopment," chiefly through the extraction of economic surplus, which development policy ostensibly seeks to

overcome (see Frank 1969; Kearney 1986:338–41). This perspective has been extended by proponents of the world systems paradigm (see Nash 1981). An alternative view, sometimes termed articulation theory, emphasizes the complex character of production relations in the "underdeveloped" world, as seen in the coexistence of traditional patterns of subsistence production with commodity production for national or international markets (Kearney 1986:341–45; see also MATERIALISM; MODE OF PRODUCTION). Both approaches have stimulated considerable research by anthropologists.

References

De Gregori, Thomas R., and Oriol Pi-Sunyer. 1969. *Economic Development: The Cultural Context*. New York: Wiley. An introductory text.
Frank, Andre Gunder. 1969. *Capitalism and Underdevelopment in Latin America*. Rev. ed. New York: Monthly Review Press. An important expression of dependency theory.
Hoselitz, Bert F. 1960. "Theories of Stages of Economic Growth." B. F. Hoselitz et al., *Theories of Economic Growth*. Glencoe, Ill.: Free Press. A historical review.
Kearney, Michael. 1986. "From the Invisible Hand to Visible Feet: Anthropological Studies of Migration and Development." *ARA* 15:331–61.
Moore, Wilbert E. 1963. *Social Change*. Englewood Cliffs, N.J.: Prentice-Hall. Embodies the perspective of modernization theory.
Nash, June. 1981. "Ethnographic Aspects of the World Capitalist System." *ARA* 10:393–423. Offers the perspective of world systems theory.
Schneider, Harold K. 1975. "Economic Development and Anthropology." *ARA* 4:271–92. An extensive review, emphasizing the formalist perspective in economic anthropology.
Srinivas, M. N. 1966. *Social Change in Modern India*. Berkeley and Los Angeles: University of California Press.
Tipps, Dean C. 1973. "Modernization Theory and the Comparative Study of Societies: A Critical Perspective." *Comparative Studies in Society and History* 15:199–226. A useful and highly critical assessment.

Sources of Additional Information

George Dalton, ed., *Economic Development and Social Change*, Garden City, N.Y.: Natural History Press, 1971, offers a useful selection of studies with an anthropological emphasis. Carol S. Holzberg and Maureen J. Giovannini, "Anthropology and Industry: Reappraisal and New Directions," *ARA* 10:317–60, 1981, discusses the anthropological literature on industrialization. In "Anthropologists and Development," *ARA* 11:349–75, 1982, Allan Hoben reviews the work of applied anthropologists, particularly through government service, in implementing development programs. A history and critique of governmental efforts at planned development is provided by A. F. Robertson, *People and the State: An Anthropology of Planned Development*, Cambridge: Cambridge University Press, 1984.

DIFFUSION. The transfer of discrete CULTURE traits from one society to another, through MIGRATION, trade, WAR, or other contact.

The diffusion of culture traits contrasts with ACCULTURATION, which describes a process of systematic cultural transformation through the involvement of an alien, politically dominant society.

In Renaissance thought, diffusion as a source of cultural diversity was acknowledged but deprecated. Given a biblical theory of social origins, the facts of CULTURE CHANGE, diversity, and diffusion could only be interpreted as manifestations of decline from an original Adamic condition (Hodgen 1964:269). This essentially negative view of diffusion was reinforced by the static and hierarchical ordering of human societies implied in the Renaissance conception of a "Great Chain of Being" (see Formigari 1973; Hodgen 1964: ch. 10). A more tolerant view of diffusion emerged in the seventeenth and eighteenth centuries, although biblical doctrine was often replaced by equally simplistic reconstructions. Thomas Hobbes (d. 1679), William Temple (d. 1699), Lord Monboddo (d. 1799), and Johann Gottfried von Herder (d. 1803), among others, speculated on diffusionist influences between Asian and European CIVILIZATIONS (Slotkin 1965:100–101, 229–30).

Theories of Diffusion

The rise of evolutionary thought in nineteenth century ANTHROPOLOGY served to set EVOLUTION and diffusion as rival theoretical systems, with proponents of each advancing highly speculative accounts of the development of world cultures. At the root of this debate was a philosophical disagreement regarding human creativity. Evolutionary theory presumes that innovation is a common feature of social life and that the shared mental characteristics of our species make it inevitable that significant inventions (e.g., percussion flaking, pottery, unilineal DESCENT, writing) will be developed independently in numerous societies (see PSYCHIC UNITY). Diffusionist theory, in contrast, presumes that humans are inherently conservative and uninventive and that the major route of progress in culture history has been through the spread of civilization from a very few culture centers.

The theories of the English scholar Grafton Elliot Smith provide an extreme example of diffusionist thought. He considered Egypt the primary source of high culture, providing "the essential elements of the ancient civilizations of India, Further Asia, the Malay Archipelago, Oceania, and America" (Smith 1931:393–94). As clues to the diffusionist puzzle, Smith cited the distribution of mummification, megalithic monuments, sun worship, phallic cults, and intensive agriculture. In comparison, the German and Austrian diffusionists, often referred to as the Culture-Circle School or *Kulturkreislehre*, took a more sober approach, arguing for a number of culture centers. Here diffusion was thought to proceed not via the adoption of isolated elements, but through the transmission (chiefly through migration) of a whole culture complex, "a group of elements in organic connection" (eine Gruppe von Dingen als zusammengehörig) (Gräbner 1905:28; see also CULTURE AREA).

Through at least the 1920s, American anthropology under the leadership of Franz Boas (1858–1942) was aggressively atheoretical, rejecting as unsubstantiated assumptions the grand reconstructions of both evolutionists, such as Lewis Henry Morgan and Herbert Spencer, and diffusionists, such as G. E. Smith and Fritz Gräbner. Although diffusion was emphasized as the primary means of culture change, American anthropologists such as Boas, Robert Lowie, and Ralph Linton depicted this process as both contingent and arbitrary, each society being influenced by many sources, making any given culture a "planless hodgepodge, that thing of shreds and patches" (Lowie 1920:441; see HISTORICISM). Linton popularized this view in his satire of American insularity: his model householder read "the news of the day, imprinted in characters invented by the ancient Semites upon a material invented in China by a process invented in Germany . . . [while thanking] a Hebrew deity in an Indo-European language that he is 100 percent American" (Linton 1936:327).

Beyond Diffusion

Diffusion has been largely supplanted as a focus of anthropological research. Although American historicist anthropology began with detailed studies of culture trait variation among neighboring Native American tribes, yielding reconstructions of diffusionist influences (e.g., Kroeber 1941), interest soon passed to more holistic and psychologically nuanced interpretations of CULTURE and culture change. In the place of diffusion came studies of acculturation, culture PATTERNS, and the relation of culture and PERSONALITY (Boas 1936:311). Evolutionary studies of the 1940s, emphasizing CULTURAL ECOLOGY and ADAPTATION, made diffusion appear theoretically irrelevant, "a mechanical and unintelligible, though universal, cause . . . stating distributions in historical terms but failing to explain process" (Steward 1949:4). The concept of diffusion retains importance in ethnological studies but now has at best a secondary role in analyzing the processes of culture change.

References

Boas, Franz. 1936 [1966]. "History and Science in Anthropology: A Reply." Franz Boas, *Race, Language and Culture*. New York: Free Press.
Formigari, Lia. 1973. "Chain of Being." *DHI* 1:325–35.
Gräbner, Fritz. 1905. "Kulturkreise und Kulturschichten in Ozeanien." *Zeitschrift für Ethnologie* 37:28–53. An early work of the German diffusionist school.
Hodgen, Margaret T. 1964. *Early Anthropology in the Sixteenth and Seventeenth Centuries*. Philadelphia: University of Pennsylvania Press.
Kroeber, Alfred. 1941 [1952]. "Salt, Dogs, Tobacco." A. Kroeber, *The Nature of Culture*. Chicago: University of Chicago Press.
Linton, Ralph. 1936. *The Study of Man: An Introduction*. N.p.: Appleton-Century-Crofts.
Lowie, Robert. 1920 [1961]. *Primitive Society*. New York: Harper & Brothers. An early text on social structure.
Slotkin, J. S., ed. 1965. *Readings in Early Anthropology*. Chicago: Aldine. A useful, pre-Victorian anthology.
Smith, Grafton Elliot. 1931. "The Influence of Ancient Egyptian Civilization in the East and in America." V. F. Calverton, ed., *The Making of Man: An Outline of*

Anthropology. New York: Modern Library. A now discredited, extreme diffusionist perspective.

Steward, Julian. 1949. "Cultural Causality and Law: A Trial Formulation of the Development of Early Civilizations." *AA* 51:1–27. A pioneering article in cultural evolution.

Sources of Additional Information

For general discussions of diffusion see Robert Lowie, *The History of Ethnological Theory*, New York: Rinehart, 1937, chs. 10, 11; and Marvin Harris, *The Rise of Anthropological Theory*, New York: Crowell, 1968, ch. 14. For examples see Alfred Kroeber, *Anthropology*, New York: Harcourt, Brace, 1948, particularly chs. 12–14. The relation of diffusion and innovation is discussed in Homer G. Barnett, *Innovation: The Basis of Cultural Change*, New York: McGraw-Hill, 1953. See also Peter J. Hugill and D. Bruce Dickson, eds., *The Transfer and Transformation of Ideas and Material Culture*, College Station: Texas A&M University Press, 1988.

E

ECOLOGY. See CULTURAL ECOLOGY.

ECONOMY. The production and distribution of goods and services possessing culturally defined value for use or exchange.

Economic activity—the transformation of NATURE to meet material ends—is a human universal, yet the values that guide economic life, and the ways in which economic activity is organized, are specific to each CULTURE. As a first approximation, differences in economy reflect differences in modes of ADAPTATION. Thus the social organization and values of a small and materially simple hunter-gatherer BAND will necessarily differ from those of a large pastoralist TRIBE, where surplus can be accumulated in the form of herd animals. Either will differ markedly from the economic scale, complexity, and surplus attained in an urban, industrialized STATE (see also DEVELOPMENT; PEASANTRY).

The terms economics and economy are derived from the Greek *oikonomia*, meaning "the art of household management" (from *oikos*, the household + *nomos*, law or rule), in contrast to a narrower, profit-oriented (if more modern) concept of "the art of money-making," *chrematistike* (Finley 1974:40–41). The Greek idea of *oikonomia*, designating activity aimed at maintaining or provisioning the social unit, broadly characterizes the aims and organization of economic life in most nonindustrial, relatively nonmonetized societies.

The concepts of economy and economics should be distinguished. An economy is a pattern of activity directed at material ends; economics is a body of theories or assumptions used to analyze that activity. Every society will possess a system of ideas that classifies and guides economic activity, in short an indigenous economics. The economics of Aristotle depended upon the values of distributive justice and the maintenance of COMMUNITY, and in this way reflected—albeit in idealized form—the social life of fourth-century Greece (Finley 1974). Similarly, the economic assumptions of Thomas Aquinas (1225–1274) reflected the social institutions of the High Middle Ages, notably the feudal order and the Catholic church (see Bell 1953:70–73). The degree to which the economic science of the modern West is likewise culture-bound remains controversial. Are, for example, the guiding assumptions of Adam Smith's *Wealth of Nations* (Smith 1776)—the human propensity to exchange, the guiding motive of individual advantage, and the social harmony that results from the pursuit of self-interest—universal truths relevant to all cultures and eras, or elements of an ideology reflecting the culture and history of industrializing Britain?

Emergence of Economic Anthropology

The description of economic activities has been a standard element of ETH-NOGRAPHY. J.-M. Degérando, in his early manual on field methods, specified inquiry regarding how "territory is used, and its resources exploited; whether any cultivation is practiced or known . . . how readily [a tribe engages] in barter with strangers it visits" (Degérando 1800:95–97). By the 1920s and 1930s, a number of sophisticated studies with a distinctly economic focus had appeared. Notable examples included Bronislaw Malinowski's study of the Melanesian *kula* trade (Malinowski 1922), Marcel Mauss's essay on gifts and exchange (Mauss 1925), Raymond Firth's analysis of the economy of Tikopia, in Polynesia (Firth 1965, 1st ed., 1938), and general texts by Richard Thurnwald and Melville Herskovits (Thurnwald 1932; Herskovits 1952, 1st ed., 1940). By the 1960s, economic anthropology, the study of economic systems in cross-cultural perspective, had become a recognized subdiscipline (see Burling 1962; Cook 1973).

Despite the fact that economy and ecology are both derived from the Greek *oikos*, the fields of economic ANTHROPOLOGY and CULTURAL ECOLOGY have shown little convergence. Ecological models have been criticized for reductionism, "the reduction of economics to nutrition and of production to the creation of calories rather than the creation of use and exchange values through the appropriation and transformation of natural resources" (Cook 1973:849). On the other hand, formalist economic models (see below), based on the rational calculation of individual benefit, have been inhospitable to systemic perspectives that seek to model the interaction of culture and environment (see SYSTEM). A more recent emphasis on production within economic anthropology may provide a better ground for theoretical synthesis (Ellen 1982:277–79).

The Formalist/Substantivist Debate

What constitutes the domain of economic phenomena has been widely argued, both in Western economics and in anthropology (see Herskovits 1952: ch. 3; Burling 1962; Kirzner 1976; Godelier 1977). Modern economics claims as its subject the process of allocating resources under conditions of scarcity so as to maximize advantage: "human behaviour as a relationship between ends and scarce means which have alternative uses" (Robbins 1952:16). In reality, economists investigate a more limited domain, maximizing as it guides a system of prices and markets. The formalist position in economic anthropology seeks to translate this perspective to the domain of non-Western, nonmonetized or only partially monetized economies. Concepts such as capital, credit, and profit, and analytic techniques such as indifference curves and decision trees are used to model the behavior of putatively rational individuals acting to maximize personal advantage (Plattner, ed., 1975; see also RATIONALITY).

The substantivist position denies the validity of models generated in a monetized, capitalist economy for non-Western, kin-based societies. Malinowski was in effect an early substantivist, ridiculing "the Primitive Economic Man ... this fanciful, dummy creature ... prompted in all his actions by a rationalistic conception of self-interest" (Malinowski 1922:60). For Karl Polanyi (1957), who was chiefly responsible for articulating the substantivist program, the characteristics of an economy derive in the first instance not from the decisions of individuals but from the constraints of institutions.

In particular Polanyi distinguished between institutions based on (1) reciprocity, where exchanges proceed symmetrically between individuals and groups bound by wider social ties (e.g., KINSHIP); (2) redistribution, where exchange is asymmetrical, moving to and from an economic center, whether this be the senior male of an extended household, or the imperial tax collector of Rome or China; and (3) market exchange, where advantage as defined by price governs the interaction of otherwise unassociated individuals (Polanyi 1957). In this view, neither reciprocity nor redistribution could be analyzed with assumptions derived from the study of market exchange. Economic action does not occur in a social vacuum, but through the culturally constituted institutions of a society, such as kinship, RELIGION or politics (see INEQUALITY).

The Role of Marxist Theory

Marxism has contributed to anthropology, and to Western social science more generally, in numerous ways: in the concept of ideology, the analysis of social stratification (see SOCIAL STRUCTURE), and the theory of cultural EVOLUTION. In economic analysis, Marxist anthropology superficially resembles the substantivist viewpoint, holding that the production process cannot be separated from the social relationships through which it occurs (Godelier 1977:33–34). However, while the substantivist school emphasizes distribution, and sees social institutions as determining economic patterns, Marxist anthropology gives analytic primacy to the production process itself. For Karl Marx, "through estranged labour man ... creates the relationship in which other men stand to his production and to his product, and the relationship in which he stands to these other men" (Marx 1844:71).

Paradoxically, the economy is not a significant Marxist category. Just as the substantivist perspective rejects a distinctly economic motivation, Marxism rejects the analytic validity of a distinctly economic domain. Rather, in analyzing the interrelation of production, distribution, and surplus in non-Western societies, the concept of MODE OF PRODUCTION (integrating the technical means and the social relations of the production process) has become a primary tool of Marxist anthropology (see also MATERIALISM).

References

Bell, John Fred. 1953. *A History of Economic Thought*. New York: Ronald Press.

Burling, Robbins. 1962. "Maximization Theories and the Study of Economic Anthropology." *AA* 64:802–21. Considers the disparate meanings of economy in economic anthropology.

Cook, Scott. 1973. "Economic Anthropology: Problems in Theory, Method, and Analysis." John J. Honigmann, ed., *Handbook of Social and Cultural Anthropology*. Chicago: Rand McNally. A broad survey, emphasizing a formalist position.

Degérando, Joseph-Marie. 1800 [1969]. *The Observation of Savage Peoples*. F. C. T. Moore, trans. Berkeley and Los Angeles: University of California Press. A very early manual of ethnographic field methods.

Ellen, Roy. 1982. *Environment, Subsistence and System*. Cambridge: Cambridge University Press. A broad overview of cultural ecology.

Finley, M. I. 1974. "Aristotle and Economic Analysis." M. I. Finley, ed., *Studies in Ancient Society*. London: Routledge and Kegan Paul.

Firth, Raymond. 1965 [1975]. *Primitive Polynesian Economy*. New York: Norton. 1st ed., 1938.

Godelier, Maurice. 1977. "Anthropology and Economics." M. Godelier, *Perspectives in Marxist Anthropology*. Robert Brain, trans. Cambridge: Cambridge University Press. The entire collection provides a challenging introduction to Marxist theory in anthropology.

Herskovits, Melville. 1952. *Economic Anthropology: The Economic Life of Primitive Peoples*. New York: Norton. 1st ed., 1940.

Kirzner, Israel M. 1976. *The Economic Point of View*. 2d ed. edition. Kansas City, Kansas: Sheed and Ward. Kirzner outlines major disagreements over the concept of economy within the discipline of economics.

Malinowski, Bronislaw. 1922 [1961]. *Argonauts of the Western Pacific*. New York: Dutton. A classic ethnography.

Marx, Karl. 1844 [1974]. *Economic and Philosophic Manuscripts of 1844*. Moscow: Progress Publishers. An early statement of Marx's views.

Mauss, Marcel. 1925 [1967]. *The Gift: Forms and Functions of Exchange in Archaic Societies*. Ian Cunnison, trans. New York: Norton. This theoretically sophisticated essay foreshadowed later structuralist approaches.

Plattner, Stuart, ed. 1975. *Formal Methods in Economic Anthropology*. American Anthropological Association (Washington, D.C.), *Special Publication*, 4.

Polanyi, Karl. 1957 [1968]. "The Economy as Instituted Process." George Dalton, ed., *Primitive, Archaic, and Modern Economies: Essays of Karl Polanyi*. Boston: Beacon Press. The collection offers a good introduction to the substantivist perspective in economic anthropology.

Robbins, Lionel. 1952. *An Essay on the Nature and Significance of Economic Science*. 2d ed. London: Macmillan. An important statement of economic formalism.

Smith, Adam. 1776 [1937]. *The Wealth of Nations*. New York: Modern Library.

Thurnwald, Richard. 1932 [1969]. *Economics in Primitive Communities*. London: Oxford University Press.

Sources of Additional Information

A number of essays by Marshall Sahlins that have helped shape a distinctly anthropological approach to economics are reprinted in his *Stone Age Economics*, Chicago:

Aldine, 1972. David Kaplan's "The Formal-Substantive Controversy in Economic Anthropology: Reflections on Its Wider Implications," *Southwestern Journal of Anthropology* 24:228–51, 1968, is a useful introduction to that debate. Edward E. LeClair and Harold K. Schneider, eds., *Economic Anthropology: Readings in Theory and Analysis*, New York: Holt, Rinehart and Winston, 1968, provides readings with a formalist slant. A range of theoretical controversies are surveyed in John Clammer, ed., *Beyond the New Economic Anthropology*, Basingstoke, England: Macmillan, 1987. H. T. van der Pas, *Economic Anthropology: 1940–1972*, Oosterhout (Netherlands): Anthropological Publications, 1973, provides a helpful annotated bibliography. A valuable review is *Research in Economic Anthropology: A Research Annual*, Greenwich, Conn.: JAI Press, 1978–.

EMIC/ETIC. Contrasting ethnographic perspectives: the emic view is based on native knowledge, the etic view on the scientifically grounded categories of an observer.

The terms emic and etic refer to alternative perspectives for analyzing CULTURE: emic data are derived from an indigenous (actor's) perspective, etic data from a scientific (observer's) viewpoint.

By way of example, both Clyde Kluckhohn and Edward Evans-Pritchard published highly acclaimed studies of witchcraft in tribal societies. Kluckhohn's analysis of Navajo witchcraft emphasized a social-psychological explanation, focusing on concepts of aggression, anxiety, and socialization (Kluckhohn 1944). Evans-Pritchard's account of Azande witchcraft, in contrast, was concerned with the Azande perspective, depicting the logic and consistency of their beliefs regarding witchcraft, misfortune, magic, and divination (Evans-Pritchard 1937). In these terms, Kluckhohn's study was primarily etic and comparative, Evans-Pritchard's primarily emic and particularistic.

While the emic/etic distinction is relatively recent, it epitomizes a debate regarding the nature of ethnographic knowledge and the appropriate means of explaining cultural data which has a much longer history. Two questions are of particular importance. First, are the most valid ethnographic data derived from the more readily verifiable statements of an observer or the more subjective understandings of a native participant? Second, should the goal of ANTHROPOLOGY be the search for social laws of general validity (thus abstracting data from their context) or the description and INTERPRETATION of cultural phenomena in their distinctiveness? Presumably, an etic account is better suited to the former goal, an emic account to the latter (see COMPARATIVE METHOD; HISTORICISM).

For the first half of the twentieth century, at least in anglophone anthropology, what came to be termed the "native's point of view" (i.e., an emic perspective) has had priority. Bronislaw Malinowski set forth this argument in 1922 in *Argonauts of the Western Pacific*: "The final goal, of which an Ethnographer should never lose sight . . . [is] to grasp the native's point of view, his relation to life, to realise *his* vision of *his* world" (Malinowski 1922:25). Franz Boas (in 1943) argued similarly: "If it is our serious purpose to understand the thoughts of a people the whole analysis of experience must be based on their concepts, not ours'' (in Harris 1968:317). The emergence of participant observation as the dominant method of ETHNOGRAPHY reflected the concern to capture an indigenous cultural perspective with fidelity.

The Emic/Etic Distinction

The terms emic and etic were coined by Kenneth Pike in 1954, in analogy to phonemic and phonetic approaches in linguistics: phonemic referring to that set of sound contrasts significant for speakers of a particular language; phonetic to an objective description of sound patterns applicable to any language (Pike 1967). The emic/etic contrast thus reflects the strong influence of linguistics upon American cultural anthropology in the mid-twentieth century (see LANGUAGE). In considering Pike's ideas, it is appropriate to differentiate between the conceptual distinction he sought to draw, the goal of ethnographic research he envisioned, and the methods he proposed. The first has attained a permanent place in anthropological thought, the second is widely debated, and the third largely ignored.

Pike described the emic/etic contrast in the following terms: ''It proves convenient—though partially arbitrary—to describe behavior from two different standpoints, which lead to results which shade into one another. The etic viewpoint studies behavior as from outside of a particular system, and as an essential initial approach to an alien system. The emic viewpoint results from studying behavior as from inside the system'' (Pike 1967:37). The two perspectives may be further contrasted as follows: (1) the etic perspective is applicable to all cultures or languages and is thus inherently comparative; the emic perspective is ''culturally specific, applicable to one language or culture at a time'' (Pike 1967:37); (2) etic units of analysis are determined in advance, that is, they are a priori in character; emic units, in contrast, can only emerge in the course of studying a particular linguistic or cultural domain; and (3) etic categories can be established through a logic alien to the SYSTEM of belief under examination; emic categories must be based on criteria relevant to the system itself.

The goal of ethnography, for Pike, was to achieve an emic account of behavior: ''The initial etic description gradually is refined, and is ultimately—in principle, but probably never in practice—replaced by one which is totally emic'' (Pike 1967:39).

Finally, as regards method, Pike sought a common framework within which both verbal and nonverbal behavior could be described and interpreted, the behavioral stream of events providing the focus of inquiry. Pike envisioned a microscopic analysis of behavior (verbal and non-verbal), organized through a complex set of categories derived from linguistics, with ''kinemes,'' ''behavioremes,'' ''tagmemes,'' and other neologisms paralleling phonemes, morphemes, sentences, and the like (Pike 1967).

Later Trends

In certain respects Pike's work resembles later kinesic research and anticipates the study of language in its communicative context (ethnography of speaking), as developed for example, by Dell Hymes (see COMMUNICATION). However, the premise of a language-like, hierarchical structuring to the minutiae of human behavior has been largely rejected or ignored by later anthropologists (see Gregersen 1977:90–91; cf. Harris 1976).

Although anthropologists have long acknowledged the importance of rendering "the native's point of view," there is no agreement as to how this goal is to be reconciled with the need to create a cross-cultural body of theory. Thus the relationship between emic and etic knowledge in anthropology remains controversial. Many anthropologists consider emic and etic approaches as complementary, or maintain that emic approaches can in fact produce comparative, testable propositions (see Goodenough 1970: ch. 4; Feleppa 1986:244–45). Under the rubric of cognitive anthropology or ETHNOSCIENCE, much research has been conducted with the aim of systematically codifying native knowledge in particular cultural domains (such as KINSHIP, color categories, and ethnobotany).

The perspective of cultural MATERIALISM is rather different. In the view of Marvin Harris, for example, emic accounts are biased toward idealist forms of explanation and, by emphasizing the uniqueness of cultural systems, impede the formulation of testable, cross-cultural laws. Harris has embraced the emic/etic distinction, although his use of emic and etic diverges somewhat from that of Pike (Harris 1976; Harris 1979: chs. 2 and 3; for a critique, see Wallace 1980).

While Pike's conception of the emic/etic contrast was closely tied to principles of structural linguistics (i.e., the determination of complementarity and contrast between significant units), these subtleties of usage have largely disappeared in later anthropological writings. In terms of current usage, emic data are those internal to a culture; etic data are those generated from a detached, "scientific" perspective (see Marano 1982). However, in weighing the value of these terms, one can legitimately ask whether an etic perspective in fact represents an objective, Archimedean vantage point for ethnography or merely the culture of Western science.

References

Evans-Pritchard, E. E. 1937. *Witchcraft, Oracles and Magic Among the Azande*. Oxford: Clarendon Press. A classic study, exemplifying an emic perspective.

Feleppa, Robert. 1986. "Emics, Etics, and Social Objectivity." *CA* 27:243–55. The article provides a good summary of the debates over the emic/etic distinction.

Goodenough, Ward H. 1970. *Description and Comparison in Cultural Anthropology*. Chicago: Aldine. A statement from the ethnoscience perspective, envisioning a complementary relation between emic and etic views.

Gregersen, Edgar A. 1977. "Linguistic Models in Anthropology." W. C. McCormack and Stephen A. Wurm, eds., *Language and Thought: Anthropological Issues*. The Hague and Paris: Mouton. A review and critique of linguistically oriented theory in cultural anthropology.

Harris, Marvin. 1968. *The Rise of Anthropological Theory*. New York: Crowell. A highly polemical history.

———. 1976. "History and Significance of the Emic/Etic Distinction." *ARA* 5:329–50.

————. 1979. *Cultural Materialism: The Struggle for a Science of Culture*. New York: Random House. The emic/etic contrast figures prominently.

Kluckhohn, Clyde. 1944 [1967]. *Navaho Witchcraft*. Boston: Beacon Press. Incorporates a predominantly etic analysis of witchcraft beliefs.

Malinowski, Bronislaw. 1922 [1961]. *Argonauts of the Western Pacific*. New York: Dutton. A classic ethnography.

Marano, Lou. 1982. "Windigo Psychosis: An Emic-Etic Confusion." *CA* 23:385–412.

Pike, Kenneth L. 1967. *Language in Relation to a Unified Theory of the Structure of Human Behavior*. 2d ed. The Hague and Paris: Mouton. The origin of the emic/etic distinction.

Wallace, A. F. C. 1980. "Review of: Marvin Harris, *Cultural Materialism: The Struggle for a Science of Culture*." *AA* 82:423–26. Includes a critique of Harris's use of the emic/etic distinction.

Sources of Additional Information

Pertti J. and Gretel H. Pelto, *Anthropological Research: The Structure of Inquiry*, 2d ed., Cambridge: Cambridge University Press, 1978, ch. 4, provides a useful introduction to these contrasting perspectives.

ETHNICITY. The existence of culturally distinctive groups within a society, each asserting a unique identity on the basis of a shared TRADITION and distinguishing social markers such as a common LANGUAGE, RELIGION, or economic specialization.

Ethnic is derived from the Greek *ethnos*, a group sharing common CUSTOMS (see also ETHNOLOGY). It occurs in English from the late fifteenth century, originally signifying "nations not Christian or Jewish; Gentile, heathen, pagan"; the more modern sense of "peculiar to a race or nation" appears in the mid-nineteenth century (*OED*). The abstraction "ethnicity," denoting the existence of distinctive ethnic groups or identities, is a twentieth century usage.

Until perhaps the 1970s anthropologists remained generally indifferent to ethnicity as a research problem. The major exception was the concern within American psychological ANTHROPOLOGY with the study of national character, beginning in the 1940s (see PERSONALITY). This indifference is now changing.

Ethnicity implies the existence of social markers, recognized means for differentiating groups coexisting within a wider field of social interaction. Distinctions are made on various grounds, including physical appearance (see RACE), geographic origins (see MIGRATION), economic specialization, religion, language, and such expressive PATTERNS as clothing and diet. Regardless, however, of the particular criteria utilized, ethnicity implies distinctions that are cultural as well as social. Unlike the divisions of class within a state, or of age-group (see ASSOCIATION) and clan (see DESCENT) within a tribe, ethnicity involves the assertion of a distinctive tradition, and an ideology of separate origin and cultural independence (De Vos 1975:9).

The phenomenon of ethnicity is ubiquitous, illustrated by the relation of Pathans, Kohistanis, and Gujars in Pakistan (Barth 1956); of Pueblos, Navajos,

Hispanics, and Anglos in New Mexico; or of ethnic Lithuanians, Poles, Germans, Byelorussians, Jews, and Tatars in Lithuaria (Milosz 1975). Assertions of ethnic identity can be readily transformed into movements for political separatism: obvious examples from the 1970s and 1980s include the demands of Basques in Spain, Quebecois in Canada, Tamils in Sri Lanka, and Sikhs in India.

Ethnicity and Culture

In the field of anthropology, ethnicity does not constitute a new domain of research but a challenge to the adequacy of conventional CULTURE theory. Studies of ethnicity have brought into question several dicta of traditional anthropology: the assumptions of cultural homogeneity, cultural assimilation, and cultural objectivity.

(1) In their concern to counter the weaknesses of evolutionist culture theory, advocates of both HISTORICISM and FUNCTIONALISM were led to stress the intensive study of village COMMUNITIES, understood to represent in microcosm a total culture or SOCIAL STRUCTURE. Tribal societies were treated as though culturally homogeneous and effectively isolated from wider economic and political influences. These assumptions were even less valid when applied to STATE-level societies, which are almost universally multiethnic collectivities.

(2) Evidence for the multicultural character of most societies has also been disregarded because of an essentially static view of tribal cultures, leading to the assumption that any change imposed by contact with a politically dominant state must result in irreversible ACCULTURATION. However, more recent studies have revealed the striking endurance of ethnic identities and distinctive traditions as cultural enclaves within larger, multicultural states (see Castile and Kushner 1981).

(3) Anthropology's predominant perspective has been one of cultural realism. Cultures have been treated as though existing sui generis, "species objects" with objectively describable characteristics (cf. Leach, in Naroll 1964:299; see SUPERORGANIC). The phenomenon of ethnicity throws this view into question, for ethnic identity is commonly ambiguous, subjective, and situational (Southall 1970; R. Cohen 1978; see TRIBE).

Primordial and Instrumental Perspectives

Reflecting differing emphases on the issues noted above, anthropological studies have been characterized by two general approaches, one stressing ethnicity as cultural persistence (the primordialist viewpoint), the other as adaptive strategy (the instrumentalist viewpoint). The underlying debate concerns whether an ethnic group "is to be conceived of as a primordially constituted entity based on ancestry and racial descent; or as a situationally constituted entity, an organizational design for the pursuit of collective goals" (Casino 1985:25). (For works guided by a primordialist perspective, see Spicer 1971, and Castile and Kushner 1981; for those taking an instrumentalist view, see Barth 1969, and Skinner 1975.)

The primordialist position has been argued by Clifford Geertz, claiming that "the congruities of blood, speech, custom, and so on, are seen to have an ineffable, and at times overpowering, coerciveness in and of themselves" (Geertz 1973:259). Yet as Fredrik Barth has noted, in the emergence of ethnic categories, "the features that are taken into account are not the sum of 'objective' differences, but only those which the actors themselves regard as significant" (Barth 1969:14). Thus from the instrumentalist viewpoint, the fundamental research problems do not involve describing and classifying objective and unchanging ethnic formations, but understanding the processes by which ethnic identities and boundaries are created, modified, and maintained (see also INTERPRETA- TION).

However, the instrumentalist position also has major weaknesses. As Gary Cohen has asked, "If the persistence or strengthening of ethnic identity derives simply from the pursuit of social or economic interests, why do individuals articulate an ethnic identity rather than merely a class or interest-group identity, and why does ethnic identity have a different value content from other group identities?" (G. Cohen 1984:1037). More generally, primordialist and instru- mentalist views share a broader flaw: an inability to explain "how people rec- ognize the commonalities (of interest or sentiment) underlying claims to common identity" (Bentley 1987:26; see also Winthrop 1990).

Nationalism, Pluralism and the State

The relationship between ethnicity and state-level polity is obviously complex, and terms such as nation and nationalism are used with great inconsistency. One can agree with George De Vos that, while strictly speaking nationality and ethnicity are equivalent terms, "in a looser sense, the words 'nation' and 'na- tionality' very often encompass diverse groups that have achieved political uni- fication" (De Vos 1975:11). While "nationalism" served to justify the numerous anticolonial movements of this century (as it served the efforts of European ethnic minorities in the nineteenth century), many of the postcolonial states such as India and Nigeria have themselves had to struggle with the challenge of supplanting divisive ethnic oppositions with a unifying allegiance to a nation- state (see Geertz 1973).

The reverse situation also holds: Enforced division between ethnic groups can become an object of state policy, a condition generally characterized as pluralism or the plural society. The result is a state divided into distinct, unequal social spheres, under the overall political dominance of one ethnic segment. The regime of apartheid in modern South Africa is a notable example. According to M. G. Smith, pluralism "simultaneously connotes a social structure characterized by fundamental discontinuities and cleavages, and a cultural complex based on systematic institutional diversity" (Smith 1969:27). Whether ethnic pluralism can best be understood as a unique institutional form, or as another, particularly pernicious, variant of social INEQUALITY (see also CASTE) remains a matter of debate (see R. Cohen 1978:398–400).

References

Barth, Fredrik. 1956. "Ecological Relationships of Ethnic Groups in Swat, Pakistan."
     AA 58:1079–1089. A pioneering article.
———. 1969. "Introduction." Fredrik Barth, ed., *Ethnic Groups and Boundaries*. Bos-
     ton: Little, Brown. An influential collection of essays from the instrumentalist
     perspective.
Bentley, G. Carter. 1987. "Ethnicity and Practice." *Comparative Studies in Society and
     History* 29:24–55. A critique of prevailing ethnicity theory, from the perspective
     of Pierre Bourdieu's theory of practice.
Casino, Eric S. 1985. "The Parameters of Ethnicity Research." Fred W. Riggs, ed.,
     Ethnicity/Intercocta Glossary: Concepts and Terms Used in Ethnicity Research.
     Pilot ed. Department of Political Science, University of Hawaii.
Castile, George, and Gilbert Kushner, eds. 1981. *Persistent Peoples: Cultural Enclaves
     in Perspective*. Tucson: University of Arizona Press. A selection of readings from
     the primordialist viewpoint.
Cohen, Gary B. 1984. "Ethnic Persistence and Change: Concepts and Models for His-
     torical Research." *Social Science Quarterly* 65:1029–42.
Cohen, Ronald. 1978. "Ethnicity: Problem and Focus in Anthropology." *ARA* 7:379–
     403. A valuable review.
De Vos, George. 1975. "Ethnic Pluralism: Conflict and Accommodation." George De
     Vos and Lola Romanucci-Ross, eds., *Ethnic Identity: Cultural Continuities and
     Change*. Palo Alto, Calif.: Mayfield Publishing.
Geertz, Clifford. 1973. "The Integrative Revolution: Primordial Sentiments and Civil
     Politics in the New States." C. Geertz, *The Interpretation of Cultures: Selected
     Essays*. New York: Basic Books.
Milosz, Czeslaw. 1975. "Vilnius, Lithuania: An Ethnic Agglomerate." George De Vos
     and Lola Romanucci-Ross, eds., *Ethnic Identity: Cultural Continuities and
     Change*. Palo Alto, Calif.: Mayfield Publishing.
Naroll, Raoul. 1964. "On Ethnic Unit Classification." *CA* 5:283–312. Naroll expresses
     the view of cultural realism.
Skinner, Eliott P. 1975. "Competition Within Ethnic Systems in Africa." Leo A. Despres,
     ed., *Ethnicity and Resource Competition in Plural Societies*. The Hague and Paris:
     Mouton. Discusses political and economic factors shaping ethnic groupings in
     modern Africa.
Smith, M. G. 1969. "Institutional and Political Conditions of Pluralism." Leo Kuper
     and M. G. Smith, eds., *Pluralism in Africa*. Berkeley and Los Angeles: University
     of California Press.
Southall, Aidan W. 1970. "The Illusion of Tribe." *Journal of Asian and African Studies*
     5:28–50.
Spicer, Edward H. 1971. "Persistent Identity Systems." *Science* 174:795–800. An in-
     fluential statement, from the primordialist perspective.
Winthrop, Robert H. 1990. "Persistent Peoples: Mechanisms of Cultural Survival in
     Southern Oregon and Northwestern California." Nan Hannon and Richard K.
     Olmo, eds., *Living With the Land: The Indians of Southwest Oregon*. Medford,
     Oreg.: Southern Oregon Historical Society.

Sources of Additional Information

A useful overview is provided by George L. Hicks,` "Introduction: Problems in the Study of Ethnicity," in George L. Hicks and Philip E. Leis, eds., *Ethnic Encounters: Identities and Contexts*, North Scituate, Mass.: Duxbury Press, 1977. A somewhat more traditional ethnological treatment is provided in John W. Bennett, ed., *The New Ethnicity: Perspectives From Ethnology* American Ethnological Society, *Proceedings, 1973*, St. Paul, Minn.: West Publishing, 1975. A brief introduction to the debate on plural societies is given by Cyril S. Belshaw, *Traditional Exchange and Modern Markets*, Englewood Cliffs, N.J.: Prentice-Hall, 1965, ch. 4.

ETHNOGRAPHY. The analysis of the CULTURE of a COMMUNITY or other distinctive social unit, grasped through the method of participant observation; the written account of such a study.

An ethnography is literally a written account of an alien nation (Gk. *ethnos*), a people bound by common CUSTOMS. Ethnography, the detailed study of a distinct culture, is traditionally contrasted with ETHNOLOGY, the comparative and classificatory treatment of cultural data. Thus, "ethnography embraces the descriptive details, and ethnology the rational exposition, of the human aggregates and organizations" (E. Reclus [1878], in *OED*). Ethnography is both the characteristic activity and expression of cultural ANTHROPOLOGY.

Interest in describing the distinctive characteristics of unfamiliar peoples dates to antiquity, with Herodotus (fifth century B.C.) and Tacitus (second century A.D.) producing notable studies, the *Persian Wars* and the *Germania*, respectively. Beginning in the Renaissance, European travelers, soldiers, and missionaries compiled numerous accounts (occasionally of high quality) of the societies they encountered. In Europe antiquarians collected with equal interest, and with much the same understanding, minerals and fossils, plants and insects, obscure artifacts, and written accounts of alien customs (see Hodgen 1964).

With occasional exceptions, until the nineteenth century ethnography did not exist as an independent inquiry, but was carried out rather casually in the course of other studies, typically geological, botanical, or zoological. An early effort to systematize ethnographic research was undertaken in 1800 by J.-M. Degérando, whose manual for the collection of field data was intended to guide the efforts of the French Société des Observateurs de l'Homme (Degérando 1800). This proved a precursor of more elaborate guides, notably the *Notes and Queries on Anthropology, for the Use of Travellers and Residents in Uncivilized Lands*, produced (in various editions) by the British Association for the Advancement of Science, beginning in the 1870s (Stocking 1983:72).

Patterns of Research

It is a commonplace that the dominant figures of Victorian anthropology— for example, Edward Tylor (1832–1917) or James Frazer (1854–1941)—did little if any first hand ethnography. What might be termed the "notes and queries" approach, with amateur observers providing information on demand to scholars at a distance, remained common until at least 1900. Henry Schoolcraft (1793–1864) employed this technique in compiling his synoptic ethnology of the North American tribes in the 1840s and 1850s, as did Lewis Henry Morgan (1818–1881) in his global studies of systems of KINSHIP and DESCENT during the 1860s (Hallowell 1960:42–51), though both men were unusual in also having conducted firsthand field studies.

Nonetheless, by the 1880s two models of direct ethnographic research were taking shape: on the one hand, the systematic ethnographic survey, conceived on the pattern of the Victorian natural history surveys of unexplored lands (and often staffed by naturalists turned anthropologists); and, on the other, the more intensive study, typically involving a single researcher living within one or a few native communities for a period of months or years. Examples of the survey approach include the massive ethnographic and linguistic studies of Native American groups conducted by the U.S. Bureau of American Ethnology, beginning in 1879, under the direction of John Wesley Powell (Hinsley 1981: ch. 6); and the British expedition to the Melanesian Torres Straits in 1898–99, led by Alfred Haddon (Stocking 1983:75–77). Early examples of intensive, sustained ethnographic research include Frank Cushing's studies at Zuni Pueblo from 1879 to 1884 (Hinsley 1983) and the research on central Australian aboriginal BANDS carried out by Baldwin Spencer and F. J. Gillen in the 1890s (Spencer and Gillen 1899).

The eventual acceptance of sustained, focused field research as the norm for ethnography was stimulated by later exemplars, notably Franz Boas's studies of the Kwakiutl of the Northwest Coast, conducted in numerous trips between 1895 and 1930 (Codere 1966), and Bronislaw Malinowski's research in the Melanesian Trobriand Islands between 1914 and 1918 (Malinowski 1922). Among the Kwakiutl, Boas "lived with the people and ate their food, gave feasts and was invited to them in turn, gave and received in potlatches . . . attended and took part in winter dance ceremonials" (Codere 1966:xxiv). Malinowski's participation in Trobriand life was, if anything, more extensive (Kaberry 1957:77–79). Each man saw his work as guiding a transformation of anthropological theory and practice: Boas seeking a detailed, historically grounded treatment of cultures (see HISTORICISM), Malinowski arguing for the study of communities as complex, integrated systems shaped by human needs (see FUNCTIONALISM). Unlike their fieldworking predecessors, each found a significant academic base (Boas in the United States, Malinowski in Britain) from which to shape an intellectual tradition.

The Ideal of Participant Observation

The notion of participant observation, a legacy of Boas and Malinowski, has become something of a shibboleth for modern anthropology. The task of ethnography, in this view, involves a necessary tension between the intimate and the detached, between the experiential and the scientific, in short, between indigenous and imposed frameworks of understanding (see EMIC/ETIC). To a greater degree than in perhaps any other social science, there is in anthropology a strong dialectic between the conduct of research and the molding of theory. The anthropologist's attempt to interact within an existing but alien framework of social relations involves an affirmation of the essential humanity of the "Other," the ethnographic subject. If this understanding is today self-evident, it nonetheless represented a fundamental transformation of the Victorian conception of the PRIMITIVE. Furthermore, by recognizing that field research required participation, anthropologists were forced to confront the fact that each culture constituted an indigenous world of meaning, the interpretation of which became an essential task of any ethnography (see RELATIVISM; SYMBOLISM).

Contemporary ethnography exhibits a bewildering range of methods and assumptions (see Pelto and Pelto 1978). There remains major disagreement on the balance to be struck between the ethnographer's stance as engaged participant and as detached observer. While a valid ethnography must penetrate the culture-specific premises of an alien society, its findings cannot be utilized to build a broader anthropological understanding unless they are expressed in terms that permit comparison and the testing of theory. By recognizing the necessity and interdependence of both modes of inquiry, cultural anthropology can be distinguished in its intent both from the other social sciences and from the humanities (see COMPARATIVE METHOD; INTERPRETATION; MATERIALISM).

References

Codere, Helen. 1966. "Introduction." In Franz Boas, *Kwakiutl Ethnography*. Helen
     Codere, ed. Chicago: University of Chicago Press. Useful for Boas's methods of
     research.
Degérando, Joseph-Marie. 1800 [1969]. *The Observation of Savage Peoples*. F. C. T.
     Moore, trans. Berkeley and Los Angeles: University of California Press. An early
     ethnographic field manual.
Hallowell, A. Irving. 1960. "The Beginnings of Anthropology in America." Frederica
     de Laguna, ed., *Selected Papers from the American Anthropologist, 1888–1920*.
     Washington, D.C.: American Anthropological Association. A good historical
     summary.
Hinsley, Curtis M., Jr. 1981. *Savages and Scientists: The Smithsonian Institution and
     the Development of American Anthropology, 1846–1910*. Washington, D.C.:
     Smithsonian Institution Press.
————. 1983. "Ethnographic Charisma and Scientific Routine: Cushing and Fewkes in
     the American Southwest, 1879–1893." George W. Stocking, Jr., ed., *Observers
     Observed: Essays on Ethnographic Fieldwork*. Madison: University of Wisconsin
     Press. Hinsley contrasts two approaches to ethnography: interpretive and positiv-
     istic.
Hodgen, Margaret. 1964. *Early Anthropology in the Sixteenth and Seventeenth Centuries*.
     Philadelphia: University of Pennsylvania Press.
Kaberry, Phyllis. 1957. "Malinowski's Contribution to Fieldwork Methods and the Writ-
     ing of Ethnography." Raymond Firth, ed., *Man and Culture: An Evaluation of
     the Work of Bronislaw Malinowski*. London: Routledge & Kegan Paul.
Malinowski, Bronislaw. 1922 [1961]. *Argonauts of the Western Pacific*. New York:
     Dutton. A classic study, setting a standard for later ethnography.

Pelto, Pertti J., and Gretel H. Pelto. 1978. *Anthropological Research: The Structure of Inquiry*. 2nd ed. Cambridge: Cambridge University Press. Emphasizes scientific, hypothesis-testing approaches to research.

Spencer, Baldwin, and F. J. Gillen. 1899 [1968]. *The Native Tribes of Central Australia*. New York: Dover.

Stocking, George W., Jr. 1983. "The Ethnographer's Magic: Fieldwork in British Anthropology from Tylor to Malinowski." George W. Stocking, Jr., ed., *Observers Observed: Essays on Ethnographic Fieldwork*. Madison: University of Wisconsin Press.

Sources of Additional Information

The accounts collected in George D. Spindler, ed., *Being an Anthropologist: Fieldwork in Eleven Cultures*, New York: Holt, Rinehart and Winston, 1970, provide insight into the process of ethnography. A readable text on ethnographic method, emphasizing linguistic models of research, is Michael Agar, *The Professional Stranger: An Informal Introduction to Ethnography*, New York: Academic Press, 1980. A more technical handbook of method, with a strong emphasis on ethnoscience, is Oswald Werner and G. Mark Schoepfle, *Systematic Fieldwork*, 2 vols., Beverly Hills: Sage Publications, 1987.

ETHNOLOGY.   The classification and comparison of CULTURES, often emphasizing their DEVELOPMENT and historical interrelationships.

Ethnology is derived from the Greek *ethnos*, a people linked by common CUSTOMS, a nation. Ethnology is a comparative discipline; its goal is to describe the cultural (and originally, physical) differences between peoples and to explain these differences by reconstructing the history of their development, MIGRATION, and interaction. Ethnological studies emerged from a more general, prescientific literature of the exotic, those collections of odd customs and summaries of travelers' tales—such as Johann Boemus's sixteenth-century *Fardle of Facions*—common from the Middle Ages through at least the seventeenth century (see Hodgen 1964: ch. 4). Nonetheless, it was the Renaissance concern with the understanding of a distant cultural world (that of ancient Greece and Rome) which made a more general effort at cross-cultural interpretation possible, for "it created a 'perspective distance' at which antiquity or any more recent culture might be seen whole and observed with a respect that would make it an acceptable object of study" (Rowe 1965:14).

A notable Renaissance work of ethnology was Joseph de Acosta's *The Natural and Moral History of the Indies*. This study described with considerable fidelity the peoples and institutions of Mexico and Peru and weighed alternative theories for their origin, suggesting as the most plausible their entry from the Old World via a northerly land bridge (Acosta 1590, bk. 1, ch. 20). Acosta was at considerable pains to counter the "common and ignorant contempt in which the Indians are held by Europeans who think that these peoples have none of the qualities of rational men" (in Pagden 1982:157). In affirming what would later be termed the PSYCHIC UNITY of mankind, works such as this laid the foundation for an essential principle of modern ANTHROPOLOGY, the explanation of distinctive

PATTERNS of belief and behavior in terms of cultural learning rather than innate biological difference (see also SUPERORGANIC).

Ethnology as a Victorian Discipline

An explicit concept of ethnology appears to date from the late eighteenth century; it was defined by Chavannes in 1787 as "l'histoire des progrès des peuples vers la civilisation," the history of the progress of peoples toward CIVILIZATION (in Brinton 1892:264). The emergence of ethnology as the label for a coherent scholarly perspective can be documented through the history of institutions: the Société Ethnologique de Paris was founded in 1839, the American Ethnological Society in 1842, and the Ethnological Society of London in 1843 (Stocking 1987:243–44; Hallowell 1960:92). In 1847 James Prichard described the goals of ethnology in terms that are still broadly accurate: "to trace the history of the tribes and races of men from the most remote periods which are within reach of investigation, to discover their mutual relations, and to arrive at conclusions, either certain or probable, as to their affinity or diversity of origin" (in Stocking 1987:52). As thus defined, ethnology synthesized the data of what today would be termed physical anthropology, linguistics, archaeology, and ETHNOGRAPHY.

Mid-nineteenth century anthropology was molded by debate on several major issues. Among these were the validity and significance of biblical doctrine for reconstructing human prehistory; the respective roles of DIFFUSION and EVO-LUTION in the development of human societies; and the biological relationship holding between the various RACES, the monogenist position affirming the underlying unity of humankind, the polygenist position explaining cultural difference by the racialist postulate of multiple, unequal species. In the controversy over race, notably in Britain, ethnology was associated with the monogenist perspective, a view justified in part by biblical teaching. Although sympathetic to evolutionist ideas, the ethnologists emphasized historical reconstruction of the development of societies (Stocking 1973:ci). Anthropology in contrast became the banner of the polygenist opposition, institutionalized in the 1860s by the Anthropological Society of London. Guided by the model of a non-Darwinian comparative anatomy, the perspective of the "anthropologicals" consisted essentially of a racist, rigidly typological physical anthropology. The goal of "anthropology," so defined, was to explain cultural difference by means of an assumed biological inequality between races.

By the 1870s the monogenist view was broadly accepted, and under the influence of Darwinian theory "anthropology" had been transformed into an evolutionist discipline, drawing on physical, archaeological, and ethnographic data alike (Stocking 1987: ch. 7). Accordingly the earlier tradition of ethnology as a study combining physical and cultural data—epitomized by the work of James Prichard (see Prichard 1813)—gave way to a more restricted sense of the term. From the position of a contending paradigm, ethnology was reduced to the status of a subdiscipline: the comparative study of culture (Stocking 1987:245–62). By a similar logic, ethnology came to be contrasted with ethnography, the description of particular societies (see *OED*, s.v. "ethnography"; Brinton 1892).

Twentieth Century Ethnology

In the United States anthropologists such as Franz Boas, Alfred Kroeber, Robert Lowie, and Leslie Spier stressed the investigation of culture history, utilizing diffusion rather than evolution as an explanatory principle, and the concept of CULTURE AREA as a basic analytic device. In this regard American anthropology showed continuities with earlier British and continental ethnology, though with a far higher standard of ethnographic research than had previously been common. At the same time, American ethnology was transformed by a gradual acceptance of cultural RELATIVISM, a recognition of the meaningful relation between the various elements of a culture (see PATTERN), and the need to accommodate questions of CULTURE CHANGE and ACCULTURATION. Anthropologists were "no longer satisfied with the systematic enumeration of standardized beliefs and customs of a tribe . . . [seeking instead how] the individual reacts to his whole social environment" (Boas 1920:316). In this perspective, each culture involved a distinct, historically constituted world of value and meaning (see HISTORICISM), which it was ethnology's task to understand.

The changing emphasis of British anthropology, from the 1930s onward, on SOCIAL STRUCTURE rather than culture is reflected in the separation of social anthropology from ethnology (Radcliffe-Brown 1951:53–54). The ethnological tradition has remained strong in European anthropology (see Birket-Smith 1965). As a descriptive term, ethnology is today broadly synonymous with cultural anthropology.

References

Acosta, Joseph de. 1590 [1970]. *The Natural and Moral History of the Indies*. Edward Grimston, trans. [Hakluyt Society, 1st ser., vols. 60, 61] New York: Lenox Hill, Burt Franklin (reprint). An influential Renaissance study of New World cultures.

Birket-Smith, Kaj. 1965. *The Paths of Culture: A General Ethnology*. Karin Fennow, trans. Madison: University of Wisconsin Press. A general text in the ethnological tradition by an eminent Danish anthropologist.

Boas, Franz. 1920. "The Methods of Ethnology." *AA* 22:311–321.

Brinton, Daniel G. 1892. "The Nomenclature and Teaching of Anthropology." *AA* [o.s.] 5:263–266.

Hallowell, A. Irving. 1960. "The Beginnings of Anthropology in America." In Frederica de Laguna, ed., *Selected Papers from the American Anthropologist, 1888–1920*. Washington, D.C.: American Anthropological Association.

Hodgen, Margaret T. 1964. *Early Anthropology in the Sixteenth and Seventeenth Centuries*. Philadelphia: University of Pennsylvania Press. Hodgen's study describes the Renaissance foundations of ethnology.

Pagden, Anthony. 1982. *The Fall of Natural Man: The American Indian and the Origins of Comparative Ethnology*. Cambridge: Cambridge University Press. A significant study stressing Spanish sources.

Prichard, James C. 1813 [1973]. *Researches into the Physical History of Man*. George

W. Stocking, Jr., ed. Chicago: University of Chicago Press. A major work of
  early nineteenth-century ethnology.
Radcliffe-Brown, A. R. 1951 [1977]. "The Comparative Method in Social Anthropology." Adam Kuper, ed., *The Social Anthropology of Radcliffe-Brown*. London:
  Routledge & Kegan Paul.
Rowe, John H. 1965. "The Renaissance Foundations of Anthropology." *AA* 67:1–20.
Stocking, George W., Jr. 1973. "From Chronology to Ethnology: James Cowles Prichard
  and British Anthropology, 1800–1850." In Prichard 1813.
———. 1987. *Victorian Anthropology*. New York: Free Press.

Sources of Additional Information

For a sense of the scope of contemporary ethnology, see the journals *Ethnology* and
American Ethnologist.

ETHNOSCIENCE. The description of a CULTURE in terms of its characteristic
  patterns of cognition, that is, its rules for categorizing experience.

Ethnoscience (literally, the knowledge of a cultural group) is a postwar development within cultural ANTHROPOLOGY that advocates the attainment of reliable ethnographic knowledge through a comprehensive analysis of indigenous
systems of categorizing experience. In practice this has involved quite limited
domains (e.g., the classification of KINSHIP, diseases, colors, or plant forms).
This approach has also been termed, with polemical intent, the New Ethnography,
or when emphasizing the influence of psychology, linguistics, or formal logic,
cognitive anthropology (Tyler 1969). Ethnoscience represents the expansion of
a familiar anthropological principle into a program of research and a theory of
culture, namely, that meaningful description requires an understanding of the
assumptions by which actors (rather than observers) structure experience—what
is often termed the "native's point of view."

As the ethnographer and linguist Edward Sapir once noted, consider an observer

> making a painstaking report of [actions] . . . to which he has not the cultural key. If
> he is a skillful writer, he may succeed in giving a picturesque account of what he
> sees and hears, or thinks he sees and hears, but the chances of his being able to
> give a relation of what happens in terms that would be intelligible and acceptable
> to the natives themselves are practically nil. (Sapir 1927:546–47)

For ethnoscience, the objective of a cultural description (an ETHNOGRAPHY) is
to identify those standards of thought and action that are "intelligible and acceptable" to the native (whether the native be found in New Guinea, Bombay,
or Akron, Ohio). Culture, from this viewpoint, is "a set of standards that seems
to be authoritative" (Goodenough 1970:103). The concern is not with behavior
but with cultural knowledge, the goal for ethnoscience being "to penetrate
beyond mere material representations [i.e., events] to the logical nexus of underlying concepts" (Tyler 1969:14).

While ethnoscience is not unique in stressing an indigenous cultural perspective, it is distinctive in its search for rigorous and formal methods by which the native's point of view can be transcribed. These goals and methods reflect the influence of linguistics on anthropology in the postwar period (Keesing 1972; see LANGUAGE). The search for underlying codes, standards, or paradigms that guide behavior parallels the linguist's search for the rules of phonology and syntax which order speech. As in linguistics, advocates of ethnoscience have sought to discover for any given domain a minimum number of rules through which all known forms may be generated, for example, the reduction of the complexities of kin terminology to a few rules based on specification of gender, generation, connection between kin, and the like (Lounsbury 1969). The influence of linguistics is also evident in the ethnoscientific contrast of emic and etic description, referring respectively to culture-bound and culture-independent categories, a usage drawn from the linguistic distinction between phonemic and phonetic analysis (see EMIC/ETIC).

Examples of Research

Studies of culturally patterned classification have a considerable history in anthropology. In the 1840s Lewis Henry Morgan noted among the Iroquois a distinctive approach to designating and classifying kin, a discovery that led to his pioneering treatment of systems of kin terminology (see KINSHIP). In 1903 Emile Durkheim and Marcel Mauss published a comparative study of the relation between cosmological categories and SOCIAL STRUCTURE, noting (among other examples) a correspondence among the Zuni of the American Southwest between a division of society into seven clans and a corresponding sevenfold classification of nature: directions, seasons, elements, animals, and the like (Durkheim and Mauss 1903:42–45).

Studies conducted from an explicitly ethnoscientific standpoint have generally been more limited in aim and programmatic in character. Charles Frake has studied the ethnomedicine of the Subanum of Mindanao, describing their complex disease taxonomy and criteria for diagnosis (Frake 1964). Brent Berlin, Dennis Breedlove, and Peter Raven (1966) have studied Tzeltal (Mexican) ethnobotany, contrasting the indigenous classification of flora with the familiar Linnaean classification of scientific botany; considerable discrepancy between the two systems was found. James Spradley (1972) has used ethnoscience to document the lifeways of the tramp subculture in the urban United States. One of the most productive studies has been Brent Berlin and Paul Kay's comparative analysis of basic color terms. They discovered considerable regularity, concluding that "a total universal inventory of exactly eleven basic color categories exists from which the eleven or fewer basic color terms of any given language are always drawn" (Berlin and Kay 1969:2).

The Critique of Ethnoscience

The importance of ethnoscience lies in the intent of its proponents to create an explicitly scientific, formal, and verifiable mode of ethnography. Their insistence on reducing the study of a culture to a system of underlying rules or categories marks a radical break with anthropological tradition and excludes much of the scope of more conventional ethnographic inquiry. Critics have not been lacking.

Roger Keesing has argued that the assumptions of descriptive or taxonomic linguistics, which provided the theoretical inspiration for ethnoscience, have been rendered obsolete by the advent of transformational (Chomskyean) linguistics. While, for example, an earlier linguistic theory assumed the structural uniqueness of each language (or for ethnoscience, each culture), which must thus be studied on its own terms, transformational theory suggests "a universal language design, of which each natural language represents one possible expression" (Keesing 1972:311).

Clifford Geertz, taking an interpretive perspective, attacks as reductionist the ethnoscientific search for culture in what are psychological data, namely, individually acquired rules, classifications, or concepts. Rather, he argues, culture is necessarily public and social: it is not encoded, but transacted (Geertz 1973:10–13; see also INTERPRETATION; SUPERORGANIC).

Finally, Gerald Berreman has criticized the formalist goals of ethnoscience for narrowing the scope of cultural anthropology to a quasi-linguistic search for rules and typologies devoid of any humanistic insight. The result, he claims, is "astoundingly pallid, sterile, and fragmentary ethnography" (Berreman 1966:349).

References

Berlin, Brent, Dennis Breedlove, and Peter Raven. 1966 [1969]. "Folk Taxonomies and Biological Classification." Stephen Tyler, ed., *Cognitive Anthropology.* New York: Holt, Rinehart and Winston.
Berlin, Brent, and Paul Kay. 1969. *Basic Color Terms.* Berkeley and Los Angeles: University of California Press.
Berreman, Gerald. 1966. "Anemic and Emetic Analyses in Social Anthropology." *AA* 68:346–54. A strong critique.
Durkheim, Emile, and Marcel Mauss. 1903 [1963]. *Primitive Classification.* Rodney Needham, trans. Chicago: University of Chicago Press. A pioneering study.
Frake, Charles O. 1964. "The Diagnosis of Disease Among the Subanum of Mindanao." Dell Hymes, ed., *Language in Culture and Society.* New York: Harper & Row.
Geertz, Clifford. 1973. "Thick Description: Toward an Interpretive Theory of Culture." C. Geertz, *The Interpretation of Cultures.* New York: Basic Books. Offers a significant critique of the philosophical premises of ethnoscience.
Goodenough, Ward. 1970. *Description and Comparison in Cultural Anthropology.* Chicago: Aldine. An important statement of the ethnoscience perspective.
Keesing, Roger M. 1972. "Paradigms Lost: The New Ethnography and the New Linguistics." *Southwestern Journal of Anthropology* 28:299–331. Highly recommended for its analysis of the weaknesses and possibilities of a cognitive anthropology.
Lounsbury, Floyd G. 1969. "A Formal Analysis of the Crow- and Omaha-Type Kinship Terminologies." Stephen Tyler, ed., Cognitive Anthropology. New York: Holt, Rinehart and Winston.

Sapir, Edward. 1927 [1949]. "The Unconscious Patterning of Behavior in Society."
    David G. Mandelbaum, ed., *Selected Writings of Edward Sapir in Language,
    Culture and Personality*. Berkeley and Los Angeles: University of California
    Press.
Spradley, James P. 1972. "Adaptive Strategies of Urban Nomads: The Ethnoscience of
    Tramp Culture." Thomas Weaver and Douglas White, eds., *The Anthropology
    of Urban Environments*. Society for Applied Anthropology, Monograph 11.
Tyler, Stephen. 1969. "Introduction." Stephen Tyler, ed., *Cognitive Anthropology*. New
    York: Holt, Rinehart and Winston.

Sources of Additional Information

William C. Sturtevant, "Studies in Ethnoscience," Robert A. Manners and David
Kaplan, eds., *Theory in Anthropology*, Chicago: Aldine, 1968, provides a useful introduction. The ethnoscientific approach to ethnography is presented in detail in Oswald
Werner and G. Mark Schoepfle, *Systematic Fieldwork*, 2 vols., Beverly Hills: Sage,
1987.

EVOLUTION. (1) Change with direction. (2) In cultural anthropology, the
reorganization of a social SYSTEM involving an increase in scale, complexity,
or heterogeneity.

Evolution implies directional change, that is, change which is cumulative
rather than random. Evolution can also involve the emergence of novelty, the
qualitative transformation of a system resulting from an increase in complexity
and heterogeneity. These two senses are sometimes referred to respectively as
microevolution and macroevolution. In the biological realm, microevolution is
illustrated by the gradual modification of Galapagos finches into a number of
species with beaks adapted to distinct diets (Bowler 1989:163), macroevolution
by the successive emergence of fish, amphibians, reptiles, and mammals. In the
domain of CULTURE, microevolution is illustrated by the ADAPTATION of Atha-
paskan peoples to varied North American environments by means of a range of
subsistence strategies, macroevolution by the emergence of larger, more complexly organized TRIBES from smaller hunter-gatherer BANDS.

Philosophical Background

For writers of the eighteenth century Enlightenment, human history reflected
a movement age by age toward ever greater achievement and wisdom. In short,
the providential history of Christian faith was transformed into the rationalist
aspirations of secular philosophers (see Burrow 1966:8–9). For Jacques Turgot
(1727–1781) this progressive movement was inevitable and universal: "The
human species considered from its origin appears to the eyes of a philosopher
as an immense whole, which has, like every individual, its childhood and its
progress" (in Frankel 1948:122). Turgot's speculations on "universal history"
announced themes that were to appear prominently in the writings of Victorian
evolutionists a century later: the positing of stages, the insistence on the universal
character of progress, embracing all societies, and the identification of various

institutions each with its upward trajectory: governments, LANGUAGES, morals, manners, sciences, and arts (Frankel 1948:122–23).

Another theme that was to reappear in Victorian writings, the ubiquitousness of error or irrationality, formed a notable part of Enlightenment thought. From a narrowly rationalist perspective a vast range of belief and behavior in any society must appear fallacious or inexplicable. For a philosopher such as the Marquis de Condorcet (1743–1794) such persistence of ignorance and superstition had itself a rational explanation: The ruling classes perpetuated such beliefs to keep their inferiors in servitude (Frankel 1948:136–40). Yet this tension between rationalist premises and seemingly irrational CUSTOM could not be so easily dismissed. For both the Victorian evolutionists and their later critics this problem helped to shape the development of culture theory, notably in the concepts of FOLKLORE, MYTH, RATIONALITY, RITUAL, SURVIVAL, and SYMBOLISM.

A third element, developed in particular by Scottish writers, was the reliance on the data of so-called PRIMITIVE societies in order to reconstruct the earlier stages of human progress, aptly described as "the illumination of the past by the exotic present" (Burrow 1966:12). As Adam Ferguson wrote (in 1767), "It is in their [the Indians'] present condition that we are to behold, as in a mirror, the features of our own progenitors" (in Burrow 1966:12). Here philosophy and the incipient science of ETHNOLOGY merged.

The Victorian Context

The emergence of an explicit theory of cultural evolution in the middle to late nineteenth century reflected several influences.

(1) By 1850 many of the natural sciences had achieved dramatic success and, more importantly, prestige through the systematic collection and classification of observable facts: the positivist method. There was considerable impetus to extend this approach to all domains of knowledge, including the study of customs and social institutions (Burrow 1966:102 ff.).

(2) The emerging science of geology had revealed the complexity and depth of the fossil record. One consequence was the demonstration of both the transformation of the biological world over time and the immense duration of this process (Bowler 1989: ch. 5). Applied to the human sphere, this provided an intellectual context for a developmentally oriented archaeology and ethnology (Daniel 1976; Grayson 1983).

(3) By the mid-nineteenth century utilitarian philosophy, which explained human action through the supposedly universal calculus of pleasure and pain, appeared inadequate when set beside the bewildering variety of human customs that ethnologists were then documenting. A theory of cultural evolution offered a way out of this impasse, by "reformulating the essential unity of mankind, while avoiding the current objections to the older theories of a human nature everywhere essentially the same. Mankind was one not because it was everywhere

the same, but because the differences represented different stages in the same process'' (Burrow 1966:98).

(4) In contrast to these factors, the influence of Darwinian thought in shaping Victorian cultural evolutionism was—in any direct sense—surprisingly limited (see Burrow 1966:19–21; Stocking 1987: ch. 5; Bowler 1989:233). Darwin's problem was to explain the emergence of diversity (the origin of species), while the proponents of cultural evolution began with a wholly different need: to demonstrate the common goal (CIVILIZATION) of societies currently at very different levels of cultural achievement. In contrast to the Darwinians, cultural evolutionists sought ''an explanation that was uniformitarian not only in process but in outcome'' (Stocking 1987:178).

Classical Evolutionism

By the mid-nineteenth century, the cycle of European exploration, conquest, and colonization had yielded vast possessions with a multitude of peoples culturally alien to European experience, and thus both politically and scientifically problematic. The discipline of anthropology arose in large measure in response to this encounter between cultures (see ETHNOGRAPHY; ETHNOLOGY). Cultural evolution—anthropology's first systematic ethnological theory—was intended to order and explain this diversity, while justifying (however unconsciously) Euro-American dominance.

Fundamental to this endeavor was the notion of dividing the ethnological record into evolutionary stages, ranging from most primitive to most civilized. In *Ancient Society* (1877), Lewis Henry Morgan (1818–1881) commented, ''As it is undeniable that portions of the human family have existed in a state of savagery, other portions in a state of barbarism, and still other portions in a state of civilization, it seems equally so that these three distinct conditions are connected with each other in a natural as well as necessary sequence of progress'' (Morgan 1877:3). Each stage (and its subdivisions) had its identifying benchmarks. Thus middle savagery was marked by the acquisition of a fish diet and the discovery of fire; upper savagery by the bow and arrow; lower barbarism by pottery; middle barbarism by animal domestication and irrigated agriculture; upper barbarism by the manufacture of iron; and civilization by the phonetic alphabet (Morgan 1877: ch. 1). The Victorians were quite unselfconscious in equating their own institutions with the acme of evolutionary achievement.

Such stages served to classify both the archaeological past and the ethnological present. Thus the evolutionary record could be retraced in both time and space, in time back to the earliest archaeological remains, and in space to those contemporary societies deemed by Victorian observers to be the most remote from their own ways of life (see BAND). The so-called primitive societies of modern times were seen as analogous to the earliest human or protohuman groups, an assumption illustrated by John Lubbock's popular exposition *Prehistoric Times* (1872), subtitled *As Illustrated by Ancient Remains and the Manners and Customs of Modern Savages*. Gaps in the archaeological record could be filled—by this logic—by conveniently chosen examples from contemporary groups. ''What the opossum and the sloth are to the geologist,'' wrote Lubbock, so were the natives of South America or Van Diemen's Land (Tasmania) to the antiquarian: evolutionary survivals of a more primitive era (Lubbock 1872:428; see also Stocking 1987:150–56). Finally, because contemporary societies were measured against the emergence of protohuman groups in the archaeological record, cultural difference could be equated not only with cultural but biological inferiority. To a great extent, RACE and culture were understood as interchangeable categories (cf. SUPERORGANIC).

Edward Tylor's *Primitive Culture*, published in 1871, represented an epitome of the evolutionist perspective. There he noted that

> The condition of culture among the various societies of mankind . . . is a subject apt for the study of laws of human thought and action. On the one hand, the uniformity which so largely pervades civilization may be ascribed, in great measure, to the uniform action of uniform causes; while on the other hand its various grades may be regarded as stages of development or evolution, each the outcome of previous history, and about to do its proper part in shaping the history of the future. (Tylor 1871:1:1)

This statement suggests several elements of the evolutionist program. The concept of culture was placed at the center of anthropological inquiry. (Tylor in fact introduced the modern, technical sense of this term to the English-speaking world; see Leopold 1980.) Culture was, moreover, understood in the singular, embracing all societies. The investigation was cast on positivist lines, seeking laws of human thought and action. Change occurred chiefly through multiple, independent invention—manifesting the uniform action of uniform causes—rather than through the historical interaction of societies (DIFFUSION), an assumption justified by the premise of PSYCHIC UNITY.

Writers such as Tylor or Lubbock framed their arguments in part to serve polemical ends, to argue the case for evolution against what were for Victorians two serious alternatives. Against polygenism, the racialist argument that humans comprised multiple, unequal species, the evolutionists postulated a common human NATURE—the doctrine of psychic unity—though this did not prevent them from postulating at the same time the inequality of RACES (see ETHNOLOGY).

Against degenerationism, the explanation of so-called savage societies in terms of a decline from original high cultures divinely instituted, they argued that civilized society was the result of the gradual development of culture from an earlier, ruder state (see Hodgen 1936: ch. 1). To bolster this argument evolutionists invoked the concept of SURVIVAL, a practice or belief preserved from an earlier era, assumed to lack function or rationality in its modern setting, that is, a ''superstition.'' Through this device the record of evolutionary development could be read not only in contemporary ''primitive'' societies, but within civilization itself. James Frazer's mammoth study of magic and religion, *The Golden Bough* (1890), used this device to particular advantage.

The intent of works such as *Primitive Culture*, *Prehistoric Times*, or *Ancient Society* was not so much to depict ethnographic data for their own sake, but to argue the plausibility of cultural evolution. What this meant in practice was a concern with describing, not whole ways of life occurring at particular developmental stages, but the evolutionary path of one or another element of culture— garments, weapons, MARRIAGE patterns, or supernatural beliefs.

Thus KINSHIP patterns were thought to have evolved from promiscuity through matrilineal to patrilineal systems of DESCENT (see also GENDER). Systems of belief were thought—by Frazer (1890:648), for example—to have evolved from MAGIC through RELIGION to science. (See also ANIMISM, LAW, MARRIAGE, and TOTEMISM.) To effect these reconstructions, evolutionists utilized the COMPARATIVE METHOD, the comparison of multiple examples of a given culture element, widely dispersed in time and space and thus divorced from their ethnographic contexts, so as to substantiate the reconstructions of an evolutionary pedigree.

The doctrine of cultural evolution, combined with the comparative method, allowed writers such as Tylor, Morgan, and Frazer to undertake vast—and for Victorian readers, fascinating—syntheses, combining data from diverse times and places to support their reconstructions of human experience. By 1900, with the advent of new understandings of culture and new techniques of ethnography, both doctrine and method came under sharp attack. Nonetheless, classical cultural evolutionism provided the rationale for a scientific anthropology and the focus for a newly emerging discipline.

The Critique of Evolutionism

By the time of the First World War evolutionism had been roundly attacked on both sides of the Atlantic. In America Franz Boas (1858–1942) offered a measured critique centering on the weaknesses of the comparative method, advocating historically oriented research (see HISTORICISM) while acknowledging the validity of both invention and diffusion as mechanisms of CULTURE CHANGE (Boas 1896; see Stocking 1968; Kuper 1988: ch. 7). As Marvin Harris has remarked, Boas did not oppose evolutionism per se; rather, he rejected biological reductionism, cultural parallelism—the assumption that all societies follow the same path of cultural transformation—and universal standards of progress (Harris 1968:295).

A number of Boas's colleagues drew sharper battle lines. Berthold Laufer described the doctrine of cultural evolution as "inane, sterile, and pernicious," insisting that valid ethnographic investigation was necessarily limited to the study of "each cultural phenomenon as exactly as possible in its geographical distribution, its historical development and its relation or association with other kindred ideas" (1918, quoted in Harris 1968:293–94).

In Britain the critique of evolution came originally (as in America) from the perspective of historicism, notably through the writings of W. H. R. Rivers (1864–1922) (see Kuper 1988: ch. 8). The emergence of FUNCTIONALISM as the dominant perspective of British anthropology in the inter-war period, through the work of Bronislaw Malinowski (1884–1942) and A. R. Radcliffe-Brown (1881–1955), proved even more damaging to the evolutionist cause. The functionalist insistence on the detailed study of living communities was diametrically opposed to that a priori reconstruction of the development of institutions which formed the central task of classical evolutionism.

Later Developments

In the history of evolutionary thought, change has been explained both as the gradual unfolding of that which is predestined by design (preformationism) and as a process of immutable progress toward a preestablished goal (orthogenesis; see Bowler 1989:57–62, 268–70). Progress in biological theory came by abandoning such ideas in favor of explaining evolution as an open-ended process of change guided by certain underlying mechanisms, notably natural selection and Mendelian genetics.

In studies of cultural evolution the ethnocentric Victorian faith in the inexorable movement of societies toward rationality and civilization was replaced with a more cautious search for mechanisms of change, emphasizing material factors in the shaping of culture. A series of changes in culture theory, beginning in the 1930s, served to reopen interest in evolutionary perspectives. A concern with environmentally based CULTURE AREAS was replaced by more sophisticated attempts to describe patterns of adaptation, manifested through complex interrelations of technology, ECONOMY, and SOCIAL STRUCTURE.

Beginning with a series of articles in the 1940s, Leslie White (1900–1975) championed an evolutionary and materialist interpretation of the broad sweep of culture history, identifying energy utilization as the key variable underlying cultural transformation. He formulated this as the "law of cultural development": "Culture advances as the amount of energy harnessed per capita per year increases, or as the efficiency or economy of the means of controlling energy is increased, or both" (White 1959:56). White was concerned not with specific societies but with the evolutionary transformation of culture generally. In viewing culture as a single, global development, White's work—despite its materialist viewpoint—shows strong affinities with the evolutionism of Edward Tylor (White 1959:ix; see also Sahlins et al. 1960).

Victorian anthropologists had been heavily criticized for formulating universal evolutionary sequences describing the developmental path all societies must follow (unilinear evolution). Julian Steward (1902–1972) counterposed to this the perspective of multilinear evolution: multiple, alternative developmental paths reflecting the specific adaptive strategies appropriate to varying environmental conditions. Beginning with studies in the 1930s (Steward 1936), he sought to identify "recurrent causal relationships in independent cultural traditions" (Steward 1955:27). In describing the evolution of band-level societies, Steward argued that "the functional relations and cultural-ecological adaptations which led to a patrilineal band, consisting of a localized lineage, were very different from those which produced a nomadic, bilateral band composed of many unrelated families. . . . [These in turn may be distinguished from] dispersed family groups, such as the Shoshoni and Eskimo, and . . . cohesive tribelets, such as those of California" (Steward 1955:24–25). Such studies established the field of CULTURAL ECOLOGY.

Since the 1960s, cultural evolutionism has served less as a contending doctrine than as a general perspective implicit in all materialist versions of culture theory, Marxist and non-Marxist alike (see MATERIALISM). The study of microevolutionary change has become an essential part of anthropological studies of ecology and adaptation (see also DEVELOPMENT). The nature and causes of macroevolutionary change remain—as in biology—less well understood. Nonetheless, macroevolutionary problems such as the origins of agriculture or the emergence of STATE-level societies (involving dramatic changes in scale, ECONOMY, and structured inequality) have been of major theoretical interest in this period. In the 1980s a new and strongly Darwinian version of evolutionary culture theory emerged under the banner of SOCIOBIOLOGY.

References

Boas, Franz. 1896 [1940]. "The Limitations of the Comparative Method of Anthropology." F. Boas, *Race, Language and Culture*. New York: Free Press.

Bowler, Peter. J. 1989. *Evolution: The History of an Idea*. Rev. ed. Berkeley and Los Angeles: University of California Press. An excellent history of evolutionary theory in biology.

Burrow, J. W. 1966. *Evolution and Society: A Study in Victorian Social Theory*. Cambridge: Cambridge University Press. An excellent source on the intellectual background of cultural evolutionism.

Daniel, Glyn. 1976. *A Hundred and Fifty Years of Archaeology*. Cambridge, Mass.: Harvard University Press.

Frankel, Charles. 1948 [1969]. *The Faith of Reason: The Idea of Progress in the French Enlightenment*. New York: Octagon Books.

Frazer, James George. 1890 [1959]. *The New Golden Bough*. 1 vol, abr. Theodor H. Gaster, ed. New York: Criterion. A classic study of the evolution of magic and religion.

Grayson, Donald K. 1983. *The Establishment of Human Antiquity*. New York: Academic Press. Describes the transformation of European thought resulting from the development of geology and archaeology.

Harris, Marvin. 1968. *The Rise of Anthropological Theory*. New York: Crowell.

Hodgen, Margaret T. 1936. *The Doctrine of Survivals*. London: Allenson.

Kuper, Adam. 1988. *The Invention of Primitive Society: Transformations of an Illusion*. London: Routledge.

Leopold, Joan. 1980. *Culture in Comparative and Evolutionary Perspective: E. B. Tylor and the Making of* Primitive Culture. Berlin: Dietrich Reimer Verlag. An important study of Tylor's intellectual development.

Lubbock, John. 1872. *Prehistoric Times: As Illustrated by Ancient Remains and the Manners and Customs of Modern Savages*. New York: Appleton. An influential Victorian text.

Morgan, Lewis H. 1877. *Ancient Society*. Chicago: Charles H. Kerr.

Sahlins, Marshall D., et al. 1960. *Evolution and Culture*. Ann Arbor: University of Michigan Press.

Steward, Julian H. 1936. "The Economic and Social Basis of Primitive Bands." *Essays in Anthropology Presented to A. L. Kroeber*. Berkeley and Los Angeles: University of California Press.

————. 1955. *Theory of Culture Change: The Methodology of Multilinear Evolution*. Urbana: University of Illinois Press.

Stocking, George W., Jr. 1968. "Franz Boas and the Culture Concept in Historical Perspective." G. Stocking, *Race, Culture, and Evolution*. New York: Free Press.

————. 1987. *Victorian Anthropology*. New York: Free Press. An excellent intellectual history.

Tylor, Edward. 1871 [1958]. *Primitive Culture*. 2 vols. New York: Harper Torchbook. One of the definitive works of classic cultural evolution.

White, Leslie. 1959. *The Evolution of Culture*. New York: McGraw-Hill.

Sources of Additional Information

An excellent source for understanding the outlook (and failings) of Victorian anthropology is John Lubbock (Lord Avebury), *The Origin of Civilization and the Primitive Condition of Man*, Chicago: University of Chicago Press, orig. ed. 1870, reprinted 1978. An introduction to evolutionary culture theory is provided by Robert L. Carneiro, "The Four Faces of Evolution," John J. Honigmann, ed., *Handbook of Social and Cultural Anthropology*, Chicago: Rand McNally, 1973. A modern treatment of the broad theoretical implications of cultural evolution is provided in Tim Ingold, *Evolution and Social Life*, Cambridge: Cambridge University Press, 1986.

F

FAMILY. A core group of closely related, cooperating kin, encompassing two or more generations, whose members (affines excluded) are prohibited from sexual relations.

Family is both a key anthropological concept and a powerful symbol in Western social thought. Efforts at a cross-culturally valid definition of family have been complicated by assumptions and values specific to Euro-American societies. This entry reviews the development of family as an analytic category, together with the associated topics of residence patterns, the contrast of family and household, and the prohibition of incest. For related entries see DESCENT, KINSHIP, MARRIAGE, and SOCIAL STRUCTURE.

English usage reflects the complexity of the concept. Its meanings have included (1) those claiming descent from a common ancestor, that is, a lineage (from the early fifteenth century); (2) "the body of persons who live in one house or under one head, including parents, children, servants, etc.," that is, a household (from the mid-sixteenth century); and (3) "the unity formed by those who are nearly [i.e., closely] connected by blood or affinity" (from the late seventeenth century), the sense closest to modern anthropological usage (see *OED*). Family, at least in this last sense, implies a set of individuals sharing bonds of kinship, sufficiently close in relationship to form a cooperating unit.

Several anthropological efforts at definition suggest the range of issues in question. Robert Lowie defined the family as "the group comprising a married couple and their children," arguing that it forms a distinguishable unit in all societies, regardless of other kinship principles. "Everywhere the husband, wife and immature children constitute a unit apart from the remainder of the community" (Lowie 1920:63, 67). This is echoed by Bronislaw Malinowski's dictum (in 1930): "The family is always the domestic institution *par excellence*" (in Goody 1958:56).

Such statements beg the issue of why a distinct social unit of this type should exist. This problem has most frequently been attacked by postulating certain functions universally fulfilled by the family. In G. P. Murdock's influential work *Social Structure*, for example, the family is defined as "a social group characterized by common residence, economic cooperation, and reproduction. It includes adults of both sexes, at least two of whom maintain a socially approved sexual relationship, and one or more children, own or adopted, of the sexually cohabiting adults" (Murdock 1949:1). Murdock sees in the two-generation (or nuclear) family a "universal human social grouping," providing four indispensable functions, "sexual, economic, reproductive, and educational" (Murdock 1949:2, 3).

Structural Variations

Later research has strongly challenged the assumption that the nuclear family constitutes the fundamental kin unit in all societies. Although the bonds of husband/wife and parent/child may be considered nearly universal, they do not consistently combine to form a distinct nuclear family. Rather, these bonds exist within a wider structure of relationships, both positive and negative: relationships of propinquity developed through principles of descent, marriage, kin classification, and common residence; and relationships of avoidance required by rules of exogamy (outmarriage) and sexual prohibition (the incest taboo).

The result is a wide variety of family structures, based on ties through multiple generations (the extended family), multiple marriage partners (the polygamous family), or multiple, cooperating nuclear units linked by siblings (the collateral family). These can generate numerous specific forms (see Buchler and Selby 1968:23–28). Furthermore, the family unit need not be based on the conjugal (i.e., husband/wife) bond, though Euro-American practice has so colored our theorizing that, as Ralph Linton noted, "we tend to think of marriage and the family as inseparably linked." Rather, many societies place primary emphasis on consanguine (blood) ties in structuring the family unit (Linton 1936:159).

Residence and Domestic Groups

One of the most basic questions posed in field ETHNOGRAPHY is the physical organization of the family unit, the issue of residence pattern. Because the location of the family unit has important logistical consequences, residence patterns have a long history of study: Edward Tylor (1832–1917), for example, investigated the association between residence and such CUSTOMS as kin avoidance and teknonymy (naming parent after child; see Tylor 1889). Anthropologists have traditionally analyzed residence in relation to marriage, based on the kin group with which the newly married couple resides. This approach yields a few basic patterns: uxorilocal residence (Lat. *uxor*-wife), where the couple resides with the wife's kin group; virilocal residence (Lat. *vir*-man, husband), where they reside with the husband's kin; and neolocal residence, where a new and independent household is established. Where residence reflects the dominance of a unilineal decent system, an older terminology can be used: patrilocal, describing residence with the husband's father, in a patrilineal system; matrilocal, describing residence with the wife's mother, in a matrilineal system (see Pehrson 1954:194–95). However, such classifications can be misleading, and several alternative approaches to the analysis of family and residence have been proposed.

(1) Paul Bohannon has suggested that residence patterns be described in terms of the "basic family relationship for domestic grouping": that relationship in a given society which is most valued, and thus most likely to prevail in the case of conflict. Most family units are based on one of five relationships: husband-wife, father-son, mother-daughter, father-daughter, or brother-sister (Bohannon 1957:318–19). In many societies, lineage ties expressed through father-son or mother-daughter may overshadow the conjugal bond: Among the East African Basoga, for example, "the solidarity of exogamous patrilineages is strong and nuclear families tend to be split by the conflicting loyalties of the spouses" (Levy and Fallers 1959:218). The sibling households of the traditional Ashanti illustrate another form of family organization (Bender 1967:495).

(2) According to Donald Bender, ethnographic analyses would be improved by distinguising three categories generally collapsed into the notion of family: family considered in a strict sense, as a relationship based on close kinship ties; co-residence, as a relationship of physical propinquity; and domestic unit, as a relationship of cooperation providing "the day-to-day necessities of living, including the provision and preparation of food and the care of children" (Bender 1967:499). For example, the Mundurucu traditionally utilize two forms of residential unit: one of adult males, another of women and children. Since the husband provides his wife with fish and game, the nuclear family functions as a domestic but not a co-residential unit (Bender 1967:495).

(3) Meyer Fortes and other Cambridge anthropologists have stressed the dynamic character of domestic groups. In this view, the predominant household composition and residence pattern observed in a given society should not be reified as a permanent cultural attribute. Thus diversity in family form does not represent a deviation from the culturally "correct" pattern, but an expression of "phases in the growth cycle of a joint family." Speaking of the Tallensi of West Africa, Fortes wrote (in 1949), "The domestic group grows, changes, and dissolves with the growth cycle of . . . [the] lineage" (in Goody 1958:53).

The Incest Taboo

Incest involves prohibited sexual relations with family members; normally this is taken to include consanguines within the nuclear family, and a varying array of extended and collateral kin, often including affines. The prohibition on incest (see TABOO) is apparently culturally universal, although the range of kin considered to fall within this prohibition varies dramatically from culture to culture. That is, at its narrowest, certain cultures apply the stigma of incest only to sexuality between immediate family members; at its broadest it is applied "beyond relatives with whom an actual genealogical connection can be traced, such as in the case of clans, phratries, and moieties" (Leavitt 1989:120; see DESCENT).

Nonetheless, the prohibition of incest within the family appears to form both the emotional and theoretical core of the phenomenon. The family is in a sense defined by two complementary cultural values: positively, by what Fortes has termed the "axiom of amity," the requirement that close kin interact through trust and solidarity (see KINSHIP); negatively, by the incest taboo, the insistence that the emotional force of sexuality be directed outward, widening rather than constricting the ties of social life.

The cause of the incest taboo remains controversial; few topics in ANTHRO-POLOGY have received so many, generally contradictory, efforts at explanation. The following three views have been particularly prominent.

(1) The explanation of incest has played a prominent role in psychoanalytic theory, beginning with the work of Sigmund Freud, notably in *Totem and Taboo* (Freud 1913; see TOTEMISM). Freudian theory assumes that incest is an intensely desired act (manifested, for example, in the mother/son fixation of the Oedipus complex), which is both strongly repressed in the course of individual psychological development and strongly prohibited through the cultural postulate of incest. Freud, reflecting the anthropological knowledge of his day, assumed the original existence of a primal horde, presided over by a tyrannical father with sexual control of all women in the group. The beleaguered sons at some point banded together and overpowered, killed, and ate their father. Filled with remorse, they then established in expiation a totemic ritual, protecting in symbolic form the father they had murdered, and instituting the prohibition against incest, thereby renouncing "the women whom they desired and who had been their chief motive for despatching their father" (Freud 1913:144). Although this account is at best unverifiable, the underlying psychology of the Freudian position continues to influence anthropological debate (see Spain 1987).

(2) A second prominent view, propounded in particular by Leslie White (1948) and Claude Lévi-Strauss (1949) is cultural rather than psychological in character. Here the essential function of the incest prohibition is the widening of social ties, signifying in a real sense the creation of a society. Thus, for White, "rules of exogamy originated as crystallizations of processes of a social system. . . . Inbreeding was prohibited and marriage between groups was made compulsory in order to obtain the maximum benefits of cooperation" (White 1948:426). Lévi-Strauss saw the emergence of the incest taboo as the fundamental cultural act, the transformation of NATURE into CULTURE. "Before it, culture is still non-existent; with it, nature's sovereignty over man is ended. The prohibition of incest is where nature transcends itself" (Lévi-Strauss 1949:25).

(3) While differing in other respects, the theories of Freud and Lévi-Strauss are in agreement in assuming that the incest taboo reflects a transformation of nature and that among nonhumans mating between close consanguines is common. At least in Freud's view incest is an act strongly desired, which if not prohibited would be widely performed. The view advanced originally by Edward Westermarck (1853–1936), and developed more recently by bioevolutionary theorists (sometimes termed the aversion hypothesis), is categorically opposed to those assumptions.

According to Westermarck, "There is a remarkable absence of erotic feelings between persons living very closely together from childhood." Such persons generally being close relatives, "their aversion to sexual relations with one another displays itself in custom and law as a prohibition of intercourse between near kin" (Westermarck 1925:2:192–93). In this theory, the ultimate rationale for the incest prohibition is the evolutionary advantage conferred through the avoidance of inbreeding. Finally, Westermarck noted that far from being a uniquely human creation, the avoidance of sexual relations with close kin occurs in many species. Considerable evidence has now been amassed in support of both points (see McCabe 1983; Shepher 1983; see also SOCIOBIOLOGY).

Family and Social Structure

Anthropological research has demonstrated the complexity and adaptability of the family when viewed in comparative perspective. If the family is defined as a core group of closely related, cooperating kin, encompassing two or more generations, then this institution is highly variable, its structure and functions differing from society to society. The question of the universality of the family (see Spiro 1954) has given way to more productive questions: the relationship between adaptive constraints and the patterning of residence, between core kin groups and wider kin structures, and between the functioning household and the ties of marriage.

Studies of these questions have altered the traditional view of the family as existing within a distinct, domestic sphere of nurturance, analytically separable from wider arrangements of politics and ECONOMY. As Sylvia Yanagisako has noted, "The units we label as families are undeniably about more than procreation and socialization. They are as much about production, exchange, power, inequality, and status" (Yanagisako 1979:199). Because anthropological theory has traditionally viewed the domestic sphere as the domain of female identity and responsibility, such reevaluations of the nature of the family have broad implications for the cross-cultural study of GENDER.

References

Bender, Donald R. 1967. "A Refinement of the Concept of Household: Families, Co-residence, and Domestic Functions." *AA* 69:493–504.
Bohannon, Paul. 1957 [1968]. "An Alternate Residence Classification." Paul Bohannon and John Middleton, eds., *Marriage, Family, and Residence*. Garden City, N.Y.: Natural History Press. Advocates that residence be analyzed in terms of the dominant kin bond.
Buchler, Ira, and Henry Selby. 1968. *Kinship and Social Organization*. New York: Macmillan. An advanced text.
Freud, Sigmund. 1913 [1950]. *Totem and Taboo*. James Strachey, trans. New York: Norton. A classic work of the psychoanalytic perspective.
Goody, Jack. 1958 [1971]. "The Fission of Domestic Groups Among the Lodagaba." J. Goody, ed., *The Developmental Cycle in Domestic Groups*. Cambridge: Cambridge University Press.

Leavitt, Gregory. 1989. "Disappearance of the Incest Taboo: A Cross-Cultural Test of General Evolutionary Hypotheses." *AA* 91:116–31.

Lévi-Strauss, Claude. 1949 [1969]. *The Elementary Structures of Kinship*. J. H. Bell, J. von Sturmer, and R. Needham, trans. Boston: Beacon Press. A classic study.

Levy, M. J., Jr., and L. A. Fallers. 1959 [1968]. "The Family: Some Comparative Considerations." Paul Bohannon and John Middleton, eds., *Marriage, Family, and Residence*. Garden City, N.Y.: Natural History Press.

Linton, Ralph. 1936. *The Study of Man*. N.p.: Appleton-Century-Crofts.

Lowie, Robert H. 1920 [1961]. *Primitive Society*. New York: Harper & Brothers.

McCabe, Justine. 1983. "FBD Marriage: Further Support for the Westermarck Hypothesis of the Incest Taboo?" *AA* 85:50–69. Supports the Westermarck avoidance theory.

Murdock, George Peter. 1949. *Social Structure*. New York: Macmillan. An important compendium of data.

Pehrson, Robert N. 1954 [1971]. "Bilateral Kin Groupings as a Structural Type: A Preliminary Statement." Nelson Graburn, ed., *Readings in Kinship and Social Structure*. New York: Harper & Row.

Shepher, Joseph. 1983. *Incest: A Biosocial View*. New York: Academic Press. Takes a sociobiological perspective.

Spain, David H. 1987. "The Westermarck-Freud Incest-Theory Debate." *CA* 28:623–45. A pro-Freudian account.

Spiro, Melford E. 1954 [1968]. "Is the Family Universal?" Paul Bohannon and John Middleton, eds., *Marriage, Family, and Residence*. Garden City, N. Y.: Natural History Press. Discusses the Israeli kibbutz.

Tylor, Edward B. 1889 [1961]. "On a Method of Investigating the Development of Institutions; Applied to Laws of Marriage and Descent." Frank W. Moore, ed., *Readings in Cross-Cultural Methodology*. New Haven, Conn.: HRAF Press.

Westermarck, Edward. 1925. *The History of Human Marriage*. 5th ed., 3 vols. London: Macmillan. 1st ed., 1891. Advocates the aversion theory of incest taboo.

White, Leslie. 1948. "The Definition and Prohibition of Incest." *AA* 50:416–35.

Yanagisako, Sylvia J. 1979. "Family and Household in the Analysis of Domestic Groups." *ARA* 8:161–205. An excellent review, with extensive bibliography.

Sources of Additional Information

Claude Lévi-Strauss, "The Family," Harry L. Schapiro, ed., *Man, Culture and Society*, New York: Oxford University Press, 1956, provides a perceptive introduction to the topic.

FOLK CULTURE.   A model of the peasant COMMUNITY characterized by economic self-sufficiency, intimate social ties, the strong role of RITUAL and TRADITION, and relative isolation from urban centers.

The concept of folk culture (or its near synonym, folk society) represents an attempt to characterize the values and SOCIAL STRUCTURE of traditional, rural communities existing within complex societies. Folk has been a highly polarized term in social thought. For many European folklorists and anthropologists of the nineteenth and early twentieth centuries, folk or folk stratum (*couche inférieure, Unterschicht, Volksschicht*, etc.) signified an ignorant and conservative peasant or proletarian majority, standing in strong contrast to a progressive urban elite, a view that animated both William Sumner's *Folk-Ways* (1906) and James Frazer's *Golden Bough* (1890) (see also FOLKLORE; and *GEC*, s.v. "Lower Stratum").

However, a more benign view of traditional, rural communities also developed in this period, stemming from concern for the cultural stability and social solidarity of emerging industrial societies. In Steven Lukes's words, "If pre-industrial societies were held together by common ideas and sentiments, by shared norms and values, what holds an industrial society together?" (Lukes 1973:141).

The view of Ferdinand Tönnies's *Gemeinschaft und Gesellschaft* (1887) is indicative of this phase of European thought. He contrasted the intimate social bonds and respect for tradition of the folk community (Gemeinschaft) with the less personal ties of ASSOCIATION (Gesellschaft) existing within a large-scale society (see also URBANISM). As Tönnies wrote, "All praise of rural life has pointed out that the Gemeinschaft among people is stronger there and more alive; it is the lasting and genuine form of living together. In contrast to Gemeinschaft, Gesellschaft is transitory and superficial" (Tönnies 1887:35). Although less enamored than Tönnies with the primitive rural virtues, the works of Henry Maine (1861) and Emile Durkheim (1893) also fostered an analytic opposition between folk and urban, industrial ways of life (see Miner 1968).

Redfield's Folk Culture

The idea of folk culture emerged in the first ethnographic studies of PEASANTRY, beginning in the 1930s. Peasantries exist within STATE-level societies; they are in fact "part-societies," dominated economically and politically by metropolitan centers and rural elites. Unlike tribal societies (see TRIBE), peasant communities could not be treated as social isolates, but had to be understood in relation to a larger state and CIVILIZATION. Largely through the Mesoamerican studies of Robert Redfield (1897–1958), the notion of folk culture emerged as a focus for ethnographic research (see Redfield 1930; Redfield and Villa Rojas 1934).

Three problems came to dominate Redfield's writings, and by extension, the analysis of peasantries by American anthropologists, at least through the 1950s. (1) What is the role of tradition, ritual, and ritualized social ties in the social organization of the folk community as opposed to the urban center? (2) What is the relation between the CULTURE of the folk and that of the urban elite? (3) By what processes does CULTURE CHANGE occur in the folk community?

Redfield variously spoke of "folk society" and "folk culture," stressing in the first case a distinctive social structure, in the second a distinctive PATTERN of beliefs and values. Folk culture, in Redfield's view, rested on a moral consensus: "It is a state of society in which the technical order is still subordinated to the moral order, in which the local community is a single, well-integrated moral community, without separation of classes by important differences in knowledge or in faith" (Redfield 1953:63).

In "The Folk Society" (1947), Redfield described the major characteristics of this social and cultural pattern. Referring explicitly to the writings of Maine, Tönnies, and Durkheim, Redfield described the folk society as "small, isolated, non-literate, and homogeneous, with a strong sense of group solidarity," and characterized by economic self-sufficiency and a minimal division of labor. The folk society is "traditional, spontaneous, and uncritical": behavior is highly conventionalized, and there is no encouragement to reflect critically upon traditional ways. Finally, the folk society is a "sacred society," in which tradition carries the weight of religious conviction (Redfield 1947:235–45).

Much of Redfield's research was explicitly comparative: In the Yucatan (Mexico) he sought to map the cultural relationships between a village (Chan Kom), a town (Dzitas), and a city (Merida), the first exemplifying a folk culture, the last an urban, relatively sophisticated, community (Redfield and Villa Rojas 1934:ix). For Redfield such studies had historical as well as ethnological value, for the notion of folk culture was utilized to provide a baseline in reconstructing the cultural EVOLUTION of complex states out of localized village communities (see Redfield 1953).

Critique of the Model

The model of folk culture, presuming the existence of isolated, highly traditional, and harmonious communities, has been challenged in several ways. Redfield's ethnography of the Mexican village of Tepoztlan (Redfield 1930) received a searching examination from Oscar Lewis, who undertook a systematic restudy of the community and came to dramatically different conclusions. According to Lewis; "The impression given by Redfield's study of Tepoztlan is that of a relatively homogeneous, isolated, smoothly functioning, and well-integrated society made up of a contented and well-adjusted people. His picture of the village has a Rousseauan quality which glosses lightly over evidence of violence, disruption, cruelty, disease, suffering, and maladjustment" (Lewis 1951:428–29). Conversely, Sidney Mintz has argued that many of the characteristics of a folk culture may be retained within an industrial setting—what he terms a "rural proletarian community"—as in the case of a sugar plantation (Mintz 1953, 1956).

Larger trends within ANTHROPOLOGY, in particular an emphasis on MATERIALISM in culture theory, have overtaken Redfield's model of the folk culture. Later peasant studies have given greater weight to issues of ADAPTATION, DEVELOPMENT, ECONOMY, and INEQUALITY, factors that help explain—as the folk-urban continuum cannot—the profound differences in wealth and power characterizing most peasant communities (see Silverman 1979). Perhaps the most important legacy of Redfield's studies of folk culture has been the understanding of tradition that he developed (see Redfield 1956: ch. 3). His contrast of "Great Tradition" and "Little Tradition," one codified and self-reflective, the other informal and unsophisticated, has had a major influence on the postwar study of complex societies.

References

Durkheim, Emile. 1893 [1933]. *The Division of Labor in Society*. George Simpson, trans. New York: Free Press. Important for its contrast of mechanical (folk) and organic (urban) patterns of social organization.

Frazer, James G. 1890 [1959]. *The New Golden Bough*. 1 vol., abr. Theodore H. Gaster, ed. New York: Criterion Books.

Lewis, Oscar. 1951. *Life in a Mexican Village: Tepoztlan Restudied*. Champaign: University of Illinois Press.

Lukes, Steven. 1973. *Emile Durkheim, His Life and Work: A Historical and Critical Study*. Harmondsworth, England: Penguin. Lukes provides (in chap. 7) the intellectual background regarding the folk/urban contrast.

Maine, Henry. 1861 [1972]. *Ancient Law*. London: Dent, Everyman's Library. Contrasts status (in folk societies) and contract (in the modern world).

Miner, Horace. 1968. "Community-Society Continua." *IESS* 3:174–80. Miner describes sociological approaches to the folk/urban contrast.

Mintz, Sidney. 1953. "The Folk-Urban Continuum and the Rural Proletarian Community." *American Journal of Sociology* 59:136–43. Mintz suggests the possibility of a proletarian folk.

———. 1954. "On Redfield and Foster." *AA* 56:87–92.

Redfield, Robert. 1930. *Tepoztlan: A Mexican Village*. Chicago: University of Chicago Press. A report of Redfield's early Mexican research.

———. 1947. "The Folk Society." *American Journal of Sociology* 52:293–308.

———. 1953. *The Primitive World and Its Transformations*. Ithaca, N.Y.: Cornell University Press.

———. 1956. *Peasant Society and Culture: An Anthropological Approach to Civilization*. Chicago: University of Chicago Press. Introduces the important Great Tradition/ Little Tradition contrast.

Redfield, Robert, and Alfonso Villa Rojas. 1934 [1962]. *Chan Kom: A Maya Village*. Chicago: University of Chicago Press.

Silverman, Sydel. 1979. "The Peasant Concept in Anthropology." *Journal of Peasant Studies* 7:49–69.

Sumner, William Graham. 1906 [1940]. *Folk-Ways*. New York: Mentor. Exemplifies the negative perception of folk.

Tönnies, Ferdinand. 1887 [1963]. *Community and Society*. Charles Loomis, trans. New York: Harper & Row. An influential work idealizing the traditional rural community. The original title, *Gemeinschaft und Gesellschaft*, would be more accurately translated as Community and Association.

Sources of Additional Information

Robert Redfield's *The Folk Culture of Yucatan*, Chicago: University of Chicago Press, 1941, is a basic source on the concept. George Foster's "What is Folk Culture?" *AA* 55:159–74, 1953, gives a useful overview. The Redfield-Lewis debate regarding Tepoztlan and its folk culture is reviewed in George Foster, "Interpersonal Relations in Peasant Society," *Human Organization* 19:174–78, 1960–61. Robert Paine, "A Critique of the Methodology of Robert Redfield: 'Folk Culture' and Other Concepts," *Ethnos* 31:161–72, 1966, examines the assumptions underlying Redfield's work.

FOLKLORE. (1) Verbal art; the spoken, expressive, orally transmitted creations of any group. (2) The systematic collection and analysis of these materials.

The term was introduced in English in 1846 by William Thoms, who argued that the then-prevailing phrase "popular antiquities" be replaced by "a good Saxon compound, Folklore, —the Lore of the People" (Thoms 1846). Folklore includes both a certain body of TRADITIONS and the methods by which these are studied. This entry will consider the concept of folk, folklore as a body of data, and folklore as a discipline. See also MYTH.

The Concept of Folk

The term folk has Germanic roots, deriving from Old English *folc*, a people. Three senses of the term, as it emerged in the late medieval period, are relevant. First, folk has signified people in an indefinite sense: Chaucer wrote in the fourteenth-century *Canterbury Tales* "than longen folk to goon on pilgrimages." Second, folk has served as a vague ethnological grouping: "Brytones were [th]e firste folc [th]at to Engelond come" (1297). Third, the term has implied persons subordinated to and distinguished from a superior, be this God, royalty, or (in later usage) an upper class. In a translation of Psalms (1549) we read, "we are his folke, he doth us feede" (see *OED*). From these three strands come the later connotations of folk: an anonymous (and frequently nonliterate) rural population, culturally conservative, ethnically distinctive, and socially subordinate.

Many European folklorists have interpreted the concept in highly negative and class-conscious terms, as an inferior stratum, an *Unterschicht*. In Hoffmann-Krayer's words (1902), this is "the enduring folk—lower, primitive in thought, and lacking individuality" ("das niedere, primitiv denkende, von wenigen Individualitäten durchdrungene Volk": in *GEC*, 178). In this sense, folk played much the same role within a European context as did the term PRIMITIVE within ETHNOLOGY. A similar but less invidious construction was given by the American anthropologist Robert Redfield in his concept of FOLK CULTURE, equating folk with the highly traditional, unsophisticated and unacculturated PEASANTRY within a larger society (Redfield 1930:1–14; see also TRADITION).

Alternatively, folk has been defined not as a distinctive stratum of a society (see INEQUALITY), but as a group of individuals united by common experience. Richard Weiss has defined this as "a spiritual and mental attitude determined by community and tradition" ("eine durch Gemeinschaft und Tradition bestimmte geistig-seelische Haltung": in *GEC*, 128). Alan Dundes has defined folk more broadly as "any group of people whatsoever who share at least one common factor" (Dundes 1977:22). In these terms, it is possible to have a folk (and thus a folklore) on the basis of occupation, ethnicity, region, dialect, or any other distinctive characteristic.

The Emergence of Folklore

The study of folklore grew out of the antiquarianism of the sixteenth and seventeenth centuries, a concern for the rare and obscure among customs and artifacts, particularly those of distant peoples (see Hodgen 1964). However, folklore emerged as a distinct field of study under the dual influence of European romanticism and nationalism. An emphasis on the unusual and subjective in human experience, an interpretation of society as a natural unity grounded in tradition, and an exhalting of cultural distinctiveness as the basis of politics— these themes motivated the search for the characteristic folklife of each nation as epitomized in lore and CUSTOM (see ETHNICITY).

The romantic philosopher J. G. von Herder (1744–1803) was particularly influential in establishing the category of folk in European thought and the various folk traditions as worthy objects of study. The most natural polity (*Staat*), he noted characteristically, is that containing one folk with its own national character (Herder 1791:269 [*Ideen* 9.4.2]; see also Rotenstreich 1973). One of the earliest attempts at systematic collection was undertaken by Jacob and Wilhelm Grimm, with their compilation of German folk tales, the *Kinder- und Haus-Märchen* (1815). The study of folklore became a growth industry over the course of the nineteenth century in most of the European countries; its development in Britain has been described by Dorson (1968).

Defining Folklore

The scope of folklore has been variously defined. In the nineteenth century, anthropological views of folklore (dominated by ideas of cultural EVOLUTION) interpreted these materials as evolutionary SURVIVALS, discordant or irrational elements originating in an earlier stage of CULTURE. According to Andrew Lang, folklore "collects and compares the . . . immaterial relics of old races, the surviving superstitions and stories, the ideas which are in our time but not of it" (Lang 1910:11). In this view, the folklore gathered in European societies could be utilized, via the COMPARATIVE METHOD, as a means of understanding the ideas and institutions of so-called primitive societies. This was the central idea animating James Frazer's twelve-volume *Golden Bough* (Frazer 1890).

Twentieth-century folklorists have commonly defined their discipline simply as the study of traditional materials. According to Stith Thompson, "the common idea present in folklore is that of tradition, something handed down from one person to another and preserved either by memory or practice rather than written record. It involves the dances, songs, tales, legends, and traditions, the beliefs and superstitions, and the proverbial sayings of peoples everywhere" (in Leach and Fried, eds. 1972:403). Alternatively, stress is placed on the nonreflective or unsophisticated character of folklore materials: for André Varagnac, folklore involves "collective beliefs without doctrine, collective practices without theory" ("croyances collectives sans doctrine, practiques collectives sans théorie," in *GEC*, 136).

Anthropologists on the whole have defined the topic of folklore far more narrowly. For George Foster, folklore is "the unwritten literary manifestations of all peoples, literate or otherwise" (in Leach and Fried, eds. 1972:399). Similarly, William Bascom speaks of folklore as "verbal art" (in *GEC*, 137). More explicitly, Bascom argues that folklore "includes myths, legends, tales, proverbs, riddles, the texts of ballads and other songs, and other forms of less importance, but not folk art, folk dance, folk music, folk costume, folk medicine, folk custom, or folk belief'' (Bascom 1953:28; see also Herskovits 1946).

The Study of Folklore

Folklore is studied both within and outside ANTHROPOLOGY. Folklore studies, as a distinct discipline, treats traditional texts or practices as ends in themselves, abstracted from their broader social context. A major aim is to organize data in comparative fashion to establish parallels among motifs and tale-types and their DIFFUSION through time and space (see Dorson 1972; Levin 1973). Anthropology, in contrast, has generally studied folklore for the evidence it offers regarding culture and SOCIAL STRUCTURE. However, convergences are occurring. Anthropology has given insufficient attention to the expressive dimension of culture, including narrative. One trend discernible, in both anthropology and folklore studies, is a concern for understanding narrative as a communicative performance, ''as a totality encompassing not only the verbal story but the entire narrative experience, auditory and visual, of spectator and actor'' (Colby and Peacock 1973:624; see also Ben-Amos 1977; Murphy 1978).

References

Bascom, William R. 1953 [1965]. "Folklore and Anthropology." Alan Dundes, ed., *The Study of Folklore*. Englewood Cliffs, N.J.: Prentice-Hall.

Ben-Amos, Dan. 1977. "The Context of Folklore: Implications and Prospects." William Bascom, ed., *Frontiers of Folklore*. Boulder, Colo.: Westview Press.

Colby, Benjamin N., and James L. Peacock. 1973. "Narrative." John J. Honigmann, ed., *Handbook of Social and Cultural Anthropology*. Chicago: Rand McNally. Reviews new approaches to expressive form in cultural analysis.

Dorson, Richard M. 1968. *The British Folklorists: A History*. Chicago: University of Chicago Press. An exhaustive study of the development of folklore studies in Britain.

———. 1972. "Techniques of the Folklorist." R. Dorson, *Folklore: Selected Essays*. Bloomington: Indiana University Press.

Dundes, Alan. 1977. "Who are the Folk?" William Bascom, ed., *Frontiers of Folklore*. Boulder, Colo.: Westview Press. A reinterpretation of the folk category.

Frazer, James G. 1890 [1959]. *The New Golden Bough*. 1 vol., abr. Theodor H. Gaster, ed. New York: Criterion Books. A classic of anthropology and folklore.

Grimm, Jakob, and Wilhelm Grimm. 1815 [1960]. *The Grimms' German Folk Tales*. Francis Magoun and Alexander Krappe, trans. Carbondale: Southern Illinois University Press. One of the first systematic folkloristic studies.

Herder, J. G. von. 1791 [1964]. *Ideen zur Philosophie der Geschichte der Menschheit*. *Herders Werke*, vol. 4. Berlin and Weimar: Aufbau-Verlag. Stresses the role of context in cultural understanding and the appreciation of cultural diversity.

Herskovits, Melville J. 1946. "Folklore after a Hundred Years: A Problem in Redefinition." *Journal of American Folklore* 46:89–100. Argues for defining folklore as oral literature.

Hodgen, Margaret T. 1964. *Early Anthropology in the Sixteenth and Seventeenth Centuries*. Philadelphia: University of Pennsylvania Press.

Lang, Andrew. 1910. *Custom and Myth*. London: Longmans, Green. An evolutionist perspective of folklore as survivals.

Leach, Maria, and Jerome Fried, eds. 1972 [1984]. *Funk & Wagnalls Standard Dictionary of Folklore, Mythology, and Legend*. New York: Harper & Row. A standard reference.

Levin, Harry. 1973. "Motif." *DHI* 3:235–244. A review of the concept of motif in poetics and folklore.

Murphy, William P. 1978. "Oral Literature." *ARA* 7:113–36. Emphasizes the communicative context of folklore.

Redfield, Robert. 1930. *Tepoztlan: A Mexican Village*. Chicago: University of Chicago Press.

Rotenstreich, Nathan. 1973. "Volksgeist." *DHI* 4:490–96. An intellectual history of the folk concept.

Thoms, William. 1846 [1965]. "Folklore." Alan Dundes, ed., *The Study of Folklore*. Englewood Cliffs, N.J.: Prentice-Hall. Introduced folklore into the English vocabulary.

Sources of Additional Information

Alan Dundes, "Suggestions for Further Reading in Folklore," A. Dundes, ed., *The Study of Folklore*, Englewood Cliffs, N.J.: Prentice-Hall, 1965, is a useful bibliographic essay. Changing perspectives are illustrated by comparing Alexander Krappe, *The Science of Folklore*, New York: Norton, 1964 (orig. published 1930), and Barre Toelken, *Dynamics of Folklore*, Boston: Houghton Mifflin, 1979. See also Richard Dorson, "Current Folklore Theories," *Current Anthropology* 4:93–112, 1963. The range of folklore research is surveyed in Elliott Oring, ed., *Folk Groups and Folklore Genres: An Introduction*, Logan: Utah State University Press, 1986.

FUNCTIONALISM. (1) As a postulate of ethnographic method, the assumption that the elements of a sociocultural system are meaningfully interrelated and should be studied accordingly; (2) as a social theory, the doctrine that most or all culturally patterned belief and behavior serve to perpetuate a social system.

Functionalism is an important yet ambiguous word in the anthropological vocabulary. It can be understood (1) as a dictum of method, emphasizing a holistic approach to research and the need to seek interrelationships among social facts; and (2) as a specific theory explaining CUSTOMS and beliefs in terms of their role in maintaining a total SOCIAL STRUCTURE. The first view was propounded most forcefully by Bronislaw Malinowski (1884–1942); the second in particular by A. R. Radcliffe-Brown (1881–1955). As method, functionalism has long been an accepted principle of ETHNOGRAPHY; as theory, it has been highly influential (particularly in British ANTHROPOLOGY), but since the 1950s much criticized for both its logical and substantive failings.

In fact, if not in name, functional analyses have a long history. Cicero recognized the political significance of RITUAL for Roman society. While expressing scepticism as to the reality of divination, he noted that "out of respect for the opinion of the masses and because of the great service to the State we maintain

the augural practices, discipline, religious rites, and laws" (*De divin.* 2.33).
Montesquieu (1689–1755), in *The Spirit of Laws*, propounded a sophisticated
analysis of the interrelationships of various PATTERNS of government, LAW, and
ECONOMY. A successful democracy, he argued, requires economic equality;
hence, laws of bequest, dowry, and the like must conform so as to maintain a
relatively even distribution of wealth within each family line (Montesquieu 1748:
Bk. 5.5).

Functionalism (in its various forms) emerged in early twentieth century anthropology as a response to the inadequacies of existing theory. In British anthropology, the period immediately after 1900 was marked by an increasingly
futile controversy between proponents of cultural EVOLUTION (see also COM-
PARATIVE METHOD) and those who assumed DIFFUSION to be the basic mechanism
underlying variation and CULTURE CHANGE. This disagreement notwithstanding,
the actual research inspired by either perspective was much the same. Tribal
societies were treated as convenient repositories of data (generally obtained
secondhand from missionaries and colonial administrators) and invoked rather
arbitrarily to reconstruct the global movement of CULTURE traits or the evolution
of particular institutions.

Functionalism marked a departure from existing anthropology in at least two
respects. First, it presumed a holistic sense of social life, viewing BANDS and
TRIBES as living systems, cultural worlds of intrinsic value and significance. This
contrasted strongly with the then-predominant concern with isolated culture traits
compared in diverse eras and societies. Second, functionalism insisted on the
RATIONALITY or meaningful character of behavior in supposedly PRIMITIVE societies, in contrast to the evolutionists' INTERPRETATION of tribal ritual and belief
as the result of ignorance or irrationality. In both respects functionalism marked
a major advance.

Functionalism as a Heuristic Method

Although Bronislaw Malinowski was certainly not the first British anthropologist to undertake systematic, firsthand research—a notable example being the
interdisciplinary Torres Straits Expedition in 1898 (Stocking 1987:320)—his
work in the Melanesian Trobriand Islands between 1914 and 1918 set a new
standard. For Malinowski the overarching goal of ethnography was "to grasp
the native's point of view, his relation to life, to realise his vision of his world"
(Malinowski 1922:25). A key to this goal, in Malinowski's view, was to interpret
social life by tracing the myriad interrelations between seemingly disparate acts,
and thus to understand culture as a lived reality. Cultural understanding was
necessarily contextual; it implied—to quote a later anthropologist—that "no
human custom exists in vacuo; there must always be an interplay between the
component elements of a social system" (Spencer 1965:13). American anthropologists pursued a similar course in the 1920s and 1930s by seeking to identify
an integrated pattern of cultural themes or values underlying the life of each
society.

Starting from the premise that culture is intrinsically adaptive, meeting challenges posed by both social life and the environment, Malinowski viewed belief and behavior in pragmatic terms. His statement on MYTH is indicative: "Myth fulfills in primitive culture an indispensable function: it expresses, enhances, and codifies belief; it safeguards and enforces morality; it vouches for the efficiency of ritual and contains practical rules for the guidance of man" (Malinowski 1926:101). Accordingly, he strongly criticized the evolutionist stereotype of tribal life as a slavish and irrational obedience to custom.

Malinowski sought to elaborate and justify his functionalist position by transforming it into a formal theory that explained culture in terms of underlying biological needs, and the institutions that are called into existence to meet them. This project was not a success, seldom if ever rising above a restatement of the obvious ("each partial activity in the food-providing process, from the planting of seed, the catching of the quarry, right up to biting, chewing, and swallowing, is normed and regulated" [Malinowski 1944:98]). Arguably, Malinowski's attempt at a formal theory of needs in fact demonstrated the opposite of its thesis: namely that socio-cultural facts cannot meaningfully be explained solely or predominantly through the psychology of the individual (see SUPERORGANIC).

Functionalism as a Theory of Society

Like Malinowskian functionalism, what has come to be termed structural functionalism also rejected the evolutionist model of research. However, this approach, associated particularly with A. R. Radcliffe-Brown, differed significantly from the Malinowskian version in both its understanding of society and its interpretation of rationality.

A point of departure for this tradition of thought was the analytic priority placed on social action (most notably ritual) over individual belief, thus contrasting strongly with the intellectualist bias of evolutionary theory. Here the biblical scholar W. Robertson Smith (1846–1894) was a pioneer. In *The Religion of the Semites* he wrote: "In the study of Semitic religion, we must not begin by asking what was told about the gods, but what the working religious institutions were, and how they shaped the lives of the worshippers" (Smith 1889:21–22).

This perspective was extended and transformed by the French sociologist Emile Durkheim (1858–1917), who made of it both social theory and moral philosophy. Regarding the role of worship in social life, he claimed that "the effect of the cult [i.e., ritual] really is to recreate periodically a moral being upon which we depend as it depends upon us. Now this being does exist: it is society" (Durkheim 1915:389). Society was thus reified, and the rationality of social action was equated with that which served to perpetuate the social organism.

The social metaphysics of Durkheim was rendered both more prosaic and more empirical by Radcliffe-Brown. Custom and ritual—including both acts and avoidances—were understood as the means by which the sentiments underlying social relationships were expressed, reinforced, and communicated from generation to generation (Radcliffe-Brown 1922:233–34). Thus, "the function of any recurrent activity, such as the punishment of a crime, or a funeral ceremony, is the part it plays in the social life as a whole and therefore the contribution it makes to the maintenance of the structural continuity'' (Radcliffe-Brown 1935:180).

The concept of society that Radcliffe-Brown propagated within anthropology was highly artificial: static, harmonious, and insulated from any wider influences. In his view, ''all parts of the social system work together with a sufficient degree of harmony or internal consistency'' so that any conflict which arises is either regulated or resolved (Radcliffe-Brown 1935:181). Within this ''functional unity'' the institutions of KINSHIP and DESCENT were given explanatory emphasis, and Radcliffe-Brown assumed that—at least within tribal societies—these facts determined in large measure the character of FAMILY organization, politics, the economy, and inter-group relations. This perspective guided the work of most British (and British-trained) anthropologists from the 1930s through the 1950s (Fortes and Evans-Pritchard 1940; Kuper 1973: chs. 3, 4).

The Legacy of Functionalism

Credit for some of functionalism's lasting contributions can rightly be shared by Malinowski and Radcliffe-Brown. Despite their major differences, both approaches marked a shift in the assumptions of ethnography, from a concern with isolated traits to the interpretation of social life. The logic of anthropological explanation was permanently altered by their insistence on the rationality of human action.

These considerations aside, Malinowski's primary contributions have been in field method. His insistence on seeking the meaningful interrelation between seemingly isolated acts and beliefs has become axiomatic. His concern with ''the native's point of view'' as a criterion of ethnographic authenticity has had a pervasive influence (see EMIC/ETIC; ETHNOSCIENCE). Finally, his pragmatism, understanding culture as a mechanism for meeting individual needs, has had an enduring significance. Although relatively unproductive as a formal theory, this perspective has influenced a later generation of anthropologists to interpret social action as the outcome of individual decision making in the context of competing interests—a view sometimes termed methodological individualism (see Kuper 1973:164–67).

The theoretical influence of Radcliffe-Brown has unquestionably been greater than that of Malinowski, and as such it has also engendered more sustained criticism. Through perhaps the 1950s British research showed strong continuity with the tradition of structural functionalism, while extending and, in significant areas, revising basic assumptions. One of Radcliffe-Brown's key premises, the harmonious and changeless character of tribal society, represented such a divergence from reality that theoretical revisionism was inevitable.

Here the work of Max Gluckman was particularly significant, emphasizing the study of dispute settlement and so-called rituals of rebellion, mechanisms that in his view contained and channeled discord, and thus resolved conflict short of social transformation (see Gluckman 1965). While guided by a functionalist perspective, Gluckman and his colleagues reacted to the overemphasis on formal institutions inherent in structural functionalism, turning to the study of social

NETWORKS, often in the context of urbanization and culture change. Finally, SYMBOLISM became a prominent topic for research, understandable in light of the Durkheimian emphasis on the representation of social relations through myth and ritual.

Radcliffe-Brown advocated that social anthropology should be a naturalistic discipline, concerned not with contingent issues of history and change, nor with cultures as distinctive worlds of meaning, but with laws of social form and process, derived through the classification and comparison of societies. Structural functionalism, in his view, provided the theory and method to accomplish these goals (Kuper 1973: ch. 2). Nonetheless, this conception of anthropology has not fared well in the postwar period. Many critics have pointed to the conservative implications of functionalism, masking the tension and social change that were an inherent part of British colonialism (Asad 1973). The claim that functionalism in fact constitutes an explanatory theory has been strongly questioned (Jarvie 1965). Finally, Radcliffe-Brown's fundamental contention that anthropological theory and method should be naturalistic and classificatory, on the supposed model of the physical or biological sciences, has been emphatically rejected from the standpoint of both HISTORICISM (Evans-Pritchard 1950) and STRUCTURALISM (Leach 1961).

References

Asad, Talal, ed. 1973. *Anthropology & the Colonial Encounter*. London: Ithaca Press. A series of historical studies, emphasizing British social anthropology in Africa.

Durkheim, Emile. 1915 [1965]. *The Elementary Forms of the Religious Life*. Joseph W. Swain, trans. New York: Free Press.

Evans-Pritchard, E. E. 1950 [1962]. "Social Anthropology: Past and Present." E. E. Evans-Pritchard, *Social Anthropology and Other Essays*. New York: Free Press. A strong critique of Radcliffe-Brown's anthropology from the perspective of historicism.

Fortes, Meyer, and E. E. Evans-Pritchard. 1940 [1969]. "Introduction." M. Fortes and E. E. Evans-Pritchard, eds., *African Political Systems*. London: Oxford University Press.

Gluckman, Max. 1965. *Politics, Law and Ritual in Tribal Society*. Oxford: Basil Blackwell.

Jarvie, I. C. 1965. "Limits of Functionalism and Alternatives to It in Anthropology." Don Martindale, ed., *Functionalism in the Social Sciences*. American Academy of Political and Social Science, *Monograph 5*.

Kuper, Adam. 1973. *Anthropologists and Anthropology: The British School, 1922–1972*. New York: Pica Press. A readable intellectual history.

Leach, E. R. 1961. *Rethinking Anthropology*. London: Athlone Press. The title essay contains an influential critique of functionalism.

Malinowski, Bronislaw. 1922 [1961]. *Argonauts of the Western Pacific*. New York: Dutton. A classic ethnography.

———. 1926 [1954]. "Myth in Primitive Psychology." B. Malinowski, *Magic, Science and Religion, and Other Essays*. Garden City, N.Y.: Doubleday/Anchor.

————. 1944. *A Scientific Theory of Culture and Other Essays*. Chapel Hill: University of North Carolina Press.

Montesquieu, Baron de (Charles-Louis de Secondat). 1748 [1949]. *The Spirit of Laws*. Thomas Nugent, trans. New York: Hafner Press/Macmillan.

Radcliffe-Brown, A. R. 1922 [1964]. *The Andaman Islanders*. New York: Free Press. His major monograph.

————. 1935 [1965]. "On the Concept of Function in Social Science." A. R. Radcliffe-Brown, *Structure and Function in Primitive Society*. New York: Free Press.

Smith, W. Robertson. 1889 [1972]. *The Religion of the Semites: The Fundamental Institutions*. New York: Schocken.

Spencer, Robert F. 1965. "The Nature and Value of Functionalism in Anthropology." Don Martindale, ed., *Functionalism in the Social Sciences*. American Academy of Political and Social Science, *Monograph 5*.

Stocking, George W., Jr. 1987. *Victorian Anthropology*. New York: Free Press.

Sources of Additional Information

For an attempt to refurbish a functionalist perspective for postwar anthropology, see Walter Goldschmidt, *Comparative Functionalism*, Berkeley and Los Angeles: University of California Press, 1966. Annemarie deWaal Malefijt, *Images of Man: A History of Anthropological Thought*, New York: Knopf, 1974, ch. 10, offers an introduction to the functionalist outlook.

G

GENDER. The cultural construction of roles and status on the basis of sex.

The respective place of biology and CULTURE in shaping sex-specific status and roles—the issue of gender—has assumed increasing importance in anthropological theory since the 1970s. This entry considers the intellectual background to the problem provided by nineteenth century writers; the complexities inherent in the problem of defining women's (or men's) status; criticisms of traditional ethnographic method for its ostensible gender bias; and various interpretations of the place of culture in constructing gender.

Although the factors shaping gender in human societies constitute a problem of obvious theoretical importance, the issue has been significant in anthropology mainly in those periods (the late nineteenth century and from 1970 to 1990) in which feminism held a prominent place in Western social thought. Feminist concerns have to a significant extent centered on the need for social equality between men and women, an insistence that has done much to shape the direction of anthropological discussions of gender. Thus John Stuart Mill, in the influential essay "The Subjection of Women" (1869), criticized the legal subordination of women then existing in Great Britain, claiming that this principle "is wrong in itself, and now one of the chief hindrances to human improvement; and that it ought to be replaced by a principle of perfect equality, admitting no power or privilege on the one side, nor disability on the other" (Mill 1869:225). The philosophical abstraction represented by Mill's "principle of perfect equality" has proved difficult to apply to ethnographic reality. Such an essentially unidimensional comparison between the status of men and women ignores the diversity of roles in any society, the universality of a sexual division of labor, and the multiple dimensions of belief and behavior through which gender relations can be expressed.

This artificially simple image of SOCIAL STRUCTURE was reflected in Victorian theories regarding the EVOLUTION of gender relations, a question that drew the attention not merely of a small group of specialists, but a much wider audience concerned with the position of women in Victorian society (see Stocking 1987:197–208). The idea of PRIMITIVE matriarchy had a prominent place in such discussions, a postulated stage in which politics, DESCENT, and ideology all reflected the primacy of women over men. The Swiss classicist Johann Bachofen (1815–1887) was a major proponent of this evolutionary reconstruction, holding that "matriarchy belongs to an earlier stage of civilization than the patriarchal system and its full and unlimited strength crumbled before victorious paternity" (Bachofen 1861:159).

The evolutionary priority of matrilineal over patrilineal descent was also suggested by other writers, for example John McLennan (1827–1881), without, however, the assumption of the dominance of the female principle in all aspects of culture that had animated Bachofen (McLennan 1865; see also MARRIAGE). Even this milder theory had political implications. As George Stocking has commented, the "evolutionary rejection of divinely instituted patriarchalism" in McLennan's *Primitive Marriage* "was felt to be subversive of existing domestic order" (Stocking 1987:206). Yet despite a recent revival by certain feminist writers, theories of primitive matriarchy have little if any factual support (Rosaldo and Lamphere 1974:2–4).

Assessing Women's Status

E. E. Evans-Pritchard, writing in the mid–1950s, could complain of the "entire inadequacy, indeed almost complete lack, of serious scientific research" regarding relations between men and women cross-culturally (Evans-Pritchard 1955:57). Indeed, until the 1960s few anthropologists had given detailed attention to gender. In 1894 Otis Mason published a survey, *Women's Share in Primitive Culture*, depicting through the COMPARATIVE METHOD supposedly characteristic female roles: the weaver, the potter, the food-bringer, the beast of burden, and so forth (Mason 1894). In his influential text *Primitive Society*, Robert Lowie included a perceptive chapter on gender, noting the marked divergence between ideology and practice in many societies regarding the relative status of men and women (Lowie 1920: ch. 8). The work of Margaret Mead in Oceania, beginning in the 1920s, has had particular importance for understanding the respective roles of culture and biology in shaping gender (see below).

In his 1955 review, Evans-Pritchard made certain generalizations which at the time at least would have received wide agreement from other anthropologists. In tribal societies, he argued, a woman's status is defined fundamentally through the tie of marriage: she is "above all a wife." Reversing the optimism of certain evolutionist writers, Evans-Pritchard argued that in all societies "regardless of the form of social structure, men are always in the ascendancy, and this is perhaps the more evident the higher the civilization" (Evans-Pritchard 1955:46, 54). Almost two decades later, another writer could state flatly, "The secondary status of woman in society is one of the true universals, a pan-cultural fact" (Ortner 1974:67).

Nonetheless, later scholars have questioned the utility of such sweeping assessments. Naomi Quinn has suggested that gender status be understood "as a composite of many different variables, often causally independent one from another." She would distinguish between questions of women's political participation, their control over the ECONOMY, their personal autonomy, the degree of deference they display, their level of prestige, ethnotheories of women's status, and stylistic differences between men and women in language and behavior (Quinn 1977:183).

Gender and Ethnography

Any cross-cultural assessment of the relation of gender and status raises the question of the accuracy of ethnographic data. Many anthropologists would agree with Michelle Rosaldo and Louise Lamphere in claiming that, with few exceptions, "anthropologists in writing about human culture have followed our own culture's ideological bias in treating women as relatively invisible and describing what are largely the activities and interests of men" (Rosaldo and Lamphere 1974:2). Certainly male voices are far more prominently represented in the ethnographic record (Quinn 1977:184). More recent studies suggest that simply identifying women's roles with the domestic sphere, as held by Evans-Pritchard among others, involves a serious distortion (see FAMILY). More sweepingly, Edwin Ardener has suggested that in a given society men and women may possess quite distinct ideologies, with the male perspective more readily articulated within the ethnographic process (Ardener 1972).

The Cultural Construction of Gender

The degree to which sex roles are molded by culture rather than biological inheritance remains a key problem for ANTHROPOLOGY. Research bearing on this question is extremely diverse, and the conclusions contradictory. Beginning in the 1920s with *Coming of Age in Samoa*, Margaret Mead (1901–1978) undertook a series of studies that examined sex roles in Melanesia, Polynesia, Bali, and (more anecdotally) the United States, combining modern ethnographic methods with a theoretical concern with culture and PERSONALITY (Mead 1928, 1949). Mead's writings developed two related themes: That the expression of gender is highly variable cross-culturally and that this variability reflects the coercive power of cultural patterning. As she noted, "Whether we deal with small matters or with large . . . we find this great variety of ways, often flatly contradictory one to the another, in which the roles of the two sexes have been patterned" (Mead 1949:8).

It is indicative of the complexities of the issues involved that Mead's work has been criticized from opposing viewpoints. Her interpretation of Samoan adolescence stressed a contrast with American mores, notably in a widespread sexual permissiveness and a low incidence of rape and other violent behavior (Mead 1928). Derek Freeman (1983) has presented a rebuttal to Mead, contesting her interpretation at almost every point. He has depicted Samoan sexual PATTERNS as restrictive and often violent, seeing in this revisionist account strong support for a primarily biological rather than cultural determination of gender and sexuality.

Mead's writings on the Chambri (Tchambuli) of Papua New Guinea depicted gender patterns as the reverse of those in the United States, with women assertive and brisk, men responsive and subservient. In a position diametrically opposed to that of Freeman, Frederick Errington and Deborah Gewertz have criticized Mead's studies of the Chambri for failing "to take seriously enough the extent of cultural differences" (Errington and Gewertz 1987:7). They contend instead that the Chambri possess culturally distinctive concepts of self and other, male and female, which cannot be rendered as analogies of American gender constructs, however transposed.

A variety of empirical studies since the 1970s suggest the complex interactions of biology and culture shaping gender in any given society. Two examples must stand for a far larger literature.

(1) A growing body of research has documented the widespread distribution of ritualized homosexuality in Melanesia. Such practices are frequently associated with male initiation rites (see RITE OF PASSAGE), guided by a complex belief system regarding male roles and powers within the maturation process. The Melanesian evidence—regarding both the complex interrelation of sexual, RITUAL, and political domains, and the expectation that culturally patterned homosexual and heterosexual activities will coexist in the same life course—demonstrates that anthropology's Western-derived concepts of gender and sexuality remain seriously deficient (see Herdt, ed. 1984).

(2) One of the goals of the Israeli kibbutz movement was to create a social world in which women "were to be fully emancipated . . . by a radical transformation in the traditional systems of marriage, the family, and sex-role differentiation" (Spiro 1979:5). Yet despite both this radical ideology and an ostensibly gender-blind socialization process, as the kibbutz movement has matured many of the most innovative changes have been rejected by the kibbutz membership, male and female. Melford Spiro has suggested on this evidence that pre-cultural (or biological) patterning plays a larger role than anticipated in shaping the distribution of gender roles and the character of interaction between the sexes (Spiro 1979).

Finally, other scholars have approached the problem of the construction of gender by drawing on the categorical oppositions of STRUCTURALISM, specifically the categories of NATURE and culture, which Claude Lévi-Strauss has argued form a fundamental cognitive contrast in all societies. Sherry Ortner has attempted to account for the supposedly universal subordination of women to men by positing a cross-cultural logic in which women are seen as more natural and thus less cultural (or culturally developed) than men, and on a cognitive level are thereby distinguished and demeaned (Ortner 1974:73). This influential thesis has received both support and criticism (see MacCormack and Strathern, eds. 1980).

References

Ardener, Edwin. 1972. "Belief and the Problem of Women." J. S. LaFontaine, ed., *The Interpretation of Ritual: Essays in Honor of A. I. Richards*. London: Tavistock. Ardener suggests men and women may possess distinct world views.

Bachofen, Johann. 1861 [1931]. "Das Mutterrecht" [excerpt]. V. F. Calverton, ed., *The Making of Man: An Outline of Anthropology*. New York: Modern Library. A classic statement regarding primitive matriarchy.

Errington, Frederick, and Deborah Gewertz. 1987. *Cultural Alternatives and a Feminist Anthropology*. Cambridge: Cambridge University Press. A symbolically oriented analysis of gender among the Chambri of New Guinea.

Evans-Pritchard, E. E. 1955 [1965]. "The Position of Women in Primitive Societies and In Our Own." E. E. Evans-Pritchard, *The Position of Women in Primitive Societies and Other Essays in Social Anthropology*. New York: Free Press.

Freeman, Derek. 1983. *Margaret Mead and Samoa: The Making and Unmaking of an Anthropological Myth*. Cambridge, Mass.: Harvard University Press. A controversial attack on Mead.

Herdt, Gilbert, ed. 1984. *Ritualized Homosexuality in Melanesia*. Berkeley and Los Angeles: University of California Press.

Lowie, Robert H. 1920 [1961]. *Primitive Society*. New York: Harper & Brothers.

MacCormack, Carol P., and Marilyn Strathern, eds. 1980. *Nature, Culture and Gender*. Cambridge: Cambridge University Press. A critique of Ortner's structuralist interpretation of gender and status.

McLennan, John F. 1865 [1970]. *Primitive Marriage: An Inquiry into the Origin of the Form of Capture in Marriage Ceremonies*. Peter Rivière, ed. Chicago: University of Chicago Press.

Mason, Otis T. 1894. *Woman's Share in Primitive Culture*. New York: D. Appleton.

Mead, Margaret. 1928 [1961]. *Coming of Age in Samoa*. New York: Dell. The classic ethnography of gender.

———. 1949. *Male and Female: A Study of the Sexes in a Changing World*. New York: William Morrow.

Mill, John Stuart. 1869 [1977]. "The Subjection of Women." Rosemary Agonito, ed., *History of Ideas on Woman: A Source Book*. New York: G. P. Putnam's Sons. An influential feminist essay.

Ortner, Sherry B. 1974. "Is Female to Male as Nature Is to Culture?" M. Rosaldo et al., eds., *Woman, Culture, and Society*. Stanford, Calif.: Stanford University Press.

Quinn, Naomi. 1977. "Anthropological Studies on Women's Status." *ARA* 6:181–225. A useful review article, with extensive bibliography.

Rosaldo, Michelle Z., and Louise Lamphere. 1974. "Introduction." M. Rosaldo et al., eds., *Woman, Culture, and Society*. Stanford, Calif.: Stanford University Press.

Spiro, Melford E. 1979. *Gender and Culture: Kibbutz Women Revisited*. Durham, N. C.: Duke University Press.

Stocking, George W., Jr. 1987. *Victorian Anthropology*. New York: Free Press.

Sources of Additional Information

Judith Shapiro, in "Gender Totemism," Richard R. Randolph et al., eds., *Dialectics and Gender: Anthropological Approaches*, Boulder, Colo.: Westview Press, 1988, discusses the anthropological study of gender in relation to contending theories of contemporary feminism. See also Susan Carol Rogers, "Woman's Place: A Critical Review of Anthropological Theory," *Comparative Studies in Society and History* 20:123–62, 1978. An overview of research since the mid-seventies is provided by C. C. Mukhopadhyay and P. J. Higgins, "Anthropological Studies of Women's Status Revisited: 1977–1987," *ARA* 17:461–95, 1988. The Mead-Freeman debate is reviewed from a variety of perspectives in Ivan Brady et al., "Speaking in the Name of the Real: Freeman and Mead on Samoa," *AA* 85:908–47, 1983. An interesting intellectual history is provided by Sharon W. Tiffany and Kathleen J. Adams, *The Wild Woman: An Inquiry into the Anthropology of an Idea*, Cambridge, Mass.: Schenkman, 1985.

H

HISTORICISM. A doctrine holding that explanation in the social sciences is necessarily historical, and that the interpretation of cultural phenomena requires the preservation of context; stronger versions also hold that a historical or cultural pattern possesses uniqueness and exists sui generis.

Method and theory in historiography and ANTHROPOLOGY have reflected certain common intellectual influences. One example involves the debate over historicism, the claim that "events and situations are unique and non-repeatable and therefore cannot be understood in universal terms but only in terms of their own particular contexts" (Ritter 1986:183). This entry describes the significance of historicism (and more generally, the idea of history) in the development of anthropological theory (see also RELATIVISM).

Historians of the mid-eighteenth century Enlightenment sought common standards by which to evaluate the achievements of every era. The world of antiquity—specifically classical Greece and Rome—provided this guide, epitomizing for them the rule of reason in politics, the sciences, and the arts (see Gay 1966: ch. 1). In contrast, the writings of Johann Gottfried von Herder (1744–1803) foreshadowed the historicist view. Human understanding, he held, is not universal, but is "a Blossom of the Genius of the People, a Son of Tradition and Custom" (Herder 1791:50). Herder's sense of history, in the words of Hans-Georg Gadamer, acknowledged that "each period has its own right to exist, and its own perfection" (Gadamer 1975:176). This is the essence of the historicist viewpoint.

Historicism as a doctrine developed in the nineteenth century within a debate over method. While positivism proclaimed that the methods of the natural sciences (notably physics) were equally applicable to the historical or social sciences, advocates of historicism stressed the contrasting character of the two domains. For Wilhelm Windelband (1848–1915) the contrast lay between the general and the particular: the natural sciences are nomothetic or law-making (from Gk. *nomos*, law), formulating general propositions; the human sciences are idiographic (from Gk. *idios*, one's own), describing particular events in their distinctiveness (Cassirer 1944:186).

Wilhelm Dilthey (1833–1911) posed the distinction rather differently. Research in the human sciences (Geisteswissenschaften) involves understanding (see INTERPRETATION), rather than the observation of external phenomena, which characterizes the natural sciences. Furthermore, in his later work Dilthey stressed that this process of understanding depends upon a world of shared meaning: "The individual always experiences, thinks, and acts in a common sphere" (in Makkreel 1975:309). Thus the data of the human sciences are mute when deprived of their meaningful context, or (to anticipate an anthropological usage) their distinctive CULTURE.

Boasian Anthropology

Franz Boas (1858–1942)—arguably the individual most responsible for molding American anthropology in the twentieth century—reflected in his research and teaching several tenets of historicism (Stocking 1974:11). The Boasian research program, sometimes described as historical particularism (Harris 1968: ch. 9), arose in reaction to the simplistic reconstructions of a unilineal cultural EVOLUTION. In the latter perspective, any given institution, such as KINSHIP or RELIGION, could be assumed to have evolved through a uniform developmental sequence in all societies. The chief goal of anthropology was to formulate the lawlike regularities of such development; in this respect, the research aims of cultural evolution resembled those of the natural sciences.

For Boas, in contrast, a cultural pattern existing in a given society—a geometric style of ornamentation, or a concept of clan membership—had to be understood in its individuality. Criticizing the a priori categorizing characteristic of evolutionist writings, he argued that "the fact that we designate certain tales as myths, that we group certain activities together as rituals . . . does not prove that these phenomena . . . have the same history or spring from the same mental activities" (Boas 1916:317).

This reflected the historicist program in two respects. First, understanding must be historical, achieved typically by examining the DIFFUSION of a culture trait from one society to another. This, rather than reference to a posited PSYCHIC UNITY as in evolutionism, constituted explanation of the phenomenon. Thus, "to learn the reasons why [particular] . . . customs and beliefs exist," was for Boas, "to discover the history of their development" (Boas 1896:276). Second, understanding must be contextual, a point on which Boas strongly faulted the evolutionist COMPARATIVE METHOD. What was needed in ETHNOGRAPHY, for Boas, was "a detailed study of customs in relation to the total culture of the tribe practicing them" (Boas 1896:276).

Later Developments

Within what Harris has aptly termed the "Boasian milieu" (Harris 1968:290), the historicist perspective took several directions, exemplified in the contrasting approaches of Paul Radin (1883–1959) and Alfred Kroeber (1876–1960). Perhaps more than any other prominent anthropologist, Radin stressed individual experience as the touchstone of cultural insight. The goal of ethnography was not a generalized account of cultural norms. What was needed, instead, was "the description of a culture in such a way that we feel that we are dealing with real and specific men and women, with real and specific situations, and with a real and specific tradition" (Radin 1933:177). Radin's *Autobiography of a Winnebago Indian* (1920) demonstrated that the life history—however idiosyncratic—could provide significant insight into fundamental cultural values.

The necessity of understanding cultural phenomena in context, an argument made in different ways by both Dilthey and Boas, received particular emphasis in the work of Kroeber. He addressed the methodological distinction between science and history explicitly, characterizing the historical approach of cultural anthropology as "an endeavor at descriptive integration . . . [in which] the phenomena are preserved intact as phenomena." The sciences, in contrast, "decompose phenomena in order to determine processes as such" (Kroeber 1935:63). The British anthropologist E. E. Evans-Pritchard has argued similarly (Evans-Pritchard 1950:152).

Kroeber went further than most Boasian anthropologists, however, in regarding culture as a reality sui generis, a view summarized in his doctrine of the SU-PERORGANIC. A given culture or CIVILIZATION (for Kroeber interchangeable terms) was not an arbitrary or purely contingent arrangement of traits; rather, each possessed a characteristic PATTERN, expressed with greater or lesser fidelity by one or another social group. It is in this sense that Kroeber could write, referring to aboriginal California, that "the innermost core of northwestern civilization is more nearly represented by the Yurok than by any other group" (Kroeber 1925:7). Similarly, while the type of detailed diffusionist reconstruction advocated by Boas might prove impossible in aboriginal North America, the true goal in any case should be "the determination of the civilization in its most exquisite form, with an understanding, so far as may be, of its coming into being" (Kroeber 1925:8). It is doubtful that any other American anthropologist has argued the historicist position in so uncompromising a fashion.

Historicism remains a significant element of the theoretical landscape of postwar anthropology. Nonetheless, the alternatives in this debate have become more numerous, and the issues more complex. Historical research per se, sometimes under the rubric of ethnohistory, has become more widely integrated into anthropological studies (see Hudson 1973). The growth of interest in Marxist approaches has encouraged a historicist perspective, expressed in the formulation of a series of historically constituted MODES OF PRODUCTION to describe the interdependence of ECONOMY and SOCIAL STRUCTURE. Finally, a fundamental concern of Wilhelm Dilthey—how we understand that which is historically al-ien—has become a key issue in debates over the process of cultural interpretation and the limits of ethnographic knowledge.

References

Boas, Franz. 1896 [1940]. "The Limitations of the Comparative Method of Anthro-pology." F. Boas, *Race, Language and Culture*. New York: Free Press.
———. 1916 [1940]. "The Origin of Totemism." F. Boas, *Race, Language and Culture*. New York: Free Press.
Cassirer, Ernst. 1944. *An Essay on Man: An Introduction to a Philosophy of Human Culture*. New Haven, Conn.: Yale University Press.
Evans-Pritchard, E. E. 1950 [1962]. "Social Anthropology: Past and Present." E. E. Evans-Pritchard, *Social Anthropology and Other Essays*. New York: Free Press. Argues for anthropology as a historical discipline.
Gadamer, Hans-Georg. 1975. *Truth and Method*. New York: Seabury Press.
Gay, Peter. 1966. *The Enlightenment, an Interpretation: The Rise of Modern Paganism*. New York: Random House/Vintage.
Harris, Marvin. 1968. *The Rise of Anthropological Theory*. New York: Crowell. Though tendentious, Harris provides a useful discussion of Boas and his students.
Herder, Johann Gottfried von. 1791 [1968]. *Reflections on the Philosophy of the History of Mankind*. Abr. Frank E. Manuel, ed. Chicago: University of Chicago Press. An early example of the historicist viewpoint.
Hudson, Charles. 1973. "The Historical Approach in Anthropology." John J. Honig-mann, ed., *Handbook of Social and Cultural Anthropology*. Chicago: Rand McNally. A useful overview, with bibliography.
Kroeber, Alfred L. 1925 [1976]. *Handbook of the Indians of California*. New York: Dover. One of the major achievements of North American ethnology.
———. 1935 [1952]. "History and Science in Anthropology." A. L. Kroeber, *The Nature of Culture*. Chicago: University of Chicago Press.
Makkreel, Rudolf A. 1975. *Dilthey: Philosopher of the Human Studies*. Princeton, N.J.: Princeton University Press.
Radin, Paul. 1920 [1963]. *The Autobiography of a Winnebago Indian*. New York: Dover. A pioneering example of the ethnographic life history.
———. 1933. *The Method and Theory of Ethnology: An Essay in Criticism*. New York: McGraw-Hill.
Ritter, Harry. 1986. *Dictionary of Concepts in History*. Westport, Conn.: Greenwood Press.
Stocking, George W., Jr. 1974. "Introduction: The Basic Assumptions of Boasian An-thropology." G. Stocking, ed., *The Shaping of American Anthropology, 1883–1911: A Franz Boas Reader*. New York: Basic Books.

Sources of Additional Information

For a brief though unsympathetic treatment of historicism, with references, see Geoffrey Barraclough, *Main Trends in History*, New York: Holmes & Meier, 1978, pp. 11–17. A readable introduction to the intellectual foundations of historicism is offered in H. Stuart Hughes, *Consciousness and Society: The Reconstruction of European Social Thought, 1890–1930*, New York: Random House/Vintage, 1958, ch. 6.

I

INEQUALITY. Systematic, culturally patterned differentiation within a society, ranking groups or individuals on the basis of power, wealth, or prestige.

Inequality is a pervasive fact of social life, reflecting the EVOLUTION of societies with centralized polities and economies yielding significant surplus. The data of ANTHROPOLOGY take on particular importance in discussions of inequality because—alone among the social sciences—anthropology studies societies spanning the entire evolutionary range from egalitarian to highly stratified. Three questions are relevant here: (1) What forms does socially patterned inequality take? (2) How are the differences in degree and form of social inequality to be explained? (3) What are the moral implications of inequality? The last, though more strictly a question for political philosophy or ethics, has certainly motivated much and perhaps most of the social scientific study of organized inequality (see PRIMITIVE).

The analysis of social ranking has been a prominent topic for political theorists since antiquity. Aristotle described three classes in Greek society (*Pol.* 4.11); medieval writers described three orders: those who fight, those who pray, and those who toil (Coser 1968:443). Discussions of the legitimacy of inequality have been equally prominent, Jean-Jacques Rousseau and Edmund Burke offering a characteristic contrast. In the "Discourse on the Origin and Basis of Inequality Among Men" (1754) Rousseau decried distinctions of rank, wealth, and power not reflecting natural differences in strength or ability. Burke, in *Reflections on the Revolution in France* (1790), upheld the value of TRADITION and the political institutions such as monarchy that it sanctioned. Philosophical differences of this sort continue to guide the methods and assumptions with which social inequality is examined.

Forms of Institutionalized Inequality

The study of both BANDS and relatively egalitarian (acephalous) TRIBES has provided abundant evidence of societies organized with a bare minimum of formalized rank. E. E. Evans-Pritchard's sketch of the Nilotic Nuer offers an example: "The Nuer is the product of a hard and egalitarian upbringing, is deeply democratic, and is easily roused to violence. His turbulent spirit finds any restraint irksome and no man recognizes a superior" (Evans-Pritchard 1940:181). Nonetheless, no known society is without politically significant differentiations. Even the San (Bushmen) hunter-gatherers, with less surplus and fewer social distinctions than the pastoralist Nuer, allow greater influence to males than to females, and to the more experienced individuals than to those younger and less knowledgeable (Lee 1982). In kin-based societies generally, GENDER and age, often through formalized age-grades (see ASSOCIATION), are common bases of inequality.

More formal expressions of inequality take a variety of forms. A basic distinction may be made between ranked and stratified societies. In ranked societies, such as the CHIEFDOM, leaders and followers possess unequal status but are nonetheless joined (and at the same time differentiated) by bonds of KINSHIP (see Codere 1957). In stratified societies, whether dominated by agriculture (see PEASANTRY) or URBANISM, larger populations and more intensive patterns of production make possible relatively permanent and autonomous institutions of political authority (see STATE), with far greater social and economic differentiation. In general terms, stratified societies involve stable social groups that (1) are ranked hierarchically; (2) differ in their political power and control of resources, relative to their ranking; and (3) are separated by "cultural and invidious distinctions" (see Plotnicov and Tuden 1970:4–5). Most commonly, such units are termed classes, "basic social aggregates with contradictory interests" (Jerome Rousseau 1979:216), though there is little agreement on how to analyze class structure, or even how to identify consistently the number of classes in a society (see Coser 1968).

In addition to the more general category of class, several patterns of extreme inequality are commonly noted. Slavery involves the treatment of persons as commodities; in the formula of H. J. Nieboer, the slave "is the property of another, politically and socially at a lower level than the mass of the people, and performing compulsory labour" (in Kopytoff 1982:211). CASTE involves a hierarchy of hereditary, endogamous social units with traditional occupations, this systematic social differentiation justified by a dominant ideology, in the Indian case centering on a conception of RITUAL purity. Pluralism—seen for example in the South African system of apartheid—involves subordination and separation on the basis of ETHNICITY, producing a state divided into distinct, unequal social spheres with parallel institutions, under the dominance of one ethnic segment (see Van den Berghe 1973).

Stratification and Culture

Fundamental disagreement exists on the cross-cultural significance of stratification. The contrasting approaches can for convenience be distinguished as materialist and interpretive.

From a materialist perspective, state-level societies are necessarily stratified, composed of a hierarchy of antagonistic classes. As Karl Marx and Friedrich Engels wrote (in 1848), "The history of all hitherto existing society is the history of class struggles" (in McLellan 1971:162). In this view, social inequality is a reflection of objective differences between groups in the organization of production and ownership of property, yielding a consistent hierarchy of wealth, power, and prestige (see Plotnicov and Tuden 1970; see also MODE OF PRODUCTION; MATERIALISM).

From an interpretive perspective, in contrast, social inequality is culturally mediated. For Lloyd Fallers, "what are often called 'objective' inequalities— inequalities of wealth and power—can be understood only in their cultural contexts—only in the context of their meaning to those involved in them" (Fallers 1973:5). Hence, class and stratification are considered specifically Western cultural constructs. Rather than a consistent hierarchy, a SOCIAL STRUCTURE can involve multiple, inconsistent codes for dominance, for example, in matters political, economic, and religious (see Goldberg 1968).

These conflicting perspectives are illustrated in the debate over the appropriate study of caste. From an interpretive perspective, anthropologists such as Louis Dumont view caste as a specifically Indian phenomenon, predicated upon hierarchy as a social ideal, a structure of oppositions expressed in terms of purity and pollution, and the disjunction of power and ritual status (Dumont 1970). From a materialist standpoint, in contrast, caste ranking is not the expression of uniquely Indian values but an ideological reflection of institutionalized inequality in access to wealth and power. As such it is open to comparison with functionally similar systems, for example the traditional black/white interaction of the American South (see Mencher 1974).

References

Burke, Edmund. 1790 [1968]. *Reflections on the Revolution in France*. Harmondsworth, England: Penguin.
Codere, Helen. 1957 [1967]. "Kwakiutl Society: Rank Without Class." Tom McFeat, ed., *Indians of the North Pacific Coast*. Seattle: University of Washington Press. Originally published in *AA* 59:473–84 (1957).
Coser, Lewis A. 1968. "Class." *DHI* 1:441–49.
Dumont, Louis. 1970. *Homo Hierarchicus: The Caste System and Its Implications*. Chicago: University of Chicago Press. Interprets caste as a system of inequality unique to Indian civilization.
Evans-Pritchard, E. E. 1940 [1969]. *The Nuer*. New York: Oxford University Press.
Fallers, Lloyd A. 1973. *Inequality: Social Stratification Reconsidered*. Chicago: University of Chicago Press. A critique of the concept of stratification.

Goldberg, Harvey. 1968. "Elite Groups in Peasant Communities: A Comparison of Three Middle Eastern Villages." *AA* 70:718–30.

Kopytoff, Igor. 1982. "Slavery." *ARA* 11:207–30. A review with extensive bibliography.

Lee, Richard. 1982. "Politics, Sexual and Non-Sexual, in an Egalitarian Society." Eleanor Leacock and Richard Lee, eds., *Politics and History in Band Societies.* Cambridge: Cambridge University Press.

McLellan, David. 1971. *The Thought of Karl Marx: An Introduction.* New York: Harper & Row.

Mencher, Joan P. 1974. "The Caste System Upside Down, or The Not-So-Mysterious East." *CA* 15:469–93. A materialist intepretation of caste.

Plotnicov, Leonard, and Arthur Tuden. 1970. "Introduction." L. Plotnicov and A. Tuden, eds., *Essays in Comparative Social Stratification.* Pittsburgh: University of Pittsburgh Press. A materialist viewpoint.

Rousseau, Jean-Jacques. 1754 [1974]. "Discourse on the Origin and Basis of Inequality among Men." Lowell Bair, trans., *The Essential Rousseau.* New York: New American Library.

Rousseau, Jerome. 1979. "Kayan Stratification." *Man* 14:215–36.

Van den Berghe, Pierre L. 1973. "Pluralism." John J. Honigmann, ed., *Handbook of Social and Cultural Anthropology.* Chicago: Rand McNally.

Sources of Additional Information

Frank Cancian, "Social Stratification," *ARA* 5:227–48, 1976, provides an introduction to the anthropological debate on this topic. A useful reader is provided by André Béteille, ed., *Social Inequality: Selected Readings*, Baltimore: Penguin Books, 1969. The issue of class is ably reviewed in Raymond T. Smith, "Anthropology and the Concept of Social Class," *ARA* 13:467–94, 1984.

INTERPRETATION. A distinctive approach to ETHNOGRAPHY, emphasizing understanding over explanation and the role of the ethnographer as a mediator (rather than autonomous observer) of cultural experience.

Interpretation is derived from the Latin *interpres*, an agent between two parties, in short, a negotiator, a go-between. Interpretation is thus an act of translation, a mediation of two perspectives. It figures within a debate regarding the role of the observer in understanding an alien society, and more generally, the limits of empiricism in ANTHROPOLOGY. The issue of interpretation arises from the problematic character of ethnography. Insofar as each CULTURE provides a holistic frame of reference for analyzing experience and guiding behavior, how can an observer raised in one culture understand another and communicate this understanding to a wider audience?

The problem of interpretation, both logically and historically, begins with texts; specifically with religious or philosophical texts whose meaning is obscure. Thus Saint Augustine, in his study of scriptural interpretation *On Christian Doctrine* (completed A.D. 427), sought to describe "a way of discovering those things which are to be understood, and a way of teaching what we have learned" (Augustine [1958]:7). Such issues formed the basis for a long literature on the science of interpretation (or hermeneutics) in Christian theology, intended to clarify texts so as to guide the tasks of preaching and pedagogy.

Philosophers of the romantic movement transformed this tradition of hermeneutics in several significant ways. For Friedrich Schleiermacher (1768–1834), the question of interpretation was not an anomalous problem raised by occasional obscurities, but was rather inherent in the character of texts, resulting from the historical distance separating author and reader. In short, the historical (or better, cultural) situation of the interpreter poses a barrier to understanding, which can only be overcome by recourse to critical interpretive method (Linge 1976:xiii).

The work of Wilhelm Dilthey (1833–1911) expanded this perspective. Dilthey demonstrated that the problem of interpretation extended beyond texts to include the entire sphere of human interaction. Furthermore, he argued that the tasks of interpretation and understanding provided a distinctive basis for the social, cultural, or human sciences (German *Geisteswissenschaften*), distinguished from the natural sciences by both method and subject matter. Thus, "insofar as man experiences human states, gives expression to his experience and understands the expressions, mankind becomes the subject of the human sciences" (Dilthey 1910:71). Particularly in his later writings Dilthey stressed the social and collective (rather than merely psychological) character of meaning and expression, a view that anticipated (and influenced) the anthropological conception of cultures as distinctive worlds of meaning (see Outhwaite 1975:26–27).

Interpretation in Anthropology

The prominence accorded interpretation in postwar anthropological theory is the result of both developments internal to anthropology and the assimilation of a wider hermeneutic tradition. Comprehending and describing the meanings underlying behavior—in Bronislaw Malinowski's influential phrase "the native's point of view" (Malinowski 1922:25)—has long been recognized as one of the ethnographer's essential tasks. Theory aside, this focus was an inevitable consequence of the advent of intensive fieldwork (see ETHNOGRAPHY). A concern with interpretation has also resulted from recognition of the fallibility or bias inherent in ethnographic method. Several well-publicized debates over the adequacy of particular ethnographies—for example, concerning Robert Redfield's and Oscar Lewis's conflicting accounts of politics, religion, and interpersonal behavior in the Mexican village of Tepoztlan (Pelto and Pelto 1978:23–24), and Margaret Mead's and Derek Freeman's contradictory understandings of Samoan PERSONALITY and behavior (Brady et al. 1983)—have made this a problematic issue. Finally, the analysis of SYMBOLISM, which has formed such an important element of postwar anthropological theory, made the problem of interpretation a central concern.

If interpretation has always been an element of the ethnographic craft, only in the postwar period has it been offered as a theoretical alternative for anthropology, counterposed to an empiricist tradition of research which has derived its assumptions from the natural sciences. In large part, this development stems from the exhaustion of what were dominant theories in the prewar period. FUNC-

TIONALISM, as propounded by A. R. Radcliffe-Brown, which explained belief and CUSTOM in terms of their contribution to social solidarity, was perceived as overly abstract, static, and unconvincing. For one prominent critic, "social anthropology is a kind of historiography, and therefore ultimately [a kind] of philosophy or art." Accordingly, anthropology should study societies "as moral systems and not as natural systems," concerning itself with design rather than process, PATTERN rather than law, and interpretation rather than explanation (Evans-Pritchard 1950:152).

A similar collapse of faith can be seen regarding the classic conception of culture in the HISTORICISM of Boasian anthropology—each culture supposedly a unified and consistent world of meaning, patterning the thoughts and actions of its members. From the interpretive perspective, in contrast, culture is not a "power" determining behavior, but a context of meanings within which human action is made intelligible (Geertz 1973:14). In this vein Clifford Geertz has argued that the cultures depicted in traditional ethnographies are in fact reifications: "What we call our data are really our own constructions of other people's constructions of what they and their compatriots are up to" (Geertz 1973:9).

This theoretical shift within anthropology—from Radcliffe-Brown to Evans-Pritchard, or from Boas to Geertz—has been paralleled and reinforced by a transformation of the concept of interpretation in modern philosophy. Although Dilthey, for example, viewed the interpreter's first task as one of removing all preconceptions so as to understand an alien reality without distortion, more recent discussions of hermeneutics—for example, in the work of Hans-Georg Gadamer—assume this to be an impossibility. Understanding, in this view, "is not reconstruction but mediation" (Linge 1976:xvi; see also Gadamer 1975).

The goal of anthropology, from the empiricist perspective, is objectively controllable and communicable knowledge, expressed ideally as laws of behavior, obtained by a combination of observation, abstraction, and theoretical inference. Conceptually at least, the ethnographer belongs to another world, and it is the logic of that world which imposes questions and methods for which the field experience is to provide answers. If, however, the interpretive premise is accepted, then there is no Archimedean point, no position from which an autonomous observer can encounter an alien reality uninfluenced by his or her own historical and cultural situation. Proponents of this view thus assume that culture is "composed of seriously contested codes and representations . . . that the poetic and the political are inseparable, that science is in, not above, historical and linguistic processes" (Clifford 1986:2). Particularly because of its radically relativist implications, the interpretive perspective is, and is likely to remain, controversial.

References

Augustine, Saint. [1958]. *On Christian Doctrine*. D. W. Robertson, Jr., trans. Indianapolis: Bobbs-Merrill.
Brady, Ivan, et al. 1983. "Speaking in the Name of the Real: Freeman and Mead on Samoa." *AA* 85:908–47.

Clifford, James. 1986. "Introduction: Partial Truths." James Clifford and George E. Marcus, eds., *Writing Culture: The Poetics and Politics of Ethnography*. Berkeley and Los Angeles: University of California Press. An important collection of essays illustrating the interpretive perspective.

Dilthey, Wilhelm. 1910 [1961]. *Pattern and Meaning in History*. H. P. Rickman, ed. New York: Harper & Row.

Evans-Pritchard, E. E. 1950 [1964]. "Social Anthropology: Past and Present." E. E. Evans-Pritchard, *Social Anthropology and Other Essays*. New York: Free Press. A critique of functionalism from the interpretive standpoint.

Gadamer, Hans-Georg. 1975. *Truth and Method*. New York: Seabury Press.

Geertz, Clifford. 1973. "Thick Description: Toward an Interpretive Theory of Culture." C. Geertz, *The Interpretation of Cultures*. New York: Basic Books. An influential critique of empiricism in anthropology.

Linge, David E. 1976. "Editor's Introduction." Hans-Georg Gadamer, *Philosophical Hermeneutics*. David E. Linge, trans. Berkeley and Los Angeles: University of California Press. A helpful introduction to modern hermeneutic philosophy.

Malinowski, Bronislaw. 1922 [1961]. *Argonauts of the Western Pacific*. New York: Dutton.

Outhwaite, W. 1975. *Understanding Social Life*. London: George Allen & Unwin.

Pelto, Pertti J., and Gretel H. Pelto. 1978. *Anthropological Research: The Structure of Inquiry*. 2d ed. Cambridge: Cambridge University Press.

Sources of Additional Information

The implications of the interpretive perspective are assessed in George Marcus and Michael Fisher, *Anthropology as Cultural Critique*, Chicago: University of Chicago Press, 1986. The interpretive stance is illustrated effectively by Paul Rabinow in *Reflections on Fieldwork in Morocco*, Berkeley and Los Angeles: University of California Press, 1977. A number of essays bearing on the theme of anthropological interpretation are included in Clifford Geertz, *Local Knowledge*, New York: Basic Books, 1983. Modern theorists (and their debates) regarding interpretation and rationality are ably surveyed in Robert C. Ulin, *Understanding Cultures: Perspectives in Anthropology and Social Theory*, Austin: University of Texas Press, 1984.

K

KINSHIP. (1) A culturally defined relationship established through the premise of DESCENT, between two individuals or through common descent from a third person; that set of social relationships, particularly beyond the FAMILY unit, established on this basis. (2) More broadly, a network of consanguineal and affinal relations (i.e., ties established through descent or MARRIAGE).

The idea of kinship provides one of the most basic principles for the organization of human societies. With more than a century of research, several well-articulated theoretical schools, and a distinctive terminology, kinship is arguably the most mature topic of contemporary cultural ANTHROPOLOGY. Three reasons can be suggested for the importance of kinship as an anthropological concern. First, marriage and sexuality are highly polarized topics; quite literally, they strike close to home, and thus cross-cultural differences are inevitably of great interest. Second, because in both BANDS and TRIBES social organization is predicated upon relations of kinship, the development of accurate field methods in ETHNOGRAPHY necessitated a sophisticated analysis of kinship and marriage. Third, being inherently relational in nature, the facts of kinship lend themselves more readily to formal and mathematical treatment than any other ethnographic topic, and thus kinship has been pursued avidly by those anthropologists who equate formalism with theoretical insight.

In English the word kinship is quite recent, dating only to the nineteenth century, but the root "kin" is ancient, seen in the Latin *genus* or Greek *genos*, meaning equally a RACE or stock; a class or kind; or GENDER (see *OED*). The underlying notion is that of propagation of kind. Three other concepts are associated with it, namely descent, marriage, and family. Collectively these three terms define the domain of kinship: first, association of individuals through the premise of descent and the creation of wider groups and networks on this basis; second, the socially recognized RITUAL bonding of male and female, evolving through the tie of marriage intimacy, sexuality, economic interdependence, and the legitimation of offspring; and third, the formation of primary groups (families) through which society is reproduced over the generations. The term kinship is thus ambiguous: construed narrowly it refers to the phenomenon of descent alone, as in the phrase "kinship and marriage." More broadly, it encompasses both consanguineal and affinal relationships (i.e., ties respectively of descent and marriage).

There are numerous early examples of the study of kinship. Tacitus (first century A.D.) discussed such topics as inheritance, *wergild* (compensation for assault or homicide), and the avunculate (the distinctive role of the maternal uncle) in the German tribes (*Germ.* 20–21). Among the classical authors Andrew Lang cited for their descriptions of kinship patterns are Hesiod, Herodotus, Aristotle, Diodorus Siculus, Varro, Caesar, Polybius, Strabo, and Apuleius (Lang 1892). Isidore of Seville's seventh century compilation, the *Etymologiae*, included an elaborate analysis of Roman kin terminology and marriage patterns (Isidore [1982]; *Etym.* 9.6–7).

Serious analysis of kinship patterns began with the European exploration literature of the seventeenth century. In 1672 John Lederer identified the phenomena of CLAN, matrilineality, and exogamy among an eastern Siouan tribe (see DESCENT; MARRIAGE), while J. F. Lafitau (in 1724) described a classificatory system of kin terminology among the Iroquois (Tax 1955:445). Nonetheless, a theoretically grounded approach emerged only in the nineteenth century, where the topics of kinship and marriage provided a major realm of debate for evolutionist anthropology (see EVOLUTION). Since that time kinship studies have figured prominently in most theoretical developments, including DIFFUSION, FUNCTIONALISM, ETHNOSCIENCE, and STRUCTURALISM.

Kinship and Culture

Kinship is ostensibly a cultural codification of biological fact, interpreting through the frame of marriage and descent the facts of procreation and parentage. In reality, the relation between kinship and biology is far more complex, both because the manner in which kin ties are conceived and organized is highly variable cross-culturally, and because kinship frequently involves relationships in which biology serves as no more than a metaphor and model for framing social ties. The first point is illustrated by the variability of kin classification, for example, the decidedly different classification of "father's brother" in India, native North America, and the contemporary United States. The second point is demonstrated by the social mechanism of fictive kinship, social ties based on the metaphor of biological relation, manifested in rituals of adoption, godparenthood, and blood brotherhood.

However, the recognition that kinship is the product of a complex dialectic of NATURE and CULTURE was slow to develop (see Lévi-Strauss 1949: chs. 1–2). Lewis Henry Morgan (1818–1881) was a pioneer in the anthropological study of kinship systems, arguing that a comparison of systems of kin classification could reveal the path of cultural EVOLUTION, on the assumption that the contemporary usages of non-Western peoples were SURVIVALS of earlier stages of society. In this view, the Hawaiian (Morgan's "Malayan") system, in which the same kin term is used for all relatives of common sex and generation (father/father's brother; mother/mother's sister, etc.), derived from the earliest stratum of human experience, that of group marriage. This "consanguine family," Morgan felt, had "originated in plural marriages of consanguinei, including own brothers and sisters" (Morgan 1877:417). Thus Morgan presumed that kinship—in particular the so-called classificatory systems which group diverse kin relations under a common term—derived from a folk biology, mirroring the limited understanding of physiological paternity of so-called PRIMITIVE peoples, and the actual sexual-marital arrangements of a given era (see Buchler and Selby 1968:2–4; Tax 1955:456–66).

Morgan's narrow biological understanding of consanguinity was challenged in 1906 by the Belgian ethnologist Arnold van Gennep in his distinction between *parenté physique* and *parenté sociale*, biological and social parenthood, a perspective reinforced by the teachings of Durkheimian sociology on the collective and compelling character of social knowledge (Buchler and Selby 1968:3–4; see also SUPERORGANIC). Bronislaw Malinowski reflected this new understanding in his argument (in 1913) that "consanguinity (as a sociological concept) is therefore not the physiological bond of common blood, it is the social acknowledgement and interpretation of it" (in Buchler and Selby 1968:4).

In the same era, the work of Alfred Kroeber and W. H. R. Rivers provided, in different ways, important directions for the subsequent study of kinship in anthropology. Both were concerned with the analysis of kin terminology, a seemingly obscure topic that—because it provides a window into the emic (indigenous) understandings of kinship within a given society—has received enormous attention and debate (see EMIC/ETIC). Kroeber introduced a formal approach to kinship studies, seeking the "principles or categories of relationship" underlying the surface variety of kin systems, among these key variables being generation, comparative age, and the gender of speaker and relative (Kroeber 1909:176). Kroeber's insistence on analyzing the internal logic of kinship systems was the forerunner of the mathematical and ethnoscientific treatment of kinship semantics in the postwar period (see Buchler and Selby 1968: chs. 8, 9).

On the level of method, Rivers provided a detailed procedure for eliciting genealogies in the field setting and established a precedent for the inclusion of detailed kinship information as a standard element of ethnography. On the level of theory, Rivers argued that kin terminology and patterns of kin relations provided a key to understanding the institutional arrangements of a society, as seen in the organization of descent groups, the inheritance of property, and the conduct of ritual (Rivers 1910; see also Tax 1955:471–74). This insight provided a foundation for what was later elaborated as functionalism in British anthropology.

Later Theory

It is conventional to distinguish between four primary institutions in ethnographic analysis: economics, politics, religion, and kinship (see Schneider

1984:181–85). The nature of their interrelation, or conversely the relative autonomy of each of these cultural systems, has been a fundamental issue of anthropological theory since the 1930s.

Applied to band and tribal societies (see also PRIMITIVE), the doctrines of structural functionalism dictated that kinship be seen as the fundamental ordering principle of SOCIAL STRUCTURE. This view was emphasized in the writings of A. R. Radcliffe-Brown: "The characteristic of most of these societies that we call primitive is that the conduct of individuals to one another is very largely regulated on the basis of kinship, this being brought about by the formation of fixed patterns of behaviour for each recognised kind of kinship relation" (Radcliffe-Brown 1924:29). In this view the facts of kinship determine, in whole or part, such matters as the composition of family and household; the assignment of rank; the definition of group membership (in lineages, clans, and the like); the arrangement of marriage, and through this, alliances between groups; the regulation of succession and inheritance, and the control of economic resources; and, with the exception of STATE societies, the organization of political control (see Radcliffe-Brown 1950).

An argument for the relative autonomy of kinship has been forcefully restated by Meyer Fortes: "The realm of custom, belief, and social organization, which we descriptively identify by the overall rubric of kinship, is both analytically distinguishable and empirically specifiable as a relatively discrete domain of social structure founded upon principles and processes that are irreducible" (Fortes 1969:250). The most fundamental principle of kinship, for Fortes, is what he terms the axiom of amity: kin are obliged to interact through trust, solidarity, and mutual support, not by virtue of some personal affection or contractual obligation, but simply and solely because of their common kinship (Fortes 1969: ch. 12).

Yet there have been many dissenting voices. The functionalist position has been criticized as ignoring the degree to which patterns of kinship are determined by material conditions, a point made by Kroeber in the 1930s: "Instead of considering the clan, moiety, totem, or formal unilateral group as primary in social structure and function, the present view conceives them as secondary and often unstable embroideries on the primary patterns of group residence and subsistence associations" (Kroeber 1938:298; see also Kuper 1982:78). Edmund Leach (in 1961) argued in similar terms: "Kinship . . . is not a 'thing in itself.' The concepts of descent and affinity are expressions of property relations. . . . Marriage unifies; inheritance separates; property endures" (in Fortes 1969:222; see also ADAPTATION; MATERIALISM).

More far-reaching critiques have also been made. Anthropologists have assumed that the concept of kinship and its constituent elements (descent, exogamy, lineage, clan, etc.) are relevant to all human societies, that kinship constitutes a universal system for interpreting social existence and organizing group behavior. From the perspective of symbolic anthropology (see SYMBOLISM), however, this assumption is ethnocentric and unproven. As David Schneider has insisted, "it [should] no longer be assumed that the genealogical grid is universal or has the same value and meaning in all cultures. . . . The assumed primacy or high value attached to engendering must be treated as a question and not taken as universally true" (Schneider 1984:200). In this view, while descent is implied by procreation and marriage is ubiquitous, the value and organizational relevance of descent and marriage must be recognized as symbolic constructs, whose cross-cultural significance must be demonstrated rather than assumed.

References

Buchler, Ira R., and Henry A. Selby. 1968. *Kinship and Social Organization: An Introduction to Theory and Method*. New York: Macmillan. An advanced text.
Fortes, Meyer. 1969. *Kinship and the Social Order*. Chicago: Aldine. A historical and theoretical synthesis.
Isidore of Seville. [1982]. *Etymologias: Edicion bilingue (Etymologiae)*. Jose Oroz Reta and Manuel-A. Marcos Casquero, trans. 2 vols. Madrid: Biblioteca de autores cristianos. A compilation of early medieval knowledge including Roman kinship and family patterns.
Kroeber, A. L. 1909 [1952]. "Classificatory Systems of Relationship." A. L. Kroeber, *The Nature of Culture*. Chicago: University of Chicago Press. An early statement on the analysis of kinship terminology.
———. 1938 [1968]. "Basic and Secondary Patterns of Social Structure." Paul Bohannan and John Middleton, eds., *Kinship and Social Organization*. Garden City, N.Y.: Natural History Press.
Kuper, Adam. 1982. "Lineage Theory: A Critical Retrospect." *ARA* 11:71–95. Reviews the modern debate on kinship.
Lang, Andrew. 1892. "Family." *Encyclopaedia Britannica*. 9th ed. R. S. Peale reprint. Chicago: R. S. Peale.
Lévi-Strauss, Claude. 1949 [1969]. *The Elementary Structures of Kinship*. J. H. Bell, J. von Sturmer, and R. Needham, trans. Boston: Beacon Press. A structuralist classic.
Morgan, Louis Henry. 1877. *Ancient Society*. Chicago: Charles H. Kerr.
Radcliffe-Brown, A. R. 1924 [1952]. "The Mother's Brother in South Africa." A. R. Radcliffe-Brown, *Structure and Function in Primitive Society*. New York: Free Press. An early exposition of the structural-functional approach.
———. 1950. "Introduction." A. R. Radcliffe-Brown and Daryll Forde, eds., *African Systems of Kinship and Marriage*. London: Oxford University Press.
Rivers, W. H. R. 1910 [1971]. "The Genealogical Method of Anthropological Inquiry." Nelson Graburn, ed., *Readings in Kinship and Social Structure*. New York: Harper & Row. An early statement on the methods of kinship analysis.
Schneider, David M. 1984. *A Critique of the Study of Kinship*. Ann Arbor: University of Michigan Press.
Tax, Sol. 1955. "From Lafitau to Radcliffe-Brown: A Short History of the Study of Social Organization." Fred Eggan, ed., *Social Anthropology of North American Tribes*. 2d ed. Chicago: University of Chicago Press. A useful history.

Sources of Additional Information

For an introduction, see Robin Fox, *Kinship and Marriage*, Harmondsworth, England: Penguin, 1967. A useful reader on kinship is Jack Goody, ed., *Kinship: Selected Readings*,

Harmondsworth: Penguin, 1971. J. A. Barnes, *Three Styles in the Study of Kinship*, Berkeley and Los Angeles: University of California Press, 1971, offers a digestible introduction to the major debates of modern kinship theory, reviewing the work of Murdock, Fortes, and Lévi-Strauss. On W. H. R. Rivers and his influence on British kinship studies, see Ian Langham, *The Building of British Social Anthropology*, Dordrecht, the Netherlands: D. Reidel, 1981. The development of Morgan's theories of kinship and cultural evolution are treated in Thomas R. Trautmann, *Lewis Henry Morgan and the Invention of Kinship*, Berkeley and Los Angeles: University of California Press, 1987.

L

LANGUAGE. Systematic human vocal communication in which meanings are represented through a structured arrangement of arbitrary sound elements. Also, the transcription of vocal symbols by other means, as in writing or signing.

The capacity for language is fundamental to human ADAPTATION. Few human activities are as distinctive, and as crucial, for characterizing our species. The word "language" is derived (via French) from the Latin *lingua*, meaning literally a tongue. It appears in Middle English in the thirteenth century, in the sense of the speech of a particular nation or people. From about 1600 language also takes on the more abstract sense of all human speech (see *OED*).

Language is inherently arbitrary: Words are formed from sound combinations that (with a few exceptions) have no intrinsic relation to the concepts they represent, as Aristotle recognized (*On Interp.*, 16a). Furthermore, each lexicon reflects a distinctive life world, while each grammar molds speech into distinctive patterns in the expression of time, cause, possession, relationship, attribute, and so forth. In this way the diversity of languages mirrors the diversity of cultures, each a distinct refraction of the world of experience.

Although linguistics originated with the need to understand languages grown historically remote (Homeric Greek, classical Latin), linguistic anthropology developed through the need to analyze languages within social contexts that were both geographically and culturally alien. Thus linguistic studies formed a part of anthropological research from its inception, as a tool of ETHNOGRAPHY, as a key to reconstructing ethnological relationships, and ultimately, as a model of CULTURE as a whole. This entry considers the concept of language as it has influenced the development of anthropological methods and theory (see also COMMUNICATION).

Primitive Language

From at least the eighteenth century, the origin of language was recognized as a central problem for understanding the emergence of human society and of those human capacities that today would be subsumed by the term culture (see Lounsbury 1968:160–65). Jean-Jacques Rousseau (1712–1778) conceived of language and society as developing by stages, simultaneously (Rousseau 1754:191–200). Lord Monboddo (d. 1799), in contrast, viewed language as a relatively late development: "There must have been society before language was invented, . . . [and] it must have subsisted a considerable time, and other arts have been invented, before this most difficult one was found out" ([1792] in Slotkin 1965:451).

These disagreements aside, there was consensus through the nineteenth century on the existence of PRIMITIVE languages, languages of existing "savage" societies, intermediate in EVOLUTION between the cries of animals and the fully developed speech of civilized peoples. So-called primitive languages were assumed to lack the capacity for abstraction: "Savages will have twenty independent words each expressing the act of cutting some particular thing, without having any name for the act of cutting in general" (E. J. Payne [1899] in Henson 1971:7). Rather inconsistently, such languages were thought to have limited vocabularies and thus "were incapable of precision and specification" (Henson 1971:7). Pronunciation was considered to be inexact and shifting. Thus Hugh Goldie [1868] wrote, regarding the Efik language of Nigeria: "B is frequently interchanged with p; or rather, a sound between the two, is very frequently employed" (in Henson 1971:8).

In a similar vein, languages were ranked in terms of their morphological patterns, as isolating (e.g., Chinese), agglutinative (Turkish), and inflecting languages (Sanskrit, Latin) (see Lyons 1968:187–91). Isolating languages (in which words are unvarying) were considered the most primitive, followed by the agglutinative (which add morphemes to unvarying roots) and the inflecting languages (in which words are transformed to reflect case and number). These three morphological patterns were widely considered to reflect three levels of evolutionary achievement and intellectual ability: "The mental aptitude of a nation is closely dependent upon the type of its idiom. . . . it is no mere coincidence that those peoples who have ever borne the banner in the van of civilization have always spoken inflected tongues. The world will be better off when all others [i.e., isolating and agglutinative] are extinguished" (Brinton 1901:66–67). For nineteenth century ANTHROPOLOGY, the ideas of RACE, language, and culture were entirely confounded (see Lounsbury 1968:186–206).

Language and Ethnography

The value of language for ethnological reconstructions (see ETHNOLOGY) has long been recognized. Because a language's grammar and core vocabulary change slowly, systematic resemblances between languages are sensitive indicators of historic relationships between peoples, which William Jones (1746–

1794) demonstrated by identifying the common origin of Sanskrit and Greek in early Indo-European society (in Slotkin 1965:230-33, 240). However, the beginnings of systematic ethnography about 1900 transformed the anthropological understanding of language.

Anthropologists came to insist on competence in the native language as a prerequisite for adequate field research (Hymes 1983:139). This stance had theoretical as well as practical consequences. A strong linguistic RELATIVISM developed in American anthropology in particular, emphasizing the inappropriateness of applying the traditional phonetic and grammatical categories of European linguistics to the non-European languages encountered by anthropologists. In 1889 Franz Boas showed that the supposedly inexact or inconsistent pronunciation of "primitive" languages merely reflected the observer's linguistic bias: "Each [linguist] apperceives the unknown sounds by the means of the sounds of his own language" (Boas 1889:51).

Out of this insight the anthropologist Edward Sapir developed the phonemic principle, positing a unique set of relevant sound contrasts for each language, a key concept of modern linguistics (Sapir 1925). A phonemic (or phonological) account thus describes speech through those sound contrasts significant for the speakers of a particular language. It is distinguished from a phonetic account, utilizing an objective description of sound patterns applicable to any language (Lyons 1968: ch. 3).

Language and Cognition

The science of linguistics began as an Indo-European field of study. Yet the range of significant sounds (phonology) and acceptable sentence structure (syntax) within the European and South Asian languages represents only a narrow sample of world languages. Beginning in the late eighteenth century, the advance of linguistic studies brought the Asian, Amerindian, Oceanic, and African languages into scientific notice, while ethnographic studies dramatically conveyed a sense of wide cultural variation. Out of this encounter came the idea of a relationship between the patterning of language and the modes of thought characteristic of a culture.

The idea of "self" offers an example. Although in English the distinction of self and other is clear, this is not the case in Wintu, a California Indian language. As Dorothy Lee has noted, for the Wintu the self is neither bounded nor named (Lee 1950:132). The expression of identity, relation, and otherness in Wintu suggests that the self is merely a social focus, "which gradually fades and gives place to the other" (Lee 1950:134).

The argument for a link between language, cognition, and culture has a considerable history. The German philosopher Johann Gottfried von Herder (1744–1803) proposed that language could shape WORLD VIEW. The linguist Wilhelm von Humboldt (1767–1835) argued that "the peculiarity of the spirit and the structure of the language of a nation are so intertwined internally that if we have one we can deduce the other from it" (in Schaff 1973:13). Through von Humboldt the relation of language and thought became a significant issue in nineteenth-century linguistics and philosophy (see Penn 1972; Schaff 1973: ch. 1).

In American anthropology, Franz Boas (1858–1942), Edward Sapir (1884–1939), and Benjamin Whorf (1897–1941) pursued the idea that the structure of a language exerts significant constraint upon forms of thought and their codification in culture. Boas demonstrated that the unfamiliar grammatical patterns of North American Indian languages were not evidence of linguistic inferiority, as the evolutionists had argued, but of distinctive approaches to interpreting experience. In this way, the study of language was an avenue to the understanding of culture. "The purely linguistic inquiry," Boas argued, "is part and parcel of a thorough investigation of the psychology of the peoples of the world" (Boas 1911:59). The work of Sapir and Whorf extended this insight by analyzing how specific grammatical patterns of non-Western languages implied markedly different views of time, person, causality, and the like. As Whorf commented, "We dissect nature along lines laid down by our native languages" (Whorf 1940:213).

In short, the linguistic relativity principle or, as it is more commonly termed, the Sapir-Whorf hypothesis, holds that "language functions, not simply as a device for reporting experience, but also, and more significantly, as a way of defining experience for its speakers" (Hoijer 1974: 121). This concept remains controversial (see Schaff 1973: ch. 3).

Language and Culture

Since the 1930s, in addition to investigating the interrelation of language, culture, and cognition, the anthropological study of language has influenced the development of culture theory in several ways. First, in a general sense the phenomenon of language provided anthropologists with a model of culture as a whole (see Aberle 1957). The following parallels were frequently assumed: (1) Culture, like language, involves an essentially arbitrary selection from a universe of possibilities. (2) Culture, like language, is patterned: Individual traits are meaningless when considered in isolation. (3) Culture, like language, is ordered by a complex yet unconscious system of rules, "an elaborate and secret code that is written nowhere, known by none, and understood by all" (Sapir 1927:556). In this view, the task of the anthropologist, like the linguist, is to discover and render explicit those rules that natives acquire and use unconsciously (see PATTERN; WORLD VIEW).

Second, the field of linguistics has provided several specific paradigms for the study of culture (see Greenberg 1973; Teeter 1973; Hymes 1983:177–213). The contrast of phonemic and phonetic analysis has given rise to a supposedly parallel contrast of emic and etic approaches to culture (see EMIC/ETIC). The structural linguistics associated with Ferdinand de Saussure, Roman Jakobson, and others inspired a structuralist anthropology, as seen in particular in the work of Claude Lévi-Strauss (see STRUCTURALISM). In a more empirical vein, modern linguistics also provided the model for that systematic approach to the classifi-

cation of cultural knowledge known variously as cognitive anthropology or ETH-
NOSCIENCE.

References

Aberle, David F. 1957 [1968]. "The Influence of Linguistics on Early Culture and
Personality Theory." Robert Manners and David Kaplan, eds., *Theory in Anthropology: A Sourcebook*. Chicago: Aldine. A critical examination of the ways
in which the analogy of language and culture has guided anthropological theory.
Boas, Franz. 1889. "On Alternating Sounds." *AA* [o.s.] 2:47–53. This paper anticipated
phonemic analysis.
———. 1911 [1966]. "Introduction to *Handbook of American Indian Languages*."
Bound with J. W. Powell, "Indian Linguistic Families of America North of
Mexico." Preston Holder, ed. Lincoln: University of Nebraska Press. An early
but comprehensive statement on the anthropological significance of linguistic data.
Brinton, Daniel G. 1901. *Races and Peoples: Lectures on the Science of Ethnography*.
Philadelphia: David McKay. An interesting synopsis of pre-Boasian American
anthropology.
Greenberg, Joseph H. 1973. "Linguistics as a Pilot Science." Eric P. Hamp, ed., *Themes
in Linguistics: The 1970s*. The Hague and Paris: Mouton. A critical review of
efforts to make linguistics a model for the other social sciences.
Henson, Hilary. 1971. "Early British Anthropologists and Language." Edwin Ardener,
ed., *Social Anthropology and Language*. London: Tavistock. Henson notes the
relative disregard for linguistic issues in British anthropological theory.
Hoijer, Harry. 1974. "The Sapir-Whorf Hypothesis." Ben G. Blount, ed., *Language,
Culture and Society: A Book of Readings*. Cambridge, Mass.: Winthrop. A good
introduction to the issue of language and cognition.
Hymes, Dell H. 1983. "Linguistic Method in Ethnography: Its Development in the United
States." Dell Hymes, *Essays in the History of Linguistic Anthropology*. Amster-
dam and Philadelphia: John Benjamins. An important overview of the role of
linguistic studies in American anthropology.
Lee, Dorothy. 1950 [1959]. "The Conception of the Self Among the Wintu Indians."
D. Lee, *Freedom and Culture*. N.p.: Prentice-Hall.
Lounsbury, Floyd G. 1968. "One Hundred Years of Anthropological Linguistics." J.
O. Brew, ed., *One Hundred Years of Anthropology*. Cambridge, Mass.: Harvard
University Press. Lounsbury ably summarizes the major developments in the
history of linguistic anthropology.
Lyons, John. 1968. *Introduction to Theoretical Linguistics*. Cambridge: Cambridge Uni-
versity Press. An advanced introduction.
Penn, Julia M. 1972. *Linguistic Relativity versus Innate Ideas: The Origins of the Sapir-
Whorf Hypothesis in German Thought*. The Hague: Mouton.
Rousseau, Jean-Jacques. 1754 [1967]. "Discourse on the Origin and Foundation of
Inequality Among Mankind." J.-J. Rousseau, *The Social Contract and Discourse
on the Origin and Foundation of Inequality Among Mankind*. New York: Wash-
ington Square Press.
Sapir, Edward. 1925 [1949]. "Sound Patterns in Language." David G. Mandelbaum,
ed., *Selected Writings of Edward Sapir in Language, Culture and Personality*.
Berkeley and Los Angeles: University of California Press. Develops the concept
of the phoneme.

————. 1927 [1949]. "The Unconscious Patterning of Behavior in Society." David G. Mandelbaum, ed., *Selected Writings of Edward Sapir in Language, Culture and Personality*. Berkeley and Los Angeles: University of California Press. An influential paper exploring the language-culture analogy.

Schaff, Adam. 1973. *Language and Cognition*. Olgierd Wojtasiewicz, trans. New York: McGraw-Hill. Schaff analyses the philosophical and linguistic issues underlying the Sapir-Whorf hypothesis and related concepts; extensive bibliography.

Slotkin, J. S., ed. 1965. *Readings in Early Anthropology*. Chicago: Aldine. A useful sourcebook for classical times through the eighteenth century, with considerable material on linguistic issues.

Teeter, Karl V. 1973. "Linguistics and Anthropology." *Daedalus* 102 (3): 87–98. A review of postwar developments between the two fields.

Whorf, Benjamin Lee. 1940 [1956]. "Science and Linguistics." B. Whorf, *Language, Thought and Reality*. Cambridge, Mass.: MIT Press.

Sources of Additional Information

Elementary introductions to the subfield are provided by Nancy P. Hickerson, *Linguistic Anthropology*, New York: Holt, Rinehart and Winston, 1980; and Ward H. Goodenough, *Culture, Language, and Society*, 2d ed, Menlo Park: Benjamin Cummings, 1981. Dell Hymes, ed., *Language in Culture and Society*, New York: Harper & Row, 1964, provides a good set of readings. The work of Sapir is reviewed in William Cowan et al., eds., *New Perspectives in Language, Culture, and Personality*, Amsterdam: John Benjamins, 1986. An overview of the relation of language and society is given in R. A. Hudson, *Sociolinguistics*, Cambridge: Cambridge University Press, 1980.

LAW. A body of norms whose violation is met with sanctions which are publicly acknowledged, socially approved, and (at least in principle) consistently applied.

The formulation of law has long been considered a hallmark of STATE-level societies. Many of the fundamental institutions of CIVILIZATION are bound up with a concept of law: sovereign authority to create law, courts to try disputes, a police power to prevent or punish illegal acts. Thus the jurist J. W. Salmond defined law as "the rules in accordance with which justice is administered by the judicial tribunals of the state" (in Hoebel 1954:23). Yet does the absence of a sovereign authority, courts, or a written legal code imply the absence of law? This has posed a fundamental problem for a cross-cultural understanding of political institutions and social control, and specifically for an anthropology of law.

An anthropological approach to law must be relativistic in recognizing the variety of cultural settings in which lawmaking occurs (see RELATIVISM); it should also be theoretical in attempting to explain the particular forms that legal institutions assume. From this perspective, Montesquieu (1689–1755) had an essential role in the origins of legal anthropology; his influential work *The Spirit of Laws* (1748) rejected the rationalist approach of the then-dominant natural law philosophy. Rather than developing concepts of justice and authority from philosophical assumptions regarding human reason and the character of virtue (in the manner of Aristotle or Thomas Aquinas), Montesquieu took a comparative and relativistic approach to law, recognizing it as an institution of society, functionally constrained by the character of the political order, environment, ECONOMY, and RELIGION (Pospisil 1971:128–38; see also FUNCTIONALISM). Similarly, the German scholar Friedrich von Savigny (1779–1861) fostered a historically grounded, pluralistic conception of law, arguing that each legal system constituted a unique expression of the spirit of a people, or *Volksgeist*. In this fashion Savigny argued for the Germans' rejection of the French *Code Napoléon*, advocating instead a more traditional German common law, the *Gemeinrecht* (Pospisil 1971:139–43; see HISTORICISM).

Henry Maine (1822–1888) had a particularly important role in the development of legal anthropology, notably through his classic study *Ancient Law* (Maine 1861). Maine was concerned with describing the development of legal institutions that accompanied the EVOLUTION of societies, in particular noting the shift from a SOCIAL STRUCTURE based on groups to one predicated on relatively autonomous individuals. Thus Maine held that ''starting . . . from a condition of society in which all the relations of Persons are summed up in the relations of Family, we seem to have steadily moved towards a phase of social order in which all these relations arise from the free agreement of Individuals.'' This was reflected in the changing nature of legal relationships, which he summarized in the dictum that the movement of the progressive societies has hitherto been a movement from Status to Contract'' (Maine 1861:99, 100).

Defining Law Cross-Culturally

Anthropologists have taken a variety of approaches to the problem of defining the domain of law and the applicability of a concept of law to those societies lacking clear, centralized political institutions (i.e., BANDS and TRIBES). These views differ in the distinction drawn between law and custom, and between law and more general mechanisms of social control.

One solution has been to retain an essentially Western concept. Thus A. R. Radcliffe-Brown (1881–1955) has followed the jurist Roscoe Pound's definition of law as ''social control through the systematic application of the force of politically organised society'' (in Radcliffe-Brown 1933:212). The field of law is accordingly limited to mechanisms for applying ''organised legal sanctions.'' It follows then that ''some simple societies have no law, although all have customs which are supported by sanctions'' (Radcliffe-Brown 1933:212). Yet as Leopold Pospisil has argued, law is not a phenomenon but a concept, and ''the justification for a concept of law [lies] . . . in its value as an analytic, heuristic device'' (Pospisil 1971:19). If ANTHROPOLOGY as a comparative and relativistic discipline is to include the study of law, it should utilize a concept that will not exclude on a priori grounds a significant proportion of world cultures (see Pospisil 1971:341–42).

Another approach has been to merge law into the domain of CUSTOM. As E. S. Hartland argued, ''The rules obeyed by savage peoples have been refused the name of laws and called only customs. But customs that are fixed and generally obeyed are indistinguishable from laws" (Hartland 1924:2). For a number of writers, custom was interpreted chiefly as a mechanism of social control, in keeping with a view of so-called PRIMITIVE societies as highly conservative, "bound in the chains of immemorial tradition" (Hartland (1924:138). W. H. R. Rivers argued that in primitive societies formal legal mechanisms (e.g., courts) were superfluous: "Group sentiment . . . makes unnecessary any definite social machinery for the exercise of authority" (in Pospisil 1971:12). In short, for Rivers or Hartland, in such societies obedience to custom was pervasive and spontaneous.

Like Hartland or Rivers, Bronislaw Malinowski (1884–1942) equated law with the field of effective social constraint. Nonetheless, his understanding of the nature of social control in non-state societies was diametrically opposed to theirs. Law in such societies was (to use a Western distinction) more civil than criminal. In keeping with Malinowski's view of culture as the product of the interactions of rational, pragmatic individuals, law was interpreted more as a matter of observing customary rights and obligations between individuals and kin groups than of punishing crimes against the common good. Hence his definition of law as "a body of binding obligations, regarded as a right by one party and acknowledged as a duty by the other, kept in force by a specific mechanism of reciprocity and publicity inherent in the structure of their society" (Malinowski 1926:58). Malinowski's cross-cultural view of law, persuasively argued in *Crime and Custom in Savage Society*, can be faulted as being overbroad, leaving no room for social control or even customary observance outside the domain of law. As Paul Bohannon has noted, that which is "kept in force by . . . reciprocity and publicity" is not law, but custom (Bohannon 1965:36).

A third approach—that most widely followed in contemporary legal anthropology—takes law to be culturally universal, yet distinguishable from a more general field of custom or social sanction. For E. Adamson Hoebel, "A social norm is legal if its neglect or infraction is regularly met, in threat or in fact, by the application of physical force by an individual or group possessing the socially recognized privilege of so acting" (Hoebel 1954:28). Thus in traditional Inuit (Eskimo) culture, it was customary for a recidivist murderer to be executed by the kin of one of his victims, who "seeks and obtains, in advance, community approval for his act" (Hoebel 1954:89). Thus while lacking any of the formal elements of Western law—trial, judge, jury, or legal code—such an execution would constitute a legal act by this definition, meeting three key criteria: the use of socially legitimate force, by an authorized agent, acting in a manner consistent with precedent (see Hoebel 1954:28; cf. Pospisil 1971:95).

The Ethnography of Law

On the whole, ethnographic studies of law take as a focus the resolution of specific disputes, inferring cultural principles from legal decisions viewed in their social context. The idea that law is to be studied through its practical application—rather than as an abstract compilation of rules or statutes—is hardly new. In the words of Justice Holmes (in 1881), "The life of the law has not been logic; it has been experience" (in Pospisil 1971:31).

This approach has a long history in the anthropology of law. R. F. Barton's *Ifugao Law* (1919) made extensive use of records of past disputes and their resolution. K. N. Llewellyn and E. A. Hoebel's *The Cheyenne Way* (1941) marked a significant advance not only for its more detailed ethnographic material, but also for its emphasis on procedure, an effort to analyze the character of Cheyenne legal reasoning (see Llewellyn and Hoebel 1941: ch. 12). For Hoebel, "law . . . is secreted in the interstices of procedure" (Hoebel 1954:35). Max Gluckman has provided detailed evidence regarding legal reasoning and standards of justice among the Barotse of Zambia. As he has commented, "Their jurisprudence shares with other legal systems many basic doctrines: right and duty and injury; the concept of the reasonable man; the distinctions between statute and custom and between statute and equity or justice; responsibility, negligence, and guilt; ownership and trespass" (Gluckman 1967:17). This level of formal resemblance between legal systems makes the anthropology of law a particularly useful avenue for the comparative study of cultural values and concepts of social good.

References

Barton, R. F. 1919. *Ifugao Law. University of California Publications in American Archaeology and Ethnology* 15 (1): 1–186. An early ethnography of law.
Bohannon, Paul. 1965. "The Differing Realms of the Law." *AA* 67:6, Pt. 2 (special publication: *The Ethnography of Law*), pp. 33–42. Distinguishes law and custom.
Gluckman, Max. 1967. *The Judicial Process Among the Barotse of Northern Rhodesia (Zambia)*. Manchester: Manchester University Press. First edition 1955. A major work in the ethnography of law, stressing procedure.
Hartland, E. Sidney. 1924 [1969]. *Primitive Law*. New York: Harper & Row.
Hoebel, E. Adamson. 1954 [1983]. *The Law of Primitive Man: A Study in Comparative Legal Dynamics*. New York: Atheneum. An excellent introduction.
Llewellyn, K. N., and E. Adamson Hoebel. 1941. *The Cheyenne Way: Conflict and Case Law in Primitive Jurisprudence*. Norman: University of Oklahoma Press.
Maine, Henry. 1861 [1972]. *Ancient Law*. New York: Dutton. A classic work of evolutionary anthropology.
Malinowski, Bronislaw. 1926 [1966]. *Crime and Custom in Savage Society*. London: Routledge & Kegan Paul.
Montesquieu, Baron de (Charles-Louis de Secondat). 1748 [1949]. *The Spirit of Laws*. Thomas Nugent, trans. New York: Hafner Press/Macmillan.
Pospisil, Leopold. 1971. *Anthropology of Law: A Comparative Theory*. New York: Harper & Row. Highly recommended as a technical presentation.
Radcliffe-Brown, A. R. 1933 [1952]. "Primitive Law." A. R. Radcliffe-Brown, *Structure and Function in Primitive Society*. New York: Free Press.

Sources of Additional Information

For a brief introduction, see Leopold J. Pospisil, *The Ethnology of Law*, 2nd ed., Menlo Park, Calif.: Cummings, 1978. See also Laura Nader, "The Anthropological

Study of Law," *AA* 67:6, Pt 2 (special publication: *The Ethnography of Law*), pp. 3–32, 1965. For a useful collection of readings, see Paul Bohannon, ed., *Law and Warfare: Studies in the Anthropology of Conflict*, Garden City, N.Y.: Natural History Press, 1967. A broad range of essays is provided in June Starr and Jane F. Collier, eds., *History and Power in the Study of Law: New Directions in Legal Anthropology*, Ithaca, N.Y.: Cornell University Press, 1989.

M

MAGIC. Pragmatic acts achieved through ostensibly paranormal or occult means.

Magic involves pragmatic acts based on esoteric wisdom. A magician, as Giordano Bruno wrote in the sixteenth century, is a wise man with the power to act (Atkins 1973:246). Magic, unlike RITUAL, has an optional rather than obligatory character. The scope of magical acts is highly elastic: It can include CURING, divining, casting spells, transforming the weather, making crops prosper, and summoning spirits and demons, among other feats. Magic is often strongly contrasted with RELIGION (see also WITCHCRAFT).

Magic in Western Tradition

The English "magic" derives from the Greek *magoi*, referring to the Zoroastrian priesthood of Persia (the biblical Magi), "who in Greek popular belief were associated with magical practices." The Old Irish equivalent *druidecht* has a similar origin (*DSS* 22.42). In each case, magic was associated with the ritual of a historically or geographically distant, and thus mysteriously potent, culture (see Herodotus, *Pers. Wars* 1.140). In short, the category of magic arose as a Western projection regarding non-Western peoples. The value of magic as a cross-cultural category has been limited by its origins in a distinctly European WORLD VIEW regarding NATURE, science, and religion.

Both Judaism and Christianity found magic repugnant. The Jews were instructed to avoid anyone "who practises divination, who is soothsayer, augur or sorcerer, who uses charms, consults ghosts or spirits, or calls up the dead" (Deut. 18:10–11). The Christian image of the magician was similar: one who performed wondrous feats, not through the power of the Lord, but through recourse to evil beings. Justin Martyr (*Apol.* 1.26), writing in the second century, claimed that Simon Magus "did mighty acts of magic, by virtue of the art of the devils operating in him," and Irenaeus of Lyons (*Adv. Haer.* 23.4) described Simon's followers as using exorcisms, incantations, love-potions, charms, and familiars (see also Acts 8:9–24; *NCE*, s.v. "magic").

However, the dividing line between magical arts and religious piety is not wholly clear (see Brown 1971). In Christian tradition, the saints were credited with countless wonders: events were foretold, the weather transformed, demons subdued, and sinners miraculously punished. They, too, were men and women of power, but a power made licit by their subordination to Christian orthodoxy. In later European thought the magician was a negative if somewhat obscure figure: wise, solitary, yet potentially dangerous. Freed by his powers and unlawful knowledge from the constraints of morality, he was personified in the legend of Faust (see Atkins 1973).

Magic and Rationality

For evolutionary ANTHROPOLOGY (see EVOLUTION), magic was a matter of intellectual error, a "monstrous farrago," in Edward Tylor's phrase, "mistaking an ideal for a real connection" (1871:1:116, 133). Regarding sorcery among "the wild natives of Australia," Tylor wrote, "the Australians, like other low tribes in the world whose minds are thus set on imaginary causes of death, hardly believe a man can die unless by being slain or bewitched" (Tylor 1889:199). Although the evolutionists saw magic as characteristic of less developed cultures, Tylor recognized that so-called magical practices in fact occur worldwide, a problem he resolved by treating magic as a SURVIVAL within more complex societies.

The place of magic in the evolutionary cultural sequence was elaborated on by James Frazer in *The Golden Bough*. The era of magic (an attempt to exert direct if misguided control over nature) was replaced by that of religion (a propitiation of spiritual beings) and, in turn, by that true understanding of physical causes that we term science (Frazer 1890:648–49). More usefully, Frazer also introduced a classification of magical forms. He distinguished between homeopathic magic, based on the principle of influence through similarity, as when an effigy is used to work injury on an enemy, and contagious magic, based on the principle of influence through contact, as when some severed portion of the body—umbilical cord, hair, or nails—is used to gain power over its owner (Frazer 1890:7–37).

The approach of Tylor and Frazer was intellectualist: Magic was explained as the product of faulty reasoning regarding nature and its processes (see RATIONALITY). Yet this image of the irrational PRIMITIVE was difficult to reconcile with the obvious competence of BANDS and TRIBES in adapting successfully to harsh and often dangerous environments. In contrast, R. R. Marett emphasized emotional rather than intellectual motivations underlying the performance of magic ("the emotions must find a vent somehow") and linked magic with a belief in MANA, a supernatural efficacy or power (Marett 1915). Bronislaw Malinowski reacted to the Tylorian perspective by stressing the practical character of tribal life and thought. Magic was, in this view, "an entirely sober, prosaic, even clumsy art, enacted for purely practical reasons, governed by crude and shallow beliefs, carried out in a simple and monotonous technique'' (Malinowski 1925:69–70). For Malinowski, the use of magic supplements rather than replaces practical technique when human skill alone cannot guarantee success (see also Malinowski 1935; for a critique, see Wax and Wax 1963).

Magic and Religion

Most anthropological studies presume the contrast of magic and religion, though the basis of the distinction varies greatly from author to author. Perhaps the most influential interpretation has been that of Emile Durkheim and his colleagues; it differentiates between magic and religion in terms of their respective social organization: ''There is no Church of magic. Between the magician and the individuals who consult him, as between these individuals themselves, there are no lasting bonds which make them members of the same moral community. . . . [The magician] is a recluse; in general, far from seeking society, he flees it'' (Durkheim 1915:60). For Durkheim magic was intrinsically individualistic and asocial (recalling the Faustian image), contrasting with religious rituals that create the fundamental bonds of social life (see also Mauss 1904).

Deprived of their social context by the COMPARATIVE METHOD, magical acts as depicted in nineteenth and early twentieth century studies appeared both random and irrational. Thus Marett wrote, ''Magic . . . grows not by internal systematization, but merely as does a rubbish-heap, by the casual accumulation of degraded and disintegrated rites of all kinds'' (Marett 1915:250). Later, intensive field research, such as E. E. Evans-Pritchard's *Witchcraft, Oracles and Magic among the Azande* (1937), revealed a different picture. For the Azande, as for many other societies, magical practices form part of a complex system of beliefs and rituals designed to explain and allay misfortune, a system that encompasses witchcraft, sorcery, (white) magic, and divination.

In the distinctions established in Evans-Pritchard's pioneering work, magic operates through the precise repetition of certain actions and formulae, while witchcraft functions through the intrinsic character of the witch. Sorcery in turn is a type of magic undertaken with the intent to injure. Divination, the discerning of hidden events or causes through occult means, is used to counteract the evil effects of witchcraft and sorcery. Studies such as Evans-Pritchard's, which have shown magic functioning within a comprehensible albeit alien world view, have helped transform anthropological assumptions regarding the rationality of tribal societies.

Magic is a polarized concept: From the perspective of religion it is malign, from that of science it is fraudulent. In either view magical acts are socially illegitimate (i.e., not in conformity with prevailing definitions of piety and truth). Most anthropological treatments of magic have presumed one or another of these views.

The analytic distinction between magic and religion remains unclear. So-called magic may utilize complex pantheons, while putatively religious rituals may be directed to specific, pragmatic ends, such as the increase of harvests or the exorcism of demons (see Hsu 1983: ch. 1). It may be truer to say that magic is a category through which one religious tradition interprets another, either where orthodoxies are in competition, as in the competition of Christianity and gnosticism or where the religion of a dominant society confronts that of a subordinate culture, as in the encounter of Catholicism and Mayan folk religion (see TRADITION; FOLK CULTURE).

References

Atkins, Stuart. 1973. "Motif in Literature: The Faust Theme." *DHI* 3:244–53. A brief review of the Faust motif, a crucial source for the European image of magic.
Brown, Peter. 1971. "The Rise and Function of the Holy Man in Late Antiquity." *Journal of Roman Studies* 61:80–101. On the relation of magic and religion in late antiquity.
Durkheim, Emile. 1915 [1965]. *The Elementary Forms of the Religious Life*. J. W. Swain, trans. New York: Free Press. A foundational work of anthropology, significant for its contrast of magic and religion.
Evans-Pritchard, E. E. 1937. *Witchcraft, Oracles and Magic among the Azande*. Oxford: Clarendon Press. Initiated the modern study of belief systems and rationality.
Frazer, James George. 1890 [1959]. *The New Golden Bough*. 1 vol., abr. Theodor H. Gaster, ed. New York: Criterion Books. A classic evolutionist work on magic and religion.
Hsu, F. L. K. 1983. *Exorcising the Trouble Makers: Magic, Science, and Culture*. Westport, Conn.: Greenwood Press. An ethnographic analysis of magic, science, and religion in a Chinese community.
Malinowski, Bronislaw. 1925 [1955]. "Magic, Science and Religion." Joseph Needham, ed., *Science, Religion & Reality*. New York: Braziller. A pragmatic view of magical acts; a highly influential essay.
———. 1935 [1965]. *Coral Gardens and Their Magic*. 2 vols. Bloomington: Indiana University Press. An exhaustive treatment of magic in Trobriand society.
Marett, R. R. 1915. "Magic (Introductory)." *ERE* 8:245–52. A broad review of the concept, significant in particular for its critique of intellectualist theories of magic.
Mauss, Marcel. 1904 [1972]. *A General Theory of Magic*. Robert Brain, trans. London: Routledge & Kegan Paul.
Tylor, E. B. 1871 [1958]. *Primitive Culture*. 2 vols. New York: Harper & Brothers (Harper Torchbook). Takes an intellectualist perspective.
———. 1889. "Magic." *Encyclopaedia Britannica*, 9th ed., 15:199–206. A compact, evolutionist survey.
Wax, Murray, and Rosalie Wax. 1963. "The Notion of Magic." *CA* 4:495–518. A strong critique of the concept of magic.

Sources of Additional Information

For an historical account of European magic, see E. M. Butler, *Ritual Magic*, Cambridge: Cambridge University Press, 1949. E. E. Evans-Pritchard's *Theories of Primitive Religion*, Oxford: Clarendon Press, 1965, has much material on anthropological interpretations of magic. Hutton Webster's *Magic: A Sociological Study*, Stanford: Stanford University Press, 1948, though uncritically comparative in the spirit of Frazer, does give extensive references to magic from the more modern ethnographic literature. John Middleton, ed., *Magic, Witchcraft, and Curing*, Garden City, N.Y.: Natural History Press, 1967, provides a useful set of modern anthropological readings. For an unorthodox view linking magic and parapsychology, see Michael Winkelman, "Magic: A Theoretical Reassessment," *CA* 23:37–66, 1982.

MANA. In Polynesian and Melanesian cultures, the spiritual power or efficacy underlying successful human actions.

Mana, difficult to translate, is a Melanesian and Polynesian concept that involves a generalized spiritual power or efficacy, particularly as this is manifested in human action. One of the first references to mana occurred in Lorrin Andrews's Hawaiian dictionary (published 1836) where it was translated as "power, might, supernatural power, divine power" (Firth 1964:402). The linguistic history of the term is complex: Capell (1938) has argued that it originated in the Indonesian archipelago.

The concept of mana has received considerable attention in ANTHROPOLOGY, for at least three reasons. First, an adequate translation of the term has proved elusive: does it, for example, refer to belief in an abstract force in NATURE, or an intangible potency manifested in particular individuals? Second, the mana concept was invoked by a host of early twentieth century writers in theories of the EVOLUTION of RELIGION and MAGIC. Third, the term has gained greater attention because of arguments that it has close parallels in many non-Oceanian societies, for example, in native North America.

Although the term is more widely distributed in Polynesian languages, the classic definition of mana appeared in R. H. Codrington's study *The Melanesians* (1891): "The Melanesian mind is entirely possessed by the belief in a supernatural power or influence, called almost universally *mana*. That is what works to effect everything which is beyond the ordinary power of men, outside the common processes of nature" (Codrington 1891:118–19). Codrington also noted that

> it is a power or influence, not physical, and in a way supernatural; but it shews itself in physical force, or in any kind of power or excellence which a man possesses. This Mana is not fixed in anything, and can be conveyed in almost anything; but spirits, whether disembodied souls or supernatural beings, have it and can impart it. . . . All Melanesian religion consists, in fact, in getting this Mana for one's self, or getting it used for one's benefit. (Codrington 1891:118, n. 1)

Evolutionary Views

Nineteenth century speculations on religion first centered on the theory of ANIMISM, in which earliest religious experience derived from a belief in spirits, reflecting faulty reasoning regarding the dream state, the transition from life to death, and the like. Many found this intellectualist reconstruction of the evolution of religion unconvincing or at least incomplete. For many scholars the concept of mana offered a corrective, a view advanced, for example, in John King's *The Supernatural: Its Origin, Nature, and Evolution* (published 1892). As E. E. Evans-Pritchard has summarized the argument, "The ideas of ghost and spirit are too sophisticated for rude men. . . . There must . . . be an earlier stage than animism, a mana stage in which the idea of luck, of the canny and uncanny, was the sole constitutent" (Evans-Pritchard 1965:31). On this basis, the ideas of spell, charm, and magic emerged. R. R. Marett, in *The Threshold of Religion* (1909), advanced the paired phenomena of mana and TABOO as the irreducible basis of earliest religion, not yet differentiated from magic (the "magico-religious"). For Marett, *"Tabu* . . . is the negative mode of the supernatural, to which *mana* corresponds as the positive mode" (Marett 1909:667; see also ANIMISM).

If mana, as Marett and his contemporaries assumed, represented a distinct stage in the evolution of religion, it was logical to look to other CULTURE AREAS for counterparts to the mana concept. Through application of the COMPARATIVE METHOD, mana came to represent not only a specifically Oceanian phenomenon, but also "a class-name of world-wide application" (Marett 1915:377). Thus Marett associated the mana phenomenon with *manngur* of aboriginal Australia, *baraka* of North Africa, *hasina* of Madagascar, and in native North America, the Iroquoian *orenda*, Siouan *wakan*, and Algonquian *manitu* (Marett 1915:377–78). A number of later writers took the same position (Hocart 1922; Webster 1948: ch. 1; Birket-Smith 1965:348–350).

Later Empirical Studies

Later research, based upon more careful ETHNOGRAPHY, altered this view. Three points are relevant.

First, the evolutionary association of mana with magic or an early "magicoreligious" stage appears dubious. As Bronislaw Malinowski argued, "The real virtue of magic, as I know it from Melanesia, is fixed only in the spell and in its rite. . . . It never acts 'in all ways' [as Codrington said of mana], but only in ways specified by tradition" (Malinowski 1925:75; cf. Philsooph 1971).

Second, the interpretation of mana as an abstract power is no longer tenable: "It seems clear that *mana* did not mean to those to whose languages the word belonged the impersonal force—an almost metaphysical conception—which Marett and others . . . thought it did" (Evans-Pritchard 1965:33). Raymond Firth's study of mana on Tikopia (Solomon Islands) stressed its pragmatic character: "The Tikopia view of *manu* [= mana] may be regarded as an element in a theory of human achievement. Its thesis is that success above a certain point, the 'normal', is spirit-given. . . . Uncertainty in natural phenomena, differential human ability, dependence upon spirit entities, are the three primary factors in the manu situation" (Firth 1940:191).

Third, the phenomenon of mana in Oceania appears too distinctive to permit its extension cross-culturally. In Polynesia, in particular, mana stands in a complex relation with ideas of material success, social INEQUALITY, and taboo (Steiner 1967:36–40, 106–11). Terms of native North America, which Marett and others equated with mana (*orenda, wakan, manitu*, etc.), not only occur in a vastly different social and cultural context from that of Oceania, but also differ markedly in meaning one from another (Hultkrantz 1979:10–14).

References

Birket-Smith, Kaj. 1965. *The Paths of Culture: A General Ethnology*. Karin Fennow, trans. Madison: University of Wisconsin Press.

Capell, A. 1938. "The Word Mana: A Linguistic Study." *Oceania* 9:89–96. Capell argues for the historical derivation of mana from Indonesia.

Codrington, R. H. 1891 [1957]. *The Melanesians: Studies in their Anthropology and Folk-Lore*. New Haven, Conn.: HRAF Press. A classic work of Melanesian ethnography.

Evans-Pritchard, E. E. 1965. *Theories of Primitive Religion*. Oxford: Clarendon Press.

Firth, Raymond. 1940 [1967]. "The Analysis of *Mana*—an Empirical Approach." R. Firth, *Tikopia Ritual and Belief*. Boston: Beacon Press. One of the few detailed ethnographic studies of *mana*.

———. 1964. "Mana." Julius Gould and William L. Kolb, eds., *A Dictionary of the Social Sciences*. New York: Free Press, pp. 402–3.

Hocart, A. M. 1922. "Mana Again." *Man* (o.s.), Sept. 1922, 79:139–41. Hocart stressed the relationship between mana and chiefly authority.

Hultkrantz, Ake. 1979. *The Religions of the American Indians*. Monica Setterwall, trans. Berkeley and Los Angeles: University of California Press. Reviews supposed correlates of the mana concept in native North America.

Malinowski, Bronislaw. 1925 [1955]. "Magic, Science, and Religion." J. A. Needham, ed., *Science, Religion, and Reality*. New York: George Braziller.

Marett, R. R. 1909 [1931]. "The Conception of Mana." V. F. Calverton, ed., *The Making of Man: An Outline of Anthropology*. New York: Modern Library. An excerpt from his monograph *The Threshold of Religion*.

———. 1915. "Mana." *ERE* 8:375–80. A useful overview of Marett's position.

Philsooph, H. 1971. "Primitive Magic and Mana." *Man* (n.s.) 6:182–203. A useful review of the magic/mana debate.

Steiner, Franz. 1967. *Taboo*. Harmondsworth, England: Penguin. Considers the relation of taboo and mana.

Webster, Hutton. 1948. *Magic: A Sociological Study*. Stanford, Calif.: Stanford University Press. Gives extensive references to mana and related concepts.

Sources of Additional Information

The review of the concept by F. R. Lehmann, *Mana: Der Begriff des 'ausserordentlich Wirkungsvollen' bei Sudseevölkern*, 2d ed, Leipzig: Otto Spamer, 1922, cites much of the original literature. Roger M. Keesing, "Rethinking *Mana*," *Journal of Anthropological Research* 40:137–56, 1984, reviews the comparative linguistic evidence and provides an excellent overview of the debate on the interpretation of mana.

MARRIAGE. A socially recognized bond between two persons of opposite sex, with culturally variable implications, including economic cooperation, the transfer or sharing of property rights, sanctioned sexual intimacy, and the legitimation of children resulting from the union.

Marriage, as generally understood, involves the socially recognized association of a man and a woman, involving both sexual intimacy and economic interdependence. In most societies, this couple together with their children form a significant and enduring unit, the FAMILY, and the relationship between parents and children is publicly acknowledged and legally significant. Various of these generalizations, taken singly or together, have been used to define the institution of marriage.

George Peter Murdock has stressed the conjunction of socially approved sexuality and cooperation: "Sexual unions without economic cooperation are common, and there are relationships between men and women involving a division of labor without sexual gratification . . . but marriage exists only when the economic and the sexual are united into one relationship" (Murdock 1949:8). Others have tried to define marriage in functional terms, as serving to establish certain rights or statuses. For example, marriage is said to create legitimacy; it is "a union between a man and a woman such that children born to the woman are recognized legitimate offspring of both parents" (*Notes & Queries in Anthropology*, in Gough 1959:68). Thus, through marriage, sexuality and procreation are given specific cultural meanings. In most societies, by the fact of filiation (i.e., as offspring of their parents), children possess a socially recognized relationship with them, involving mutual rights and responsibilities.

These definitions notwithstanding, it has not proved possible to define a consistent set of rights or statuses established by marriage in all societies. Edmund Leach has noted that at least ten rights can be conferred by marriage, including rights of sexual intimacy, rights of legal fatherhood or motherhood, rights in the partner's labor, and rights over property. Yet no society establishes all such rights through marriage, nor is any of the ten identified by Leach implemented in all societies (Leach 1955:107–8). In short, "marriage is . . . 'a bundle of rights'; hence all universal definitions of marriage are vain" (Leach 1955:105).

Rodney Needham has expanded on this critique, arguing that the anthropological study of KINSHIP and marriage has suffered from what the philosopher Ludwig Wittgenstein termed "the craving for generality," the misconception that there must be some property shared by all items subsumed under a general term (Needham 1971:2; see also Wittgenstein 1958:17–19). In fact, as a recognized category of social relationship 'marriage' is not universal: a number of languages lack any such term (Needham 1971:6–7). In this fashion the debate over the concept of marriage has served as a point of attack in postwar social ANTHROPOLOGY against the naturalistic "science of society" espoused by A. R. Radcliffe-Brown, which assumed that a single set of supposedly objective categories describing social relationships could be usefully applied to each and every society (see FUNCTIONALISM; KINSHIP; and INTERPRETATION).

Forms of Marriage

The study of marriage systems has resulted in a complex terminology. Such marriage patterns can be analyzed in terms of both the rules governing recruitment of marriage partners (exogamy and endogamy) and the structure of the family unit.

Patterns of exogamy and endogamy. From the standpoint of a given individual, the rest of society (of opposite sex) can be divided into those who are eligible marriage partners and those who are not. In almost all societies close consanguines (e.g., father/daughter, brother/sister) are barred from sexual relations, the violation constituting incest (see FAMILY). However, in many kin-based societies (see TRIBE), those excluded from the marriage pool may be far more numerous, encompassing the entirety of an individual's DESCENT group (for example, a lineage, clan, or moiety). Such groups, whose members are forbidden to intermarry, are termed exogamous. Conversely, many societies have rules specifying that one must marry within a given group; such groups are termed endogamous. The two are not mutually exclusive. In the Indian CASTE system, for example, one must (with certain exceptions) marry out of one's lineage but within one's caste group; there is thus lineage exogamy and caste endogamy.

Patterns of exogamy may be further analyzed in terms of status differences between the groups exchanging marriage partners. Where the groups are required or preferred to be of equal status, the marriage exchange is isogamous. Where the husband's group is to be of higher status than that of the wife's, the exchange is hypergamous. Where, in contrast, the husband's group is to be of lower status than that of the wife's, the exchange is hypogamous. (For a discussion of hypergamy in India see Dumont 1970:116–18; regarding hypogamy in highland Burma see Leach 1951.)

Structure of the family. Considerable variation in marital arrangements occurs cross-culturally. Monogamy describes marriage between one husband and one wife. Polygamy, in contrast, describes marriage involving multiple spouses, whether male or female. A situation in which one husband is married to several wives is termed polygyny; that of one wife married to several husbands (a far less common pattern) is termed polyandry. Where plural wives are also sisters the pattern is termed sororal polygyny (or the *sororate*); where plural husbands are also brothers the pattern is termed adelphic (or fraternal) polyandry. A related CUSTOM is the levirate (Lat. *levir* = husband's brother), in which a man has the right to marry the widow of his deceased brother (see Deut. 25:5).

Early Anthropology

The topics of marriage and sexuality have preoccupied the anthropological imagination from the times of the earliest ETHNOGRAPHY, muddying an already complex topic with a variety of fantasies and stereotypes. Alien CULTURES were frequently depicted as sexually promiscuous, more bestial than human in their behavior and dispositions. Herodotus (fifth century B.C.) gave a characteristic example in describing the Auseans of Libya: "These people do not marry or live in families, but copulate promiscuously like cattle. When their children are well-grown, they are brought before the assembly of the men, which is held every third month, and assigned to those whom they most resemble" (*Persian Wars* 4.180). The Roman historian Tacitus (first century A.D.) provided a more flattering (and probably more accurate) description of the marriage customs of the German tribes, noting that monogamy was predominant, the exception being those few whose "noble birth procures for them many offers of alliance" (*Germ.* 18). He also provided a careful explanation of their marriage payments from groom to bride (or more strictly, from the groom's family to the bride's family), the custom of bridewealth.

The interest in alien forms of marriage and eroticism was a significant feature of Renaissance and later exploration literature. In Johann Boemus's sixteenth-century ethnology, the *Fardle of Facions*, marital customs, including forms of plural marriage, were given particular attention, with detailed descriptions of customs in twenty-three societies. Boemus also treated related topics such as endogamy and exogamy, dowry (wealth transferred from the bride's family to her and her husband), provisions for divorce, and punishment for adultery (Hodgen 1964:138–39).

Victorian Theories of Marriage

The study of marriage systems formed a topic of particular fascination for Victorian anthropology. The writings of three scholars—Henry Maine, John McLennan, and Lewis Henry Morgan—illustrate the types of research (and speculation) characteristic of this era.

Henry Maine (1822–1888) was fundamentally a legal historian, and his anthropologically significant writings, notably *Ancient Law* (1861), reflect an effort to utilize the evidence of classical legal codes to reconstruct earlier stages of human society. Maine held that early societies were built of essentially autonomous patriarchal family units, in which the father exercised total authority. Under early Roman law the father had literally the power of life and death over his children. Furthermore, he was able to "give a wife to his son; he can give his daughter in marriage; he can divorce his children of either sex; he can transfer them to another family by adoption; and he can sell them" (Maine 1861:81). By these ancient principles, moreover, the wife took on the legal fetters of a daughter, subject in the same fashion to the total authority of her husband (Maine 1861:91). This system of patriarchal authority, termed *patria potestas*, provided Maine with his key model for the reconstruction of ancient society.

In *Primitive Marriage* (1865) John McLennan offered an ambitious interpretation of the entire evolutionary development of marriage, from earliest times (which Maine did not venture to reconstruct) to the present. McLennan (1827–1881) began with an interpretation of the "Form of Capture in Marriage Ceremonies," seeing in such RITUALS a SURVIVAL of actual bride-capture between warring societies. Such marriage by capture he associated with group exogamy (a term he coined), polyandry, and—as "certainty as to fathers is impossible where mothers are stolen from their first lords—matrilineal descent (McLennan 1865:91). As he noted, "wherever capture, or the form of capture [i.e., as a survival], prevails, or has prevailed, there prevails, or has prevailed, exogamy" (McLennan 1865:57). From this theoretical vantage point he argued both backward, to a postulated original condition of "general promiscuity," and forward, to the replacement of matrilineal with patrilineal forms of descent. In his focal stage, that of matrilineal descent, polyandry was at first general, but later was transformed into the sharing of a wife by several brothers (fraternal polyandry), which McLennan interpreted as a necessary foundation for the development of patrilineal societies, and ultimately the emergence of monogamous patterns of marriage (McLennan 1865: ch. 8).

The evolutionary stages postulated by Lewis Henry Morgan (1818–1881) follow in broad terms those advanced by McLennan. Morgan's theories of the evolution of marriage and family were distinctive, however, in being based in large part on exhaustive studies of kin terminology (see KINSHIP). Working from the assumption that kin terms must reflect ancient marriage practices (rather than patterns of ECONOMY, residence, descent, and the like), he concluded that "the classificatory system of relationship . . . originated in the intermarriage of brothers and sisters in a communal family, and that this was the normal state of marriage . . . in the early part of the unmeasured ages of barbarism" (Morgan 1871:vi). In his evolutionary scheme, an original promiscuity (the "consanguineal family"), later modified by the prohibition of marriage between siblings (the "punaluan family"), led in turn to a transient and informal marriage of individuals (the "syndyasmian family"), and culminated in the monogamous ("monogamian") families of CIVILIZATION (Morgan 1877). Like McLennan, Morgan assumed a transition from a matrilineal to a patrilineal system of descent; furthermore, he held that such descent systems implied the existence of clans, each symbolized through a clan totem (see TOTEMISM) (Morgan 1877: e.g., 155–90, 353–67).

In the main, Victorian social evolutionists accepted McLennan's major arguments: the interpretation of marriage as a mechanism for controlling sexuality; the existence of some early form of general promiscuity; and the priority of matrilineal descent, though incorporating Maine's doctrine of patriarchy as a step in the evolutionary sequence (Stocking 1987:204). Yet by the 1880s and 1890s this picture had come under serious criticism. C. Staniland Wake's *The Development of Marriage and Kinship* (1889) offered strong refutations of many of McLennan's key ideas, attacking among other points the evidence adduced for an original state of general promiscuity, and his explanation of customs symbolizing marriage by capture (Wake 1889: chs. 2, 11). Edward Westermarck's *The History of Human Marriage* (originally published in 1891) likewise strongly criticized McLennan on these points (Westermarck 1925). Finally, John Swanton (1905) examined what he termed the "totemic clan theory" (seen most clearly in Morgan's writings), refuting both the supposed priority of matrilineal over patrilineal systems of descent and the consistent association of a matrilineal principle with clans and totems.

Modern Studies of Marriage Systems

Descent and alliance theories. After 1900 interest shifted from broad reconstructions of the evolutionary development of marriage forms to detailed studies of kinship and marriage within particular societies, reflecting the growing sophistication of ethnography in this period. For the most part, marriage as an institution was analytically subordinated to kin terminology, clan organization, and residence pattern.

The gradual ascendancy of functionalism in the 1930s through the 1950s, particularly as espoused by A. R. Radcliffe-Brown, reinforced this trend. In British social anthropology in particular, the key concept of kinship studies became the unilineal descent group (clan, lineage, etc.). Affiliation based on common descent was interpreted as the key determinant not only of the domestic world of kinship, but equally of the wider political relationships organizing an entire society (Fortes 1953:23).

An alternative to this viewpoint became prominent in the 1960s, although its intellectual roots lie considerably earlier. Often termed alliance theory, this position identified relationships based on marriage rather than on an ideology of common descent as the critical factor linking localized clans or lineages within tribal societies. Alliance theory reflected the perspective of STRUCTURALISM, with its emphasis on exchange and systems of opposition. The field of kinship and marriage, in fact, provided the first significant application in anthropology of what was at the time a dramatically novel perspective. The key work for the structuralist study of marriage was Claude Lévi-Strauss's *Elementary Structures of Kinship*, originally appearing in 1949 (Lévi-Strauss 1967); however, important contributions were also made in the 1950s by Edmund Leach's studies of the Kachin of Burma (Leach 1951, 1954) and Louis Dumont's analyses of Tamil-speaking South India (Dumont 1957).

As far as kinship studies are concerned, anthropological interest has not focused on those societies (such as the contemporary United States) in which marriage involves (in Leach's phrase) "the whims of two persons acting as private individuals." The concern, rather, has been with institutionalized marriage, "a systematically organized affair which forms part of a series of contractual obligations between two social groups" (Leach 1951:56). Structuralists such as Lévi-Strauss concerned themselves specifically with those patterns of exchange or alliance generated by preferential or prescriptive marriage rules, yielding so-called elementary structures of kinship. Elementary structures are those which permit "the immediate determination of the circle of kin and that of affines, that is, those systems which prescribe marriage with a certain type of relative" (Lévi-Strauss 1967:xxiii).

Forms of alliance. The most common preferential pattern is that termed cross-cousin marriage, in which (within a society based on exogamous unilineal descent groups) the preferred marriage partner is one related through genealogical links of both genders, for example, MBD (mother's brother's daughter) or FZS (father's sister's son). Assuming either a patrilineal or matrilineal rule of descent, this pattern will assure that the match involves different lineages and is thus not incestuous. As Lévi-Strauss and Leach among others have demonstrated, the particular marriage rule followed in a given society yields a distinctive exchange relationship between the social groups involved.

Three patterns can be distinguished: (1) A bilateral or symmetrical (*Kariera* type) cross-cousin marriage rule involves two groups joined in an essentially simultaneous exchange by the rule MBD = ZHZ; that is, the spouse related to a given individual (ego) consanguineally, as the real or classificatory mother's brother's daughter, is also linked affinally through a corresponding marriage as sister's husband's sister. (2) A patrilateral (or *Trobriand* type) rule specifies FZD (father's sister's daughter) as the preferred partner, yielding a delayed exchange between two groups, involving a lag of one generation to complete the cycle. (3) A matrilateral (or *Kachin*) rule specifies MBD (mother's brother's daughter) as the preferred partner, yielding a more complex pattern in which the exchange relationship necessarily involves more than two groups (Leach 1951:59–60).

These details aside, the essential point from the structuralist perspective is that through such elementary structures marriage serves to link social groups in ongoing relations of reciprocity. As Dumont has stated, specifying the cross-cousin as marriage partner "causes marriage to be transmitted much as membership in the descent group is transmitted. With it, marriage acquires a diachronic dimension, it becomes an institution enduring from generation to generation, which I therefore call 'marriage alliance'" (Dumont 1957:24). One of the results of structuralist alliance theory was to return marriage to a central place in kinship studies. There has, however, been no shortage of controversy (see Korn 1973). There has been prolonged argument regarding whether such models involve prescribed or merely preferential marriage patterns; whether they specify actual or classificatory kin; and most importantly, whether these depict idealized, conceptual patterns underlying social life (see SOCIAL STRUCTURE), or actual, regularly occurring marriage exchange (see Buchler and Selby 1968: chs. 5–6; Kuper 1988: ch. 11).

Complex Marriage Patterns

Modern anthropology has shown less enthusiasm for the study of marriage outside such highly institutionalized kinship structures. Yet two complementary research directions are broadening the scope of the anthropological study of marriage, kinship, and family. On the one hand, anthropologists have undertaken ethnographic studies of marriage patterns and family life in urban, industrial societies: for example, in working-class London (Young and Wilmott 1957), and in black ghettos of the United States (Stack 1974). On the other hand, kinship and marriage in tribe-based societies have been studied increasingly not as abstract social-structural patterns, but as reflections of basic cultural assumptions regarding sexuality, procreation, and GENDER, for the most part interpreted from a symbolic perspective (Goodale 1980; see also SYMBOLISM).

References

Buchler, Ira R., and Henry A. Selby. 1968. *Kinship and Social Organization*. New York: Macmillan.

Dumont, Louis. 1957. "Hierarchy and Marriage Alliance in South Indian Kinship." Royal Anthropological Institute (London), *Occasional Papers*, 12. An important statement regarding relations of affinity as a key to social structure.

———. 1970. *Homo Hierarchicus: The Caste System and Its Implications*. Mark Sainsbury, trans. Chicago: University of Chicago Press.

Fortes, Meyer. 1953. "The Structure of Unilineal Descent Groups." *AA* 55:17–41. An authoritative summary of functionalist descent theory.

Goodale, Jane C. 1980. "Gender, Sexuality and Marriage: A Kaulong Model of Nature and Culture." Carol P. MacCormack and Marilyn Strathern, eds., *Nature, Culture and Gender*. Cambridge: Cambridge University Press.

Gough, E. Kathleen. 1959 [1968]. "The Nayars and the Definition of Marriage." Paul Bohannon and John Middleton, eds., *Marriage, Family, and Residence*. Garden City, N.Y.: Natural History Press.

Hodgen, Margaret T. 1964. *Early Anthropology in the Sixteenth and Seventeenth Centuries*. Philadelphia: University of Pennsylvania Press.

Korn, Francis. 1973. *Elementary Structures Reconsidered: Lévi-Strauss on Kinship*. Berkeley and Los Angeles: University of California Press. A critical examination of Lévi-Strauss's *Elementary Structures*.

Kuper, Adam. 1988. *The Invention of Primitive Society*. London: Routledge.

Leach, Edmund. 1951 [1961]. "The Structural Implications of Matrilateral Cross-Cousin Marriage." E. R. Leach, *Rethinking Anthropology*. London: Athlone Press. An early work of alliance theory.

———. 1954. *Political Systems of Highland Burma*. Boston: Beacon Press. An important study of marriage alliances and political relationships among the Kachin.

———. 1955 [1961]. "Polyandry, Inheritance and the Definition of Marriage: With Particular Reference to Sinhalese Customary Law." E. R. Leach, *Rethinking Anthropology*. London: Athlone Press.

Lévi-Strauss, Claude. 1967. *The Elementary Structures of Kinship*. Rev. ed. J. H. Bell and J. R. von Sturmer, trans. Boston: Beacon Press. 1st ed. 1949. The key work in the structuralist study of kinship and marriage.

Maine, Henry. 1861 [1972]. *Ancient Law*. New York: Everyman's Library. A Victorian classic, offering the patriarchal family as the evolutionary origin of marriage and society.

McLennan, John F. 1865 [1970]. *Primitive Marriage: An Inquiry into the Origin of the Form of Capture in Marriage Ceremonies*. Peter Rivière, ed. Chicago: University of Chicago Press. An influential text, advocating the priority of matrilineal kinship in the evolution of marriage.

Morgan, Lewis H. 1871. *Systems of Consanguinity and Affinity of the Human Family*. Washington, D.C.: Smithsonian Institution. A massive, comparative study of kinship terminology.

———. 1877. *Ancient Society*. Chicago: Charles H. Kerr.

Murdock, George Peter. 1949. *Social Structure*. New York: Macmillan. An important synthesis, from the cross-cultural survey perspective.

Needham, Rodney. 1971. "Remarks on the Analysis of Kinship and Marriage." R. Needham, ed., *Rethinking Kinship and Marriage*. London: Tavistock.

Stack, Carol. 1974. *All Our Kin: Strategies for Survival in a Black Community*. New York: Harper & Row.

Stocking, George W., Jr. 1987. *Victorian Anthropology*. New York: Free Press.

Swanton, John R. 1905. "The Social Organization of American Tribes." *AA* 7:663–73. An effective rebuttal of the supposed priority of matrilineal kinship.

Wake, C. Staniland. 1889 [1967]. *The Development of Marriage and Kinship*. Rodney Needham, ed. Chicago: University of Chicago Press. A much neglected synthesis and critique.

Westermarck, Edward. 1925. *The History of Human Marriage*. 5th ed. London: Mac-
    millan. 1st ed. 1891.
Wittgenstein, Ludwig. 1958. *The Blue and Brown Books*. New York: Harper & Row.
Young, Michael, and Peter Wilmott. 1957 [1980]. "Husbands and Mothers." George
    Gmelch and Walter Zenner, eds., *Urban Life*. New York: St. Martin's Press.

Sources of Additional Information

A useful introduction is provided by Robin Fox, *Kinship and Marriage: An Anthropological Perspective*, Harmondsworth, England: Penguin, 1967. A fairly accessible
comparison of functionalist and structuralist approaches to kinship and marriage is provided in J. A. Barnes, *Three Styles in the Study of Kinship*, Berkeley and Los Angeles:
University of California Press, 1971; a somewhat more technical comparison is provided
by Louis Dumont, *Introduction à deux théories d'anthropologie sociale: groupes de
filiation et alliance de mariage*, Paris: Mouton, 1971. Regarding the transactions of dowry
and bridewealth, see Jack Goody and S. J. Tambiah, *Bridewealth and Dowry*, Cambridge:
Cambridge University Press, 1973; and Laurel Bossen, "Toward a Theory of Marriage:
The Economic Anthropology of Marriage Transactions," *Ethnology* 27:127–44, 1988.

MATERIALISM. As a methodological principle, the explanation of events or
behavior in terms of material factors such as environment, technology, or
ECONOMY, rather than on the basis of non-material factors such as belief or
custom.

The concept of materialism encompasses several distinct though related sets
of beliefs. One should distinguish between materialism as a doctrine regarding
the nature of the universe and human existence (the realm of ontology), and
materialism as a set of principles guiding the explanation of events and human
behavior (methodology). Within the history of ANTHROPOLOGY, materialism
figured in nineteenth century debate chiefly through the opposition of materialistic
and theistic (religious) WORLD VIEWS, notably in discussions of EVOLUTION. In
the twentieth century, the concept has figured chiefly in debates over method,
material being opposed to mental or idealist factors (such as belief, personality,
or custom) in the explanation of social life. Materialist doctrine has a long history.
The Greek philosopher Democritus (fifth century B.C.) held that "there are atoms
and the void," the diversity of things arising from the movements and combinations of atoms (Hook 1933:209). Both the Epicurean and Stoic schools of
Greek philosophy had materialist premises. Mind, experience, or consciousness
were in this view reducible to more fundamental material processes. Beginning
in the later Renaissance, practical problems of engineering and warfare stimulated
the development of experimental method in the sciences, and with it the revival
of a materialist perspective in European thought (Hook 1933:210–11). The philosopher Thomas Hobbes (1588–1679) was a notable exponent of materialism:
"Life is but a motion of limbs. . . . What is the heart, but a spring; and the
nerves, but so many strings; and the joints, but so many wheels, giving motion
to the whole body" (Hobbes 1651:5).

In the eighteenth century, materialism became a key doctrine for many writers of the Enlightenment, such as Denis Diderot (1713–1784) and the Baron d'Holbach (1723–1789). For the Enlightenment, materialist philosophy and social progress were logically related. "At one stroke the doctrine of original sin and natural grace were ruled out in accounting for differences in political, social or biological status; the way was cleared for the infinite perfectibility of man through reasoned control of nature" (Hook 1933:212). This perspective had its influence on the nineteenth century, notably through the writings of Karl Marx (Lichtheim 1973:451).

The Emergence of Materialism in Anthropology

Through the nineteenth century—within scientific and lay circles alike—proponents of theological and naturalistic INTERPRETATIONS contended over the appropriate explanation of biological, geological, and archaeological data. Theories of biological evolution were criticized for effacing the sovereign place of *Homo sapiens* in the natural order and substituting for it a materialist and antitheological world view. The geologist Adam Sedgwick was characteristic of his era when, in 1845, he attacked the evolutionary theories of Robert Chambers for implying "that all the phenomena of the universe [were] the progression and development of a rank, unbending, and degrading materialism," making human law mere folly, and RELIGION a lie (in Stocking 1987:42). The debate intensified dramatically with the publication of Charles Darwin's *The Origin of Species*, in 1859. Its novel theory (that of natural selection) and wealth of data provided for the first time a convincing argument for a materialist interpretation of biological evolution (Bowler 1989: chs. 7, 8).

Darwinism had definite influence on anthropologists such as Edward Tylor and John Lubbock (Stocking 1987: ch. 5). Nonetheless, the predominant approach of Victorian evolutionary anthropology was intellectualist, not materialist. Explanation for the transformation of CULTURE was sought in the growth of knowledge or the gradual refinement of reason. For writers such as Lubbock and Tylor, it was ultimately the progressive and cumulative character of human RATIONALITY that had yielded an evolving technology, a more complex social organization, and more refined systems of religious belief (see PSYCHIC UNITY).

There were significant exceptions. The British philosopher and sociologist Herbert Spencer (1820–1903) propounded a comprehensive theory of evolution—physical, biological, and cultural—that was predominantly materialist in character. In his analysis of the factors shaping "social evolution" (written in 1876) he included environment and the effects of its transformation by human action, the scale and density of human settlement ("at once a consequence and a cause of social progress"), the interaction of societies, and the accumulation of knowledge and technique (Spencer [1972]:122–26; see also Nonini 1985:10–14). Lewis Henry Morgan (1818–1881), in *Ancient Society* (1877), advanced a reconstruction of cultural evolution that included some strongly materialist elements (notably in his discussion of the "arts of subsistence"), though taken as a whole the work was methodologically eclectic (Morgan 1877; Harding et al. 1964; Harris 1968:213–15).

Karl Marx (1818–1883), like Darwin and Spencer, must be considered one of the preeminent materialist writers of the Victorian period. Marx and his colleague Friedrich Engels (1820–1895) presented a sweeping interpretation of history based on the idea of class struggle, a process shaping the transformation of societies, as for example medieval feudalism was transformed into the capitalist production of modern Europe (Marx and Engels 1848: ch. 1).

Marx offered the social sciences a methodological program, a specifically materialist approach to history and human behavior. He wrote in 1859 that "the mode of production of material life conditions the social, political and intellectual life-process in general. It is not the consciousness of men that determines their being, but on the contrary their social being that determines their consciousness" (in Lichtheim 1973:451). In short, for Marx, historically constituted material conditions (in particular, the forms of economic production) shape the other domains of social life, notably politics, LAW, and ideology.

Twentieth Century Development

A weak form of materialist argument was implicit in the concept of CULTURE AREA: Such correlations between environmental type and cultural expression had been recognized since the later nineteenth century. Nonetheless, systematically materialist theories of culture proved uncongenial in American or British anthropology until the 1950s. Boasian HISTORICISM, which dominated American anthropology in the first several decades of the century, was explicitly inductivist, valuing data rather than theory, and implicitly idealist, recognizing CULTURE as itself an explanatory variable (Harris 1968:260–67). Franz Boas (1858–1942) was, in fact, something of an apostate from materialism. Originally trained in geography, he abandoned a geographic determinism in favor of culture as the mediating factor in our experience of the environment (Stocking 1968: ch. 7). British FUNCTIONALISM likewise discouraged the exploration of materialist hypotheses by narrowing the ethnographer's gaze to the interaction of roles within a complex SOCIAL STRUCTURE.

Within American anthropology, Leslie White (1900–1975) and Julian Steward (1902–1972) were influential in developing a materialist perspective in modern culture theory. In contrast to the dominant perspective of Boasian anthropology, White insisted that cultural evolution should be the central concern of the discipline, a process to be understood as the reflection of an ever-increasing technological complexity and utilization of energy (White 1949:363–93). Social systems, in his view, were "determined by technological systems" (1949:391). Quite inconsistently, White also insisted that culture was a phenomenon sui generis, to be explained on its own terms (White 1949:125; see also Barrett 1989, Harris 1968: ch. 22; see SUPERORGANIC). While White's focus was on energy and technology, the work of Steward emphasized culture as a mechanism of ecological ADAPTATION. His pioneering study of hunter-gatherer BANDS and their social-structural adaptations to the Great Basin environment has served as a model for later research (Steward 1938; see Harris 1968: ch. 23).

Since the 1960s, the materialist tradition in anthropology has developed into several distinct theoretical programs. One approach—building on the work of Steward—has emphasized the complex relations holding between culture and environment, understood as an ecological SYSTEM (see CULTURAL ECOLOGY; ADAPTATION). A second, cultural materialism, has combined the methodological strictures of positivism with a narrowly materialist approach to the explanation of culture. A third, broadly termed Marxist anthropology, has applied the Marxist perspective to the diverse data of ETHNOLOGY. The latter two schools are briefly treated below.

Cultural Materialism

The cultural materialist perspective, associated in particular with the work of Marvin Harris (1968, 1979), has been distinguished by its insistence on methodological explicitness (operationalism), its emphasis on observable phenomena (empiricism), and its strongly materialist determinism. Harris has argued that ethnographic analysis must rigorously distinguish the record of behavior from the record of mental states. Ethnographers should likewise differentiate between cultural interpretations based on the cognitive categories of outside observers and those based on the categories of participants (etic and emic analysis, respectively) (Harris 1979:33–34; see EMIC/ETIC). Cultural materialism has strongly emphasized the behavioral and etic over the mental and emic in seeking explanations of cultural phenomena. These preferences reflect the underlying theoretical assumptions of cultural materialism, in particular an insistence on the determining effect of material conditions on the immaterial dimensions of culture (e.g., SOCIAL STRUCTURE, MYTH, and RITUAL).

Cultural materialists (Harris 1979:55–56; Ross 1980:xviii) have stressed continuity with Marx's writings, for example, in the analytic distinction of base and superstructure. In reality, what was for Marx a rather general contrast between the organization of production and its associated political forms and ideologies became for the cultural materialists a three-tiered model of cultural analysis (infrastructure, structure, superstructure), with a more rigid determinism. For Harris, infrastructure encompasses both the mode of production ("the technology and practices employed for expanding or limiting basic subsistence production") and the mode of reproduction ("the technology and practices employed for expanding, limiting, and maintaining population size"). These are held to determine structure, comprising the domestic economy (family structure and domestic division of labor) and the political economy (political organization and social hierarchy). Structure in turn determines superstructure, the ideational realm of symbolism, myth, philosophy, religion, and TABOO (Harris 1979:52–54).

For the cultural materialists, in short, the explanation of cultural systems rests almost entirely on diet, technology, population, and environment. Thus Harris has argued that restrictions such as the Hindu taboo on killing cattle (the "sacred cow" complex) "originate as adaptive responses to infrastructural conditions and that they enhance the material well-being" of the population (Harris 1979:242–43). For Harris, it is infrastructural factors, such as the need for animal traction, rather than Hindu ideology, which explain the "sacred cow" complex (Harris 1979:247). In a similar vein, Aztec sacrifice has been explained as a cannibalistic effort at increasing protein intake (Harris 1979:336). Such interpretations, at least for the nonbeliever, can appear strongly reductionistic (Friedman 1974:466; Nonini 1985:23–49; cf. Harris 1979:70–75). For proponents, in contrast, cultural materialism offers a necessary corrective to idealist approaches (see SYMBOLISM; INTERPRETATION; ETHNOSCIENCE), which by overemphasizing belief or inward experience remove culture from the arena of the scientifically knowable (Ross 1980:xix-xx).

Marxist Anthropology

Although Karl Marx was a nineteenth-century figure, his influence on anthropology has been a twentieth-century phenomenon. What distinguishes Marx from the other figures considered here is his political intent. He wrote not to create theory, but to guide revolutionary political action: "The philosophers have only interpreted the world, in various ways; the point is to change it" (Marx 1846:123). Both the following that his ideas attracted and the violent opposition which they provoked, are part of twentieth century history.

As a consequence, any discussion of Marxist ideas in the nonsocialist countries has carried a heavy stigma, particularly in the United States. Hence the oddly truncated character of most materialist-oriented writings in twentieth-century anthropology. As Eleanor Leacock has rightly noted, Marx is "the constantly present but seldom acknowledged embarrassment when matters of fundamental theory are being discussed" (in Harding et al. 1964:110). In the 1960s this situation began to change. Both in Europe and in the United States a number of writers sought quite explicitly to apply Marxist principles to anthropological problems (see Bloch 1975; Godelier 1977).

"There is not *one* Marxism but rather many Marxist tendencies, schools, trends, and research projects" (Lefebvre 1988:75). This is also true for the more restricted realm of Marxist anthropology. Despite this diversity, there are a number of common assumptions that serve to distinguish Marxist anthropology not only from the mentalist and symbolic viewpoints, but also from seemingly related perspectives, such as cultural materialism and ecological anthropology.

Four assumptions are particularly important. (1) The act of production—the creation of utility through human labor—is central to the understanding of human societies. (2) Although material conditions are ultimately determinative, the relation of material and ideal is dialectical. History reflects a complex interplay between action and thought, economy and ideology, base and superstructure. (3) Marxist analysis is inherently social: its concern is not with the behavior of individuals considered in the abstract, but with the social relationships engendered by patterns of production, ownership, and inequality. (4) Marxist theory is dynamic and historical, assuming conflict between social groups, and seeking to explain the long-term, evolutionary transformations of societies.

Marxist approaches have been applied to many aspects of anthropology. Such perspectives have been particularly significant in the study of social stratification (see INEQUALITY), the interrelation of economic activity and social structure (see MODE OF PRODUCTION; ECONOMY), the impacts of industrial states on the agrarian economies of the Third World (see DEVELOPMENT; PEASANTRY), and processes of indigenous social transformation (see SOCIAL MOVEMENT).

References

Barrett, Richard A. 1989. "The Paradoxical Anthropology of Leslie White." *AA* 91:986–99.
Bloch, Maurice, ed. 1975. *Marxist Analyses and Social Anthropology*. London: Malaby Press. Provides a selection of both British and French Marxist views.
Bowler, Peter J. 1989. *Evolution: The History of an Idea*. Rev. ed. Berkeley and Los Angeles: University of California Press.
Friedman, Jonathan. 1974. "Marxism, Structuralism and Vulgar Materialism." *Man* (n.s.) 9:444–69.
Godelier, Maurice. 1977. *Perspectives in Marxist Anthropology*. Cambridge: Cambridge University Press. An important collection of essays, emphasizing the analysis of social structures and modes of production.
Harding, Thomas G., et al. 1964. "Morgan and Materialism: A Reply to Professor Opler." *CA* 5:109–14.
Harris, Marvin. 1968. *The Rise of Anthropological Theory*. New York: Crowell. A useful if tendentious history; an intellectual pedigree for cultural materialism.
———. 1979. *Cultural Materialism: The Struggle for a Science of Culture*. New York: Random House.
Hobbes, Thomas. 1651 [1957?]. *Leviathan*. Michael Oakeshott, ed. Oxford: Blackwell.
Hook, Sidney. 1933. "Materialism." *ESS* 10:209–20. Useful coverage of early materialist traditions.
Lefebvre, Henri. 1988. "Toward a Leftist Cultural Politics." Cary Nelson and Lawrence Grossberg eds., *Marxism and the Interpretation of Culture*. Urbana: University of Illinois Press.
Lichtheim, George. 1973. "Historical and Dialectical Materialism." *DHI* 2:450–56. Treats the shifting understandings of materialism within Marxism.
Marx, Karl. 1846 [1970]. "Theses on Feuerbach." In Karl Marx and Friedrich Engels, *The German Ideology*, abr. C. J. Arthur, ed. New York: International Publishers. The volume, fortunately abridged, provides texts of considerable relevance to anthropology.
———, and Friedrich Engels. 1848 [1965]. *Manifesto of the Communist Party*. Peking: Foreign Languages Press.
Morgan, Lewis Henry. 1877. *Ancient Society*. Chicago: Charles H. Kerr.
Nonini, Donald M. 1985. "Varieties of Materialism." *Dialectical Anthropology* 9:7–63. An intellectual history of materialism in anthropology, from a Marxist viewpoint.
Ross, Eric B. 1980. "Introduction." E. Ross, ed., *Beyond the Myths of Culture: Essays in Cultural Materialism*. New York: Academic Press.
Spencer, Herbert. [1972]. *On Social Evolution*. J. D. Y. Peel, ed. Chicago: University of Chicago Press.

Steward, Julian H. 1938. *Basin-Plateau Aboriginal Sociopolitical Groups*. Bureau of American Ethnology, *Bulletin*, 120. An influential text for ecological anthropology.

Stocking, George W., Jr. 1968. *Race, Culture, and Evolution: Essays in the History of Anthropology*. New York: Free Press.

————. 1987. *Victorian Anthropology*. New York: Free Press.

White, Leslie A. 1949. *The Science of Culture*. New York: Grove Press. Significant essays, emphasizing cultural evolution and materialism.

Sources of Additional Information

For a discussion of the place of materialism in doctrines of human nature, see Aram Vartanian, "Man-Machine from the Greeks to the Computer," *DHI* 3:131–46, 1973. For a helpful, nondoctrinaire introduction to Marx see David McLellan, *The Thought of Karl Marx: An Introduction*, New York: Harper & Row, 1971. A useful introduction to Marxist anthropology is provided by Bridget O'Laughlin, "Marxist Approaches in Anthropology," *ARA* 4:341–70, 1975. For a readable introduction to cultural materialism, see Marvin Harris, *Cows, Pigs, Wars, and Witches*, New York: Random House, 1974.

MEDICINE. See CURING.

MIGRATION. A relatively permanent movement of peoples across ethnological or political boundaries.

Migration has been a fundamental force in shaping human societies, from the mid-Pleistocene movements of *Homo erectus* into Eurasia, and the late Pleistocene peopling of the Americas, to the movement of economic and political refugees between nations and continents over the last century. However, migration entails more than movement: It implies a geographic or cultural transition in a fashion that disrupts if it does not sever ties with an original ecosystem and SOCIAL STRUCTURE (see also ETHNICITY). It therefore contrasts with movement within the bounds of an adaptive SYSTEM, as in the seasonal round of hunter-gatherers, or the transhumant movement of pastoralists (see ADAPTATION). Migration is also an emic notion (see EMIC/ETIC) occurring in many bodies of MYTH, as in the biblical account of the Israelites' departure from Egypt (Exod. 12–18).

Migration and Ethnology

Writers of the Renaissance and later periods readily speculated regarding migrations as the formative events of culture history. As Colin Renfrew has commented, "The biblical Lost Tribes, the Etruscan migrations of Herodotus, and the Phoenecian merchants of Strabo, for example, served for centuries as a model for the explanation of Europe's remote past, unsupported in many cases by any evidence whatsoever" (Renfrew 1979:263). More reasonably, various migrations were postulated to explain the American Indians. For Hugo Grotius (1583–1645) the native North Americans descended from Scandinavia, the Yucatecans from Ethiopia, Peruvians from China, while others migrated from Melanesia. Matthew Hale (1609–1676) less ingeniously derived the American Indians from Asia (Slotkin 1965:97–99).

Migration has been used to explain even the most tenuous similarities between cultures, a phenomenon that Robert Wauchope has termed the "lost tribes and sunken continents" approach to ETHNOLOGY (Wauchope 1962). Yet migration has been far less common as a formative factor in culture history than the more general process of cultural DIFFUSION without movements of population. Alfred Kroeber emphasized the fallaciousness of "invoking a national migration for every important cultural diffusion," arguing that "most culture changes from without have occurred through subtler and more gradual or piecemeal operations" (Kroeber 1948:473). Furthermore, many apparent parallels that had been ascribed to diffusion or migration (e.g., megalithic structures in European prehistory) are now recognized to be the product of multiple, independent invention (Renfrew 1979; see also EVOLUTION).

In contrast to the assumptions of the more extreme theorists of diffusion, the process of migration typically entails considerable CULTURE CHANGE for the immigrant population. As Thomas Jackson has noted regarding aboriginal California, "Newly arrived populations are often among the most culturally plastic societies, and endeavor to accommodate themselves in conjunction with in situ social groups" (Jackson 1986:9).

Migration and Adaptation

If earlier studies of migration were predominantly ethnological, focusing on the ethnic identity and culture history of groups in contact, recent research has interpreted migration primarily as a mechanism of adaptation. Such a perspective emphasizes the diversity of conditions under which migration can occur, among these being "(1) fissioning of groups due to population increase and resource shortage, (2) attraction to urban opportunities, (3) attraction to underdeveloped territories, (4) ideology, (5) disease, (6) warfare, (7) ecological crisis, [and] (8) trade" (y'Edynak 1979:99).

Just as the adaptive functions of migration vary, the scale and duration of migratory movement vary as well. On this basis one can differentiate between (1) "foraging," (2) circular migration, and (3) permanent emigration (Graves and Graves 1974:118–22). By this classification, foraging migration refers to "temporary forays into neighboring regions in order to supplement local resources," an adaptive strategy that occurs in STATES as well as TRIBES, as in the temporary migrations of labor from less industrialized to more industrialized countries of the European-Mediterranean sphere. Circular migration establishes relatively permanent ties between two social spheres, typically involving a rural/urban connection, a situation widely studied in sub-Saharan Africa. Finally, the idea of permanent emigration, a pattern familiar in the North American experience, must be qualified by the growing research on the phenomenon of return migration of supposedly permanent emigrants (Gmelch 1980). The relationship between migration and economic development remains controversial (see Ramu 1971; Kearney 1986).

References

Gmelch, George. 1980. "Return Migration." *ARA* 9:135–59. A review article.
Graves, Nancy B., and Theodore D. Graves. 1974. "Adaptive Strategies in Urban Migration." *ARA* 3:117–51.
Jackson, Thomas L. 1986. "Reconstructing Migrations in California Prehistory." Second California Indian Conference, University of California, Berkeley, 1986.
Kearney, Michael. 1986. "From the Invisible Hand to Visible Feet: Anthropological Studies of Migration and Development." *ARA* 15:331–61. A critical review, relating anthropological studies to a wider literature of historiography and political economy.
Kroeber, Alfred L. 1948. *Anthropology*. New York: Harcourt, Brace.
Ramu, G. N. 1971. "Migration, Acculturation and Social Mobility among the Untouchable Gold Miners in South India: A Case Study." *Human Organization* 30:170–78. Ramu demonstrates the social and economic benefits of migration and industrial development.
Renfrew, Colin. 1979. "Colonialism and Megalithismus." C. Renfrew, *Problems in European Prehistory*. New York: Cambridge University Press. Criticizes the overdependence on migrationist models in archaeology.
Slotkin, J. S. 1965. *Readings in Early Anthropology*. Chicago: Aldine.
Wauchope, Robert. 1962. *Lost Tribes and Sunken Continents: Myth and Method in the Study of American Indians*. Chicago: University of Chicago Press. A witty account of the more bizarre migrationist theories in prehistory.
y'Edynak, Gloria. 1979. Commentary on William H. McNeill, "Historical Patterns of Migration." *CA* 20:99–100.

Sources of Additional Information

A broad anthropological review of migration is provided by W. Y. Adams et al., "The Retreat from Migrationism," *ARA* 7:483–532, 1978. An introduction to geographic perspectives on migration is provided by Philip E. Ogden, *Migration and Geographical Change*, Cambridge: Cambridge University Press, 1984; see also Robert P. Larkin and Gary L. Peters, *Dictionary of Concepts in Human Geography*, Westport, Conn.: Greenwood Press, 1983, s.v. "Migration." A useful anthology, presenting a multidisciplinary perspective, is William H. McNeil and Ruth S. Adams, eds., *Human Migration: Patterns and Policies*, Bloomington: Indiana University Press, 1978.

MODEL. See SYSTEM.

MODE OF PRODUCTION. A specific, historically constituted combination of resources, technology, and social and economic relationships, creating use or exchange value.

Mode of production (*Produktionsweise*) is a critical concept in Karl Marx's historical MATERIALISM. Although assuming the analytic primacy of production processes in shaping social relations and modes of thought, the concept of mode of production offers for ANTHROPOLOGY a means of characterizing and contrasting the subsistence PATTERN and economic organization of diverse societies without resorting to a narrow technological determinism. Since the 1960s, particularly through French anthropology, this and related Marxist concepts (e.g., social formation, forces and relations of production) have acquired a prominent place in anthropological debate regarding the nature of cultural EVOLUTION and the analysis of non-Western economies.

The concept of mode of production was developed in a number of Marx's works, including the posthumously published manuscript *Grundrisse* (1858), *Capital* (1867), and *The German Ideology*, written with Friedrich Engels (1846). For Marx, human activity is inherently social. Human labor cannot be understood as the activity of isolated individuals, but rather must be seen as a collective process, in which the realms of economics, politics, and social organization are deeply interrelated. Thus, a "mode of production must not be considered simply as being the production of the physical existence of the individuals. Rather, it is a definite form of activity of these individuals, a definite form of expressing their life, a definite mode of life on their part" (Marx and Engels 1846:42). As Marx indicated in the *Grundrisse*, discussing precapitalist societies, the relation between a specific form of COMMUNITY and particular conditions of production constitutes a unity, a distinctive "mode of production." This "appears equally as the relationship of the individuals to one another and as their specific daily behaviour towards inorganic nature, their specific mode of labour" (Marx 1858:94).

Mode of Production in Anthropology

The anthropologist Maurice Godelier has defined mode of production in these terms: "a combination—which is capable of reproducing itself—of productive forces and specific social relations of production which determine the structure and form of the process of production and the circulation of material goods within a historically determined society" (Godelier 1977:18). A specific mode of production is not reducible to a particular labor process or subsistence pattern:

> A production process, in fact, consists not only of one or more labour processes (man's relationship to man on the material level in a determined environment on the basis of a determined technology) but man's relationship to man, producers and non-producers, in the appropriation and control of the means of production (land, tools, raw materials, manpower) and the products of labour (hunting, gathering, fishing, agriculture, breeding, grazing, planting, handicrafts, etc.). (Godelier 1977:24)

The former involves technological processes (forces of production); the latter involves social relationships (relations of production).

From the Marxist perspective, the technological processes and the social relationships involved in a mode of production stand in a complex relation of mutual constraint (see Friedman 1974:445–49; O'Laughlin 1975:354–58). Furthermore, any given society at a particular historical juncture (a social formation) may involve multiple modes of production in a specified articulation. Thus, in Godelier's analysis, the Inca Empire of the sixteenth century involved at least three modes: (1) production on a village basis through communal ownership and labor; (2) forced labor by villages functioning collectively on lands appropriated by the state; and (3) production through the direct subordination of servile individuals to aristocratic families (Godelier 1977:63–69).

Points of Controversy

Anthropologists have shown more enthusiasm than consistency in applying this concept to the analysis of non-Western economies. There is considerable disagreement regarding the number of distinct modes of production to be found and the appropriate methods by which they should be analyzed (see Terray 1969; O'Laughlin 1975; Godelier 1977: ch. 1). Eric Wolf (1982: ch. 3) has identified three: a capitalist mode, involving the monetary appropriation of labor power; a tributary mode, in which primary producers remit a portion of production to a political elite in the form of tribute; and a kin-ordered mode, in which production is organized on the basis of KINSHIP relations. Marshall Sahlins has proposed a domestic mode, characterized by a small-scale subsistence economy, based on production for use rather than exchange (Sahlins 1972). Marx spoke of "feudal" and "Asiatic" modes (Marx 1858); arguments have also been made for a characteristic "African" mode of production (Coquery-Vidrovitch 1969; cf. Meillassoux 1964).

Studies from the perspectives of cultural evolution or cultural materialism likewise utilize a notion of mode of production, though more commonly a phrase such as "techno-economic base" or "subsistence pattern" is used. However, two assumptions commonly employed in evolutionary or ecological analyses serve to differentiate them from the perspective outlined above. First, most evolutionary studies assume that a social form can be characterized by its technology (e.g., a "hunting-and-gathering society"), that is, that technological processes determine economic relations. Second, with few exceptions, such studies treat each society in terms of a single mode of production (see Legros 1977:26–31). Each represents a major contrast to the analysis of ECONOMY, SOCIAL STRUCTURE, and CULTURE CHANGE found in the Marxist tradition of anthropology.

References

Coquery-Vidrovitch, Catherine. 1969. "Recherches sur un mode de production africain."
    La pensée 144:61–78. Suggests a distinctive mode of production in sub-Saharan
    Africa.
Friedman, Jonathan. 1974. "Marxism, Structuralism, and Vulgar Materialism." *Man*
    (n.s.) 9:444–69. A critique of non-Marxist materialist approaches in anthropology.
Godelier, Maurice. 1977. *Perspectives in Marxist Anthropology*. Robert Brain, trans.
    Cambridge: Cambridge University Press. Provides a challenging exposition of
    major anthropological issues; an excellent collection.
Legros, Dominique. 1977. "Chance, Necessity, and Mode of Production: A Marxist
    Critique of Cultural Evolutionism." *AA* 79: 26–41. Contrasts the perspectives of
    cultural evolutionism and Marxism.
Marx, Karl. 1858 [1965]. *Pre-Capitalist Economic Formations*. Jack Cohen, trans. Eric

J. Hobsbawm, ed. New York: International Publishers. Selections from the *Grundrisse der Kritik der Politischen Ökonomie*.

————. 1867 [1967]. *Capital*. Vol. 1, *The Process of Capitalist Production*. Samuel Moore and Edward Aveling, trans. New York: International Publishers. A mature statement of Marx's views.

Marx, Karl, and Friedrich Engels. 1846 [1970]. *The German Ideology*, abr. C. J. Arthur, ed. New York: International Publishers.

Meillassoux, Claude. 1964. *Anthropologie économique des Gouro de Côte-d'Ivoire*. Paris and The Hague: Mouton. One of the first Marxist analyses of a tribal economy.

O'Laughlin, Bridget. 1975. "Marxist Approaches in Anthropology." *ARA* 4:341–370. A good introduction.

Sahlins, Marshall. 1972. "The Domestic Mode of Production: The Structure of Underproduction." M. Sahlins, *Stone Age Economics*. Chicago: Aldine. A theoretically eclectic approach, analyzing "underproduction" in a variety of non-capitalist economies.

Terray, Emmanuel. 1969. *Le marxisme devant les sociétés "primitives": deux études*. Paris: Maspero.

Wolf, Eric R. 1982. *Europe and the People without History*. Berkeley and Los Angeles: University of California Press. The bibliographic essay (see pages 400–404) provides extensive references regarding "mode of production."

Sources of Additional Information

David McLellan, *The Thought of Karl Marx: An Introduction*, New York: Harper & Row, 1971, provides relatively painless access to Marx's ideas. A good collection of essays, theoretical and empirical, is provided in David Seddon, ed., *Relations of Production: Marxist Approaches to Economic Anthropology*, Helen Lackner, trans., London: Frank Cass, 1978. More specialized studies are found in Anne M. Bailey and Josep R. Llobera, eds., *The Asiatic Mode of Production: Science and Politics*, London: Routledge & Kegan Paul, 1981; and Richard R. Wilk, ed., *The Household Economy: Reconsidering the Domestic Mode of Production*, Boulder, Colo.: Westview, 1989.

MYTH. A traditional, sacred prose narrative, depicting the primordial events that shaped the world.

Myth is derived from the Greek *mythos*, a tale, story, or narrative, in contrast to *logos*, a historic account (*GEL*). From antiquity, myth was considered a distinct type of narrative, recounting episodes from times beyond historic recollection: the works of the gods (see RELIGION). Myth thus involves special knowledge claims. Depending on the perspective of the hearer, myth may be interpreted as error or fiction, or as a higher truth.

The systematic study of myth dates from the Renaissance (Seznec 1973:292–93). Its study has been a multidisciplinary enterprise, involving not only ANTHROPOLOGY, but also comparative religions, philology, FOLKLORE, art history, literature, philosophy, and psychology.

Defining Myth

According to the Finnish folklorist Lauri Honko, myth can be defined as "a story of the gods, a religious account of the beginning of the world, the creation, fundamental events, the exemplary deeds of the gods as a result of which the world, nature and culture were created together with all the parts thereof and given their order, which still obtains" (Honko 1972:49). Myth is a distinctive type of narrative because it portrays paradigmatic events, events situated in a sacred time beyond history (Eliade 1954: ch. 1), which can both interpret social institutions and validate moral axioms. Thus Hindu myth justifies the ranked divisions of the CASTE system by their origin from the sacrificial division of the primordial man (Purusa): the priests deriving from his mouth, warriors from his arms, traders from his thighs, and laborers (the lowest ranked) from his feet (*Rig Veda* 10.90.12). In this sense, myth is "any presentation of the actual in terms of the ideal" (Gaster 1954:112). Its religious or symbolic significance distinguishes it from other forms of narrative.

This premise underlies the contrast of myth, legend, and folktale (Bascom 1965). Myths, in their traditional setting, are intrinsically sacred narratives dealing chiefly with nonhuman characters, depicting (as was noted) the primordial events that shaped the world. Legends, whether sacred or secular, are traditionally presented as fact, but center on the actions of human characters. In contrast to myths, legends "are set in a period considered less remote, when the world was much as it is today" (Bascom 1965:9). MIGRATIONS, WARS, and the deeds of heroes are common topics of legends; a notable example is the cycle of British legend centering on King Arthur. Folktales, encompassing a variety of genres, are secular in nature, involving human or nonhuman characters in situations understood to be fictional. Paul Bunyan, Cinderella, and Brer Rabbit are familiar characters from Western folktales. The contrast of legend and folktale parallels that common in European folklore studies between *Sagen* and *Märchen* respectively, a distinction originally drawn by the eminent nineteenth century folklorists Jakob and Wilhelm Grimm (Bascom 1965:8, n. 6).

Development of Myth Studies

The study of myth implies a certain critical distance, the development of a sceptical attitude toward the literal sense of myth, prompting the search for truth behind appearance, the symbolic meaning underlying what was once convincing narrative. Ancient Greece offers a case in point. The TRADITION recounted with apparent piety by Hesiod or Homer in the eighth century B.C. was received critically by the philosophers of the fourth century (Schuhl 1973). Myth was frequently interpreted as allegory, that is, "a fictional narrative with symbolic meaning" (Bidney 1967:304). For Aristotle, for example, myths identifying the stars with gods reflected philosophical insight, crudely anthropomorphized "with a view to the persuasion of the multitude" (*Metaphysics* 1074b).

The writers of the Enlightenment sought inspiration in classical Greek culture, in large measure because (in their view) the Greeks had replaced myth with reason, deducing their morality, as Edward Gibbon said, "from the nature of man rather than from that of God" (in Gay 1966:73). This is what the *philosophes* of the seventeenth and eighteenth centuries sought to do for their own age. A key element of their endeavor was the rational reinterpretation of the myths (both pagan and Christian) received from medieval tradition (see Gay 1966:72–94).

In this vein, Pierre Bayle (1647–1706) emphasized the scandalous inconsistency between the mythic accounts of gods and heroes, and the veneration that tradition accorded them: witness the classical Jupiter, author of numberless acts of lewdness and incestuous depravity; or the biblical King David, guilty of murder, treason, and adultery (Feldman and Richardson 1972:19–24). David Hume (1711–1776) sought to explain myth through euhemerism, the deification of once historical figures. "Most of the divinities of the ancient world are supposed to have once been men," Hume argued, whose history, "corrupted by tradition, and elevated by the marvellous, became a plentiful source of fable" (in Feldman and Richardson 1972:162).

Romanticism, in contrast, broke with the derogation of myth fundamental to the Enlightenment. For its proponents, myth now appeared "as an inexhaustible mode of truth or even power" (Feldman 1973:303). Giambattista Vico (1668–1744) anticipated the romantic perspective in arguing for the necessity of myth in human societies. Myth, for Vico, was itself a type of philosophy: "Poetic wisdom, the first wisdom of the gentile [i.e., tribal] world, must have begun with a metaphysics not rational and abstract like that of learned men now, but felt and imagined" (in Feldman and Richardson 1972:58).

For the romantics of the later eighteenth and nineteenth centuries, the study of myth offered insight into—not the frailties of human reason, as the Enlightenment believed—but the spirit or "genius" (Ger. *Geist*) of particular peoples. This appreciation in part grew from the much wider range of myth texts available in this period, for example the Norse *Eddas* and the Vedic scriptures of ancient India (Feldman 1973:304). Johann Gottfried von Herder (1744–1803) was a major proponent of the study of myth for the insight it yielded into the distinctive genius of each people (Ger. *Volk*; see FOLKLORE). Modern societies, Herder argued in 1767, fail in not recognizing their own mythologies: "Let us study the mythology of the ancients as poetical heuristics, to become inventors ourselves" (in Feldman and Richardson 1972:231). Given this perspective, it is not surprising that the romantic study of myth developed strongly nationalist overtones. In *Teutonic Mythology* (1835), for example, Jakob Grimm sought to document authentic German myth and folklore, criticizing the willingness of myth scholars to "overlook the independence of German poetry and legend" by subordinating it to that of ancient Greece and Rome (in Feldman and Richardson 1972:414).

Victorian Theories of Myth

Victorian discussions of myth were dominated by the contending perspectives of comparative mythology and evolution. The champion of comparative mythology (also termed solar mythology) was the linguist Friedrich Max Müller (1823–1900), renowned for his studies of Indo-European languages. In an influential 1856 essay Müller argued that myth could in large measure be explained as a "disease of language." Terms that originally named natural phenomena became reified over time: "As long as people thought in language, it was simply impossible to speak of morning or evening, of spring and winter, without giving to these conceptions something of an individual, active, sexual, and at last, personal character" (Müller, in Dorson 1968:1:70). Müller noted, for example, that the god Dyaus for the early Aryans, like its cognate Zeus for the ancient Greeks, originally signified "sky" (in Dorson 1968:1:81). What was once metaphor describing natural phenomena became, for a later age, transformed into myth (see Dorson 1955).

An alternative theory of myth was offered by proponents of cultural EVOLUTION, notably Andrew Lang (1844–1912). Folktale and CUSTOM, which for the solar mythologists reflected the degeneration of once coherent PATTERNS of language, represented for evolutionists the SURVIVAL of PRIMITIVE belief. For Lang, the Greek myth of Cronus devouring his sons did not require Müller's elaborate philological interpretation, but simply a recognition of the (supposed) place of cannibalism in primitive custom (Dorson 1955:21–23). The supernatural character of fairytales, Lang wrote in 1873, was better understood "as a survival of animal-worship, and of magic, than as a degraded shape of the myths of the elements, and the great vicissitudes of nature" (in Dorson 1968:1:195). For Lang the similarity of myth and folktale motifs cross-culturally reflected PSYCHIC UNITY: "The Aryan and the lower races have had to pass through similar conditions of imagination and of society, and therefore of religion" (in Dorson 1968:1:197). While both approaches have been superseded, Lang's evolutionism lay far closer to the ethnologically grounded views of later anthropologists.

Myth and Modern Anthropology

The topic of myth has been of concern to almost every tendency in modern anthropology. This entry briefly considers the understanding of myth in FUNCTIONALISM, STRUCTURALISM, and symbolic anthropology (see SYMBOLISM). In these approaches are discernible both the Enlightenment view of myth as masking a more fundamental social reality (in functionalism and structuralism), and the romantic understanding of myth as a distinctive mode of knowledge (in symbolic anthropology).

The functionalist view of myth. The essence of functionalism is to see societies live and whole, rather than as disembodied catalogs of culture traits. All aspects of culture are taken to be meaningfully interrelated, serving to preserve a social system, or to fulfill psychobiological needs. From this perspective, for Bronislaw Malinowski (1884–1942), myths were not "merely a story told but a reality lived . . . not an intellectual explanation or an artistic imagery, but a pragmatic charter of primitive faith and moral wisdom" (Malinowski 1926:100–101). The function of myth is to enhance tradition "by tracing it back to a higher, better, more supernatural reality of initial events" (Malinowski 1926:146).

The structuralist view. Structuralism is a rationalist theory of society which assumes that cultural forms reflect a series of cognitive oppositions, systems of contrasting categories modeling the characteristics of a society and, more fundamentally, the structure of the human mind. The structuralist approach is illustrated by Claude Lévi-Strauss's analysis of the Tsimshian myth of Asdiwal. This myth takes the hero through a series of adventures in which he receives magical objects, passes between earth and heaven, journeys repeatedly between mountains and sea, hunts a variety of animals, and marries a series of women, both divine and mortal. For Lévi-Strauss, the myth describes the contrasting patterns of Tsimshian life, reflecting the natural and cultural oppositions of sea/land, west/east, vegetable/animal, famine/repletion, endogamy/exogamy, and matrilocality/patrilocality (Lévi-Strauss 1967).

The structuralist method commonly considers not single myth texts, but compares multiple versions of a myth and numerous myths within a CULTURE AREA. As David Mandelbaum has commented, despite numerous problems with this approach, Lévi-Strauss's work does "direct attention to seeing relations of opposition and anomaly, of contradiction and transformation, of similarity and inclusion among seemingly disparate episodes of a myth" (Mandelbaum 1987:35).

The symbolist view. Proponents of symbolic anthropology share a concern for the INTERPRETATION of cultural expression, the relation between form, meaning, and cultural context. Victor Turner, one of the most influential theorists of symbolic anthropology, has stressed the close relation between myth and ritual, finding a link in the nature of the symbolism that animates both domains. In Turner's view myths are not (as Malinowski claimed) "to be treated as models for secular behavior" (Turner 1968:577). Rather, one of the common characteristics of both myth and ritual is their sacred character, their compelling moral power. Myths are "felt to be high or deep mysteries which put the initiand temporarily into close rapport with the primary or primordial generative powers of the cosmos" (Turner 1968:577). The Christian Eucharist, in which ritual action reenacts a sacred and mythic event—the Last Supper—exemplifies the mutual dependence of these domains.

In practice these approaches need not be mutually exclusive. Modern anthropology considers myth as a guide to RITUAL and cosmology, and as a cultural product reflecting the varied constraints of environmental ADAPTATION, SOCIAL STRUCTURE, and WORLD VIEW.

References

Bascom, William. 1965 [1984]. "The Forms of Folklore: Prose Narratives." Alan Dundes, ed., *Sacred Narrative: Readings in the Theory of Myth*. Berkeley and Los Angeles: University of California Press. A useful typology.

Bidney, David. 1967. "The Concept of Myth." D. Bidney, *Theoretical Anthropology*, 2nd ed. New York: Schocken.

Dorson, Richard M. 1955. "The Eclipse of Solar Mythology." Thomas A. Sebeok, ed., *Myth: A Symposium*. Philadelphia: American Folklore Society. A good treatment of the Müller-Lang controversy.

———, ed. 1968. *Peasant Customs and Savage Myths: Selections from the British Folklorists*. 2 vols. Chicago: University of Chicago Press.

Eliade, Mircea. 1954. *The Myth of the Eternal Return*. Willard R. Trask, trans. New York: Bollingen/Pantheon. Eliade is an outstanding scholar of myth, whose work fits better the view-point of comparative religions than anthropology.

Feldman, Burton. 1973. "Myth in the Eighteenth and Early Nineteenth Centuries." *DHI* 3:300–307.

Feldman, Burton, and Robert D. Richardson, eds. 1972. *The Rise of Modern Mythology: 1680–1860*. Bloomington: Indiana University Press. an important anthology of myth analysis and theory, with good commentary.

Gaster, Theodor H. 1954 [1984]. "Myth and Story." Alan Dundes, ed., *Sacred Narrative: Readings in the Theory of Myth*. Berkeley and Los Angeles: University of California Press.

Gay, Peter. 1966. *The Enlightenment, An Interpretation: The Rise of Modern Paganism*. New York: Random House.

Honko, Lauri. 1972 [1984]. "The Problem of Defining Myth." Alan Dundes, ed., *Sacred Narrative: Readings in the Theory of Myth*. Berkeley and Los Angeles: University of California Press.

Lévi-Strauss, Claude. 1967. "The Story of Asdiwal." E. R. Leach, ed., *The Structural Study of Myth and Totemism*. London: Tavistock. A good example of structuralist method applied to myth.

Malinowski, Bronislaw. 1926 [1954]. "Myth in Primitive Psychology." B. Malinowski, *Magic, Science and Religion, and Other Essays*. Garden City, N.Y.: Doubleday/ Anchor. A key statement of the functionalist perspective.

Mandelbaum, David. 1987. "Myths and Myth Maker: Some Anthropological Appraisals of the Mythological Studies of Lévi-Strauss." *Ethnology* 26:31–36.

Schuhl, P.-M. 1973. "Myth in Antiquity." *DHI* 3:272–75.

Seznec, Jean. 1973. "Myth in the Middle Ages and the Renaissance." *DHI* 3:286–94.

Turner, Victor. 1968. "Myth and Symbol." *IESS* 10:576–82. A statement from the viewpoint of symbolic anthropology.

Sources of Additional Information

A brief overview of major anthropological approaches to myth is offered by Percy S. Cohen, "Theories of Myth," *Man* (n.s.) 4:337–53, 1969. Maria Leach and Jerome Fried, eds., *Funk & Wagnalls Standard Dictionary of Folklore, Mythology, and Legend*, New York: Harper & Row, 1972, remains a major reference source. A variety of anthropological approaches are demonstrated in Melville Jacobs and John Greenway, eds., *The Anthropologist Looks at Myth*, Austin: University of Texas Press, 1966. A good bibliography of myth texts is provided by Roy Smith, ed., *Mythologies of the World: A Guide to Sources*, Urbana, Ill.: National Council of Teachers of English, 1981. In *Four Theories of Myth in Twentieth-Century History: Cassirer, Eliade, Lévi-Strauss and Malinowski*, Iowa City: University of Iowa Press, 1987, Ivan Strenski considers the intellectual background of these four theorists.

N

NATURE. (1) The evolutionary continuum of matter and life; the totality of life-forms, considered in their interrelation. (2) The pre-cultural world. (3) Those traits and predispositions characteristic of the human species generally, rather than of a particular culture, (i.e., human nature).

Nature is derived from the Latin *natura*, from *nasci*, to be born. As a translation of the Greek *physis* (cf. physics, physician), *natura* absorbed much of the Greek term's semantic complexity. The words nature and natural contrast with other terms in a bewildering variety of contexts (see *OED*). That which is natural is spontaneous and unforced, rather than artificial and insincere, that is, dictated by CUSTOM. That which is natural is also pure rather than adulterated, produced without alteration by technology. Natural occurrences are those which are attributable to physical or biological forces (an earthquake), in contrast to events resulting from human agency (a war).

The common element in these contrasts is the estrangement of the human realm (encompassing actions, customs, and experience) from the realm of nature. In the vernacular of ANTHROPOLOGY, these are the contrasting domains of nature and CULTURE (see also SUPERORGANIC). Much of the theoretical debate in twentieth century anthropology can in fact be ascribed to disagreement regarding the meaning of these two concepts and their interrelation. The concept of nature will be considered briefly as it bears upon (1) the supposed contrast of PRIMITIVE and civilized society; (2) the process of human ADAPTATION to the environment; and (3) the problem of biological continuity and the human capacity for culture. (For the role of nature in shaping ideas of male and female domains and capacities, see GENDER.)

Nature and the Primitive

For the Greeks, that which occurs *physei*, by nature, is spontaneous and instinctive, prior to reason or experience, and because of that a more reliable gauge of human capacities and the appropriateness of political and social institutions (Lovejoy and Boas 1935: ch. 3). This distinction, perpetuated in Western thought, formed an essential tenet of romanticism. As a contemporary wrote of Mme. de Staël, she showed "primitive, incorruptible, naive, passionate nature in conflict with the barriers and shackles of conventional life" (in Babbitt 1919:49). In the work of Jean-Jacques Rousseau (d. 1778), nature rather than custom and artifice guided humans in their primitive condition, an argument that provided him with a perspective from which to criticize the complexity and INEQUALITY of CIVILIZATION.

> If I consider him [the primitive], in a word, such as he must have issued from the hands of nature . . . I see him satisfying his hunger under an oak, and his thirst at the first brook; I see him laying himself down to sleep at the foot of the same tree that afforded him his meal; and there are all his wants completely supplied. (Rousseau 1754:179)

The association of so-called primitive societies with the state of nature was not unique to the romantics, for it was perpetuated in evolutionary anthropology as well (see EVOLUTION). In this vein, the German ethnologists contrasted Kulturvölker (the civilized) and Naturvölker (the primitive): "We speak of natural races [Naturvölker], not because they stand in the most intimate relations with Nature, but because they are in bondage to Nature" (Ratzel 1896:14).

Nature and Adaptation

Arguably, the experience of nature by living things is as various as their modes of adaptation. Our species, however, is an extreme generalist, within the broad lines laid down by our primate heritage. Capable of surviving in a bewildering range of terrestrial environments, humans are specifically fitted to none. Rather, our cultures (in the plural) provide the knowledge and techniques needed for survival in one or another habitat. Considered more closely, however, culture does not merely adapt a population to its environment—it mediates the human experience of nature, and this is equally true of societies at the level of the BAND, the TRIBE, or the STATE. Nature does not exist for us as an external and objective reality; rather, "nature is seen by humans through a screen of beliefs, knowledge, and purposes, and it is in terms of their images of nature, rather than of the actual structure of nature, that they act" (Rappaport 1979:97). Or, as Marshall Sahlins has written, it is "culture that is the context of nature," and not the reverse (Sahlins 1977:20; see also ETHNOSCIENCE).

Culture and Human Nature

In the context of anthropology, a concept of nature has had its greatest importance by implying the existence of a pan-human essence or character, more fundamental and more revealing than the accidental variety of belief and custom, which necessarily vary from one society to another. In Greek thought *physis* was that which was of universal human validity. It was counterposed to the *nomoi*, the variegated and inconsistent laws and customs of one or another region, which because of their multiplicity could not be fundamentally valid (see Lovejoy and Boas 1935:107–8). In later periods this concept appeared under a variety of names: the classical *consensus gentium*, or general opinion of peoples; the medieval *lumen naturale*; or the PSYCHIC UNITY of the evolutionists (see Boas 1973:348).

In a world after Darwin, these considerations have become more complex. One must contend not only with the problem of the underlying relation between diverse peoples, but also with the problem of continuity or discontinuity between humans and other species. Fields such as ethology and SOCIOBIOLOGY have sought the basis of human sexuality, aggression, or territoriality through comparisons with other species. Once again, nature is sought in the universal. Regarding studies by the Austrian ethologist Konrad Lorenz on the nature of human aggression (Lorenz 1963), Harvey Sarles has commented that he "wants to describe what he believes is deeply, fundamentally human, solely by observing other species—what is 'natural' to humans is what we share with others" (Sarles 1979:13). Yet this is by no means obvious.

The task of anthropology is not to comprehend "the passage from nature to culture," as Lévi-Strauss (1969:142) has argued, but to reconcile the emergence of culture with the evolutionary continuity that manifestly exists between our species and other mammals, and in particular other primates. The capacity for culture is our nature, or at least our *physis*. In the Greek view—lost in later Roman and European thought—the nature of any kind of being is its pattern of growth, "the immanent cause or self-active principle of its self-realization" (Lovejoy and Boas 1935:450, sec. 28; see also Bauman 1973:7–10). The human species achieves this self-realization in cultural expression, not by transcending nature, but by manifesting one distinctive evolutionary pattern within the innumerable adaptations of the natural world. For anthropology to perpetuate the misleading opposition of nature and culture serves to negate both the supposed unity of the discipline and the evolutionary distinctiveness of our species.

References

Babbitt, Irving. 1919 [1977]. *Rousseau and Romanticism*. Austin: University of Texas Press.
Bauman, Zygmunt. 1973. *Culture as Praxis*. Boston: Routledge & Kegan Paul.
Boas, George. 1973. "Nature." *DHI* 3:346–51.
Lévi-Strauss, Claude. 1969. *Le totémisme aujourd'hui*. Paris: Presses Universitaires de France.
Lorenz, Konrad. 1963. *On Aggression*. Marjorie K. Wilson, trans. New York: Harcourt, Brace & World. Considers war and aggression as expressions of human nature.
Lovejoy, Arthur O., and George Boas. 1935. *Primitivism and Related Ideas in Antiquity*. Baltimore, Md.: Johns Hopkins University Press. An essential source on the classical concept of nature.
Rappaport, Roy A. 1979. "On Cognized Models." R. Rappaport, *Ecology, Meaning, and Religion*. Richmond, Calif.: North Atlantic Books.
Ratzel, Friedrich. 1896. *The History of Mankind*. A. J. Butler, trans. London: Macmillan. An influential work of nineteenth-century ethnology.
Rousseau, Jean-Jacques. 1754 [1967]. "Discourse on the Origin and Foundation of

Inequality Among Mankind.'' Lester G. Crocker, ed. *The Social Contract, and Discourse on the Origin and Foundation of Inequality Among Mankind.* New York: Washington Square. A basic text of Enlightenment anthropology.

Sahlins, Marshall. 1977. ''The State of the Art in Social/Cultural Anthropology: Search for an Object.'' Anthony F. C. Wallace et al., eds., *Perspectives on Anthropology, 1976.* Washington, D.C.: American Anthropological Association, *Special Publication,* 10.

Sarles, Harvey. 1979. ''Reflections on Human Nature: An Anthropologist's Perspective.'' Paper presented at the Department of Anthropology, University of Chicago, 50th Anniversary Celebration.

Sources of Additional Information

Clarence J. Glacken's *Traces on the Rhodian Shore: Nature and Culture in Western Thought from Ancient Times to the End of the Eighteenth Century,* Berkeley and Los Angeles: University of California Press, 1967, is an immense and valuable study, considering the theme of nature and culture from the perspective of geography. Clifford Geertz's ''The Impact of the Concept of Culture on the Concept of Man,'' C. Geertz, *The Interpretation of Cultures,* New York: Basic Books, 1973, provides a significant critique of the quest for a universal human nature. A range of challenging essays with a psychoanalytic emphasis is given in Melford E. Spiro, *Culture and Human Nature,* Benjamin Kilborne and L. L. Langness, eds., Chicago: University of Chicago Press, 1987. For a brief, anthropologically oriented review of the nature/culture dialectic, see Stephen Horigan, *Nature and Culture in Western Discourses,* London: Routledge, 1988.

NETWORK. A real or potential chain of social interaction reckoned from the perspective of a given individual.

Network analysis is a postwar innovation aimed at increasing the realism and detail of ETHNOGRAPHY by examining the relatively informal and often transient links through which individuals interact in a given social setting. The study of networks thus complements the examination of more formal and relatively permanent social forms, such as unilineal DESCENT groups or age-sets (see ASSO-CIATION). The aims of network analysis, according to Jeremy Boissevain, are three: ''it asks questions about who is linked to whom, the nature of that linkage, and how the nature of the linkage affects behaviour'' (Boissevain 1979:393).

Networks are quite literally ''non-groups.'' Members of a network do not necessarily know one another or even know of each other's existence; such social forms often lack either a collective purpose or ''consciousness of kind'' (Boissevain 1968:542). Two related concepts are the action set and the quasi-group. An action set is a subset of a personal network utilized with a particular aim, for example, the individuals brought into play in support of an election campaign by virtue of their ties with the candidate (Harries-Jones 1969:302). A quasi-group, in contrast, possesses somewhat greater structure and ideological coherence: ''a coalition of persons, recruited according to structurally diverse principles by one or more existing members, between some of whom there is a degree of patterned interaction and organization'' (Boissevain 1968:550). One could include here factions, clienteles, and SOCIAL MOVEMENTS.

The Critique of Functionalism

The emergence of network analysis in the 1950s, notably in British social anthropology, constituted in part a refinement, and in part a critique, of the tenets of structural FUNCTIONALISM. Functionalist doctrine advocated, even when it did not employ, a rather simplistic empiricism: "The concrete reality with which we are concerned is the set of actually existing relations, at a given moment of time, which link together certain human beings" (Radcliffe-Brown 1940:192). In fact, this stance was realized far better through the later methods of network analysis than it was in the earlier and more orthodox functionalist studies. However, network analysis also developed as one reaction to the obvious insufficiencies of the functionalist approach: among these were the almost exclusive concern with formal institutions, and its correlate, an essentially static image of permanent social equilibrium (see SOCIAL STRUCTURE).

Among the developments in theory and method that sought to transcend these limitations were an attention to systems of LAW; the interpretation of RITUAL as an expression of social tension and factionalism; the extended case study, examining in detail the interactions of particular individuals in the context of dispute; and, stimulated by studies of URBANISM and DEVELOPMENT in sub-Saharan Africa, the analysis of the more diffuse and transient interactions of social networks. These approaches shared an interest in power, competition, and conflict, and a methodological insistence on illuminating general principles through specific case studies of interacting individuals. Moreover, this research direction was strengthened by a common institutional base provided by the anthropology department at the University of Manchester, under the leadership of Max Gluckman—hence, the common appellation of *Manchester School* to describe this tendency within postwar British anthropology (see Kuper 1973: ch. 6).

Varieties of Network Analysis

Network analysis has, broadly speaking, taken two distinct approaches, one showing continuity with functionalism, the other marked divergence—orientations that can be described respectively as structural and transactional (see Mitchell 1974:285–86). The structural method takes an existing pattern of social ties (the network) as a given, reflecting some wider social system, and explains behavior in terms of the patterning of this network. In this fashion A. L. Epstein, in his analysis of patterns of gossip in an African town, argued that the concept of network clarified "some of the problems of social control in African urban society: how norms of behaviour come to be set, how they are maintained or sanctioned, and how they come to be diffused" (Epstein 1969:117). Similarly, Peter Harries-Jones (1969) examined the effect of social ties based on shared village origins (*bakumwesu* or home-people) on political organizing by migrants to the industrial Copperbelt of Zambia.

The transactional method, in contrast, takes as its starting point various ends pursued by individuals—such as political advantage or economic sufficiency—

and examines how networks are forged to further these ends. Questions of reciprocity are central to this perspective, thus showing an affinity with theories of exchange (see SOCIAL STRUCTURE). Adrian Mayer's study of an election campaign in Madhya Pradesh (India) offers an example. Political supporters were recruited into this "action set" through diverse linkages, including KINSHIP, party membership, common occupation, common CASTE, common religious sect, village membership, and such economic ties as employer-employee and creditor-debtor (Mayer 1966:108–10). Similarly, in her study of "kin structured local networks" in an American black ghetto, Carol Stack noted that "flexible expectations and the extension of kin relationships to non-kin allow for the creation of mutual aid domestic networks which are not bounded by genealogical distance or genealogical criteria" (Stack 1974:61).

An unresolved issue concerns the aims of network analysis. Is it a heuristic method—simply a useful addition to the ethnographic tool kit—or do social networks form a class of phenomena to be investigated for their intrinsic formal properties, particularly through the medium of graph theory (see Harary et al. 1965)? Network analysis developed in ANTHROPOLOGY as a means of enhancing the realism and detail of ethnographic description. Critics of the increasingly formal and mathematical approach to network studies in the social sciences (see Boissevain 1979:393) fear that this is likely to yield an analysis devoid of human detail or cultural content, a result alien to the underlying goals of anthropology.

References

Boissevain, Jeremy. 1968. "The Place of Non-Groups in the Social Sciences." *Man* 3:542–56. Boissevain suggests network analysis as a corrective to the overemphasis on formal groups in social anthropology.
———. 1979. "Network Analysis: A Reappraisal." *CA* 20:392–94.
Epstein, A. L. 1969. "Gossip, Norms and Social Network." J. Clyde Mitchell, ed., *Social Networks in Urban Situations*. Manchester, England: Manchester University Press.
Harary, Frank, et al. 1965. *Structural Models: An Introduction to the Theory of Directed Graphs*. New York: John Wiley & Sons.
Harries-Jones, Peter. 1969. "'Home-Boy' Ties and Political Organization in a Copperbelt Township." J. Clyde Mitchell, ed., *Social Networks in Urban Situations*. Manchester, England: Manchester University Press.
Kuper, Adam. 1973. *Anthropologists and Anthropology: The British School, 1922–1972*. New York: Pica Press. An incisive history of modern British anthropology.
Mayer, Adrian. 1966. "The Significance of Quasi-Groups in the Study of Complex Societies." Michael Banton, ed., *The Social Anthropology of Complex Societies*. London: Tavistock. A study of Indian politics.
Mitchell, J. Clyde. 1974. "Social Networks." *ARA* 3:279–99. A good overview.
Radcliffe-Brown, A. R. 1940 [1965]. "On Social Structure." A. R. Radcliffe-Brown, *Structure and Function in Primitive Society*. New York: Free Press.
Stack, Carol B. 1974. *All Our Kin: Strategies for Survival in a Black Community*. New York: Harper & Row.

Sources of Additional Information

A general review with extensive bibliography is presented in Norman E. Whitten, Jr., and Alvin W. Wolfe, ''Network Analysis,'' John J. Honigmann, ed., *Handbook of Social and Cultural Anthropology*, Chicago: Rand McNally, 1973. For a brief introduction to network methods see David Knoke and James H. Kuklinski, *Network Analysis*, Beverly Hills, Calif.: Sage, 1982.

P

PATTERN. A relatively stable arrangement of culture traits; more strongly, the coherence underlying cultural expression within a society.

The idea of culture pattern represents an effort to depict the unity underlying the diversity of cultural data, the sense and order involved in a distinctive way of life. According to Melville Herskovits, culture patterns are "the designs taken by the elements of a culture which . . . give to this way of life coherence, continuity, and distinctive form" (Herskovits 1956:202). The pattern concept has been described with a variety of terms, others including configuration, ethos, style, theme, WORLD VIEW, and *Zeitgeist* (the characteristic spirit of an age). Pattern theories in anthropology represent one approach to the identification of lawlike regularities in culture. These contrast with theories based on noncultural factors, for example those giving explanatory value to SOCIAL STRUCTURE (structural FUNCTIONALISM), or to processes of ADAPTATION (CULTURAL ECOLOGY; MATERIALISM).

The writings of G. W. F. Hegel (1770–1831) established a philosophical rationale for seeking the characteristic idea or world view underlying the outward diversity of a culture. As Isaiah Berlin has commented, "Hegel transferred the concept of the personal character of the individual, the aims, logic, quality of his thoughts, his choices . . . to the case of entire cultures and nations" (Berlin 1963:42). For Hegel the spirit (*Geist*) of a nation found its expression in the varied phenomena of cultural life, manifested through "the law known to everybody, familiar and recognized . . . everyday Customary Convention (*Sitte*)" (Hegel 1807:467; see CUSTOM). By this logic, in any era or society such diverse fields as art, science, and RELIGION might all reflect some common style or impulse (see Berlin 1963:42–43). This perspective was transmitted to ANTHROPOLOGY through the HISTORICISM of Wilhelm Dilthey (1833–1911). Relativizing the Hegelian perspective, Dilthey offered a "concept of discrete individual *Geis-*

ten associated with specific historical periods or cultural traditions,'' a view which had a profound influence on anthropologists such as Franz Boas and Alfred Kroeber (Stocking 1974:11).

The adoption of a pattern concept in American anthropology between approximately 1915 and 1930 reflected dissatisfaction with existing approaches to ETHNOGRAPHY, characterized by a trait-oriented collection of data, and explanation in terms of DIFFUSION. One of the earliest formulations of the idea within anthropology came from Clark Wissler (1870–1947). He noted, in 1917, that "in certain phases of culture each social unit develops a style, or pattern, for its traits and . . . borrowed traits will be worked over to make them conform to this pattern" (in Freed and Freed 1983:814). Similarly, Franz Boas (1858–1942) argued in 1920 for "the study of [the] inner development" of cultures, a problem to be investigated in "processes of acculturation and . . . the interdependence of cultural activities," that is, the phenomenon of pattern (Boas 1920:284–85; see also Stocking 1976:14–16).

Pattern and Personality

In the 1920s and 1930s, in addition to the influence of German historicism, interest in the idea of culture pattern was encouraged by contemporary psychology. For many anthropologists of that period, PERSONALITY offered a model for the understanding of culture, suggesting a parallel in its integration of numerous discrete traits into a single goal-directed system. The idea of culture pattern was particularly encouraged by Gestalt psychology, with its emphasis on part-whole relationships (Wertheimer 1925).

The work of Ruth Benedict (1887–1948) reflected both influences (see Benedict 1934: ch. 3). For example, Benedict characterized the culture of the Pueblo as integrated by values of sobriety and restraint. "The whole interest of the culture is directed toward providing for every situation sets of rules and practices by means of which one gets by without resort to the violence and disruption that their culture distrusts" (Benedict 1932:6).

Later Approaches

A number of psychologically oriented studies such as Benedict's assumed that a single focal value or orientation could usefully characterize a whole society. In contrast, many later studies employed the notion of pattern or configuration to describe a system of interrelated values, which interact to produce a distinctive outlook and a characteristic behavior. Proposing the notion of cultural theme, Morris Opler contended "that a limited number of dynamic affirmations, which I shall call themes, can be identified in every culture and that the key to the character, structure, and direction of the specific culture is to be sought in the nature, expression, and interrelationship of these themes" (Opler 1946:198). In describing the Chiricahua Apache, Opler cited the themes of male superiority; the importance of the quest for long life; and the pervasive danger of sorcery. Each of these themes was manifested in a number of expressions, some formal and ritualized (see RITUAL), others informal and fluid (Opler 1946).

Alfred Kroeber, taking a rather different approach, contrasted several types of pattern phenomena (Kroeber 1948: ch. 8). Among these he included styles ("a particular method or manner" of carrying out an activity), art historical styles providing the most obvious examples; systemic patterns, coherent systems of interrelated traits, such as plow agriculture or the alphabet, which are transmitted readily from society to society; and total-culture patterns, characteristic of an entire CIVILIZATION, which in Kroeber's view possess their own inherent cycles of growth and decay (see SUPERORGANIC).

Proponents of the pattern concept assume that cultures are relatively coherent systems of meaning, that there is an order that the observer describes rather than imposes. Gregory Bateson expressed this assumption in arguing that "if it were possible adequately to present the whole of a culture, stressing every aspect exactly as it is stressed in the culture itself, no single detail would appear bizarre or strange or arbitrary" (Bateson 1958:1). Yet it is equally plausible to assume that any culture is likely to involve irreconcilable principles or domains—for example, KINSHIP and ECONOMY in the United States—which follow divergent assumptions. One could thus agree with Clifford Geertz that "the problem of cultural analysis is as much a matter of determining independencies as interconnection, gulfs as well as bridges" (in Keesing 1974:80).

The idea of pattern was a useful analytic device within prewar Boasian cultural anthropology and was essential to the historicist CULTURE concept then in vogue. In the postwar period, many of the same concerns that prompted the search for themes, values, or configurations have been pursued with greater analytic refinement—usually without the assumption of a global coherence within culture—through the approaches of ETHNOSCIENCE, SYMBOLISM, INTERPRETATION, and SYSTEMS theory.

References

Bateson, Gregory. 1958. *Naven*. 2d ed. Stanford, Calif.: Stanford University Press.
Benedict, Ruth. 1932. "Configurations of Culture in North America." *AA* 34:1–27.
———. 1934. *Patterns of Culture*. Boston: Houghton Mifflin. An influential presentation of the pattern concept.
Berlin, Isaiah. 1963. *Karl Marx*. New York: Time.
Boas, Franz. 1920 [1940]. "The Methods of Ethnology." F. Boas, *Race, Language and Culture*. New York: Free Press.
Freed, Stanley A., and Ruth S. Freed. 1983. "Clark Wissler and the Development of Anthropology in the United States." *AA* 85:800–825.
Hegel, G. W. F. 1807 [1967]. *The Phenomenology of Mind*. J. B. Baillie, trans. New York: Harper & Row. The foundation of historicist ideas of culture pattern.
Herskovits, Melville J. 1956. *Man and His Works: The Science of Cultural Anthropology*. New York: Knopf.
Keesing, Roger M. 1974. "Theories of Culture." *ARA* 3:73–97.
Kroeber, Alfred L. 1948 [1963]. *Anthropology: Culture Patterns and Processes*. New York: Harcourt, Brace & World. Abridged from the textbook *Anthropology*, this is a useful presentation of the concept of culture pattern.

Opler, Morris E. 1946. "Themes as Dynamic Forces in Culture." *American Journal of Sociology* 51:198–206.

Stocking, George W., Jr. 1974. "Introduction: The Basic Assumptions of Boasian Anthropology." G. Stocking, ed., *The Shaping of American Anthropology, 1883–1911: A Franz Boas Reader*. New York: Basic Books.

————. 1976. "Ideas and Institutions in American Anthropology: Toward a History of the Interwar Period." G. Stocking, ed., *Selected Papers from the American Anthropologist, 1921–1945*. Washington, D.C.: American Anthropological Association.

Wertheimer, Max. 1925 [1955]. "Gestalt Theory." Willis D. Ellis, ed., *A Source Book of Gestalt Psychology*. London: Routledge & Kegan Paul.

Sources of Additional Information

An introduction is provided in Elizabeth E. Hoyt, "Integration of Culture: A Review of Concepts," *CA* 2:407–26, 1961. See also A. Hultkrantz, *GEC*, s.v. "culture pattern." For a study of one pattern theorist, see Judith S. Modell, *Ruth Benedict: Patterns of a Life*, Philadelphia: University of Pennsylvania Press, 1983.

PEASANTRY. Traditional agriculturalists within a state-level society, whose life is characterized by technological simplicity, economic and political subordination within a rural hierarchy, and dominance of the household as the unit of production.

The term peasant has as its primary association the idea of a rural dweller, a rustic. Peasant is derived from the Latin *pagensis*, the territory of a *pagus* or canton, in short, the countryside; pagan developed from the same root. It appeared in English from the late fifteenth century (see *OED*). Peasantries are an ancient form of social life: They emerged as the rural dimension of the first civilizations, at least six thousand years ago. Peasantries have been a dominant feature in the civilizations of China, India, Southeast Asia, the Near East, and Europe for most of their histories, and in parts of the Americas (for example, among the Mayans) from the first millenium A.D.

The word peasant has generally held negative connotations. Karl Marx described peasant life as "rural idiocy"; as Ernestine Friedl has noted, the common conception of peasantry has been that of "stupidity and stubborn resistance to change" (in Thorner 1968:508; Dalton 1972:386). Stated less pejoratively, peasantries are culturally stable and traditional, and socially or geographically remote from the sophistication of dominant elites and urban centers.

Anthropology came late to the study of peasantries. Historians have documented the feudal relationships and agrarian conditions of medieval European peasantries (see Duby 1968; Dalton 1972); folklorists (see FOLKLORE) have recorded peasant CUSTOMS, legends, and beliefs, in short the material of "folk life" (Redfield 1956: ch. 1). In contrast, ANTHROPOLOGY began with the ETHNOGRAPHY of tribal societies (see TRIBE). It was not until the 1930s that ethnographic studies of peasantries began to appear, for example, in Mexico (Redfield 1930), Ireland (Arensberg 1937), and Japan (Embree 1939). After the

Second World War, anthropological studies of peasant societies increased dramatically, and "peasant" began to be used as a theoretically significant, explicitly defined term (Silverman 1979:51–53).

Peasantry as a Part-Society

Reinforced by the orientation of FUNCTIONALISM, peasantries were first approached in anthropology as another manifestation of the village COMMUNITY, as integrated, small-scale social isolates. Anthropologists were among the first to examine modern peasantries as functioning social groups rather than as repositories of antiquarian data. Here the ethnographic experience of tribal societies provided an influential model (Arensberg 1937:27).

However, the isolation of peasant communities is relative, not absolute. In contrast to tribal groups, peasant communities exist culturally within an encompassing CIVILIZATION, and politically within a superordinate STATE. According to Alfred Kroeber, peasantries "constitute part-societies with part-cultures. They lack the isolation, the political autonomy, and the self-sufficiency of tribal populations; but their local units retain much of their old identity, integration, and attachment to soil and cults" (Kroeber 1948:284). The relative autonomy of peasantries has provided a major focus for research. The peasant community exhibits a tension between the stability of TRADITION and the forces of ACCULTURATION exerted by dominant urban centers. This is, in Robert Redfield's formulation, the FOLK CULTURE (Redfield 1930:1–14; Silverman 1979:52–57).

Peasantry as an Economic Pattern

Peasantries have also been defined in terms of a distinctive economic formation. One approach, taken by Raymond Firth, has been to treat a peasantry as any self-sufficient agrarian group: "small-scale producers, with a simple technology and equipment often relying primarily for their subsistence on what they themselves produce" (in Dalton 1972:386). The weakness of this approach is that it fails to distinguish between tribal producers and near-subsistence agriculturalists within a monetized, state-level society.

Among BANDS and TRIBES "surpluses are exchanged directly among groups or members of groups; peasants, however, are rural cultivators whose surpluses are transferred to a dominant group of rulers" (Wolf 1966:3–4). Put another way, tribal agriculturalists normally have direct access to productive resources, particularly land; peasants, in contrast, normally must appropriate a portion of their surplus to elites in the form of rent. Peasant households are linked to both superior and inferior groups within a rural hierarchy through a variety of social and economic mechanisms, often taking the form of patron/client relationships. Examples include the *compadrazgo* (godparenthood) complex of Latin America (Gudeman 1972), and the *jajmani* system, involving economic and ritual ties between service and agriculturalist CASTES, in rural India (Dumont 1970: ch. 4). Whether such hierarchical relations are inherently exploitative has been widely debated (see Roseberry 1976).

The Russian economist A. V. Chayanov (d. 1939) emphasized the distinctiveness of peasant economies, contrasting them with both capitalist and socialist forms of production (see MODE OF PRODUCTION). In the peasant sector the household is the unit both of production and (to a large but variable extent) of consumption. Thus the criterion of economic success is not profit as measured in monetary terms, but the survival of the peasant family (see Chayanov 1925; Kerblay 1971). These characteristics have significance for social change programs that attempt economic DEVELOPMENT of peasant societies (see also ECONOMY).

Types of Peasantries

The description given above, while offering a general picture, obscures the diversity of social contexts within which peasantries exist and neglects the role of history in the transformation of agrarian societies. Peasantry as a mode of life can be differentiated by a number of variables, among them the extensiveness of cash cropping and involvement in regional and national markets, the nature of landholding (rights of alienation, rights of usufruct, sharecropping, squatting, etc.), the range of obligatory payments to superiors (taxes, rents, corvée labor, payment in cash versus payment in kind), and the character of relations between peasants and landless agricultural workers (see Wolf 1966; Shanin 1971; Mintz 1973).

A more differentiated use of the peasant concept can be seen in Eric Wolf's distinction between the closed, corporate peasant communities of the Latin American highlands, and the culturally heterogeneous communities of lowland Latin America, characterized by quite different patterns of landholding and extensive involvement in cash cropping (Wolf 1955). Paul Friedrich's analysis of CULTURE CHANGE and peasant politics in Michoacan (Mexico) exemplifies the greater attention to historical forces in more recent studies of peasantries (Friedrich 1977; see also Dalton 1972). Peggy Barlett's review of research on adaptive strategies in peasant decision making suggests the sophisticated mix of theory (emphasizing ADAPTATION, CULTURAL ECOLOGY, and microeconomic modeling) that has been applied since the 1970s to understanding the range of variation in peasant agricultural production (Barlett 1980).

References

Arensberg, Conrad. 1937 [1968]. *The Irish Countryman*. New York: Natural History Press. An early (and highly readable) study of a peasant community.
Barlett, Peggy. 1980. "Adaptive Strategies in Peasant Agricultural Production." *ARA* 9:545–73. Summarizes recent research on peasantry from the perspectives of cultural ecology and economic anthropology.
Chayanov, A. V. 1925 [1986]. *The Theory of Peasant Economy*. Daniel Thorner et al., eds. Madison: University of Wisconsin Press. Includes translations of major works by Chayanov on the nature of the peasant economy, with extensive essays on his work.
Dalton, George. 1972. "Peasantries in Anthropology and History." *CA* 13:385–415. Dalton analyzes stages in the modernization of European peasantry.
Duby, Georges. 1968. *Rural Economy and Country Life in the Medieval West*. Cynthia

Postan, trans. Columbia: University of South Carolina Press. An example of the enormous historical literature bearing on peasantries.

Dumont, Louis. 1970. *Homo Hierarchicus: The Caste System and Its Implications*. Mark Sainsbury, trans. Chicago: University of Chicago Press.

Embree, John F. 1939. *Suye Mura: A Japanese Village*. Chicago: University of Chicago Press.

Friedrich, Paul. 1977. *Agrarian Revolt in a Mexican Village*. Chicago: University of Chicago Press. An ethnohistorical study of revolutionary peasant politics.

Gudeman, Stephen. 1972. "The Compadrazgo as a Reflection of the Natural and Spiritual Person." Royal Anthropological Institute, *Proceedings, 1971*, pp. 45–71.

Kerblay, Basile. 1971. "Chayanov and the Theory of Peasantry as a Specific Type of Economy." Teodor Shanin, ed., *Peasants and Peasant Societies: Selected Readings*. Harmondsworth, England: Penguin. Kerblay provides a useful introduction to Chayanov's work.

Kroeber, Alfred. 1948. *Anthropology*. New York: Harcourt, Brace.

Mintz, Sidney. 1973. "A Note on the Definition of Peasantries." *Journal of Peasant Studies* 1:91–106. Suggests the need for a more differentiated, historically grounded understanding of peasantries.

Redfield, Robert. 1930. *Tepoztlan: A Mexican Village*. Chicago: University of Chicago Press. A classic work.

————. 1956. *Peasant Society and Culture*. Chicago: University of Chicago Press.

Roseberry, William. 1976. "Rent, Differentiation, and the Development of Capitalism among Peasants." *AA* 78:45–58. Considers the supposed exploitation of peasantries from a Marxist perspective.

Shanin, Teodor. 1971. "Peasantry: Delineation of a Sociological Concept and a Field of Study." *Archives européenes de sociologie* 12:289–300. Reviews the differing theoretical perspectives on peasant studies.

Silverman, Sydel. 1979. "The Peasant Concept in Anthropology." *Journal of Peasant Studies* 7:49–69. Contrasts the influences of Redfield and Steward in shaping an anthropology of peasant societies.

Thorner, Daniel. 1968. "Peasantry." *IESS* 11:503–11.

Wolf, Eric. 1955. "Types of Latin American Peasantry: A Preliminary Discussion." *AA* 57:452–71.

————. 1966. *Peasants*. Englewood Cliffs, N.J.: Prentice-Hall. A good introduction.

Sources of Additional Information

Several readers provide good selections. These include Jack M. Potter et al., eds., *Peasant Society: A Reader*, Boston: Little, Brown, 1967; George Dalton, ed., *Tribal and Peasant Economies*, Garden City, N.Y.: Natural History Press, 1967; and Teodor Shanin, ed., *Peasants and Peasant Societies: Selected Readings*, Harmondsworth, England: Penguin, 1971. Eric Wolf, *Peasant Wars of the Twentieth Century*, New York: Harper & Row, 1969, highlights the role of peasantries in modern revolutionary movements. In the very readable study *Villages*, Garden City, N.Y.: Doubleday, 1983, Richard Critchfield provides the perspective of a journalist on peasant life and problems in the Third World. See also *The Journal of Peasant Studies* (London), 1973–.

PERSONALITY. The characteristic modes of thought, motivation, and feeling, conscious and unconscious, which guide the behavior of an individual.

Personality is derived from the Latin *persona*, denoting originally the mask worn by an actor on assuming a role. In common usage personality is linked with individuality: "that quality or assemblage of qualities which makes a person what he is, as distinct from other persons" (*OED*). The term has served as a point of orientation for the discipline of psychology and as its basic integrating concept. In the anthropological domain, the study of personality has been a key concern of psychological ANTHROPOLOGY, which involves the study of mental processes viewed in cross-cultural perspective and through ethnographic method (Bourguignon 1973). Until the 1970s this area of research, particularly in the United States, was more narrowly construed as the study of CULTURE and personality. This entry describes anthropological views regarding the interrelation of personality and culture—two of the most ambiguous terms in the entire social science lexicon.

However varied the definitions of personality may be, most acknowledge several common principles: (1) it is interactional, for personality is conditioned by the social field within which an individual exists; (2) it is patterned, involving consistency in behavior (narcissism or aggression, for example, can be manifested in numerous contexts); and (3) it is dynamic, for personality develops through the life cycle. These facts are recognized in the definition offered by Gordon Allport: "Personality is the dynamic organization within the individual of those psychophysical systems that determine his unique adjustments to his environment" (Allport 1937:48). The problems involved in appropriating the idea of personality for anthropology are exacerbated by the theoretical disagreements among psychologists. Very different concepts of personality, and methods for its study, are implied by Freudian or neo-Freudian psychoanalytic theory, behaviorist learning theory, and humanistic psychology (Wepman and Heine 1963).

Early Studies in Culture and Personality

Arguably, the central issue in psychological anthropology has been the correlation of distinctive personality types with particular cultures, or more briefly, the problem of national character. This issue has a long history. The thirteenth-century writer Bartholomaeus Anglicus offered many capsule descriptions of distinctive peoples: the Cantabrians of Spain were "unsteadfast in heart, apt to steal and [rob]"; the people of Flanders mild, honest, and peaceful; the Germans bold, hardy, and wild (in Hodgen 1964:63–64). Five centuries later, in the work of the German historian J. G. von Herder (1744–1803), the analysis was not markedly different: the seamen of Phoenecia were sensual and treacherous; the Egyptians quiet and industrious, and their art characterized by fidelity and precision; the Romans known for their courage and fortitude, and so forth (Herder 1791:145, 153, 253).

The first sustained consideration of the relation between personality and culture occurred in American anthropology in the early twentieth century. Margaret Mead's *Coming of Age in Samoa* (1928) asserted the importance of culture in shaping personality, citing the untroubled character of adolescent development in Samoa as a result of permissive sexual norms, in contrast with the conflict-filled adolescence in the more sexually repressive United States. On a more theoretical level, the personality concept was invoked as a means of overcoming the limitations of the diffusionist culture trait studies of Boasian anthropology (see HISTORICISM). For Edward Sapir (1884–1939) personality provided a model for cultural analysis, a basis for viewing cultures not as atomistic collections of traits, but as coherent patterns of thought and behavior. "The more fully one tries to understand a culture," Sapir argued, "the more it seems to take on the characteristics of a personality organization. . . . A word, a gesture, a genealogy, a type of religious belief may unexpectedly join hands in a common symbolism of status definition" (Sapir 1934:594).

This type of analysis, sometimes termed configurationism, was developed more fully by Ruth Benedict (1887–1948) in the widely read *Patterns of Culture* (1934). Cultures were distinctive and in a sense incommensurable because each was the result of a gradual process of selection, transforming an accumulation of unrelated behaviors into a distinctive pattern "in accordance with unconscious canons of choice that develop within the culture" (Benedict 1934:48). For Benedict a given culture could be characterized by a specific psychological config-uration. She viewed the Pueblo of the American Southwest as Apollonian (after Nietzsche's contrast of Apollonian and Dionysian perspectives), valuing restraint and ceremoniousness over excess and ecstasy. In contrast the Kwakiutl of the Northwest Coast, in their emphasis upon rank and wealth, and their seemingly frenzied competition for prestige through ritualized destruction of goods (the potlatch) were characterized as megalomaniac (Benedict 1934:129, 222; see also PATTERN; RELATIVISM).

Psychodynamic Approaches

In contrast to the essentially intuitive depiction of personality seen in the works of Sapir, Benedict, or the early Mead, later studies took as a point of departure existing psychological theory (usually Freudian), and sought to adapt it to the unfamiliar context of cross-cultural research. Freudian psychoanalytic theory assumed an essentially invariant process of personality formation, which in large measure determined cultural expression. For Sigmund Freud, "the beginnings of religion, morals, society and art converge in the Oedipus complex" (Freud 1913:156). Abram Kardiner offered a significant modification of this simplistic reduction of culture to psychology. Kardiner's schema gave logical priority to "primary institutions," those patterns of social organization and subsistence that mold early childhood experience and thereby establish a culture-specific basic personality structure, which in turn gives rise to "secondary institutions," for example, MYTH and RELIGION (Kardiner 1945:111).

Thus among the Alorese of Indonesia, by Kardiner's interpretation, females' exclusive involvement in horticulture led to maternal neglect of children; con-sequently, "the image of the parent as a persistent and solicitous helper . . . was not built up." As a result social interaction was characterized by distrust, an attitude also projected in the character of supernatural beings in Alorese religion

(Kardiner 1945:115–16; see also DuBois et al. 1944). While collaborating with Kardiner, Cora DuBois nonetheless argued that considerable variability in personality type can exist in any society, and she formulated as a more modest goal of research the identification of modal personality, the "central tendencies in the personalities of a group of people" (DuBois et al. 1944:xix).

Later Research

In the postwar period, the study of culture and personality has taken several directions.

(1) Efforts to identify a single personality profile for a given society faltered. According to Anthony Wallace, although anthropologists had assumed that psychological development within a given culture and society involved the "replication of uniformity" (creation of a common personality type), in fact, the process was one of "the organization of diversity," yielding a society of varied but interdependent personality types (Wallace 1970: ch. 4).

(2) Adapting techniques of controlled cross-cultural comparison to psychological anthropology (see COMPARATIVE METHOD), John and Beatrice Whiting pioneered a systematic research program on child development, investigating the interaction of culture, environment, and personality. Drawing on both behaviorist and psychoanalytic theory, their studies have given a more rigorous understanding of enculturation, the process by which culturally salient values and behaviors are internalized in the developing personality (see Beatrice Whiting et al. 1975, 1988).

(3) Particularly since the 1960s, research in psychological anthropology has broadened beyond a concern with personality per se, to encompass such topics as altered states of consciousness (see TRANCE), cross-cultural perspectives on illness and CURING, and the interpretation of SYMBOLISM and RITUAL. There has been renewed interest in the long-standing debate over the respective significance of panhuman (innate) and culture-specific (learned) psychological patterning, investigated in such domains as aggression (see WAR), GENDER, and RATIONALITY (see NATURE; PSYCHIC UNITY; SOCIOBIOLOGY).

References

Allport, Gordon W. 1937. *Personality: A Psychological Interpretation*. New York: Henry Holt. Offers considerable material on the history of the concept.
Benedict, Ruth. 1934 [1959]. *Patterns of Culture*. Boston: Houghton Mifflin. A classic statement of the configurationist view.
Bourguignon, Erika. 1973. "Psychological Anthropology." John J. Honigmann, ed., *Handbook of Social and Cultural Anthropology*. Chicago: Rand McNally. A useful overview.
DuBois, Cora, et al. 1944 [1961]. *The People of Alor: A Social-Psychological Study of an East Indian Island*. 2 vols. New York: Harper & Brothers. A pioneering, collaborative study.
Freud, Sigmund. 1913 [1950]. *Totem and Taboo: Some Points of Agreement Between the Mental Lives of Savages and Neurotics*. New York: Norton.

Herder, Johann Gottfried von. 1791 [1968]. *Reflections on the Philosophy of the History of Mankind*. Abr. Frank E. Manuel, ed. Chicago: University of Chicago Press.

Hodgen, Margaret T. 1964. *Early Anthropology in the Sixteenth and Seventeenth Centuries*. Philadelphia: University of Pennsylvania Press.

Kardiner, Abram. 1945. "The Concept of Basic Personality Structure as an Operational Tool in the Social Sciences." Ralph Linton, ed., *The Science of Man in the World Crisis*. New York: Columbia University Press. A pioneering effort at a cross-cultural model of personality formation.

Mead, Margaret. 1928 [1968]. *Coming of Age in Samoa*. New York: Dell. A classic of psychological anthropology.

Sapir, Edward. 1934 [1951]. "The Emergence of the Concept of Personality in a Study of Cultures." David Mandelbaum, ed., *Selected Writings of Edward Sapir in Language, Culture and Personality*. Berkeley and Los Angeles: University of California Press.

Wallace, Anthony F. C. 1970. *Culture and Personality*. 2d ed. New York: Random House.

Wepman, Joseph M., and Ralph W. Heine, eds. 1963. *Concepts of Personality*. Chicago: Aldine. A good survey of personality theories in psychology.

Whiting, Beatrice B., et al. 1975. *Children of Six Cultures*. Cambridge: Harvard University Press.

————. 1988. *Children of Different Worlds: The Formation of Social Behavior*. Cambridge: Harvard University Press.

Sources of Additional Information

For an accessible introduction, see Philip K. Bock's *Continuities in Psychological Anthropology*, San Francisco: Freeman, 1980. A valuable overview of research, with extensive references, is provided by Francis L. K. Hsu, ed., *Psychological Anthropology*, rev. ed., Cambridge, Mass.: Schenkman, 1972. George D. Spindler, ed., *The Making of Psychological Anthropology*, Berkeley and Los Angeles: University of California Press, 1978, offers a revealing series of professional self-portraits by major figures in psychological anthropology. In *Freud and Anthropology: A History and Reappraisal*, New York: International Universities Press, 1983, Edwin R. Wallace IV reviews Freud's study of, and reception in, anthropology.

POLITICS. See INEQUALITY.

PRIMITIVE. (1) (Adjective) The moral or intellectual condition of BANDS or TRIBES, by implication inferior to that of civilizations (an obsolete usage). (2) (Noun) A member of such a society.

The concept of the primitive has been anthropology's lodestone, polarizing and orienting its research. This invidious term, like the still more negative "savage" or the now ironic "barbarian," has served to divide the social world in two: on the one side CIVILIZATION, on the other those alien, less powerful, and little known societies that have comprised (at least until recently) the anthropological subject matter. Etymologically, the primitive is that which appeared first (from the Latin *primus*, first): "of or belonging to the first age, period, or stage; pertaining to early times. . . . [and as a noun] an original inhabitant, an aboriginal'' (OED). In the context of ANTHROPOLOGY, however, "primitive" perpetuates a double misconception. First, it implies a spurious unity, grouping together societies that vary radically in size, complexity, and mode of life. Second, it suggests that such living peoples are culturally similar to the men and women of early prehistory, an implication that is false.

So-called primitive societies have been peripheral to the European heartland. For the ancient Greeks and Romans, this periphery included the tribes of Britain, Gaul, Germany, Asia Minor, and north Africa. The exploration and conquest initiated in the Renaissance pushed back the margins of the known world, eventually embracing Africa and the Near East, the Americas, Oceania, Australia, and Asia. The most salient feature of these cultures was their radical unfamiliarity, their "otherness." As such they could be viewed positively or negatively, as the argument demanded.

In the ancient world several lines of thought converged to paint such alien cultures in flattering terms. The German tribes could be viewed realistically, as with Tacitus (d. A.D. 117), though he used their customs as a telling criticism of Roman decadence—"Good morality is more effective in Germany than good laws are elsewhere" (German. 19). But for many classical authors (Seneca, for example) the Germans, the Scythians, and other tribes, real or imagined, were seen as exemplars of the Noble Savage, a view encouraged by the primitivism of both Cynic and Stoic philosophies, with their idealizing of NATURE and depreciation of civilization (see Lovejoy and Boas 1935).

Christian writers were on the whole far more negative regarding tribal peoples, a tendency that has persisted to the present day. Clement of Alexandria (d. ca. 215) could use the primitive rhetorically: "When he wished to humiliate the Greeks, he called to their attention the legendary nobility of their savage contemporaries. When . . . he wished to praise the Christians, he contrasted their life with the horrors of savagery" (Boas 1948:135). The consistently negative views of Tertullian (d. ca. 230), however, were more typical. He described the nomadic Scythians in acid terms: "Their domicile is unsettled, their life is rude [vita cruda], their lust is promiscuous and for the most part open" (in Lovejoy and Boas 1935:342–43).

The Primitive in the Rise of Anthropology

From the accounts of Renaissance explorers through the evolutionary reconstructions of Victorian anthropologists, a strongly negative view of the primitive world has predominated. Christian belief, medieval legend, and rationalist philosophy alike had little use for a doctrine of the noble primitive (see Hodgen 1964:358–62; George 1968; Bitterli 1976). The pessimistic description that Thomas Hobbes presented in the Leviathan (1651) of the "natural condition of mankind," that is, before the establishment of political harmony through the STATE, is indicative: "There is no place for industry, because the fruit thereof is uncertain . . . no knowledge of the face of the earth; no account of time; no arts; no letters; no society; and which is worst of all, continual fear, and danger

of violent death; and the life of man, solitary, poor, nasty, brutish, and short"
(Sec. 1.13; Hobbes 1651:161).

If ethnological diversity was, to the pagan Greeks and Romans, simply a fact
to be noted, to Renaissance writers it posed a crucial problem: explaining the
existence of nonbiblical peoples (Boas 1948:129). Being non-Christian in manner
and belief (even when these were recounted with a semblance of accuracy, which
was seldom), these alien cultures were morally as well as ethnologically problematic. In broad terms, two solutions were available. The first was to amend,
if not to reject, the adequacy of biblical testimony by positing the existence of
multiple creations, yielding at different times the various human species, with
their diverse characteristics and abilities—the doctrine of polygenesis (see RACE).
The second alternative, accepting the biblical doctrine of a single creation (mon-
ogenesis), was to explain the existence of "primitives" as a degeneration from
the innocence and perfection of the time of Adam.

At the same time, their presence in lands far from the Mediterranean heartland
implied a history of MIGRATION, in the course of which knowledge of true
morality and religion had been replaced by ignorance and superstition. William
Strachey, writing in 1612, explained savage peoples as descendants of the wan-
dering Ham: "Yt is observed that Cham, and his famely, were the only far
Travellors, and Straglers into divers unknowne countries . . . as also yt is said
of his famely, that what country soever the Children of Cham happened to
possesse, there beganne both the Ignorance of true godliness" (in Hodgen
1964:262).

The emergence of EVOLUTION as the dominant paradigm for anthropology in
the late eighteenth and nineteenth centuries transformed the theoretical basis for
explaining cultural difference and, in particular, the existence of "savage societies." Nonetheless, the image of such peoples in the anthropological imagination was little changed. If anything, the rigid stages (e.g., savagery, barbarism,
civilization) presumed by evolutionist writers served to make the picture of the
"primitive" more homogeneous and stereotypic (cf. PSYCHIC UNITY). The result
is what might be termed the "generic savage." To quote John Lubbock, "The
mind of the savage, like that of the child, is easily fatigued. . . . Such ideas
[regarding the relation of earth and sun] are, in fact, entirely beyond the mental
range of the lower savages, whose extreme mental inferiority we have much
difficulty in realising" (Lubbock 1870:4, 5). Similarly, "There is no individual
thought, his emotions are collective, and—as collective emotions always are—
are emphasized until they become an obsession. . . . Since, from his ignorance,
the savage draws no line between the natural and the supernatural, or rather
everything is equally natural to him, mysteries are a part of his daily life"
(Hartland 1924:79–80). Such views have extended—as the last quotation
shows—well into the twentieth century.

Side by side with the predominantly negative view of tribal peoples has been
a quite different (albeit minority) tendency, a sympathetic and tolerant interest
in the cultural alternatives that so-called primitive societies offer to European

civilization. This can be seen notably in the works of the Enlightenment *philosophes* of the eighteenth century, Diderot, Rousseau, and Montesquieu among others. Yet these views must not be exaggerated. Jean-Jacques Rousseau (d. 1778)—to cite the best known—was no primitivist, despite his erroneous reputation as an glorifier of the "noble savage" (see Rousseau 1754; Cassirer 1932). The closest approximation to a primitivist perspective in the modern era occurs in literature (inspired or at least abetted by anthropology), as seen in the works of Herman Melville, William Butler Yeats, and D. H. Lawrence (see Bell 1972).

Modern Usage

The position of a modern, post-Boasian or post-Malinowskian anthropology is more complex. Many decades of careful ETHNOGRAPHY have revealed the gross ethnocentrism and error of this predominant, negative image of "the primitive." Yet while no contemporary anthropologist would endorse the views of John Lubbock or Thomas Hobbes, the categorical distinction of primitive and civilized cultures has shown remarkable longevity, even in anthropology. Here several viewpoints should be distinguished.

(1) Certain writers, Lucien Lévy-Bruhl most notably, developed at length an argument for two contrasting modes of thought, primitive and civilized, reflected in the "primitive's" understandings of causation, the relation between individual and group, or the so-called mystical participation between (to us) unrelated phenomena, for example, between an individual and his shadow, his name, or his totem animal. Lévy-Bruhl did not argue (in the fashion of Lubbock) that primitives were unintelligent, but that their intelligence was applied through an alien reasoning, as manifested in MAGIC, RELIGION, RITUAL, and TOTEMISM (Lévy-Bruhl 1927; Evans-Pritchard 1965: ch. 4). Although the categorical contrast of two such mentalities has few defenders today (but see Schweder 1982), the issues raised by Lévy-Bruhl have prompted recognition of the difficulties inherent in the INTERPRETATION of religion and ritual and in the complexities presented by the concept of RATIONALITY.

(2) A second approach, exemplified in the work of Stanley Diamond, resurrects primitivism as a critique of civilization, in the tradition of Tacitus or Seneca. In this view, primitive societies are characterized by a complex of positive features, among these a stable, communalistic economy, a collective and traditional pattern of leadership, and an integration of religion and healing with all other aspects of culture. Diamond's aim is to revitalize "primitive" as an analytic term of anthropology, as a point of reference against which the psychological and social inadequacies of state-level societies can better be measured. Thus, "the search for the primitive is the attempt to define a primary human potential. Without such a model . . . , it becomes increasingly difficult to evaluate or understand our contemporary pathology and possibilities" (Diamond 1974:119).

(3) The most common pattern of usage in postwar anthropology has been neither to deprecate nor to exhalt the primitive, but rather to use the term haphazardly, without theoretical justification, or to seek more palatable synonyms ("nonliterate" and "native" among them) for what is recognized to be an

invidious term. This suggests that the category of primitive has endured in anthropology more from intellectual inertia than analytic precision. Certainly its usage is highly inconsistent, as several writers have documented (e.g., Hsu 1968). Yet the problem lies less with the connotations of primitive than with the class of societies it denotes. As Sol Tax has argued, "The anthropological use of *primitive* is not a legitimate concept deserving a single term. We lump together all of the peoples of the world, past and present, except those which are part of Western Civilization and its ancient progenitors" (Tax 1968:65).

More than a century after Lubbock, anthropology is equipped with several sets of theoretically robust categories through which societies can be objectively contrasted. The political categories of BAND, TRIBE, CHIEFDOM, and STATE offer one possibility; contrasts based on subsistence forms or economic patterns offer others. Any or all would seem preferable to the outdated contrast of primitive and civilized.

References

Bell, Michael. 1972. *Primitivism*. London: Methuen. A short work on primitivism in modern literature.

Bitterli, Urs. 1976. *Die "Wilden" und die "Zivilisierten."* Munich: C. H. Beck. Has an excellent bibliography on the exploration literature.

Boas, George. 1948. *Essays on Primitivism and Related Ideas in the Middle Ages*. Baltimore: Johns Hopkins University Press.

Cassirer, Ernst. 1932 [1963]. *The Question of Jean-Jacques Rousseau*. Peter Gay, trans. and ed. Bloomington: Indiana University Press. Clarifies the complex ideas of Rousseau, including his view of the noble savage.

Diamond, Stanley. 1974. *In Search of the Primitive: A Critique of Civilization*. New Brunswick, N.J.: Transaction Books. An eloquent appeal for a positive interpretation of the primitive in anthropology.

Evans-Pritchard, E. E. 1965. *Theories of Primitive Religion*. Oxford: Clarendon Press. This excellent study reveals the inadequacies of early anthropological stereotypes regarding primitive thought and society.

George, Katherine. 1968. "The Civilized West Looks at Primitive Africa: 1400–1800: A Study in Ethnocentrism." Ashley Montagu, ed., *The Concept of the Primitive*. New York: Free Press. A historical review of changing perceptions in culture contact.

Hartland, E. Sidney. 1924 [1969]. *Primitive Law*. New York: Harper. Hartland holds to the "custom-bound" image of primitive culture.

Hobbes, Thomas. 1651 [1939]. *Leviathan*. Edwin A. Burtt, ed., *The English Philosophers from Bacon to Mill*. New York: Modern Library.

Hodgen, Margaret T. 1964. *Early Anthropology in the Sixteenth and Seventeenth Centuries*. Philadelphia: University of Pennsylvania Press.

Hsu, Francis L. K. 1968. "Rethinking the Concept 'Primitive.'" Ashley Montagu, ed., *The Concept of the Primitive*. New York: Free Press. A critical review of the inconsistent uses of primitive in anthropology.

Lévy-Bruhl, Lucien. 1927 [1963]. *L'âme primitive*. Paris: Presses Universitaires de France. Suggests a distinctive logic in primitive thought.

Lovejoy, Arthur O., and George Boas. 1935 [1965]. *Primitivism and Related Ideas in*

Antiquity. New York: Octagon Books. A major compilation of primitivist texts by classical writers.

Lubbock, John. 1870 [1978]. *The Origin of Civilization and the Primitive Condition of Man*. Peter Rivière, ed. Chicago: University of Chicago Press. A characteristic— and immensely popular—work of Victorian anthropology.

Rousseau, Jean-Jacques. 1754 [1967]. *Discourse on the Origin and Foundation of Inequality among Mankind*. Lester G. Crocker, ed., *The Social Contract* and *Discourse on the Origin and Foundation of Inequality among Mankind*. New York: Washington Square Press. A much cited, less frequently read text, impressive for its anthropological insight.

Schweder, Richard A. 1982. "On Savages and Other Children." *AA* 84:354–66. A critique of recent efforts to revive the idea of a primitive mentality.

Tax, Sol. 1968. "'Primitive' Peoples." Ashley Montagu, ed., *The Concept of the Primitive*. New York: Free Press. Another critique of the concept of primitive. The entire volume of essays is highly recommended.

Sources of Additional Information

Jacob Pandian, *Anthropology and the Western Tradition: Toward an Authentic Anthropology*, Prospect Heights, Ill.: Waveland, 1985, offers a readable introduction to the stereotypes of the primitive and alien in anthropological—and more broadly, Western— thought. In *Primitive Heritage: An Anthropological Anthology*, New York: Random House, 1953, Margaret Mead and Nicholas Calas provide a provoking set of texts recording the alien qualities in belief and behavior frequently subsumed by the term primitive.

PSYCHIC UNITY. Those common human capacities and characteristics that transcend the diversity of cultural expression; human nature.

Psychic unity—the postulate of a common human condition or capacity transcending cultural diversity—has been an enduring theme in ANTHROPOLOGY, as in moral philosophy. The concept of psychic unity has taken a variety of forms: sometimes understood substantively, as a particular set of characteristics shared by all peoples; and sometimes formally, as an explanatory principle (e.g., human reason) justifying a claim for the possibility of cross-cultural understanding, or a postulated uniformity in the course of cultural EVOLUTION.

A concept of psychic unity can be found in classical philosophy, notably in the Stoic emphasis on *consensus gentium*, the general opinion of nations. The goal of Stoic ethics, as taught by Zeno of Citium (4th century BC), was to act in harmony with God or NATURE, the natural being that which is universal. Human nature, accordingly, is revealed in those patterns of thought and behavior that are invariant, which stand out against the variegated background of local CUSTOM (Boas 1973; Long 1973).

Far closer to our own era, the philosophers of the Enlightenment—themselves much influenced by Stoicism—grappled with similar concerns (see Gay 1966:296–304). In seeking to ground ethics, politics, and religion in a universal human reason, rather than inherited TRADITION, these writers were led to contrast the multiplicity (and thus arbitrariness) of custom with the supposed constancy of human nature. Thus Voltaire (1694–1778) argued that "whatever concerns human nature is the same from one end of the universe to the other, and . . . what is dependent upon custom differs" (in Slotkin 1965:382). Differences in custom were explained as the result of culturally determined learning, not innate character. According to the English philosopher Bernard de Mandeville (d. 1733), "There is no Difference between the original Nature of a Savage, and that of a civiliz'd Man," a view whose implications were rather tolerant and benign (in Slotkin 1965:260). The Scot William Robertson (1721–1793) made a still stronger claim for psychic unity, namely the constancy of mental processes: "The human mind . . . holds a course so regular, that in every age and country the dominion of particular passions will be attended with similar effects" (in Slotkin 1965:427).

Victorian Anthropology

By the early nineteenth century a sufficient body of data in ETHNOGRAPHY, prehistory, physical anthropology, and linguistics had accumulated to provide a reasonable starting point for a discipline concerned with explaining the diversity and historical development of peoples and customs. At least in Britain, theorizing was originally dominated by a diffusionist ETHNOLOGY. The work of James Prichard (1786–1848), for example, sought to demonstrate human psychic unity by reconstructing the origins of all peoples through DIFFUSION and MIGRATION from a common original population, in a manner compatible with biblical orthodoxy (Stocking 1987:48–53).

By the 1870s, however, the older ethnological approach had been superseded by an evolutionary paradigm. Anthropologists were now concerned not with questions of origin and derivation, but with progress and DEVELOPMENT, demonstrating, according to Edward Tylor (1832–1917), "the uniformity with which like stages in the development of art and science are found among the most unlike races" (Tylor 1878:232). Psychic unity was no longer—as with Prichard's ethnology—a hypothesis to be demonstrated but rather an essential working assumption. Without it the evolutionists' COMPARATIVE METHOD would have no meaning. Their ethnographic examples (e.g., concerning RELIGION, LAW, or MARRIAGE), culled from the most diverse societies, could only be taken to exemplify the various stages of a developmental sequence if one assumed that a common human mentality necessitated a uniform path for cultural evolution (see Stocking 1987: chs. 2, 5).

A very different approach can be seen in German ethnology. Adolf Bastian (1826–1905) explored the problem of psychic unity in terms strongly influenced by the philosophical tradition of German idealism, by means of the paired concepts of *Völkergedanken* and *Elementargedanken* ("folk ideas" and "elementary ideas"). Bastian postulated a series of panhuman mental principles or archetypes, each manifested through a variety of empirical folk ideas, as for example the elementary idea of deity is realized empirically in very different ways in the religious systems of ancient Greece, Polynesia, and South Asia (Koepping 1983:51).

Modern Approaches

The evolutionists' espousal of psychic unity coexisted uneasily with a strong emphasis on the inequality of cultural attainment between PRIMITIVE societies and CIVILIZATIONS, a contrast often justified by a form of racial determinism, a correlation of RACE and CULTURE (see Stocking 1987:245–62). To a significant extent twentieth-century anthropological theory was created in the course of disproving such radical and invidious distinctions between societies and affirming a panhuman psychic unity. Thus in American anthropology the HISTORICISM of Franz Boas and Alfred Kroeber rejected any explanation of culture in terms of biology (see SUPERORGANIC) and emphasized the need for RELATIVISM in interpreting each culture as a reality sui generis. In British FUNCTIONALISM, Bronislaw Malinowski affirmed psychic unity by demonstrating the RATIONALITY underlying belief and RITUAL in tribal societies. Finally, a major concern of French STRUCTURALISM, as seen in the work of Claude Lévi-Strauss, has been to demonstrate a common order underlying such diverse realms as MYTH and SOCIAL STRUCTURE, imposed by the character of the human mind, in all societies.

These perspectives notwithstanding, the problem of psychic unity remains a significant issue for contemporary anthropology. An adequate anthropology must be able to explain the range of cultural diversity existing in the human species while avoiding both horns of a dilemma: either losing any grasp of what is generically human by an overemphasis on variability and relativism; or trivializing culture in the name of a universal but essentially empty category of "human nature" (see Geertz 1973).

References

Boas, George. 1973. "Nature." *DHI* 3:346–51.
Gay, Peter. 1966. *The Enlightenment, an Interpretation: The Rise of Modern Paganism*. New York: Vintage. Treats a philosophical movement foundational for anthropology.
Geertz, Clifford. 1973. "The Impact of the Concept of Culture on the Concept of Man." In Clifford Geertz, *The Interpretation of Cultures*. New York: Basic Books. A valuable essay on the problem of psychic unity from the perspective of symbolic anthropology.
Koepping, Klaus-Peter. 1983. *Adolf Bastian and the Psychic Unity of Mankind*. New York: University of Queensland Press.
Long, Anthony A. 1973. "Ethics of Stoicism." *DHI* 4:319–22.
Slotkin, J.S. 1965. *Readings in Early Anthropology*. Chicago: Aldine. A significant anthology emphasizing the seventeenth and eighteenth centuries, with much relevance regarding psychic unity and human nature.
Stocking, George W., Jr. 1987. *Victorian Anthropology*. New York: Free Press. A valuable historical study.
Tylor, Edward B. 1878 [1964]. *Researches into the Early History of Mankind and the Development of Civilization*. 3d ed., abr. Chicago: University of Chicago Press. An important text of evolutionist anthropology.

Sources of Additional Information

For a discussion of structuralist anthropology that pays significant attention to the problem of psychic unity, see Edmund Leach, *Lévi-Strauss*, London: Fontana, 1970.

PSYCHOLOGY. See PERSONALITY.

R

RACE. (1) One of a number of broad divisions of the human species, based on a common geographic origin and certain shared physical characteristics. (2) In more recent usage, a group of human breeding populations distinguished from other such groups by a characteristic distribution of gene frequencies.

Race is one of the most symbolically weighted terms of the social science vocabulary. At the root of the concept is the idea of common ancestry, but this has been construed both very narrowly and very broadly. Narrowly, race was understood as an individual's offspring, as in the "race and stock of Abraham" (1570); broadly, as humanity as a whole, the "human race," a usage also dating to the late sixteenth century (see *OED*). Between these two extremes lies its main—and controversial—sense, as one of a series of major social groupings, based on a common biological heritage and shared physical characteristics.

Homo sapiens is markedly polytypic. That is, the human species is expressed through a number of physical types, involving characteristic combinations of stature, head form, skin color, and the like, each reflecting some balance of common DESCENT and evolutionary ADAPTATION to a common environment. Han Chinese, Kashmiri Brahmans, Russians, Nigerian Ibos, Navahos, and Australian Aborigines—these groups suggest the range of physical differences to be found in our species. Nonetheless, although there is obvious physical variation within the human population, the interpretation of this diversity—the process of sorting individuals into races—has to a large extent reflected cultural presuppositions, particularly ethnocentrism (see RELATIVISM).

Efforts at a systematic classification of the human races, though seldom consistent, date from the seventeenth century. Francois Bernier (1620–1688) identified four races: the peoples of Europe (including much of western and southern Asia), Africa, the rest of Asia, and the Lapps. The natives of the Americas, however, were not considered sufficiently distinct to merit a separate category (in Slotkin 1965:94–95). In 1781 Johann Friedrich Blumenbach (1752–1840), who originated—quite arbitrarily—the notion of a "Caucasian" race, argued for the existence of five races. In addition to Caucasian he identified Mongolian, Ethiopian (referring to sub-Saharan Africa), American, and Malayan (Slotkin 1965:190). This influential model provided the now-familiar "white," "yellow," "black," and "red" of Western folk classification, supplemented by the Malayan racial grouping to account for Southeast Asia and Oceania. A modern, though nonetheless controversial, classification identifies seven races: Caucasoid, Mongoloid, full-sized Australoid, dwarf Australoid (e.g., Negritos), full-sized Congoid, dwarf Congoid (e.g., Pygmies), and Capoids (e.g., San ["Bushmen"]) (Coon and Hunt 1965:11–13). Other racial classifications devised over the past century have shown similar inconsistency (see Nelson and Jurmain 1982:196–97).

Race and Ideology

Prejudice against alien peoples and ways of life—particularly those belonging to technologically simple BANDS and TRIBES—was not invented by the Victorians. Rather, a perceived dichotomy between PRIMITIVE and civilized societies has been a major element of the Western WORLD VIEW since the beginnings of worldwide European exploration in the sixteenth century. What set apart the nineteenth century understanding of human difference was the emerging prominence of biology as a scientific discipline, manifested in particular through the study of EVOLUTION, and the corresponding assumption that the true determinant of human capacities and behavior was heredity, as expressed in race. As Stephen Gould has commented, "Racial prejudice may be as old as recorded human history, but its biological justification imposed the additional burden of intrinsic inferiority upon despised groups, and precluded redemption by conversion or assimilation" (Gould 1981:31).

Aside from a naive biological determinism, any prospect of an objective investigation of human variation was rendered impossible by political controversies of the nineteenth and early twentieth centuries (see Barzun 1965). The concept of race in this period became inextricably connected with arguments in defense of slavery, colonialism, and nationalism. Furthermore, the entirely distinct domains of human biology, LANGUAGE, and CULTURE were frequently treated as interchangeable, with social or linguistic traits considered permanent and inherent characteristics of a people, rooted in biology. Even the eminent nineteenth century linguist Max Müller, discussing the Indo-Aryan language family of South Asia, implied the existence of an "Aryan" race and commented on the character of the "Aryan mind" (Stocking 1987:59). More sweepingly, the American paleontologist Henry Fairfield Osborn argued (in 1916) that "race implies heredity, and heredity implies all the moral, social, and intellectual characteristics and traits which are the springs of politics and government" (in Montagu 1965:32).

Monogenism and Polygenism

Arguments regarding race and biology were rendered more complex by a debate between monogenists and polygenists, the former believing all races constitute one species, the latter holding various races to constitute distinct and unequal species (see Stanton 1960). Polygenist doctrine has a considerable history. In the sixteenth century Isaac de la Peyrère (1594–1676) postulated the existence of a "pre-Adamic" race, supplementing the narrative offered in Genesis (Slotkin 1965:81–82). Not surprisingly, the doctrine of polygenesis was employed as a justification for slavery (Haller 1971: ch. 3). Edward Long (1734–1813) claimed that blacks constituted a separate species, holding that they were "void of genius, and seem almost incapable of making any progress in civility or science" (in Slotkin 1965:209). Similar arguments were advanced for the biological inferiority of the American Indians (Stanton 1960:82–99). The renowned French anatomist Paul Broca (1824–1880) defended the polygenist position not only on biological but also on cultural grounds, claiming as evidence (incorrectly) the existence of peoples lacking any religious conceptions, speaking languages unrelated to any other, and being "altogether anti-social" (in Count 1950:69).

The monogenists, in contrast, had biblical orthodoxy on their side. "We know, with infallible certainty," William Robertson (1721–1793) proclaimed, "that all the human race spring from the same source, and that the descendants of one man . . . multiplied and replenished the earth" (in Slotkin 1965:202). The monogenist position nonetheless raised problems. Before the acceptance of Darwinian theory it was difficult to reconcile the radical cultural differences between so-called primitive and civilized peoples with belief in the unity of the human species. One answer was the doctrine of degenerationism, holding that the cultural and moral qualities (as well as physical form) of various peoples had declined from an earlier, higher level. This was, in fact, the reverse of the evolutionist perspective. As Blumenbach phrased the argument, if "the causes of degeneration are sufficient to explain the phenomena of the corporeal diversity of mankind, we ought not to admit" the premise of multiple human species (in Count 1950:26). In practical terms, the degenerationist argument did not survive the nineteenth century.

The Reinterpretation of Race

The quite different problems involved in interpreting human physical and cultural diversity led ANTHROPOLOGY in divergent directions in the late nineteenth and early twentieth centuries. Within physical anthropology the investigation of racial diversity shifted from anecdotal and subjective description to the quantitative study of bodily form (anthropometry), with an emphasis on the skull. In Europe such research was pioneered by the anatomists Anders Retzius (1796–1860) and Paul Broca (see Count 1950: ch. 9). In the United States, the physician Samuel Morton (d. 1851) accumulated a collection of more than one thousand skulls to document the anthropometry of racial difference (Gould 1981:51).

Until well into the twentieth century such racially oriented anthropometric studies dominated physical anthropology (see Hrdlicka 1914). In large part the field remained within the polygenist tradition, with its key corollaries the essential fixity of racial types and the racial determination of cultural expression (Stocking 1968:55–56; see also Brinton 1901). In this context, these ever more precise efforts to determine the quantitative characteristics of racial distinctiveness proved largely self-defeating. The range of human diversity within any given population became increasingly evident, and the idea of pure and primordial racial types ever less plausible (Stocking 1968:164–65).

The resolution of this impasse can be attributed both to a change of perspective within cultural anthropology (see ETHNOLOGY) and the transformation of biological thought, resulting from the acceptance of Mendelian genetics. Within the emerging field of cultural anthropology, the work of Franz Boas (1858–1942) had particular importance. In physical anthropology, Boas challenged the doctrine of stability of forms by demonstrating the considerable role the environment played in determining stature and rate of growth. In a study of European immigrants and their American-born children, he concluded (in 1911) that "while heretofore we had the right to assume that human types are stable, all the evidence is now in favor of a great plasticity of human types, and permanence of types in new surroundings appears rather as the exception than as the rule" (in Stocking 1968:178; see also Boas 1913).

From an early date Boas had expressed scepticism regarding the supposed relation between cultural achievement and intellectual capacity in the various races (Boas 1894). The most significant legacy of Boas's mature thought was, in this regard, an understanding of culture as a reality sui generis, to be understood on its own terms, the product of historical and social, rather than biological forces (Stocking 1968:212–22; see HISTORICISM). The independence of culture and biology (or race)—an accepted tenet of cultural anthropology in the first half of this century—was a proposition developed more fully by Boas's students, notably by Alfred Kroeber (1876–1960) in his concept of the SUPERORGANIC.

Recent Approaches to Biological Variation

In the biological sciences, by the 1940s, the gradual synthesis of Darwinian evolutionary theory with Mendelian population genetics had transformed the scientific understanding of race. Two important changes resulted. First, the diagnostic concern shifted from expressed form (phenotype), such as stature or hair color, to inherited genetic information (genotype). Second, rather than defining races in terms of an idealized and static typology of physical traits, they came to be understood as genetically heterogeneous breeding populations. From this perspective, Theodosius Dobzhansky defined races simply as "populations differing in the incidence of certain genes" (in Molnar 1983:17). For others, the advent of population genetics rendered the race concept obsolete, not because variation in the human species is insignificant, but because—in the view of many anthropologists—its complexity cannot be characterized accurately by any racial typology (see Livingstone 1964).

The popular understanding of race has been rather different. As the UNESCO statement on race noted, "The biological fact of race and the myth of 'race' should be distinguished; for all practical social purposes 'race' is not so much a biological phenomenon as a social myth" (in Montagu 1951:15). Such myths, in the form of racial typologies, remain strongly represented in the folk knowledge of various cultures (see ETHNOSCIENCE). Not surprisingly, these folk typologies are highly inconsistent: compare the relatively simple fourfold scheme common in the United States (white, black, red, yellow) with the much more complex and fluid racial classification common in Brazil (van den Berghe 1967:71). Furthermore, race and ETHNICITY (the recognition of groups on the basis of a distinctive cultural tradition and identity) have become widely confounded. In the United States, for example, government studies routinely ask individuals to classify themselves through such categories as white, Hispanic, black, Russian, and Pacific Islander—a meaningless set of alternatives.

Anthropological research since the 1960s has returned to questions of the interrelation of biology and culture, an area of investigation that earlier scholars such as Boas and Kroeber had tried to rule off limits. Yet with the exception of an unresolved and perhaps unresolvable debate over the relation of race and intelligence (Lewontin 1975), recent studies of the biology/culture interaction largely ignore racial formalism. Research on biocultural adaptation has examined the role of particular variations in genotype in adapting a population to distinctive environments and patterns of subsistence. An example is variation in the adult tolerance of milk (because of the enzyme lactase), a capacity that has been attributed to selection pressures in groups which evolved a herding-dairying way of life (Jolly and Plog 1982:394–95). In contrast, studies in SOCIOBIOLOGY have investigated the degree to which cultural forms, such as MARRIAGE rules or patterns of reciprocity, may have been determined by the same mechanisms of natural selection long identified in biological evolution.

References

Barzun, Jacques. 1965. *Race: A Study in Superstition*. Rev. ed. New York: Harper & Row. An intellectual history of racism and the race concept.
Boas, Franz. 1894 [1974]. "Human Faculty as Determined by Race." George W. Stocking, Jr., ed., *The Shaping of American Anthropology, 1883–1911: A Franz Boas Reader*. New York: Basic Books.
———. 1913 [1940]. "Changes in Bodily Form of Descendants of Immigrants." Franz Boas, *Race, Language and Culture*. New York: Free Press. An important study challenging the assumption of the fixity of racial types.
Brinton, Daniel G. 1901. *Races and Peoples: Lectures on the Science of Ethnography*. Philadephia: David McKay. Reflects the era's polygenist and racist perspective.
Coon, Carleton S., and Edward E. Hunt, Jr. 1965. *The Living Races of Man*. New York: Knopf.
Count, Earl W., ed. 1950. *This Is Race: An Anthology Selected from the International Literature on the Races of Man*. New York: Henry Schuman. An excellent anthology of scientific (rather than polemical) writings on race.

Gould, Stephen Jay. 1981. *The Mismeasure of Man*. New York: Norton. A critical study of the anthropometric tradition in physical anthropology.

Haller, John S., Jr. 1971. *Outcasts from Evolution: Scientific Attitudes of Racial Inferiority, 1859–1900*. Urbana: University of Illinois Press.

Hrdlicka, Ales. 1914. "Physical Anthropology in America: An Historical Sketch." *AA* 16:508–54.

Jolly, Clifford, and Fred Plog. 1982. *Physical Anthropology and Archaeology*. 3d ed. New York: Knopf.

Lewontin, Richard. 1975. "Race and Intelligence." Ashley Montagu, ed., *Race and IQ*. New York: Oxford University Press.

Livingstone, Frank B. 1964. "On the Nonexistence of Human Races." Ashley Montagu, ed., *The Concept of Race*. New York: Free Press. The volume is a useful collection, from a perspective critical of racial typologies.

Molnar, Stephen. 1983. *Human Variation: Races, Types, and Ethnic Groups*. 2d ed. Englewood Cliffs, N.J.: Prentice-Hall. A reliable introductory text.

Montagu, Ashley. 1951. *Statement on Race*. New York: Henry Schuman.

———. 1965. *Man's Most Dangerous Myth: The Fallacy of Race*. New York: Meridian Books.

Nelson, Harry, and Robert Jurmain. 1982. *Introduction to Physical Anthropology*. 2d ed. St. Paul, Minn.: West.

Slotkin, J. S., ed. 1965. *Readings in Early Anthropology*. Chicago: Aldine.

Stanton, William. 1960. *The Leopard's Spots: Scientific Attitudes Toward Race in America, 1815–59*. Chicago: University of Chicago Press.

Stocking, George W., Jr. 1968. *Race, Culture, and Evolution: Essays in the History of Anthropology*. New York: Free Press. Strongly recommended.

———. 1987. *Victorian Anthropology*. New York: Free Press.

van den Berghe, Pierre L. 1967. *Race and Racism: A Comparative Perspective*. New York: John Wiley.

Sources of Additional Information

For a nontechnical introduction see Michael Banton and Jonathan Harwood, *The Race Concept*, New York: Praeger, 1975.

RATIONALITY. Thought or action guided by reason or logical consistency, as in the selection of means commensurate with desired ends.

Rationality implies the application of reason to the guidance of particular processes or undertakings, acting to deduce valid consequences from initial premises, to select appropriate means for attaining desired ends, and to achieve the maximum coherence within a given system of ideas or WORLD VIEW. The value of rationality has held great attraction in the modern West, an inheritance of the eighteenth-century Enlightenment, encouraged and reinforced by the successes of scientific method and the technical constraints of industrialism.

Rationality has been a pivotal concept for ANTHROPOLOGY, providing (rightly or wrongly) a basis for differentiating the intellectual perspective of urban CIVILIZATIONS from the beliefs and CUSTOMS of small-scale, supposedly PRIMITIVE societies. When set against the intellectual and moral complexity inherent in cultural RELATIVISM—recognizing the worth of a multitude of societies, with startlingly different beliefs and values—the concept of rationality has appealed to many scholars by offering a universal standard in terms of which the diversity of human behavior can be ordered and interpreted.

Rationality and Evolutionism

The idea of a gradually increasing rationality spanning the development of human CULTURE had a major place in Victorian theories of unilineal EVOLUTION. The topics of RELIGION, MAGIC, and TABOO provided the widest field for discussions of the supposed irrationality of tribal custom or, more invidiously, "superstition" (see SURVIVAL; COMPARATIVE METHOD).

The picture of the mentality of tribal peoples sketched in evolutionist writings was inconsistent. Insofar as evolutionary theorists attributed primitive religious beliefs to fallacious reasoning, they acknowledged the psychology underlying such beliefs as rational though ignorant and uncritical, a view necessary for the evolutionary postulate of PSYCHIC UNITY. In John Lubbock's view, "Though savages always have a reason, such as it is, for what they do and what they believe, their reasons often are very absurd" (Lubbock 1870:3). More commonly, however, the childlike or dreamlike character of such thought was stressed. Thus, "primitive thinking does not distinguish between the natural and the supernatural, between subjective and objective reality" (Crawley 1927:3–4 [orig. ed. 1902]). For Herbert Spencer, similarly, the primitive mind is "unspeculative, uncritical, incapable of generalizing, and with scarcely any notions save those yielded by the perceptions" (in Evans-Pritchard 1965:105; see also Frazer 1890).

Rationality: Later Views

The Victorian image of primitive belief could not be sustained by later research. In part this was due to the technical sophistication evident in many aspects of tribal social life. As the philosopher Ludwig Wittgenstein remarked, the individual who avenges himself through magic nonetheless "really does build his hut of wood and cuts his arrow with skill and not in effigy" (Wittgenstein 1982:4). Besides this, later standards of ETHNOGRAPHY, in emphasizing the social context of behavior, demonstrated that each society possessed a relatively consistent world view, rather than the amalgam of inchoate beliefs which nineteenth century scholars had assumed.

This said, there nonetheless remains a problem of how to interpret patterns of belief and behavior that diverge so drastically from the logic of Western science. There have been several approaches taken.

(1) The French philosopher Lucien Lévy-Bruhl (d. 1939) emphasized the mental gulf between so-called primitives and moderns, explaining this not as the result of inferior reasoning but rather of altogether different logical principles, a prelogical mentality. The source of this difference was not individual but social, the result of inherited categories of thought, "the collective representations which

form an integral part of every perception" (Lévy-Bruhl 1910:781; see also PRIM-
ITIVE; SUPERORGANIC).

(2) Another approach has been to demonstrate how ostensibly erroneous assumptions can nonetheless combine to provide a consistent guide for social life.
E. E. Evans-Pritchard, in an influential study of the African Azande, stressed
the mutually reinforcing character of beliefs regarding WITCHCRAFT, magic, and
divination. Azande culture, he argued, by providing a coherent means of explaining misfortune, created an essentially unfalsifiable belief system (Evans-
Pritchard 1937).

(3) From the perspective of structural FUNCTIONALISM, religious belief and
ritual are rational because they are in fact symbolic, ultimately referring not to
the properties of illusory gods and spirits, but to real relationships between social
groups. The Kachin of Burma, for example, make sacrifices to a series of spirits
(nats), which in their cosmology possess ranks paralleling that of Kachin society.
For Edmund Leach such RITUALS, and the beliefs or MYTHS which describe them,
are purely symbolic: "The various nats of Kachin religious ideology are . . .
nothing more than ways of describing the formal relationships that exist between
real persons and real groups in ordinary Kachin society" (in Gellner 1970:40).

(4) The functionalist thesis has been vigorously challenged, in particular from
an intellectualist or neo-Tylorian perspective, recalling the work of the Victorian
evolutionist Edward Tylor. In the neo-Tylorian view, statements of belief are
attempts at explanation, in a sense comparable to statements of natural science
explaining observations of nature, and should be construed literally (see Horton
1968; Skorupski 1976).

(5) Philosophically, a more radical position involves a reexamination of the
relation of language and social action in the articulation of belief. This view
rejects the assumption that propositions possess a single linguistic function—
explanation—as in the neo-Tylorian perspective (Winch 1970:90). Rather,
"magical rites constitute a form of expression in which these possibilities and
dangers [of daily life] may be contemplated and reflected on" (Winch 1970:106;
see also Wittgenstein 1982).

Rationality and Culture

Finally, the concept of rationality also enters anthropological theory in a
broader sense, as an absolute, extra-cultural standard for explaining human action. One example is the debate over the relevance of formal microeconomic
theory (based on a universal principle of maximization of advantage) in interpreting non-Western economic systems (see Kaplan 1968); the issue occurs in
a number of other contexts as well (see ADAPTATION; ECONOMY; MATERIALISM;
SOCIOBIOLOGY). The underlying question is whether culture is to be viewed as
merely the reflection of human experience, "the codification of man's actual
purposeful and pragmatic action," or alternatively, as establishing experience,
thus mediating and transforming all extra-cultural constraints (Sahlins 1976:55).
In the former case, culture is necessarily rational in some absolute sense, because
it serves an instrumental function, reflecting the constraints of a more funda-

mental, material order (see Sahlins 1976:56). In the latter case, a notion of rationality is itself culturally determined and thus not absolute.

References

Crawley, Ernest. 1927 [1960]. *The Mystic Rose*. 2d ed. Theodore Besterman, ed. New York: Meridian Books. 1st ed., 1902.

Evans-Pritchard, E. E. 1937. *Witchcraft, Oracles and Magic among the Azande*. Oxford: Clarendon Press. A classic contribution to the study of religion and rationality.

———. 1965. *Theories of Primitive Religion*. Oxford: Clarendon Press. A useful summary.

Frazer, James. 1890 [1959]. *The New Golden Bough*. 1 vol., abr. Theodor H. Gaster, ed. New York: Criterion.

Gellner, Ernest. 1970. "Concepts and Society." Bryan R. Wilson, ed., *Rationality*. New York: Harper & Row. A good selection of the divergent views on rationality.

Horton, Robin. 1968. "Neo-Tylorianism: Sound Sense or Sinister Prejudice?" *Man* (n.s.) 3:625–34. Advances the literalist interpretation of belief statements.

Kaplan, David. 1968. "The Formal-Substantive Debate in Economic Anthropology: Reflections on its Wider Implications." *Southwestern Journal of Anthropology* 24:228–51.

Lévy-Bruhl, Lucien. 1910 [1931]. "How Natives Think" (excerpt). V. F. Calverton, ed., *The Making of Man: An Outline of Anthropology*. New York: Modern Library.

Lubbock, John. 1870 [1978]. *The Origin of Civilization and the Primitive Condition of Man*. Peter Rivière, ed. Chicago: University of Chicago Press.

Sahlins, Marshall. 1976. *Culture and Practical Reason*. Chicago: University of Chicago Press. Treats the wider issues of rationality in culture theory.

Skorupski, John. 1976. *Symbol and Theory: A Philosophical Study of Theories of Religion in Social Anthropology*. Cambridge: Cambridge University Press.

Winch, Peter. 1970. "Understanding a Primitive Society." Bryan R. Wilson, ed., *Rationality*. New York: Harper & Row. An interpretation of belief statements from the Wittgensteinian, "language-games" perspective.

Wittgenstein, Ludwig. 1982. *Remarks on Frazer's Golden Bough*. A. C. Miles, trans. Nottinghamshire: Brynmill Press.

Sources of Additional Information

A brief philosophical introduction to rationality and related issues is found in Ernest Gellner, "Reason, Rationality and Rationalism," Adam Kuper and Jessica Kuper, eds., *Social Science Encyclopedia*, London: Routledge & Kegan Paul, 1985, pp. 687–90. See also I. C. Jarvie, *Rationality and Relativism*, London: Routledge & Kegan Paul, 1984.

RELATIVISM. (1) The methodological principle that any belief or CUSTOM must be understood in its cultural context, reflecting a distinctive WORLD VIEW. (2) The ethical principle that behavior must be judged in terms of the values indigenous to a culture, rather than through alien or ostensibly universal standards of judgment.

The phenomenon of CULTURE makes each society a distinctive world, differing from its neighbors in its way of life, its values, and its conception of reality. Some observers have welcomed diversity, suspending judgment as to which

CUSTOMS should be deemed superior. The French philosopher Michel de Montaigne (1533–1592) was an outstanding example: "No propositions astonish me, no belief offends me, however much opposed to my own." And similarly, "The different customs I find in one nation after another please me by their very diversity; each custom has its reason" (in Slotkin 1965:54–55).

However, the encounter with the cultural "Other" can also involve a process of misunderstanding and denigration. Thus the French romantic the Vicomte de Chateaubriand (1768–1848) could comment on the peoples of the Middle East: "Of liberty they know nothing; of propriety, they have none; force is their God." In the same vein, the Crusades he defended as a struggle between "a cult [Islam] that was civilization's enemy, systematically favorable to ignorance . . . to despotism, to slavery, or a cult that had caused to reawaken in modern people the genius of a sage antiquity" (in Said 1978:172). The example of Chateaubriand is more characteristic than that of Montaigne, for historically it is ethnocentrism, taking one's own cultural values as a universal standard, rather than tolerance which has guided most encounters between alien peoples.

A strong, if implicit, ethnocentrism was internalized in ANTHROPOLOGY through Victorian theories of cultural EVOLUTION, which arranged societies along a continuum from PRIMITIVE to civilized in terms of the degree to which their institutions resembled those of western Europe. As John Lubbock commented on diversity in RELIGION: "The so-called religion of the lower races bears somewhat the same relation to religion in its higher forms that astrology does to astronomy, or alchemy to chemistry" (Lubbock 1870:116).

The Emergence of Relativism

Several factors contributed to the adoption of an explicit cultural relativism in anthropology. The period between 1880 and 1920 saw a shift in the aims of anthropological research, from a comparative study of discrete culture traits to an intensive examination of distinct societies. This change in itself encouraged the INTERPRETATION of beliefs and customs in terms of indigenous systems of meaning (see ETHNOGRAPHY; ETHNOLOGY; FUNCTIONALISM).

This methodological relativism, the axiom that behavior must be understood in its cultural context, was also encouraged by theoretical developments in this period.

The work of Emile Durkheim (1858–1917) and his colleagues demonstrated that categories of thought (e.g., the divisions of space or time) were not universal, but were rather collective representations specific to each society, and in their view, reflections of a distinctive SOCIAL STRUCTURE (Durkheim and Mauss 1903), a conclusion with strongly relativist implications.

The relativist perspective emerged strongly from the conception of culture that developed in American anthropology under the leadership of Franz Boas (1858–1942). Early on, Boas had stressed the significance of the individual cultural element over the abstract classifications favored by evolutionism, yet the individuality of a given form (e.g., a tool design, a MYTH element, a kin classification) existed by virtue of its context. For Boas, understanding "the single specimen" required viewing it in relation to "the productions [of a given tribe] as a whole" (Boas 1887, in Stocking 1974:5). This dictum was reinforced by the perspective of HISTORICISM. As George Stocking has commented, "Especially after 1900 . . . Boas became more concerned with the ways in which the 'genius of a people' integrated the elements that the almost accidental accumulation of historical processes brought together in a single culture" (Stocking 1974:6).

By the 1930s, a pluralistic conception of culture had become an accepted element of American anthropology. Ruth Benedict's *Patterns of Culture* (1934), a work astonishingly influential in popularizing the relativist perspective, depicted the cultures of the Dobuans, Pueblo, and Kwakiutl as unique worlds of value and meaning. For Benedict, these three cultures "are travelling along different roads in pursuit of different ends, and these ends and these means in one society cannot be judged in terms of those of another society, because essentially they are incommensurable" (Benedict 1934:223). Melville Herskovits likewise denied that there can be absolute moral standards transcending the norms of a given culture. He offered, however, as a counterargument the notion of cultural universals: every culture possesses *some* concept of time, of space, of morality, and so forth, though the particular conceptions that are held in various cultures may be wildly incompatible (Herskovits 1972:31–4).

Critiques of Relativism

As a dictum of field method, cultural relativism commands widespread support in the discipline. Further afield, it has served as a useful antidote to at least the more obvious forms of ethnocentrism.

Considered at the level of theory, however, there is no consensus on the appropriateness of relativism. There is a fundamental tension within anthropology between understanding and explanation, the former involving the interpretation of a cultural practice in its uniqueness, the latter a generalization from numerous examples to yield a statement of cross-cultural validity. Economic anthropologists have long debated whether to analyze transactions through the unique social and political institutions of a given culture or though the analytic categories of Western market economics (Kaplan 1968; see also ECONOMY). In the domain of psychological anthropology, a similar disagreement exists between those who view abnormality as a matter of cultural definition and those (notably the psychoanalytically inclined) who maintain that categories such as neurotic and psychotic are of cross-cultural, objective significance (Devereux 1956). Critics insist that a consistent relativism makes impossible either scientifically useful description (see EMIC/ETIC) or the formulation of significant cross-cultural generalizations (see COMPARATIVE METHOD; RATIONALITY).

Events of the Second World War have made an absolute ethical relativism a less palatable concept; many of the most atrocious acts of that era were encouraged by the TRADITIONS of one or another of the combatants. Although the problem of ethical relativism is certainly raised by the findings of anthropology, the issue has for the most part been debated elsewhere (see Geertz 1984).

References

Benedict, Ruth. 1934 [1959]. *Patterns of Culture*. Boston: Houghton Mifflin. An essential exposition of cultural relativism.
Devereux, George. 1956 [1980]. "Normal and Abnormal." G. Devereux, *Basic Problems of Ethnopsychiatry*. B. M. Gulati et al., trans. Chicago: University of Chicago Press. Insists that psychiatric categories are universal rather than culture-bound.
Durkheim, Emile, and Marcel Mauss. 1903 [1963]. *Primitive Classification*. Rodney Needham, trans. Chicago: University of Chicago Press.
Geertz, Clifford. 1984. "Anti Anti-Relativism." *AA* 86:263–78. An oblique defense of relativism.
Herskovits, Melville J. 1972. *Cultural Relativism: Perspectives in Cultural Pluralism*. Frances Herskovits, ed. New York: Random House.
Kaplan, David. 1968. "The Formal-Substantive Controversy in Economic Anthropology: Reflections on Its Wider Implications." *Southwestern Journal of Anthropology* 24:228–51.
Lubbock, John. 1870 [1978]. *The Origin of Civilization and the Primitive Condition of Man*. Peter Rivière, ed. Chicago: University of Chicago Press.
Said, Edward W. 1978. *Orientalism*. New York: Random House/Vintage. A study of the ethnocentrism inherent in European views of the Orient, broadly defined.
Slotkin, J. S., ed. 1965. *Readings in Early Anthropology*. Chicago: Aldine.
Stocking, George W., Jr. 1974. "The Basic Assumptions of Boasian Anthropology." G. Stocking, ed., *The Shaping of American Anthropology, 1883–1911: A Franz Boas Reader*. New York: Basic Books.

Sources of Additional Information

A readable and sophisticated introduction to these issues is provided in F. Allan Hanson's *Meaning in Culture*, London: Routledge & Kegan Paul, 1975, chs. 2 and 3. For a historically oriented analysis of the issue, see Elvin Hatch, *Culture and Morality: The Relativity of Values in Anthropology*, New York: Columbia University Press, 1983.

RELIGION. A culturally patterned system of beliefs and practices concerned with the transcendent or sacred.

Religion has been the most enduring topic in the history of ANTHROPOLOGY. Some of the field's most significant theoretical controversies, for example regarding the relation of RATIONALITY and SYMBOLISM, have resulted from its study. Of all the subjects investigated by anthropologists, religion is probably the least amenable to the ostensibly objective methods of observation and description, a fact that has made it easy for Western observers of non-Western religions to substitute their own prejudices and presuppositions in the absence of facts. This entry deals broadly with the concept of religion in anthropology and describes some prominent anthropological theories of religion. For specific topics, see the articles on ANIMISM, MAGIC, MANA, MYTH, RITES OF PASSAGE, RITUAL, SHAMANISM, TABOO, TOTEMISM, TRANCE, and WITCHCRAFT.

The Concept of Religion

In common usage the term religion suggests a set of doctrines (e.g., Original Sin, the Trinity, purgatory), together with the acts and avoidances such doctrines justify and require. Yet the term has a complex history (see W. C. Smith 1978: ch. 2). In classical antiquity the term religion (*religio*) suggested a distinctive pattern of worship; in the Renaissance it had a predominantly inward and personalistic sense: one's approach to God, one's piety. It is an inheritance of the Enlightenment, and less directly of the Reformation, to identify religion with the concept of belief, and hence with questions of truth and error. This modern sense is captured in the definition given by the sociologist Emile Durkheim (1858–1917): "a unified system of beliefs and practices relative to sacred things" (Durkheim 1915:62).

Such a model of religion presupposes a literate TRADITION, in which specialists such as theologians are responsible for codifying doctrine, regulating practice, and rationalizing apparent inconsistencies. Even as regards the Western religions this approach suggests a reification. As Cantwell Smith has remarked, "The participant is concerned with God; the observer has been concerned with 'religion' " (W. C. Smith 1978:131). Within anthropology, which is concerned primarily with kin-based, nonliterate, small-scale societies generally lacking anything resembling a distinct, doctrinally explicit sphere of religion, the concept is even more problematic.

These presuppositions are reflected in the anthropologist Edward Tylor's minimum definition of religion as "the belief in Spiritual Beings" (Tylor 1871:2:8). A century later, Melford Spiro described religion more appropriately as "an institution consisting of culturally patterned interaction with culturally postulated superhuman beings" (in Bharati 1972:238). Note that in Spiro's concept the emphasis has shifted from a concern with psychological questions of belief to a focus on cultural action patterned by WORLD VIEW and reflected in RITUAL. Alternatively, Clifford Geertz has proposed a definition that emphasizes religion's phenomenological or experiential dimension: "A religion is a system of symbols which acts to establish powerful, pervasive, and long-lasting moods and motivations in men by formulating conceptions of a general order of existence and clothing these conceptions with such an aura of factuality that the moods and motivations seem uniquely realistic" (Geertz 1973:90).

Religion and Evolutionary Anthropology

The history of the anthropological study of religion, which began seriously in the early nineteenth century, was in large measure a reflection of wider intellectual currents of the time. The Christian churches, generally literalist in biblical interpretation, were challenged by the natural sciences on such matters as biological EVOLUTION and geological dating, issues that seemed at the time to strike at the heart of faith. A number of writers—Edward Tylor among them— were ambivalent regarding the ultimate validity of religion (Stocking 1987:190– 91). Nonetheless, the Enlightenment viewpoint expressed by the philosopher

Condorcet (1743–1794)—that Christianity "feared that spirit of investigation and doubt, that confidence in one's own reason, which is the scourge of all religious beliefs" (in Gay 1966:212)—could epitomize the spirit of Victorian anthropology as well. Such antagonism to religious belief was reinforced by other intellectual currents. As E. E. Evans-Pritchard remarked, it was in the "climate of Comtism [i.e., positivism], utilitarianism, Biblical criticism, and the beginnings of comparative religion that social anthropology, as we now understand it, came into being" (Evans-Pritchard 1964:161).

In light of these debates, the particular fascination that the religious life of tribal peoples exercised for early anthropologists is understandable. Merely to find parallels to Western religious institutions among BANDS and TRIBES—as Robertson Smith claimed to have done in identifying the Christian Eucharist with the collective meal of totemic sacrifice (W. R. Smith 1889:295)—was to relativize Christianity. Given the theology of the day, the effect was to undermine Christian claims to a unique revelation. More importantly, from the perspective of cultural evolution, the religious life of so-called PRIMITIVE peoples stood at the beginnings of a developmental sequence that led to the modern religions, and beyond them to the gradually unfolding truths of science. By this logic, if the processes leading primitive peoples to religious belief (including here magic, taboo, mana and other near relatives) could be identified, the subsequent history of religion would in a sense be understood. This search was epitomized by James Frazer's monumental *Golden Bough*, which sought over the course of twelve volumes to trace the "movement of the higher thought . . . from magic through religion to science" (Frazer 1890:648).

The assumptions of evolutionism dictated a thoroughly dismal view of the mental abilities of tribal peoples. In the words of John Lubbock, "While savages show us a melancholy spectacle of gross superstitions and ferocious forms of worship, the religious mind cannot but feel a peculiar satisfaction in tracing up the gradual evolution of more correct ideas and of nobler creeds" (Lubbock 1870:114; see RATIONALITY).

Theories of Religion

The logic of evolutionism dictated a search for origins. Explanation involved a search for the peculiar mental processes by which prehistoric individuals could have been led into what, by Victorian lights, were the errors of primitive religion. Theories were numerous. Edward Tylor, in his theory of animism, proposed that religion emerged from a belief in souls and spirits, the mistaken product of primitive speculation on dreams and the transition of life into death (Tylor 1871). R. R. Marett suggested a prior stage in the origins of religion (animatism), involving an emotional rather than intellectual response, a sense of supernatural force or power at work, to which he applied the Polynesian term *mana* (Marett 1914).

In contrast, most twentieth-century theory has assumed that religion is to be explained in social rather than merely psychological terms. Being for the most part traditional, collective, and obligatory, religion must be understood as a manifestation of social life, not individual reasoning (Evans-Pritchard 1965:54–55). The sociologist Emile Durkheim, whose arguments have molded the modern anthropology of religion, proposed that the gods were a projection of society itself, its SOCIAL STRUCTURE traced in cosmology and belief, and its unity celebrated and reinforced through ritual (Durkheim 1915; see also TOTEMISM). These views were adapted to an anthropological milieu through the perspective of FUNCTIONALISM, notably in the writings of A. R. Radcliffe-Brown.

Postwar theories of religion have taken a variety of directions (for a review see Bharati 1972). Religion can be directed at changing rather than perpetuating a social order. Revitalization movements such as the North American Ghost Dance or the Melanesian cargo cults have provided a significant cultural response to oppression and ACCULTURATION (see SOCIAL MOVEMENT; CULTURE CHANGE). Religious beliefs and practices have been widely studied from the perspective of CULTURAL ECOLOGY, considering, for example, the effects of Hindu cow protection on the Indian peasant ECONOMY (see TABOO; ADAPTATION). Finally, the greater interest in symbolism and cultural INTERPRETATION in this period has allowed more serious consideration of religions on their own terms, as distinctive, culturally patterned means of transformation and transcendence (see Ray 1977).

References

Bharati, Agehananda. 1972. "Anthropological Approaches to the Study of Religion: Ritual and Belief Systems." B. J. Siegel, ed., *Biennial Review of Anthropology*. Stanford, Calif.: Stanford University Press. A useful review of postwar research.
Durkheim, Emile. 1915 [1965]. *The Elementary Forms of the Religious Life*. Joseph Swain, trans. New York: Free Press. A classic in the anthropology of religion.
Evans-Pritchard, E. E. 1964. "Religion and the Anthropologists." E. E. Evans-Pritchard, *Social Anthropology and Other Essays*. New York: Free Press. A scathing attack on the antireligious bias of the anthropology of religion.
————. 1965. *Theories of Primitive Religion*. Oxford: Clarendon Press. A resume of nineteenth- and early twentieth-century anthropological theory on religion.
Frazer, James. 1890 [1959]. *The New Golden Bough*. 1 vol. abr. Theodor H. Gaster, ed. New York: Criterion Books.
Gay, Peter. 1966. *The Enlightenment, an Interpretation: The Rise of Modern Paganism*. New York: Random House.
Geertz, Clifford. 1973. "Religion as a Cultural System." C. Geertz, *The Interpretation of Cultures*. New York: Basic Books.
Lubbock, John. 1870 [1978]. *The Origins of Civilization and the Primitive Condition of Man*. Peter Rivière, ed. Chicago: University of Chicago Press. A representative example of evolutionist thought.
Marett, R.R. 1914. *The Threshold of Religion*. 2d ed. New York: Macmillan.
Ray, Benjamin. 1977. "An Anthropologist's Pilgrimage." *History of Religions* 16:273–79. A review of symbolically oriented studies in the anthropology of religion.
Smith, W. Robertson. 1889 [1972]. *The Religion of the Semites: The Fundamental Institutions*. New York: Schocken.
Smith, Wilfred Cantwell. 1978. *The Meaning and End of Religion*. San Francisco: Harper & Row. A critical analysis of the concept of religion.

Stocking, George W., Jr. 1987. *Victorian Anthropology*. New York: Free Press.
Tylor, Edward. 1871 [1958]. *Primitive Culture*. 2 vols. New York: Harper & Brothers (Harper Torchbook).

Sources of Additional Information

A useful introduction, though rather reductionist in flavor, is provided by Anthony F. C. Wallace, *Religion: An Anthropological View*, New York: Random House, 1966. William A. Lessa and Evon Z. Vogt, *Reader in Comparative Religion: An Anthropological Approach*, 4th ed., New York: Harper & Row, 1979, collects a number of standard articles. A brief introduction to theories of the origins of religion is provided by S. G. F. Brandon, "Origins of Religion," *DHI* 4:92–99. For a study of a major Victorian figure in the anthropology of religion, see Robert Ackerman, *J. G. Frazer: His Life and Work*, Cambridge: Cambridge University Press, 1987. For an anthropological reflection on the study of religion, see Martin Southwold, *Buddhism and Life: The Anthropological Study of Religion and the Sinhalese Practice of Buddhism*, Manchester: Manchester University Press, 1983.

RITE OF PASSAGE. A RITUAL that symbolizes and effects a transition in social status.

The phrase "rites of passage" (*les rites de passages*) was coined by the French folklorist Arnold van Gennep (1873–1957) in his influential study of that name (Gennep 1908). Gennep used rite of passage to refer to any formal action that serves to effect a transition, within calendrical cycles, across spatial boundaries, or from one social status to another. Gennep's study is more notable for the wealth of examples he provided than for any enduring theoretical analysis. Nonetheless, it is through his efforts that the rite of passage has been recognized as an important category of ritual. A number of later anthropologists, among them Mary Douglas and Victor Turner, have sought to place such rituals within a wider theoretical perspective.

Anthropological recognition of rites of transition certainly preceded Gennep's work. James Frazer's *Golden Bough* described numerous rituals of this type, among them the calendrical rituals that marked the transition from one year to the next, with intercalary periods of license and social reversal. The medieval Feast of Fools was a notable example (Frazer 1890:562–69). Similarly, A. R. Radcliffe-Brown's *The Andaman Islanders* contained extensive analyses of the social functions of transition rites such as funerals (Radcliffe-Brown 1922:285–94). Although Radcliffe-Brown may have read Gennep in revising this work for publication, his analysis appears to have developed independently (Gluckman 1962:13, n. 3).

Gennep's Model

The primary concern of Arnold van Gennep lay with form rather than function (see FUNCTIONALISM). The central theme of *Rites of Passage* is the threefold sequence that supposedly characterizes all such rituals: first, acts of separation (*separation*); second, acts of transition (*marge*); third, acts of incorporation (*agrégation*). Thus in rituals of status transition, the individual is first separated from his or her old identity and surroundings, then conducted through certain rites that effect and symbolize a social transformation, and, finally, reintegrated with a new group or with a new status. As Gennep stated, "Our interest lies not in the particular rites but in their essential significance and their relative positions within ceremonial wholes—that is, their order" (Gennep 1908:191).

For Gennep, movement across physical boundaries provided both interesting examples of passage rites and a powerful metaphor for discussing transitions of status within society. Regarding boundary rites in the concrete sense, he noted, for example, that "the rituals pertaining to the door form a unit, and differences among particular ceremonies lie in technicalities: the threshold is sprinkled with blood or with purifying water; doorposts are bathed with blood or with perfumes; sacred objects are hung or nailed onto them, as on the architrave" (Gennep 1908:20). Yet Gennep's real interest lay in viewing passage as a social metaphor. Accordingly, the three stages of the rite of passage were also termed preliminal, liminal, and postliminal, respectively, liminal deriving from the Latin *limen*, a boundary or threshold (Gennep 1908:21). For Gennep SOCIAL STRUCTURE could be understood on analogy with architectural structure: "A society is similar to a house divided into rooms and corridors. . . . In a semi-civilized society . . . sections are carefully isolated, and passage from one to another must be made though formalities and ceremonies which show extensive parallels to the rites of territorial passage" (Gennep 1908:6).

Through the concept of rite of passage, a broad range of ritual events were brought together under a common analytic category. In addition to the calendrical rituals and rituals of spatial transition, Gennep studied within this conceptual frame rituals associated with pregnancy and childbirth; with the transition to adulthood (initiation rituals); with betrothal and marriage; with death and burial; and with induction into restricted groups (so-called secret societies, religious orders, etc.). In place of pursuing a theory that might have explained the prevalence and relatively constant form of such rituals, Gennep chose to make his argument through the repetition of examples, demonstrating that rites of passage "occurred very widely through many societies and in many situations in each society," this being the mode of "proof" then in anthropological vogue (Gluckman 1962:1).

Nonetheless, there are solid achievements. Meyer Fortes has assessed the theoretical accomplishments of *The Rites of Passage* in the following terms:

> Van Gennep demonstrated three significant theorems: first, that the critical stages, as he called them, of the life cycle . . . though tied to physiological events, are in fact socially defined; secondly, that entry into and exit from these critical stages— or statuses—are always marked by ritual and ceremony . . . , thirdly, that these passage rites follow a more or less standard pattern. (Fortes 1962:54–55)

Later Research

Numerous studies in the postwar period have examined rites of passage through a careful analysis of ritual SYMBOLISM and a concern with clarifying the place of such ritual in the life of a social group. Notable examples include Audrey Richards's study of female puberty ritual among the Bemba of Zambia (Richards 1956) and Gilbert Herdt's analysis of ritualized homosexuality in male initiation rites among the Sambia of Papua New Guinea (Herdt 1981).

On a more abstract level, a number of anthropologists have focused on Gennep's scheme of the rites of passage as a model of the social order as a whole (see SOCIAL STRUCTURE). In this perspective, rites of transition can be understood as acknowledging the competing principles of stability and change, of structure and spontaneity within social life. Mary Douglas has argued that any social transition is perceived as dangerous because status remains temporarily undefined (Douglas 1966:116). Thus the liminal period—the middle term of Gennep's schema—takes on particular analytic importance. "During the marginal period which separates ritual dying and ritual rebirth, the novices in initiation are temporarily outcast. For the duration of the rite they have no place in society" (Douglas 1966:117).

This argument can be taken further. In the liminal state the initiate is excluded from social status and is thus without differentiating rank or role. In this sense the liminal stage exemplifies the principle of *communitas*, an egalitarian and relatively unstructured social world, in a sense complementary to the more mundane, hierarchical social order. For Victor Turner and his students, liminality as encountered in ritual illustrated the symbolic mechanisms underlying attempts to create a sustained communitas, as seen in millenarian movements, communitarian experiments, and utopian fiction (Turner 1967, 1977; Myerhoff 1975; see also COMMUNITY).

References

Douglas, Mary. 1966. *Purity and Danger: An Analysis of Concepts of Pollution and Taboo*. Harmondsworth, England: Penguin. A series of provocative essays on the symbolic implications of order and disorder.

Fortes, Meyer. 1962. "Ritual and Office in Tribal Society." Max Gluckman, ed., *Essays on the Ritual of Social Relations*. Manchester: Manchester University Press. A consideration of tribal political institutions and the role of ritual in their legitimation.

Frazer, James George. 1890 [1959]. *The New Golden Bough*. 1 vol., abr. Theodor H. Gaster, ed. New York: Criterion Books.

Gennep, Arnold van. 1908 [1960]. *The Rites of Passage*. Monika Vizedom and Gabrielle Caffee, trans. Chicago: University of Chicago Press. The classic work on this topic.

Gluckman, Max. 1962. "Les Rites de Passage." Max Gluckman, ed., *Essays on the Ritual of Social Relations*. Manchester: Manchester University Press. A critique of Gennep from the perspective of social anthropology.

Herdt, Gilbert H. 1981. *Guardians of the Flutes: Idioms of Masculinity*. New York: McGraw-Hill. A study of ritualized homosexuality in male enculturation and maturation among the Sambia of Papua New Guinea.

Myerhoff, Barbara G. 1975. "Organization and Ecstasy: Deliberate and Accidental Communitas Among Huichol Indians and American Youth." Sally Falk Moore and

Barbara G. Myerhoff, eds., *Symbol and Politics in Communal Ideology: Cases and Questions*. Ithaca, N.Y.: Cornell University Press. Myerhoff applies Turner's concepts of liminality and communitas.

Radcliffe-Brown, A. R. 1922 [1964]. *The Andaman Islanders*. New York: Free Press. A classic functionalist study.

Richards, Audrey I. 1956. *Chisungu: A Girl's Initiation Ceremony among the Bemba of Northern Rhodesia*. London: Faber and Faber. A detailed ethnographic account.

Turner, Victor W. 1967. "Betwixt and Between: The Liminal Period in *Rites de Passage*." Victor W. Turner, *The Forest of Symbols: Aspects of Ndembu Ritual*. Ithaca, N.Y.: Cornell University Press. Provides a sophisticated exposition from the view of symbolic anthropology.

——. 1977. *The Ritual Process: Structure and Anti-Structure*. Ithaca, N.Y.: Cornell University Press. Analyzes rites of passage, liminality, and communitas.

Sources of Additional Information

For a brief overview from the standpoint of social anthropology, see J. S. La Fontaine, *Initiation*, Manchester: Manchester University Press, 1986. An introduction to Gennep's life and work is provided by Nicole Belmont, *Arnold van Gennep: The Creator of French Ethnography*, Derek Coltman, trans., Chicago: University of Chicago Press, 1979; see chap. 4 for a discussion of rites of passage. An interdisciplinary collection of essays is given in Louise C. Mahdi et al., eds., *Betwixt and Between: Patterns of Masculine and Feminine Initiation*, La Salle, Ill.: Open Court, 1987. Shamanic initiation is examined in Daniel Merkur, *Becoming Half Hidden: Shamanism and Initiation among the Inuit*, Stockholm: Almqvist and Wiksell, 1985.

RITUAL. Formalized, socially prescribed symbolic behavior.

Ritual—a handshake, a Mass, a royal coronation—is a formalized and meaningfully patterned social act. It is formal rather than haphazard in consisting of a relatively invariant sequence of actions. It is meaningful rather than utilitarian in expressing a sentiment or idea rather than performing a technical operation. It is social rather than individual in being predicated upon the understandings or usages of a society.

This entry treats ritual as a broad category. Regarding the patterns of belief associated with ritual, see MYTH. For ritual avoidances see TABOO. For related entries see MAGIC, RELIGION, RITE OF PASSAGE, SEMIOTICS, SYMBOLISM, and TOTEMISM.

Attempts at defining ritual have been numerous and contradictory. Some scholars have argued that the concept should be dropped altogether from the anthropological vocabulary (see Goody 1977). Aside from this counsel of despair, at least four approaches to defining ritual have been advanced.

(1) Ritual has been equated with nonutilitarian behavior: "prescribed formal behavior for occasions not given over to technological routine," in Ruth Benedict's phrase (1934:396). This, however, makes ritual a residual category, defining it in terms of what it is not.

(2) Another approach has focused on ritual's symbolic character. For John Beattie, "ritual is essentially expressive and symbolic. . . . It is this that distin-

guishes it from other aspects of human behaviour. . . . It is allied with art rather
than with science, and is susceptible of similar kinds of understanding'' (Beattie
1966:65). By this definition, however, it is not clear how ritual is to be distinguished from a host of other expressive cultural forms. As Roy Rappaport has
noted, ''It is in respect to its symbolic content that ritual is *least* distinctive''
(Rappaport 1979:174).

(3) Edmund Leach has extended the symbolic perspective by proposing that
ritual be understood not as a distinct cultural category, but as a dimension of
social life, ''the communicative aspect of behavior'' (1968:524). Drawing on
the viewpoint of FUNCTIONALISM, Leach has argued that ritual entails that aspect
of any activity which ''serves to express the individual's status as a social person''
(1954:10–11). This usage has not been widely followed.

(4) Approaching the problem from a phenomenological perspective, ritual is
distinguished by being not only expressive but obligatory in some extra-societal
sense. As S. P. Nagendra has defined it, ritual is ''symbolic action which is
transcendentally necessary'' (Nagendra 1971:9).

The Study of Ritual

The description and INTERPRETATION of ritual have been a staple of ethnographic accounts from antiquity. For Greek and Roman historians, descriptions
of ritual were important because they served to characterize barbarian societies,
distinguishing each from its neighbors. Thus Tacitus, writing in AD 98, described
in general terms the way of life of the Germans, and continued: ''I will now
touch on the institutions and religious rites [instituta ritusque] of the separate
tribes, pointing out how far they differ'' (*Ger.* 27). The medieval period, in
contrast, marked a low point in ethnological knowledge. The seventh-century
writer Isidore of Seville provided some detail on topics such as divination and
magic but little in the way of serious ETHNOLOGY (Isidore of Seville [1982]:
8.9, 9, 14; Hodgen 1964: ch. 2).

From the beginnings of European exploration through the eighteenth century,
descriptions of ritual held a significant place in travelers' accounts and antiquarians' collections. In *Purchas His Pilgrimage* (published 1613), Samuel Purchas described ''the ancient religions before the flood, the heathenish, the
Saracenicall . . . with their several opinions, idols, oracles, temples, priests, fasts,
feasts, sacrifices, and rites'' (in Hodgen 1964:171). Although the contrasts in
ritual observance between one's own society and that of an exotic land were of
great interest to Europeans, the existence of ritual itself was taken for granted.
Ritual as a concept did not assume an analytic distinctiveness but rather tended
to merge into the more general category of CUSTOM.

Christian theology had a significant role in shaping the Western understanding
of ritual. The medieval theologian Peter Lombard (d. 1160) defined a sacrament
(*sacramentum*) as a sign of sacred things (*sacrae rei signum*) and as the visible
form of invisible grace (*invisibilis gratiae visibilis forma*) (Webb 1960). These
views assumed that the ritual order represented or was determined by some other

order of existence: a reality transcending the capacities of verbal expression, a sacred realm dimly reflected in the world of profane things.

Protestant thought imparted a new perspective regarding the nature and validity of ritual. Martin Luther (d. 1546), for example, did not reject the significance of the Mass, but he revalued it, contrasting what he viewed as the core of the sacrament—a divinely instituted sharing of bread and wine, whose significance is only comprehended through the eyes of faith—with its outward, tangible, and, for him, extraneous additions (Luther 1520:271). The result was a more interior or psychological appreciation of religious devotion and a corresponding de-emphasis of outward devotional signs and acts, in short, of the ritual elements of religion. This dichotomy of belief versus action, or inward meaning versus (mere) outward form, given such emphasis by the Reformation, left a strong bias in the later study of ritual.

What was begun in theological dispute was completed by a broad transformation of European society. From the seventeenth through nineteenth centuries, the gradual dominance of a scientific mode of thought, the advent of industrial production, and the disruption of traditional communities combined to destroy an earlier way of life within which the performance of ritual—whether in sacraments, festivals, or daily routine—held a prominent and largely unquestioned place.

The Anthropology of Ritual

The concept of ritual has held a prominent place in most theoretical developments in ANTHROPOLOGY. The four approaches reviewed below consider ritual as a source of ethnological data; as an exemplar of nonrational thought; as a social mechanism for group cohesion; and as a key to the interpretation of symbolism.

Ritual and ethnology. Through the 1930s, the emphasis of American anthropology was largely ethnological, treating ritual not as a special subject of inquiry but as a source of data to establish culture histories through study of MIGRATION and cultural DIFFUSION, principally among the peoples of native North America (see ETHNOLOGY; HISTORICISM). An example is Franz Boas's comparative study of the rituals of secret societies among the Northwest Coast tribes (Boas 1897). By studying in exhaustive detail ritual PATTERNS occurring in a number of contiguous cultures (other examples include the Ghost Dance, the Sun Dance, and the Peyote Cult), much evidence accumulated regarding both the nature of variation in ritual and the potential independence of form and idea, issues that were crucial in the development of both symbolic anthropology (see SYMBOLISM) and STRUCTURALISM (Lowie 1914; La Barre 1938; Bennett 1944).

Ritual and rationality. As noted earlier, ritual has frequently been understood as a residual category, those formal, repetitive acts not analyzable in terms of a utilitarian logic. Anthropologists have found various ways to assimilate this dichotomy into theory. One approach has been to label technique as rational, ritual as nonrational. This dichotomy was fundamental to Victorian evolutionist anthropology, providing a key for the explanation of cultural difference. Where means and ends appeared incompatible, behavior (i.e., ritual) was presumed to result from intellectual confusion or inferiority (see EVOLUTION; PRIMITIVE; RATIONALITY).

Ritual and society. A later and more influential tradition analyzed ritual not as intellectual error but as a product of social life, which must be understood through the patterns of interaction and the collective conceptions that unite the members of a society. The work of the theologian W. Robertson Smith (1846–1894) played an important role in this transformation. His studies of the religions and cultures of the early Semitic peoples stressed the role of ritual as a *practice* binding the members of a society (Smith 1889). Smith's theories provided a foundation for the sociological understanding of religion and ritual later advanced by Emile Durkheim (1858–1917).

For Durkheim, society affirms itself through ritual, the "effect of the cult" being to recreate periodically in the realm of the sacred that "moral being" which, in this view, is a symbolic representation of society itself. Through the work of A. R. Radcliffe-Brown this theory of religion and ritual, now flying the banner of structural functionalism, became very influential in later social anthropology (see Hubert and Mauss 1899; Durkheim 1915; Radcliffe-Brown 1922).

Ritual and cultural interpretation. It is a legacy of the Durkheimian tradition to associate ritual and meaning. Yet if one asks what rituals mean, there are two ways to approach the problem. One is to impose an interpretation from without, that is, according to a theory of the observer; the other is to accept an interpretation from within, according to the understanding of the actor. Functionalist theory (as in the work of Radcliffe-Brown) provided the former approach. Yet the attractive simplicity of this position tended to exclude not only a large range of data—indigenous interpretations of ritual acts—but also an important theoretical question, how rituals convey meaning.

Symbolic anthropology (see SYMBOLISM) took the latter approach, seeking the meanings of ritual indigenous to a culture. Here the work of Victor Turner has been particularly influential. According to Turner, rituals offer "decisive keys to the understanding of how people think and feel about . . . relationships, and about the natural and social environments in which they operate" (Turner 1969:6; see INTERPRETATION). Although providing an exhaustive treatment of ritual among the Ndembu of Zambia, the foundation of Turner's work has been an effort to understand the general characteristics of ritual, in particular its fusion of ideological content, emotional power, and efficacy (Turner 1967).

New Directions

However productive the past fifty years of ritual studies may have been, there is a clear need for a consistent theory of ritual that can account both for its distinctive characteristics and, in the ideal, for its evolutionary emergence as part of the human cultural repertoire. Several research directions can be noted.

(1) Numerous studies have examined the relation between ritual and ADAPTATION. A notable example is Roy Rappaport's analysis of Maring (New Guinea)

ritual, which argued that this ritual cycle stands at the center of a complex, self-regulating ecological SYSTEM, influencing such factors as land distribution, pig husbandry, patterns of political alliance, and warfare (Rappaport 1968; see CULTURAL ECOLOGY).

(2) In ethology, ritualization has been used to describe the evolutionary process by which behavior is modified to enhance its communicative capability, usually by simplifying, exaggerating, or formalizing sequences of movements. The theoretical utility of such a concept of ritual, applicable to both human and nonhuman species, has been explored from a variety of perspectives (Huxley 1966; d'Aquili et al. 1979; see NATURE; SOCIOBIOLOGY).

(3) Research inspired by semiotics has suggested a broader basis for a theory of ritual, which might explain (as previous approaches have not) many fundamental characteristics: its formality or order, its complex communicative properties, and its performativeness, the ability to alter social reality (see Rappaport 1979).

References

Beattie, John. 1966. "Ritual and Social Change." *Man* (n.s.) 1:60–74.

Benedict, Ruth. 1934. "Ritual." *ESS* 13:396–97.

Bennett, John W. 1944. "The Development of Ethnological Theory, as Illustrated by the Plains Sun Dance." *AA* 46:162–181. Bennett uses studies of the Native American Sun Dance ritual to review theoretical developments in American anthropology before the Second World War.

Boas, Franz. 1897 [1940]. "The Growth of the Secret Societies of the Kwakiutl." In Franz Boas, *Race, Language and Culture*. New York: Free Press. An example of the ethnological treatment of ritual and myth.

d'Aquili, Eugene, et al. 1979. *The Spectrum of Ritual: A Biogenetic Structural Analysis*. New York: Columbia University Press. An application of ethological and neurological approaches to the study of ritual.

Durkheim, Emile. 1915 [1965]. *The Elementary Forms of the Religious Life*. J. W. Swain, trans. New York: Free Press. An analysis of Australian religion, fundamental for the anthropological study of ritual.

Goody, Jack. 1977. "Against 'Ritual': Loosely Structured Thoughts on a Loosely Defined Topic." Sally F. Moore and Barbara G. Myerhoff, eds., *Secular Ritual*. Amsterdam: Van Gorcum, Assen. A critique of the ritual concept.

Hodgen, Margaret. 1964. *Early Anthropology in the Sixteenth and Seventeenth Centuries*. Philadelphia: University of Pennsylvania Press. An important study of Renaissance anthropology.

Hubert, Henri, and Marcel Mauss. 1899 [1964]. *Sacrifice: Its Nature and Function*. W. D. Halls, trans. Chicago: University of Chicago Press. An early study by two of Durkheim's collaborators.

Huxley, Julian, ed. 1966. *A Discussion on Ritualization of Behavior in Animals and Man*. Royal Society (London), *Philosophical Transactions*, ser. B, vol. 251 (no. 772): 247–526.

Isidore of Seville. [1982]. *Etimologias: Edicion Bilingue*. Latin text and Spanish translation. Jose Oroz Reta and Manuel-A. Marcos Casquero, trans. Madrid: Biblioteca de Autores Cristianos. 2 vols. Isidore's work was a fundamental compendium of early medieval knowledge.

La Barre, Weston. 1938 [1975]. *The Peyote Cult.* 4th ed., enl. New York: Schocken. The key study of a major Native American revitalization movement.

Leach, Edmund. 1954 [1965]. *Political Systems of Highland Burma.* Boston: Beacon Press. Argues that ritual acts should be understood as statements regarding political relationships and the social order.

———. 1968. "Ritual." *IESS* 13:520–26.

Lowie, Robert H. 1914. "Ceremonialism in North America." *AA* 16:602–631. A survey of major ritual complexes in Native American religion, emphasizing diffusion.

Luther, Martin. 1520 [1961]. "The Pagan Servitude of the Church." John Dillenberger, ed., *Martin Luther: Selections from His Writings.* Garden City, N.Y.: Anchor/Doubleday.

Nagendra, S. P. 1971. *The Concept of Ritual in Modern Sociological Theory.* New Delhi: Academic Journals of India. Provides a critical overview of the concept.

Radcliffe-Brown, A.R. 1922 [1964]. *The Andaman Islanders.* New York: Free Press. An early expression of functionalist social anthropology, emphasizing ritual.

Rappaport, Roy A. 1968. *Pigs for the Ancestors: Ritual in the Ecology of a New Guinea People.* New Haven, Conn.: Yale University Press. A pioneering study of the interrelation of ecological adaptation and ritual.

———. 1979. "The Obvious Aspects of Ritual." Roy Rappaport, *Ecology, Meaning, and Religion.* Richmond, Calif.: North Atlantic Books. Drawing on ecology, systems theory, and semiotics, Rappaport offers a novel approach to the study of ritual.

Smith, W. Robertson. 1889 [1972]. *The Religion of the Semites: The Fundamental Institutions.* New York: Schocken.

Turner, Victor. 1967. *The Forest of Symbols: Aspects of Ndembu Ritual.* Ithaca, N.Y.: Cornell University Press. Offers an innovative theory of symbolism and ritual.

———. 1969 [1977]. *The Ritual Process: Structure and Anti-Structure.* Ithaca, N.Y.: Cornell University Press.

Webb, Clement C. J. 1960. "Sacrament." *Encyclopaedia Britannica* 19:798–801. A brief survey of the central rituals of Christianity.

Sources of Additional Information

On the relation of religion and ritual see Jack Goody, "Religion and Ritual: The Definitional Problem," *British Journal of Sociology* 12:142–64, 1961. Ronald L. Grimes, *Beginnings in Ritual Studies*, Lanham, Maryland: University Press of America, 1982, provides an interdisciplinary view of ritual, drawing on anthropology, religious studies, theology, and theater. Two collections of significant anthropological writings on ritual and symbolism are John Middleton, ed., *Gods and Rituals: Readings in Religious Beliefs and Practices*, Garden City, N.Y.: Natural History Press, 1967; and William A. Lessa and Evon Z. Vogt, eds., *Reader in Comparative Religion: An Anthropological Approach*, 4th ed., New York: Harper & Row, 1979. An interesting synthesis of symbolic and historical approaches is provided by Maurice Bloch's study of Madagascar circumcision ritual, *From Blessing to Violence*, Cambridge: Cambridge University Press, 1986. For the application of anthropological approaches to a western European context, see Ilse Hayden, *Symbol and Privilege: The Ritual Context of British Royalty*, Tucson: University of Arizona Press, 1987.

S

SEMIOTICS. A theory of signs, a study of the various modes of signification and their characteristics.

Semiotics is derived from the Greek *semeion*, a sign. In discussions of logic the latter was used by Aristotle as well as the later Stoics and Sceptics to describe the vehicle of a logical association or proposition, for example, smoke as a sign of fire (Dumont 1966:93). The scope of the sign concept is thus very broad. This entry describes various efforts by anthropologists to explore the nature of signs (including symbols), their forms and properties, as these are encountered in the context of ETHNOGRAPHY. Broader issues of symbolic anthropology are treated under SYMBOLISM, INTERPRETATION, and RITUAL; see also COMMUNICATION.

The idea of a science of semiotics was developed in the Enlightenment period by John Locke (d. 1704). In his *Essay Concerning Human Understanding* (Sec. 4.21), Locke spoke of three branches of knowledge: the *physikē*, or natural philosophy; the *praktikē*, or ethics, the study of right action; and the *sēmeiōtikē*, or logic, the aim of which was "to consider the nature of signs the mind makes use of for the understanding of things, or conveying its knowledge to others" (Locke 1690:3:175).

Over the past century the need for a science of signs was advanced (probably independently) by the American philosopher Charles Sanders Peirce (d. 1914) and the Swiss linguist Ferdinand de Saussure (d. 1913). For this study Peirce proposed the name semiotic: "Logic, in its general sense, is . . . only another name for semiotic (sēmeiōtikē), the quasi-necessary, or formal, doctrine of signs" (Peirce ca. 1900:98). Saussure, viewing the problem from the perspective of LANGUAGE rather than logic, suggested the term semiology, with a seemingly similar aim: to discover "what constitutes signs, what laws govern them" (Saussure 1915:16).

Sign and Symbol

Anthropological interest in the nature of signs and signification developed out of a need to understand the alien beliefs and behavior encountered in ethnography. The concern with (or even awareness of) comprehensive semiotic theories, such as those propounded by Peirce or Saussure, was a later development, dating to the 1960s.

Ethnographic data have always presented a dual character: on the one hand, those domains that appeared readily intelligible to the observer, such as agricultural technique or economic exchange; on the other, those that presented fundamental problems of interpretation, such as MYTH, art, or ritual. One approach has been to explain the contrast of these domains as the RATIONALITY of technique versus the irrationality of MAGIC and RELIGION, a direction much followed by evolutionist writers of the nineteenth century (see EVOLUTION). Perhaps more fruitfully, the problem can also be approached in semiotic terms, as a contrast in the mode of signification occurring in each context. In this sense there is a radical difference between the use of a tiger to represent a brand of gasoline and the use of a fish to represent Christ. There is a similar semiotic contrast between use of the figure ''$1.00'' to signify the price of bread and use of the word ''America'' to signify a blessed homeland.

The distinction these contrasts suggest is that between the representation of an essentially known concept, one which can be explicitly verbalized, and representation of an obscure, unarticulated, yet powerful experience. Dan Sperber has contrasted these as semantic and symbolic modes of knowledge, respectively, arguing that ''a representation is symbolic precisely to the extent that it is not entirely explicable, that is to say, expressible by semantic means'' (Sperber 1975:113). Similarly, Edward Sapir described these two modes respectively as referential symbolism and condensation symbolism, while Victor Turner spoke of signs and ritual symbols (Sapir 1935:493; Turner 1967:26). A century earlier, J. W. von Goethe (1749–1832) made the same distinction in contrasting allegory and symbolism: while the allegory is at root a concept remaining always defined (*begrenzt*), symbolism ''transforms phenomenon into idea, the idea into an image, so that the idea within the image remains infinitely effective and unattainable [*unendlich wirksam und unerreichbar*], uttered in all speech yet unexpressible'' (Goethe [1963]: nos. 1112–13).

Semiotics and Anthropology

Recognition of these contrasting modes of signification is indicative of a larger development, the diffusion of what Raymond Firth has termed ''the symbolic idiom'' in postwar anthropology (Firth 1973:165; see also Schwimmer 1977). The existence of a symbolic (as opposed to a semantic) domain, to follow Sperber's usage, suggests that a grasp of the ''native's point of view'' is not a matter of simple description—as ethnographers once assumed—but a complex process of interpretation mediated by a semiotic system (see EMIC/ETIC). Between the First and Second World wars, the writings of Sigmund Freud offered for a number of anthropologists the key to ethnography's semiotic puzzle. Although its influence is now considerably reduced, psychoanalytic theory continues to inform the subfield of psychological ANTHROPOLOGY (see Firth 1973:147–58; see also PERSONALITY). Since the 1960s, however, anthropologists have sought a more general theory of signs through which the disparate data of ethnography could be linked to culture theory (see Singer 1984: chs. 1, 2).

Claude Lévi-Strauss has argued that social anthropology should be equated with the semiology of Saussure, whose object was "the life of signs at the heart of social life." The task of anthropologists, in this view, would be to investigate the realm of nonlinguistic signs, "that domain of semiology which linguistics has not already claimed for its own" (Lévi-Strauss 1960:16–17). More recently the work of Peirce has been championed by a number of anthropologists, among them Milton Singer (1984). The views of Peirce and Saussure, while seemingly similar in intent, in fact differ significantly, in large measure because Saussure, unlike Peirce, took language as the model and preeminent example of a sign system. Continental anthropologists have been more influenced by the semiology of Saussure, Americans by the semiotic of Peirce. Very briefly, the two perspectives can be summarized as follows.

Saussure's semiology. Taking language as his model, Saussure considered every sign to be both binary in form and arbitrary in character. A sign is composed of a sound-image and a concept, or more broadly, a signifier and that which is signified. Thus the concept of tree is represented in English by the sound-image "tree." Yet the sign relation is inherently arbitrary, because the same concept of tree is signified by different sound-images in different languages, "Baum" in German, "arbre" in French, and so forth (Saussure 1915:66–68). A nonlinguistic example would be the system of traffic lights: green, amber, and red signifying "proceed," "caution," and "stop," respectively. For Saussure signs do not exist in isolation but are meaningful only in relation to other signs. Thus signs are not only arbitrary, but systemic in character; for example, collectively, the three colors green/amber/red constitute a closed system (a code), each meaningful only in relation to the others (Hervey 1982:12–13). The aim of Saussure's semiology is a theory of "systems of conventions for communication" (Hervey 1982:36; for a critique, see Sperber 1975).

Peirce's semiotic. A sign, for Peirce, is that "which stands to somebody for something in some respect or capacity" (Peirce ca. 1900:99). This is a more complex notion than that found in Saussure, for two reasons. First, the Peircean sign is triadic rather than dual in character, for it involves not only a "sign-vehicle" signifying its object (Saussure's signifier-signified relation), but the context (or in Peirce's phrase, the respect or capacity) in which it is so understood. For in this view, "the role of a sign is to establish a habit or general rule determining both the way the sign is to be 'understood' on the occasions of its use, and the kind of perceptible, or at least 'imaginable,' features of experience to which the sign may be applied" (Hervey 1982:28). Thus, the blink of an eye may be taken as a sign of flirtatious intent, but it is not enough to say that the blink "means" erotic approval, for the Peircean sign also implies the contextual understandings by which the blink is so interpreted, and not taken in any of its alternative meanings (ironic amusement, dust in the eye, etc.).

Second, Peirce's sign concept is far broader than Saussure's. Peirce describes three classes of signs, varying in the relation holding between sign and object. An icon denotes its object through a real similarity, typically of form: thus a road map is an icon of a city. An index denotes its object by virtue of a real causal relationship: lightning is an index of ensuing thunder, and a rash an index of measles. Finally, a symbol denotes its object by means of an arbitrary, culturally determined meaning: the word "tree" and the flirtatious wink are two examples (Peirce ca. 1900:102–3; Hervey 1982:30–31).

These two semiotic theories offer quite different directions for the development of symbolic studies within anthropology. Thus far the Saussurean model has been more influential, providing the theoretical basis for STRUCTURALISM. As Singer has aptly stated, this perspective has encouraged the study of symbolism as "cognitive systems, abstracted from their ethnographic context of social relations and individual action and feeling" (Singer 1984:6). Peirce's semiotic, in contrast, reflects the pragmatism of which he was a major exponent. In this view, symbolism is to be studied not as a series of abstract and ideal codes, but as it is used and created in the context of social life.

References

Dumont, Jean-Paul, ed. and trans. 1966. *Les Sceptiques grecs: Textes choisis*. Paris: Presses Universitaires de France. Excerpts from Sceptic writings, chiefly the *Pyrrhoniae hypotyposes* of Sextus Empiricus (third century A.D.).
Firth, Raymond. 1973. *Symbols: Public and Private*. Ithaca, N.Y.: Cornell University Press. A useful introduction to the anthropological study of symbolism.
Goethe, Johann Wolfgang von. [1963]. *Maximen und Reflexionen*. Munich: Deutscher Taschenbuch Verlag.
Hervey, Sandor. 1982. *Semiotic Perspectives*. London: George Allen & Unwin. Recommended as a clear introduction.
Lévi-Strauss, Claude. 1960 [1967]. *The Scope of Anthropology*. Sherry Ortner Paul and Robert Paul, trans. London: Jonathan Cape. An important synoptic statement by a leading structuralist.
Locke, John. 1690 [1963]. *An Essay Concerning Human Understanding*. In *The Works of John Locke*, new ed., corrected. 10 vols. Aalen, Germany: Scientia Verlag (reprint of 1823 ed.).
Peirce, Charles S. ca. 1900 [1955]. *Philosophical Writings of Peirce*. Justus Buchler, ed. New York: Dover Press. A useful collection of Peirce's writings, including excerpts bearing on semiotics.
Sapir, Edward. 1935. "Symbolism." *ESS* 14:492–95. Sapir's statement reflects the effort to synthesize cultural and psychological perspectives in the study of symbolism.
Saussure, Ferdinand de. 1915 [1966]. *Course in General Linguistics*. Charles Bally and Albert Sechehaye, eds. New York: McGraw-Hill. A transcript of lectures, this remains a fundamental work of linguistics and semiotics.
Schwimmer, Erik. 1977. "Semiotics and Culture." Thomas A. Sebeok, ed., *A Perfusion*

of Signs. Bloomington: Indiana University Press. Discusses the relation of anthropology and semiotics.

Singer, Milton. 1984. *Man's Glassy Essence: Explorations in Semiotic Anthropology.* Bloomington: Indiana University Press. Compares the semiotics of Saussure and Peirce as guides for symbolic anthropology.

Sperber, Dan. 1975. *Rethinking Symbolism.* Alice L. Morton, trans. Cambridge: Cambridge University Press. A critique of the Saussurean model of symbolism.

Turner, Victor W. 1967. "Symbols in Ndembu Ritual." Victor Turner, *The Forest of Symbols: Aspects of Ndembu Ritual.* Ithaca, N.Y.: Cornell University Press. Turner's model of symbolism combines psychoanalytic and social anthropological perspectives.

Sources of Additional Information

Julia Kristeva provides a brief statement on the scope of semiotics in "Introduction: le lieu sémiotique," J. Kristeva et al., eds., *Essays in Semiotics*, The Hague: Mouton, 1971. Umberto Eco's *A Theory of Semiotics*, Bloomington: Indiana University Press, 1976, is a major theoretical text. In "Semiotics of Culture: Great Britain and North America," *ARA* 6:121–35, 1977, D. Jean Umiker-Sebeok provides an review of anglophone research on semiotic and symbolic anthropology.

SHAMANISM. A religious complex, found most commonly in BAND and tribal societies, in which specialists undertake to heal, guide, and prophesy through TRANCE behavior and mystical flight.

Shamanism involves a religious complex characterized by trance, CURING, and an ideology of cosmic flight, centering on an ecstatic individual (the shaman) believed to possess supranormal powers. The term shaman is derived via Russian from the Tungus *saman*; synonyms for such extraordinary individuals are found in other languages of north and central Asia (Eliade 1964:4).

The ethnological scope of shamanism has been much debated. As implied by etymology, shamanism has been associated in particular with the cultures of Siberia; a number of scholars, among them Arnold van Gennep, have argued that the term should be restricted to this CULTURE AREA (see Krader 1978:231). However, shamanism is now generally recognized in a much broader range of societies. Shamanic patterns have been described in numerous aboriginal societies of the Americas (Hultkrantz 1979: ch. 6). Parallels between shamanism in the circumpolar regions of North America, Northeast Asia, and even Europe, have been widely noted, apparently the result of MIGRATION and DIFFUSION (Eliade 1964:333–36). Shamanism has also been studied in Southeast Asia and Oceania (Eliade 1964: ch. 10), and in sub-Saharan Africa (Lewis 1986: ch. 5). Furthermore, although the shamanic pattern is generally associated with bands and TRIBES, the role of the shaman has often survived the EVOLUTION of such societies into STATES. Examples include classical China, as recorded in the first century BC by the historian Ssu-ma Ch'ien (Watson 1961:2: 32, 42, 61), and probably classical Greece (Dodds 1951: ch. 5).

The Shamanic World View

Following Ake Hultkrantz, shamanism can be briefly characterized by four criteria: a supernatural world to which the shaman travels; action on behalf of a social group; inspiration through familiar spirits; and ecstatic, or trance, experience (Hultkrantz 1978:30). Although the shaman may fill a multiplicity of roles, including political leader and master teacher, the shamanic function centers on curing. The curing process, however, exists within a cosmological context that, while varying from society to society, shows certain consistent motifs, and which provides the essential cultural framework for the shaman's activities.

The shamanic WORLD VIEW presupposes a multileveled cosmos, with the heavens, and often an underworld, complementing the mundane world of everyday existence. Although such a cosmology is common to many religious systems, it is uniquely the role of the shamans to move between worlds in the exercise of their calling. In Mircea Eliade's phrase, only the shamans "transform a cosmo-theological concept into a concrete mystical experience" (Eliade 1964:265).

Mystical flight, however, is integrally connected in most versions of shamanism with two other themes: curing soul loss and interaction with spirit-beings. Although in the shamanic ideology illness may have several causes, the most significant is loss of soul. It is the task of the shaman to travel to one or another cosmic realm to retrieve the soul of the sick person and thus to restore him to health. Furthermore, the powers that the shaman exercises are attributed to his mastery over various spirits (see ANIMISM), both those who act as familiars, and those malignant spirits whose powers the shaman must overcome (Eliade 1964: ch. 3).

The shamanic quest generally occurs through trance. The concept of trance, however, constitutes a naturalistic description of a range of altered states of consciousness and should be distinguished from such emic categories as shamanism and possession, which involve cultural interpretations of behavior (see EMIC/ETIC). Possession can be defined as "the coercive seizing of the spirit of a man by another spirit, viewed as superhuman" (in Bourguignon 1976:5). It has frequently been contrasted with shamanism in the anthropological literature, for example by Mircea Eliade (1964:6) and Luc de Heusch (in Lewis 1986:81–83). In this view shamanism is seen as voluntary mystical flight, possession as the involuntary experience of descending spirits. Yet as I. M. Lewis has argued, this opposition is misleading. It is, for example, through the intervention of spirits that an individual first recognizes his or her vocation as a shaman (Lewis 1986:84–91).

Recent Research

If, as is now widely accepted, shamanism is understood as a global phenomenon, rather than merely a culture PATTERN originating in Northeast Asia and diffused to the Americas, then a biological or panhuman basis for the shamanic complex must be considered. Numerous studies on shamanism have appeared since the 1960s, broadening what had been essentially a problem of ETHNOLOGY into a focus of interdisciplinary research, drawing on medicine, psychology, and medical ANTHROPOLOGY, among other fields (for a review of research, see Hoppal 1987).

A major concern has been to distinguish ecstatic experience—which, as Eliade has argued, is the primary phenomenon of shamanism (Eliade 1964:504)—from its cultural context and validating belief system and to identify the biological and psychological foundations of such experience. At the same time the powers ostensibly associated with shamanic performance have been investigated more seriously. Joseph Long (1976) has urged that the reports of various parapsychological phenomena occurring in shamanic performances (clairvoyance, divination, etc.) be given serious attention by anthropologists. A number of studies have concerned the role of hallucinogenic drugs in establishing shamanic trance (Harner 1973). Finally, James Dow (1986) among others has argued that religious healing, shamanic curing, and Western psychotherapy be investigated as clinically efficacious and functionally equivalent phenomena.

References

Bourguignon, Erika. 1976. *Possession*. San Francisco: Chandler & Sharp.
Dodds, E. R. 1951. *The Greeks and the Irrational*. Berkeley and Los Angeles: University of California Press.
Dow, James. 1986. "Universal Aspects of Symbolic Healing." *AA* 88:56–69.
Eliade, Mircea. 1964. *Shamanism: Archaic Techniques of Ecstasy*. Princeton, N.J.: Princeton University Press. The classic study, written from the perspective of comparative religions.
Harner, Michael J. 1973. *Hallucinogens and Shamanism*. New York: Oxford University Press.
Hoppal, Mihaly. 1987. "Shamanism: An Archaic and/or Recent System of Beliefs." Shirley Nicholson, ed., *Shamanism*. Wheaton, Ill.: Theosophical Publishing. A useful guide to recent research.
Hultkrantz, Ake. 1978. "Ecological and Phenomenological Aspects of Shamanism." V. Dioszegi and M. Hoppal, eds., *Shamanism in Siberia*. Budapest: Akademiai Kiado.
————. 1979. *The Religions of the American Indians*. Monica Setterwall, trans. Berkeley and Los Angeles: University of California Press.
Krader, Lawrence. 1978. "Shamanism: Theory and History in Buryat Society." V. Dioszegi and M. Hoppal, eds., *Shamanism in Siberia*. Budapest: Akademiai Kiado. Examines shamanism in one Siberian society as a complex, historically evolving phenomenon.
Lewis, I. M. 1986. *Religion in Context: Cults and Charisma*. Cambridge: Cambridge University Press. An important study, suggesting a common theoretical basis for the study of witchcraft, possession, and shamanism.
Long, Joseph K. 1976. "Shamanism, Trance, Hallucinogens, and Psychical Events: Concepts, Methods, and Techniques for Fieldwork among Primitives." Agehananda Bharati, ed., *The Realm of the Extra-Human: Agents and Audiences*. The Hague: Mouton.
Watson, Burton, trans. 1961. *Records of the Grand Historian of China, Translated from the Shih chi of Ssu-ma Ch'ien*. 2 vols. New York: Columbia University Press.

Sources of Additional Information

Several selections on shamanism are provided in William A. Lessa and Evon Z. Vogt, eds., *Reader in Comparative Religion*, 4th ed., New York: Harper & Row, 1979. For a firsthand account by a contemporary Native American shaman, see Wallace H. Black Elk and William S. Lyon, *Black Elk: The Sacred Ways of a Lakota*, San Francisco: Harper & Row, 1990.

SOCIAL MOVEMENT. A network of individuals organized to advance a program of social change, motivated by a shared ideology.

A social movement is a NETWORK of individuals undertaking action to effect cultural or political change. In contrast to the types of groups more commonly studied in ANTHROPOLOGY—for example, village COMMUNITIES, unilineal DESCENT groups, age-sets, or religious ASSOCIATIONS—social movements can be distinguished by their fluidity of membership, their impermanence, and their ideological focus. Social movements have been of immense significance both culturally and historically. Examples include the Beghards and Taborites of the later Middle Ages, the Luddites and Chartists of nineteenth century Britain, the intolerant nativist movements of the nineteenth century United States, or (in a more traditionally anthropological vein) the Native American Ghost Dance, the Melanesian cargo cults, and the millenarian movements (such as the Congolese Kimbangu cult) of sub-Saharan Africa. In their formative phases, most of the major world religions (certainly Buddhism, Christianity, and Islam) could appropriately have been described as social movements. In the later twentieth century, pacifist and environmental movements have had major political influence in Europe and the United States (see also ASSOCIATION).

The use of ''movement'' to describe an ideologically motivated social grouping dates only to the nineteenth century (see *OED*). Although not always occurring in a context of political agitation (note the Anglo-Catholic ''Oxford Movement''), the term has frequently been used to connote a sense of popular or mass involvement in attempts at social change. The British radical William Cobbett, writing in 1812 regarding rioting by starving workers, noted that the government ''can find no agitators. It is a movement of the people's own'' (in Williams 1958:16). Similarly, Karl Marx and Friedrich Engels claimed, in the *Communist Manifesto* (1848), ''The proletarian movement is the self-conscious, independent movement of the immense majority, in the interests of the immense majority'' (in McLellan 1971:206).

In North America, tribal social movements have had a long history of study. An early example was James Mooney's account of the Ghost Dance, a millenarian movement through which the Indian peoples would be restored to a primeval felicity, while the intrusive and oppressive white settlers would vanish from the earth (Mooney 1896:19). The relationship between such movements and conditions of displacement, subjugation, and CULTURE CHANGE was obvious and widely noted. As Alfred Haddon argued (in 1916), ''The weakening or disruption of the old social order may stimulate new and often bizarre ideals, and these may give rise to religious movements that strive to sanction social or political aspirations'' (in Burridge 1960:xxi–xxii). In the context of American anthropology such movements were generally analyzed as manifestations of the AC-CULTURATION process (e.g., Stewart 1944). British anthropologists, guided by the perspective of FUNCTIONALISM, paid less attention. The functionalist emphasis on stable and traditional patterns of authority, and its assumption that societies are to be analyzed as isolates, uninfluenced by wider historical forces, made social movements theoretically problematic.

Types of Social Movements

Social movements present considerable variation, and a number of typologies have been suggested (e.g., Wallace 1956). It seems useful to make a broad distinction between movements of protest and movements of revitalization. In this sense, protest movements occur within a culturally homogeneous situation, and involve limited, focused opposition and relatively discrete goals of social or political change. Examples of protest movements in Euro-American experience include campaigns for women's suffrage, nuclear disarmament, and black civil rights. Revitalization movements, in contrast, occur in situations of culture conflict, typically between societies of unequal power, and advocate some form of total cultural transformation. As defined by A. F. C. Wallace, the revitalization movement is "a deliberate, organized, conscious effort by members of a society to construct a more satisfying culture" (Wallace 1956:265). Examples of such movements include the Ghost Dance and the Peyote Cult in native North America, and the various messianic and mystical movements of Jewish redemption (e.g., Hassidism), which occurred in Eastern Europe in the seventeenth and eighteenth centuries.

In turn, the broad category of revitalization movements can be subdivided. Somewhat arbitrarily, one can differentiate nativistic, revivalistic, and millenarian patterns, though these need not be mutually exclusive. The nativistic movement involves a rejection of "alien persons, customs, values [or] materiel" (Wallace 1956:267), an infamous example being the American Ku Klux Klan (see Higham 1968). The revivalistic movement, in contrast, seeks to revive or perpetuate certain aspects of an indigenous culture (Linton 1943:231), for example, the nineteenth-century Celtic revival in Ireland, or the return to Vedic RITUAL advocated by the Arya Samaj in late nineteenth-century India. Finally, the millenarian movement presumes a total cultural renewal effected through some cosmic transformative process, often involving a messianic intervention. The early Christian movement epitomized such millenarian expectations, anticipating "a new heaven and a new earth. . . . There shall be no more death, neither sorrow, nor crying, neither shall there be any more pain: for the former things are passed away" (Rev. 21:1, 4; cf. Tuveson 1973). The cargo cult is a particular variant of the millenarian movement, notable in Melanesia, anticipating the supernatural arrival of coveted goods, an arrival expected to inaugurate a new era of "material prosperity, spiritual salvation, and political independence" (Burridge 1960:28–9).

Recent Directions

Earlier anthropological studies of social movements (particularly movements rooted in culture conflict) tended to characterize them as pathological reactions to acculturation. For Philleo Nash, such movements sought "to restore the original value pattern . . . [through] construction of a fantasy situation," at times resulting in an "amorphous mass hysteria" (Nash 1937:377). Several developments since the 1960s have contributed to a less pejorative understanding.

Questions of SOCIAL STRUCTURE have received considerable attention. Movements are in fact ideologically motivated NETWORKS lacking a centralized or hierarchical order, the absence of which (paradoxically) can be highly adaptive for expanding a movement and reacting effectively to opposition. Luther Gerlach, on the basis of studies of American protest movements, has characterized their social organization as "segmentary, polycephalous, and reticulate." They are segmentary in being composed of numerous, diverse groups; polycephalous in lacking a central decision-making structure; and reticulate in encompassing complex networks, with crosscutting affiliations among individuals and groups (Gerlach 1971:817).

The increased interest in PEASANTRIES in the postwar period has stimulated research on agrarian social movements, the relation between revolutionary politics and traditional FOLK CULTURES, and more broadly, the economic and political context of culture change considered at a national rather than merely a local level (see Friedrich 1977). In this light, at least some millenarian belief systems can be understood not as dysfunctional reactions to acculturation, but as the precursors and stimulants of revolutionary change, couching their "political message in the familiar and powerful language and images of traditional religion" (Talmon 1962:142; see also RELIGION; SYMBOLISM).

References

Burridge, Kenelm. 1960 [1970]. *Mambu: A Study of Melanesian Cargo Movements and Their Social and Ideological Background*. New York: Harper & Row.
Friedrich, Paul. 1977. *Agrarian Revolt in a Mexican Village*. Chicago: University of Chicago Press. A study of a twentieth-century revolutionary movement.
Gerlach, Luther P. 1971. "Movements of Revolutionary Change: Some Structural Characteristics." *American Behavioral Scientist* 14:812–36.
Higham, John. 1968. *Strangers in the Land: Patterns of American Nativism, 1860–1925*. New York: Atheneum. A major historical study of American nativistic movements.
Linton, Ralph. 1943. "Nativistic Movements." *AA* 45:230–40.
McLellan, David. 1971. *The Thought of Karl Marx: An Introduction*. New York: Harper & Row.
Mooney, James. 1896 [1965]. *The Ghost-Dance Religion and the Sioux Outbreak of 1890*. Abr. A. F. C. Wallace, ed. Chicago: University of Chicago Press. One of the earliest studies of a tribal revitalization movement.
Nash, Philleo. 1937 [1955]. "The Place of Religious Revivalism in the Formation of the Intercultural Community on Klamath Reservation." Fred Eggan, ed., *Social An-*

thropology of North American Tribes. Chicago: University of Chicago Press. Concerns the Ghost Dance.

Stewart, Omer C. 1944. "Washo-Northern Paiute Peyotism: A Study in Acculturation." *University of California Publications in American Archaeology and Ethnology* 40:63–141.

Talmon, Yonina. 1962. "Pursuit of the Millenium: The Relation Between Religious and Social Change." *Archives européennes de sociologie* 3:125–48. An important review article.

Tuveson, Ernest. 1973. "Millenarianism." *DHI* 3:223–25.

Wallace, Anthony F. C. 1956. "Revitalization Movements." *AA* 58:264–81. An influential statement offering a more positive perspective on social movements.

Williams, Raymond. 1958. *Culture and Society: 1780–1950*. New York: Harper & Row.

Sources of Additional Information

An important overview of revitalization movements with a worldwide scope is provided by Vittorio Lantenari, *The Religions of the Oppressed: A Study of Modern Messianic Cults*, Lisa Sergio, trans., New York: New American Library, 1963. See also Ralph W. Nicholas, "Social and Political Movements," *ARA* 2:63–84, 1973.

SOCIAL STRUCTURE. Enduring, culturally patterned relations between individuals or groups.

Social structure constitutes one of the key concepts of ANTHROPOLOGY. Like CULTURE, social structure offers a comprehensive framework for ethnographic study. Unlike culture, which focuses attention on the products of social life (what individuals think and do), social structure stresses social life as such: individuals in their relations with one another. A concern with social structure yields several broad topics: forms of relationship (such as MARRIAGE and exchange); forms of differentiation (hierarchy, authority, status); characteristics of groups (principles of recruitment and spheres of action); and the expression of these social patterns through SYMBOLISM, RITUAL, and MYTH.

Distinct traditions of anthropology have developed by giving primary emphasis to culture or social structure. British anthropology in particular, and by extension anthropology as practiced in the countries of the British Commonwealth, has given priority to the study of social structure. There the discipline is most commonly termed social anthropology, contrasting with cultural anthropology (as in the United States), whose primary concern rests with cultural expression (for a polemical comparison, see Murdock 1951).

Nonetheless, in all of the national traditions of anthropology, social structure and culture remain theoretically interdependent. Meyer Fortes has expressed this from the perspective of social anthropology:

> We see custom as symbolizing or expressing social relations—that is, the ties and cleavages by which persons and groups are bound to one another or divided from one another in the activities of social life. In this sense social structure is not an aspect of culture but the entire culture of a given people handled in a special frame of theory. (Fortes 1953:21)

The discipline of sociology—which might appear quite similar in aim—differs from social anthropology in precisely this respect, the absence of a serious theoretical attention to culture.

Historical Development

The history of the study of social structure is so broad a topic that it is practically equivalent to the emergence of the social sciences through the eighteenth and nineteenth centuries (see Evans-Pritchard 1962:21–42). One theme of particular importance, however, was the growing awareness of societies as coherently organized systems, built of coordinated institutions. In describing how institutions or patterns of behavior were interdependent, the delineation of social structural detail proved essential. The French historian Fustel de Coulanges (1830–1889) showed this perspective in discussing the interrelation between ritual and social form in classical Greece and Rome: "Among the ancients, what formed the bond of every society was a worship. Just as a domestic altar held the members of a family grouped around it, so the city was the collective group of those who had the same protecting deities, and who performed the religious ceremony at the same altar" (Fustel de Coulanges 1864:146). The nineteenth-century concern with cultural EVOLUTION also directed attention to matters of social structure. For example, John McLennan (1827–1881) analyzed in evolutionary terms the interrelated development of systems of DESCENT, MARRIAGE, and KINSHIP (McLennan 1865).

The sociologist Emile Durkheim (1858–1917) developed a theoretical perspective recognizing social structure as a reality sui generis. In *The Rules of Sociological Method* (1895) Durkheim provided a sustained argument for the need to explain social facts on their own terms rather than by recourse to psychological explanation—a view that proved fundamental for modern social anthropology (cf. SUPERORGANIC). In *The Elementary Forms of the Religious Life* (1915) Durkheim analyzed the religious belief and worship of traditional Australia, demonstrating their functional relationship to aboriginal social structure (see TOTEMISM; regarding the elaboration of this perspective within anthropology, see FUNCTIONALISM).

Defining Social Structure

The concept of social structure has been defined in a variety of ways. E. E. Evans-Pritchard held it to involve "relations between groups which have a high degree of consistency and constancy," as between territorial groups, age-sets, or lineages (Evans-Pritchard 1940:262). In contrast, A. R. Radcliffe-Brown defined social structure more broadly as "an arrangement of persons in institutionally controlled or defined relationships" (Radcliffe-Brown 1952:11). That is, for Radcliffe-Brown, social structure entailed not only relations between groups, but also (1) "all social relations of person to person . . . as between a father and son, or a mother's brother and his sister's son"; and (2) "the differentiation of individuals and of classes by their social role," for example the distinct positions "of men and women, of chiefs and commoners" (Radcliffe-Brown 1952:191).

Social structure implies not only relationship but stability, that which is enduring within the flux of social life. "In the concept of social structure, the qualities recognized are primarily those of persistence, continuity, form, and pervasiveness through the social field" (Firth 1955:61). As Radcliffe-Brown remarked, "In the political structure of the United States there must always be a President; at one time it is Herbert Hoover, at another time Franklin Roosevelt, but the structure as an arrangement remains continuous" (Radcliffe-Brown 1952:10).

Aspects of Social Structure

The idea of social structure comprises a range of topics. Among these are concepts of total social systems (societies); the units that compose them; the principles of relationship through which individuals form groups; and the premises on which individuals are differentiated one from another. These are briefly outlined below. For further information, see the articles cited.

Societies. Every discipline needs unit concepts, words that describe the basic divisions of its object of study. Cultural anthropologists speak of culture (or cultures); social anthropologists of society. Each is in its way problematic.

Society is used in two distinct senses. First, in the singular, society is life lived in association with others. It is in this sense the precondition of human existence (cf. NATURE). As Adam Ferguson wrote, quoting Montesquieu, "Man is born in society, and there he remains" (Ferguson 1767:16). Aristotle expressed the same view, phrased in the categories of STATE and polis: "It is evident that the state is a creation of nature, and that man is by nature a political animal [i.e., a being of the polis, or city-state]. And he who by nature and not by mere accident is without a state, is either a bad man or above humanity" (*Pol.* 1253a).

Second, society is used in the plural, distinguishing one social aggregate from another. Max Gluckman, for example, has referred to "the tribal societies, with simple tools, lack of luxuries, and restricted trade" (Gluckman 1965:82). Yet this usage can be problematic, for social life lacks clear boundaries, and such boundaries as may exist are constantly transcended by exploration, trade, WAR, marriage, MIGRATION, and cultural DIFFUSION.

Social boundaries can more successfully be described by the limits of effective political control. Hence the most common ethnological categories are political, ranging in scale from the small BAND comprising a few families, through the larger and more differentiated TRIBE and CHIEFDOM, to the state, claiming sovereign control of a distinct territory, and demanding allegiance from the tens or hundreds of millions of individuals who reside within its borders.

Groups. The social structural forms given emphasis reflect the types of societies anthropologists have traditionally studied: small-scale, kin-based, and technologically simple. Most ethnographic study has centered on the COMMUNITY, a geographically localized population distinguished by extensive social interaction, relative self-sufficiency, and a common culture or identity. Within this setting, the smallest significant social unit is normally the FAMILY, a core group of closely related, closely cooperating kin, spanning two or more generations. In a large proportion of traditional societies, key political, economic, and ritual activities are organized through DESCENT groups (e.g., clans, lineages), whose membership is determined by relation to a specified ancestor. Finally, these social units are complemented by various forms of ASSOCIATION, groups organized on a basis other than descent or territory, including age-sets, secret societies, and the various forms of voluntary association common in the industrial West.

Relationships. As noted, social structure comprehends not only group organization, but patterned relations between individuals. The most significant of these is KINSHIP, a relationship based on the premise of descent (or more technically, filiation), which provides the organizing principles for a wide range of economic and political activities in traditional societies. Those sharing kinship are termed consanguines. MARRIAGE, a complementary principle of social structure, entails the socially recognized bond between a man and woman involving both sexual intimacy and economic interdependence. Those linked by marriage are termed affines. Finally, the study of social structure includes the less formal domain of the social NETWORK, a real or potential chain of interaction reckoned from the perspective of a given individual.

Social inequality. Although many principles of social structure bring individuals together, others set them apart. INEQUALITY involves the systematic ranking of individuals or groups within a society on the basis of descent, wealth, prestige, or other culturally defined principles. GENDER provides a basis for status distinctions in most societies. ETHNICITY and RACE serve to separate groups on the basis of cultural, linguistic, religious, or physical characteristics. State-level societies manifest stratification, hierarchical cleavages between status groups (such as classes or CASTES), reflecting large differences in wealth and power among members of such societies (see INEQUALITY).

Status in such systems may be ascribed or achieved. Ascribed status results from group membership on the basis of birth, for example in a descent group or caste. Achieved status results from individual action, as the accumulation of wealth provides the basis for big-man leadership in Melanesia or middle-class status in the United States. Societies may reflect multiple, inconsistent systems of status, for example the quite different rankings generated by caste and wealth in modern India.

Later Developments

With the growing influence of A. R. Radcliffe-Brown in the 1930s and 1940s, the notion of social structure assumed a central position in British anthropology (see Kuper 1973: ch. 3). This in turn provoked attempts to clarify or revise the concept. Two issues are considered briefly.

Formalists and pragmatists. For functionalists such as Radcliffe-Brown, society or social structure existed sui generis. In *The Andaman Islanders* he noted that ''the mass of institutions, customs and beliefs forms a single whole or system that determines the life of the society, and the life of a society is not less real, or less subject to natural laws, than the life of an organism" (Radcliffe-Brown 1922:229–30). Many anthropologists would reject this view as metaphysics rather than social science, insisting that explanation should be found not through the need to perpetuate a reified social structure, but in the motivations and actions of individuals. Bronislaw Malinowski's blunt comment regarding the *Andaman Islanders* was characteristic: "not 'the society,' but every bloody man and woman" (in Stocking 1984:158).

Human action is guided and constrained by the principles of social structure, for example, the solidarity of clan members, or (in a matrilineal system) the conflicting obligations of a man to his own as opposed to his sister's children. Nonetheless, as Raymond Firth noted, "the fulfillment of the moral obligations laid down by structural requirements is conditioned by individual interests" (in Kuper 1973:166). In short, the pragmatic realities of social life, the questions of conflict, choice, and strategy, can be obscured by formalism, an excessive emphasis on structural principles.

For this reason Firth proposed that the concept of social structure be balanced by that of social organization, which reflects the "diversity of the ends and activities of individuals in society, a pattern for their co-ordination in some particular sphere" (Firth 1955:60). This concern with individual strategy and the resolution of conflicting structural principles is evident in much postwar ethnography. Examples include Victor Turner's depiction of social dramas (focused incidents of social conflict and change) in African village life (see Turner 1957), and Fredrik Barth's pursuit of generative models of social organization, interpreting social life as the outcome of a continuous process of goal-seeking transactions between individuals (Barth 1966).

Empiricists and rationalists. Radcliffe-Brown viewed the task of social anthropology in uncompromisingly positivist terms. Social anthropology was to be a "theoretical natural science of human society," using methods "essentially similar" to those of the physical and biological sciences (Radcliffe-Brown 1952:189 [orig. 1940]). Its object of study was an observable reality, social relations, while his key concept, social structure, represented its continuities. The careful observation of social life would thus reveal social structure much as a time-lapse photograph of cars in motion will reveal the direction and intensity of traffic flows. In short, "the components or units of social structure are persons" and the continuing network of social relationships "constitute [sic] social structure" (Radcliffe-Brown 1952:9, 10).

Yet by the 1940s many anthropologists recognized that the study of social structure was a more complex matter. Social structure was an abstraction, an analytic construct imposed by the observer. As Meyer Fortes wrote in 1949, "When we describe structure we are already dealing with general principles far removed from the complicated skein of behaviour, feelings, beliefs, &c., that constitute the tissue of actual social life. . . . We discern structure in the 'concrete reality' of social events only by virtue of having first established structure by abstraction from 'concrete reality''' (in Kuper 1973:121). It is this process of abstraction that allowed ethnographers to distinguish kinship and politics in stateless societies, for example, and in turn to describe their functional relationship (e.g., Evans-Pritchard 1940).

Their differences notwithstanding, the views of Radcliffe-Brown and later writers such as Fortes converged in seeing empirical social life as the focus of anthropological interest. During the 1960s, however, growing interest in the work of Claude Lévi-Strauss forced a confrontation between the empiricism of such traditional social anthropology and the strikingly different assumptions of the emerging perspective known as STRUCTURALISM.

The structuralist program is rationalist in character, giving explanatory priority to the unconscious categories of thought through which the world is experienced. The primary object of study is thus not social behavior as such, but the structure of logical contrasts underlying and generating cultural expression. This was expressed cogently by Lévi-Strauss: "The term 'social structure' has nothing to do with empirical reality but with models which are built up after it." To this end he distinguished social structure from social relations, which "consist of the raw materials out of which the models making up the social structure are built" (Lévi-Strauss 1953:279).

The point can be illustrated by the contrasting approaches of descent and alliance theories in the study of marriage. The empiricist tradition (exemplified by Fortes or Radcliffe-Brown) emphasized the study of enduring social groups, in particular the multifunctioned descent groups such as clans and lineages. Marriage, from the perspective of descent theory, is analytically of secondary importance: a means of recruiting marriage partners and perpetuating the descent group. For structuralist-inspired alliance theory, in contrast, the primary significance of marriage in kin-based societies is as a mechanism for creating linkages between outmarrying kin groups through the exchange of spouses. As David Schneider has noted, "A given structural relationship in a very important sense cannot be seen or observed as such" (Schneider 1965:28).

From the structuralist perspective, social structure is constituted through a set of relations between groups persisting through time, but is not reducible to any one of these. Marriage thus forms part of a larger system of exchange. A given social structure (in the Lévi-Straussian sense) would be manifested empirically in a variety of ways, for example through specific forms of marriage transactions, gift exchange, and mythological accounts of group relations. The analytic problem, then, is "to search out the various forms of expression in order to comprehend the basic relationship which is structurally operative" (Schneider 1965:28).

As with the culture concept, the idea of social structure reflects in its ambiguity continuing debates within modern anthropology. At the level of theory, as opposed to that of description and technique, considerable difference of viewpoint remains as to the empirical character of social structure and its relative importance in relation to other factors shaping social life (see ADAPTATION; FUNCTIONALISM; MATERIALISM; MODE OF PRODUCTION; SYMBOLISM).

References

Barth, Fredrik. 1966 [1981]. "Models of Social Organization (I–III)." F. Barth, *Process and Form in Social Life*. London: Routledge & Kegan Paul. An influential call for a theory of social organization based on concepts of choice, social process, and transaction.

Durkheim, Emile. 1895 [1964]. *The Rules of Sociological Method*. S. A. Solovay and J. H. Mueller, trans. New York: Free Press. A classic work, emphasizing the autonomy of social life.

————. 1915 [1965]. *The Elementary Forms of the Religious Life*. J. W. Swain, trans. New York: Free Press. A study of Australian aboriginal society and religion, a key work of the functionalist tradition.

Evans-Pritchard, E. E. 1940. *The Nuer*. New York: Oxford University Press.

————. 1962. *Social Anthropology and Other Essays*. New York: Free Press.

Ferguson, Adam. 1767 [1966]. *An Essay on the History of Civil Society*. Edinburgh: Edinburgh University Press. A major work of social philosophy of the Scottish Enlightenment.

Firth, Raymond. 1955 [1964]. "Some Principles of Social Organization." R. Firth, *Essays on Social Organization and Values*. London: Athlone Press. Important for the contrast of social organization and social structure.

Fortes, Meyer. 1953. "The Structure of Unilineal Descent Groups." *AA* 55:17–41. An epitome of classic British social anthropology.

Fustel de Coulanges, Numa Denis. 1864. *The Ancient City*. Garden City, N.Y.: Anchor (reprint).

Gluckman, Max. 1965. *Politics, Law and Ritual in Tribal Society*. Oxford: Blackwell. An introduction to social anthropology from the functionalist perspective.

Kuper, Adam. 1973. *Anthropologists and Anthropology: The British School, 1922–1972*. New York: Pica Press. An often acerbic history of modern British anthropology.

Lévi-Strauss, Claude. 1953 [1963]. "Social Structure." C. Lévi-Strauss, *Structural Anthropology*. Claire Jacobson and B. G. Schoepf, trans. New York: Basic Books. A statement from the perspective of French structuralism.

McLennan, John F. 1865 [1970]. *Primitive Marriage*. Chicago: University of Chicago Press.

Murdock, George P. 1951 [1965]. "British Social Anthropology." G. Murdock, *Culture and Society: Twenty-four Essays*. Pittsburgh, Pa.: University of Pittsburgh Press. A critique from the viewpoint of cultural anthropology.

Radcliffe-Brown, A. R. 1922 [1964]. *The Andaman Islanders*. New York: Free Press. A key work of early British functionalism.

————. 1952. *Structure and Function in Primitive Society: Essays and Addresses*. New York: Free Press.

Schneider, David. 1965. "Some Muddles in the Models: or, How the System Really Works." *The Relevance of Models for Social Anthropology*. A. S. A. Monographs, 1. New York: Praeger. A comparison of descent and alliance theory.

Stocking, George W., Jr. 1984. "Radcliffe-Brown and British Social Anthropology." G. Stocking, ed., *Functionalism Historicized: Essays on British Social Anthropology*. Madison: University of Wisconsin Press.

Turner, Victor W. 1957. *Schism and Continuity in an African Society*. Manchester: Manchester University Press.

Sources of Additional Information

For the broader intellectual context of anthropological theories of society and social structure see Adam Kuper, *The Invention of Primitive Society*, London: Routledge, 1988. A useful overview and anthology is provided by George Park, *The Idea of Social Structure*, Garden City, N.Y.: Anchor/Doubleday, 1974. The contrast of structuralist and functionalist perspectives is delineated by David Goddard, "Conceptions of Structure in Lévi-Strauss and in British Anthropology," *Social Research* 32:408–27, 1965. An influential critique of functionalism by a rather heterodox structuralist is found in E. R. Leach, *Rethinking Anthropology*, London: Athlone Press, 1961. A significant older study, from a strongly empiricist and comparative viewpoint, is George Peter Murdock, *Social Structure*, New York: Macmillan, 1949.

SOCIETY. See SOCIAL STRUCTURE.

SOCIOBIOLOGY. A theory that explains patterns of social behavior in terms of biological ADAPTATION and EVOLUTION, in particular through the principle of natural selection.

Sociobiology represents an ambitious attempt to apply principles of evolutionary biology to the analysis of animal social behavior, human and nonhuman. Developed systematically in the 1970s and 1980s, sociobiology marks an effort to expand the application of biological theory in two ways: first, by offering a comprehensive theory of animal social behavior; and second, by applying such theory unreservedly to the analysis of human social life. The term sociobiology was effectively introduced by E. O. Wilson (1975); suggested alternative terms have included biosociology and evolutionary biology.

The concept of natural selection, first formulated by Charles Darwin (1809–1882), is central to modern biological theory. In the *Origin of Species* Darwin postulated that in particular environments selection pressures would favor certain variations of a species over others. Superior fitness would give such variants greater likelihood of surviving to the age of reproduction, thus differentially perpetuating these variants within the gene pool. As Darwin wrote in 1859, "This preservation of favourable individual differences and variations, and the destruction of those which are injurious, I have called Natural Selection, or the Survival of the Fittest" (in Appleman 1970:120).

Darwin was concerned primarily with the role of selection pressures in shaping organic form. However, natural selection can also act on patterns of behavior (mimicry, warning calls, expressions of dominance and aggression, courting rituals, etc.). Since the 1930s the study of animal behavior (ethology) has become a major discipline. Systematic efforts to include human behavior within a comparative ethological perspective, setting cultural patterns side-by-side with the postcopulatory displays of the striped goose or the mouth threats of the gelada baboon, are a more recent development (see Lorenz 1966; Eibl-Eibesfeldt 1970).

Sociobiology: Goals and Theories

The field of sociobiology builds on this research base but seeks to go beyond it by seeking a general theory of animal social behavior and structure, guided by natural selection. E. O. Wilson has defined the discipline as "the systematic study of the biological basis of all social behavior" (Wilson 1975:4). The more vocal proponents grant little if any autonomy to the cultural domain, culture and social structure being understood as a reflex of biological imperatives. Given this viewpoint, it is logical that Wilson has predicted the demise of the social sciences: "Sociology and the other social sciences, as well as the humanities, are the last branches of biology waiting to be included in the Modern Synthesis," that is, within neo-Darwinian evolutionary theory (Wilson 1975:4). The flavor of the sociobiological program is suggested by three topics: patterns of mate selection, KINSHIP and altruism, and optimal foraging strategy.

Mate selection. By Darwinian logic—a game whose goal is maximizing the perpetuation of one's genes—the dramatic differences in male and female reproductive roles should dictate significantly different strategies for the selection of mates (see also GENDER). Because the female's pregnancy involves so much greater an investment of time and energy than the male's act of insemination, in general the female will reap the greatest benefit by bonding with a single male who will assist her through pregnancy and parenthood. Conversely, the male will generally maximize his fitness by inseminating many females (Barash 1977:162–3). Applied to the human domain, "men should accordingly be sexual aggressors. Men should also compete among themselves for the sexual favors of women, and women should in turn be selected [evolutionarily] for assessing men in large part by the quality of the reproductively relevant resources they control" (Barash 1977:290–91).

Given the premise of male dominance, these factors can explain the widespread institution of polygyny, the MARRIAGE of one husband with several wives. Conversely, the adaptive value for females of mating with men controlling greater than average resources is taken to explain both the demographic fact that women frequently marry older men (but seldom the reverse) and the cultural pattern of hypergamy, in which women marry men of higher status than themselves (see Barash 1977:291).

Kinship and altruism. Human life is intrinsically social. Individuals are bound together through complex webs of obligation and cooperation, requiring frequent sacrifice of self-interest in ways large and small. This is, at first glance, difficult to reconcile with a strict biological determinism. As Wilson has phrased the problem, "How can altruism, which by definition reduces personal fitness, possibly evolve by natural selection?" (Wilson 1975:3).

The major answer for sociobiology rests with the theory of kin selection, developed by W. D. Hamilton (1964). Hamilton reasoned that an altruistic act (e.g., giving a warning call on the approach of a predator at the risk of exposing the altruist to greater likelihood of attack) could be justified if those benefited were closely related genetically. In essence, the number of individuals benefited and the degree of genetic similarity with the altruist must be weighed (through the evolutionary process) against the degree of risk or harm experienced. Altruism is adaptive if it serves to increase an individual's inclusive fitness, the perpetuation of genetic material whether through one's own reproduction or through that of kin. In the realm of human sociobiology, discussion of this topic has centered on the relation between kinship and reciprocity.

Optimal foraging theory. One domain of sociobiological theory seeks to model the patterns of foraging behavior best adapted to the environment and dietary resources available to a species, given the premise that natural selection will yield behavior that maximizes survival and reproductive success (Wilson 1975:51–57; Smith 1983:626). For ANTHROPOLOGY, such optimal foraging theories have been used to model the subsistence behavior of hunter-gatherer societies (see BAND), assuming the optimization of time and caloric returns in the food quest (see Smith 1983). Among the problems modeled in this fashion are breadth of diet, range of foraging space, and group form.

Models of diet breadth evaluate the time costs involved in pursuing alternative diets. Two components of cost are considered: search time and pursuit or handling time (the latter involving the time needed to pursue, capture, process, and consume a diet item). According to this formulation, search costs and pursuit costs yield opposing cost curves: "As a forager widens its diet by adding prey types of lower rank (i.e., higher handling time per unit return), handling costs averaged over the entire diet increase; search costs decrease because less time is spent searching for acceptable items" (Smith 1983:628). The diet breadth model thus predicts that the number of food types in the diet will increase until the marginal increase in handling time exceeds the marginal decrease in search time. This and related diet models have been tested in a number of cultures (Smith 1983:628–30).

Critiques

Publication of Wilson's study *Sociobiology: The New Synthesis* (1975) generated intense criticism for its extension of sociobiological reasoning to humans. Reactions can be summarized under three heads: criticism for its ideology, its grasp of ETHNOGRAPHY, and its alleged methodological errors.

(1) Elizabeth Allen et al. (1978) have likened sociobiology to earlier efforts to mold social policy at the behest of dubious biological theory (eugenics, racist immigration policies, etc.). In their view sociobiology—whatever its merits in the analysis of other species—serves to justify inequities of class and gender under the pretense of evolutionary inevitability.

(2) For a number of critics, efforts to apply sociobiology to cultural phenomena have been weakened by ignorance or distortion of the ethnographic record. The arguments for kin selection, for example, assume that altruistic behavior should vary with the degree of biological relationship: near genetic kin should show greater solidarity than individuals who are genetically more distant. Yet as Marshall Sahlins has observed, "There is not a single system of marriage, postmarital residence, family organization, interpersonal kinship, or common descent in

human societies that does not set up a different calculus of relationship and social action than is indicated by the principles of kin selection'' (Sahlins 1976:26).

(3) Various methodological failings have been argued. Sociobiologists too often assume rather than demonstrate that the behaviors they observe actually reflect the effects of Darwinian (natural) selection. As V. Blundell has argued, although some optimal foraging models may have predictive value, several alternatives to natural selection (e.g., behaviorist conditioning with learned transmission) can account for the models just as well (in Smith 1983:642). Furthermore, to argue the influence of genotype on cultural behavior, some intervening psychological mechanism guiding the individual to favor evolutionarily superior behaviors must be demonstrated. The sociobiologists have failed to do this (Barkow 1984:367).

Finally, sociobiology is intensely (and perhaps naively) reductive, collapsing history and culture into the expression of a narrow biological imperative. As Kenneth Bock has commented, "If we are to explain human social and cultural phenomena in terms of an evolved human nature, then we are left with no explanation of different societies and cultures in the present or of changing societies and cultures during historical time when evolutionary changes in human beings were slight" (Bock 1980:4).

In exploring the interface of biology and culture, sociobiology at first glance seems wholly compatible with longstanding anthropological interests: the insistence on a holistic, biocultural discipline (see ANTHROPOLOGY), the theoretical concern with environment and adaptation (see CULTURAL ECOLOGY), and the close attention given to the interrelation of NATURE and CULTURE (see Silverberg 1980). Nonetheless, most if not all anthropologists assume (1) that the biology/culture interaction is complex and bidirectional; (2) that the transmission of human behavior patterns is fundamentally learned, not genetic; and (3) that culture is a relatively autonomous process (see SUPERORGANIC). The tenets of at least the most far-ranging sociobiological theories appear to diverge from all three assumptions. As James Silverberg has observed, "While there is nothing wrong (or new) in the desire to synthesize sociological and biological study, anthropologists do not see reductionism as a form of synthesis" (Silverberg 1980:38).

There is every likelihood that the sociobiological paradigm will continue to generate both provocative research and controversy. At the same time, sociobiology does not represent the only road through which to explore the interaction of biology and culture. An alternative, emphasizing the neuroanatomical structuring of cultural expression, is represented by the interdisciplinary effort of biogenetic structuralism (see d'Aquili et al. 1979: ch. 1).

References

Allen, Elizabeth, et al. 1978. "Against 'Sociobiology.' " Arthur L. Caplan, ed., *The Sociobiology Debate: Readings on Ethical and Scientific Issues*. New York: Harper & Row. A strong attack on sociobiology as an ideologically motivated program.

Appleman, Philip, ed. 1970. *Darwin: A Norton Critical Edition*. New York: Norton. An excellent sourcebook of Darwinian texts and commentaries.

Barash, David P. 1977. *Sociobiology and Behavior*. New York: Elsevier. A popular account.

Barkow, Jerome H. 1984. "The Distance Between Genes and Culture." *Journal of Anthropological Research* 40:367–79.

Bock, Kenneth. 1980. *Human Nature and History: A Response to Sociobiology*. New York: Columbia University Press. An eloquent defense of the values of history, culture, and the social sciences.

d'Aquili, Eugene G., et al. 1979. *The Spectrum of Ritual: A Biogenetic Structural Analysis*. New York: Columbia University Press.

Eibl-Eibesfeldt, Irenaeus. 1970. *Ethology: The Biology of Behavior*. Erich Klinghammer, trans. New York: Holt, Rinehart, and Winston. A broad synthesis.

Hamilton, W. D. 1964 [1978]. "The Genetical Evolution of Social Behavior." Arthur L. Caplan, ed., *The Sociobiology Debate*. New York: Harper & Row. A key text in the theory of kin selection.

Lorenz, Konrad. 1966. *On Aggression*. Marjorie K. Wilson, trans. New York: Harcourt, Brace & World. An influential and widely debated ethological study.

Sahlins, Marshall. 1976. *The Use and Abuse of Biology: An Anthropological Critique of Sociobiology*. Ann Arbor: University of Michigan Press.

Silverberg, James. 1980. "Sociobiology, the New Synthesis? An Anthropologist's Perspective." George W. Barlow and James Silverberg, eds., *Sociobiology: Beyond Nature/Nurture?* Boulder, Colo.: Westview Press. The volume offers an excellent dialogue between anthropologists and biologists.

Smith, Eric. 1983. "Anthropological Applications of Optimal Foraging Theory: A Critical Review." *CA* 24:625–51. An overview, with good bibliography.

Wilson, Edward O. 1975. *Sociobiology: The New Synthesis*. Cambridge, Mass.: Harvard University Press. The classic work in sociobiology.

Sources of Additional Information

A spirited (though at times ethnographically naive) defense of sociobiology is provided by Michael Ruse, *Sociobiology: Sense or Nonsense?*, 2d ed., Dordrecht, the Netherlands: D. Reidel, 1985. Philip Kitcher's *Vaulting Ambition: Sociobiology and the Quest for Human Nature*, Cambridge, Mass.: MIT Press, 1985, provides an exhaustive critique. A brief and balanced review is offered by Henry Harpending, "Human Sociobiology," *Yearbook of Physical Anthropology* 30:127–50, 1987. Interesting collections of essays (generally critical) are provided in Michael S. Gregory et al., eds., *Sociobiology and Human Nature*, San Francisco: Jossey-Bass, 1978; and Ashley Montagu, ed., *Sociobiology Examined*, New York: Oxford University Press, 1980. Austin L. Hughes, *Evolution and Human Kinship*, New York: Oxford University Press, 1988, provides a formal development of the theory of kin selection as applied to human societies, weighed against ethnographic data.

STATE. A society characterized by autonomous political institutions, sovereign control of territory, centralized appropriation of surplus, and support of authority through legitimate force.

The state is the dominant form of society in the modern world. Beginning with the ancient states of Mesopotamia, Egypt, the Indus Valley, and China, state organizations have proliferated over the past five millennia so as to subordinate or destroy kin-based societies over practically the entire globe. Such political dominance has been made possible by (1) the relative institutional permanence of the state, afforded in particular by the creation of centralized and distinct politico-legal institutions; (2) the assertion of sovereign control over territory, preventing the social fission common to BANDS and TRIBES; (3) the capacity for indefinite geographic expansion, implemented through the twin mechanisms of a standing army and a civil bureaucracy; and (4) the systematic appropriation of surplus wealth and labor, through taxation, corvée, impressment, and other means (see Cohen 1978:4–5). The concept of CIVILIZATION describes the cultural dimensions of state societies, generally characterized by systematic social INEQUALITY, URBANISM, literacy, codified TRADITION, and extensive trade.

The term "state" (Italian *stato*, French *état*, etc.) first occurred in the political writings of the Renaissance, notably in the works of Nicolo Machiavelli (1469–1527) (see d'Entreves 1967: ch. 3). However, political theory regarding government, sovereignty, and the state is far older. In Western tradition, it derives from classical sources, exemplified by Aristotle's *Politics* of the fourth century B.C. Aristotle's concepts were derived from the segmentary (i.e., decentralized) states of contemporary Greece, organized through quasi-autarkic *oikia*, or households (*Pol.* 1253a; Weissleder 1978:200–202). In contrast, modern discussions of the state presume a unified and centralized organization of power, where society is "united by common obedience to a single sovereign" (Watkins 1968:150), a heritage of the European absolutist monarchies of the seventeenth and eighteenth centuries (see Meinecke 1925).

Origins of the State

In the postwar period, the study of state formation has been a point of convergence for cultural ANTHROPOLOGY and archaeology (see EVOLUTION). Numerous causes have been advanced for state origins: these include theories of managerial necessity, environmental circumscription, and class conflict. Julian Steward (1949:22–24), following the work of Karl Wittfogel, suggested that population pressure and the productivity afforded by irrigation agriculture would interact to require managerial control of public works, laying the political and economic foundations for state emergence. According to Robert Carneiro (1970), state formation processes are triggered in situations of land shortage (e.g., in the Peruvian Andes) when population pressures imposed by networks of agricultural village COMMUNITIES cannot be relieved by geographic expansion or MIGRATION, creating incentives for WAR as a mechanism of acquiring land. For Morton Fried (1967: chs. 5, 6), the development of social stratification (see INEQUALITY) is the precondition for state formation: the state exists to perpetuate on a stable basis conditions of inequality and exploitation. Later studies more commonly presume state formation to involve a complex SYSTEM having multiple causes, with the triggering conditions—irrigation, warfare, trade, population pressure—varying from one society to another (see Cohen 1978).

Kinship and State

From an evolutionary perspective, the institutions of the state—kingship, bureaucracy, courts and law, an army—supersede earlier principles of social organization, in particular KINSHIP and ASSOCIATION. This contrast has long been recognized. In *Ancient Society* (1877) Lewis Henry Morgan contrasted two forms of government, the earlier based on social organization through DESCENT group and tribe, the later based on political organization through territory and property (Morgan 1877:61). This dichotomy accorded well with European political tradition. In classical thought, the individual stood in relation to state power as a citizen, whose identity and rights were established through law (see Aristotle, *Pol.* 1275a), while the state afforded the supreme basis of political life within a society. Assuming kinship and state to be antithetical principles of political organization, anthropologists have classified the societies they studied accordingly. Thus Meyer Fortes and E. E. Evans-Pritchard (1940:5–6) divided the societies of sub-Saharan Africa into two forms of polity: "primitive states" and "stateless societies," the former operating through kingship and office, the latter organized chiefly through principles of descent.

However, more recent research—for example Aidan Southall's model of the African "segmentary state" and Burton Stein's study of the state in medieval south India—have suggested that this evolutionary dichotomy is misleading and ethnocentric. Rather than a centralized and absolute rule, many non-Western states appear to have involved multiple patterns of authority, subordinate yet partially independent of a state center, united more by allegiance through RITUAL than by absolute imposition of territorial sovereignty. Instead of an abstract and juridical notion of citizenship, more particularistic ties based on kinship or ETHNICITY appear to have retained their significance in the formation of many Asian and African states (see Southall 1974:154–56; Stein 1977).

References

Carneiro, Robert L. 1970. "A Theory of the Origin of the State." *Science* 169:733–38. Suggests warfare and population pressure as key causes of state formation.
Cohen, Ronald. 1978. "Introduction." Ronald Cohen and Elman R. Service, eds., *Origins of the State: The Anthropology of Political Evolution*. Philadelphia: Institute for the Study of Human Issues. An overview of an excellent collection on the evolution of the state.
d'Entreves, Alexander P. 1967. *The Notion of the State: An Introduction to Political Theory*. Oxford: Clarendon Press.
Fortes, Meyer, and E. E. Evans-Pritchard. 1940. "Introduction." Meyer Fortes and E. E. Evans-Pritchard, eds., *African Political Systems*. London: Oxford University Press. A classic work in political anthropology.
Fried, Morton H. 1967. *The Evolution of Political Society*. New York: Random House.
Meinecke, Friedrich. 1925 [1965]. *Machiavellism: The Doctrine of Raison d'Etat and its Place in Modern History*. Douglas Scott, trans. New York: Praeger.

Morgan, Lewis Henry. 1877. *Ancient Society*. Chicago: Charles H. Kerr. One of the basic works of nineteenth century evolutionist anthropology.

Southall, Aidan. 1974. "State Formation in Africa." *ARA* 3:153–65.

Stein, Burton. 1977. "The Segmentary State in South Indian History." Richard G. Fox, ed., *Realm and Region in Traditional India*. New Delhi: Vikas.

Steward, Julian H. 1949. "Cultural Causality and Law: A Trial Formulation of the Development of Early Civilizations." *AA* 51:1–27.

Watkins, Frederick M. 1968. "State: The Concept." *IESS* 15:150–57.

Weissleder, Wolfgang. 1978. "Aristotle's Concept of Political Structure and the State." Ronald Cohen and Elman Service, eds., *Origins of the State: The Anthropology of Political Evolution*. Philadelphia: Institute for the Study of Human Issues.

Sources of Additional Information

Lawrence Krader, *Formation of the State*, Englewood Cliffs, N.J.: Prentice-Hall, 1968, provides an introduction. Ernst Cassirer's *The Myth of the State*, New Haven, Conn.: Yale University Press, 1946, is an important study of the concept of the state in Western political thought. See also Christine W. Gailey, *Kinship to Kingship: Gender Hierarchy and State Formation in the Tongan Islands*, Austin: University of Texas Press, 1987. The process of state formation is considered in archaeological perspective in John Gledhill et al., eds., *State and Society: The Emergence and Development of Social Hierarchy and Political Centralization*, London: Unwin Hyman, 1988.

STRUCTURALISM. A rationalist theory of society which assumes that cultural forms manifest, through a structure of contrasting signs, the underlying properties of the human mind.

What has been termed structuralism is a rather inchoate philosophical movement, spanning a number of disciplines. As Peter Caws has noted, "There is as yet no coherent and worked-out set of propositions to constitute structuralism 'officially,' but only a series of suggestive and mutually reinforcing conjectures" (Caws 1973:329). However, at least within ANTHROPOLOGY, structuralism can be summarized by three assumptions. First, it involves an effort to explain the patterning of social life through fundamental characteristics of the human mind. Second, it assumes CULTURE to be semiotic in nature, that is, constituted through a system of signs. Third, it interprets such sign systems through notions of contrast, structure, and totality.

To a degree unusual in the development of social scientific theory, the elaboration of structuralism in anthropology has largely been associated with a single scholar, the French anthropologist Claude Lévi-Strauss (b. 1908). As Roger Keesing has characterized his approach, "Lévi-Strauss views cultures as shared symbolic systems that are cumulative creations of mind; he seeks to discover in the structuring of cultural domains—myth, art, kinship, language—the principles of mind that generate these cultural elaborations" (Keesing 1974:78).

Origins

The French sociologist Emile Durkheim and his colleagues of the *Année sociologique* school created the foundations for a structuralist perspective, notably by demonstrating the varied ways in which the social order is symbolically represented. In *Primitive Classification* (1903) Durkheim and Marcel Mauss suggested that SOCIAL STRUCTURE (e.g., the divisions of clan organization) is mirrored in cosmology, MYTH, and RITUAL. The phenomenon of TOTEMISM—a system of culturally postulated correspondences between kin groups and the species that personify them—provided a fruitful test case. Durkheim and Mauss understood totemic classification to reflect not intellectual error (as nineteenth-century anthropologists had assumed), but an inherent human capacity to order experience on the model of social life. For, "if totemism is, in one aspect, the grouping of men into clans according to natural objects . . . it is also, inversely, a grouping of natural objects in accordance with social groups" (Durkheim and Mauss 1903:17–18). A concern with the logic underlying social relations was reflected in other works by the Durkheim circle, seen for example in studies of the relation of sacred and profane realms in ritual sacrifice (Hubert and Mauss 1898:97), and the seemingly contradictory principles of avoidance, hierarchy, and economic interdependence in the Indian CASTE system (Bouglé 1900:3–4).

The structuralist movement received a more specific inspiration from linguistics (see LANGUAGE), in particular the structural linguistics inaugurated by Ferdinand de Saussure (d. 1913). Structural linguistics was a reaction "against the exclusively historical concept of language, against a linguistics that broke language down into isolated elements . . . following the changes that took place in them" (Benveniste 1971:79). In a period in which linguistics was primarily comparative and historical, Saussure—who was himself influenced by Durkheim (Ivic 1965:123)—studied language as an integrated SYSTEM of signs in which each element derived its meaning from its situation of contrast with other signs, and from its position within a linguistic totality. For Saussure, "it is from the interdependent whole [of language] that one must start and through analysis obtain its elements" (in Benveniste 1971:80). Thus understood, linguistics was envisioned as one part of a broader science that Saussure termed semiology, studying "the life of signs within society" (Saussure 1915:16; see SEMIOTICS).

The approach of structural linguistics (like the later structuralist program generally) is inherently synchronic, analyzing the nature of a linguistic system at one moment of time, rather than diachronic, examining processes of change through time (Saussure 1915: ch. 3). Equally important, the focus of analysis is not on any set of actual utterances, but on the total linguistic system which engenders speech. In Saussure's terms, the emphasis is on *langue* (language), rather than *parole* (speech, speaking) (Saussure 1915:9–15). More precisely, "*Parole* is constituted of the particular verbal acts (controlled by the conventions of *langue*) which are performed daily and forgotten, which give language its empirical and historical reality. . . . Without *langue*, *parole* would be a series of isolated and meaningless utterances; without *parole*, *langue* would be an abstract and empty system'' (Caws 1973:323–24). Applied to the realm of culture by structuralist anthropology, this distinction has meant not a concern with social behavior as such, but a search for a structure of logical contrasts underlying, and generating, cultural expression.

The Emergence of Structuralism in Anthropology

One view of the structuralist pedigree interprets it as an outgrowth of British structural FUNCTIONALISM, as seen in the work of A. R. Radcliffe-Brown (Caws 1973:325). Although Durkheim had formulated the notion of social function in the late nineteenth century, Radcliffe-Brown linked this explicitly to a concept of structure. As he wrote in 1935, structure is ''a set of relations amongst unit entities, the continuity of the structure being maintained by a life-process made up of the activities of the constituent units'' (Radcliffe-Brown 1935:180). Yet the structure Radcliffe-Brown envisioned is one of stability in the interactions of individuals within a social system; it is, in this sense, a characteristic of empirical (i.e., observable) phenomena. The concern of structuralism, however, lies not with regularities in behavior as such but with the RATIONALITY underlying social or cultural forms.

Marcel Mauss, mentioned above, has a better claim to being a founder of structuralism. In particular, his study *The Gift* (1925) offered a very influential model of social analysis. Mauss argued that the culturally mandated patterns of gift giving are, in their necessary, ongoing reciprocity, not to be understood as isolated actions between individuals but as a structure of relations engendering society (Mauss 1925:3). It is this characteristic analytic movement, from the observable acts of individuals to an underlying totality of relations, which prompted Lévi-Strauss to describe Mauss as the first ethnologist to attempt to transcend empirical observation so as to attain more profound realities (Lévi-Strauss 1966a:xxxiii). Lévi-Strauss's first major work, *The Elementary Structures of Kinship* (1949), concerned with the analysis of marital exchange in tribal societies, was clearly inspired by Mauss's study (see also Lévi-Strauss 1963:83).

Mature Structuralism

The work of Claude Lévi-Strauss can be seen as an effort to reclaim the study of mind for anthropology, to reaffirm with theoretical rigor the concept of a human PSYCHIC UNITY. He stated in a characteristic passage that ''among all [cultural] forms there exists a difference of degree rather than nature, of generality rather than type. To understand their commonality [*leur base commune*], one must seek certain fundamental structures of the human mind [*de l'esprit humain*], rather than considering this or that privileged region of the world or period in the history of civilization'' (in Bauman 1973:120, my trans.). In short, for the structuralist all patterned behavior can be seen to reflect permutations of certain universal principles inherent in the human mind: the creation of society through exchange, outmarriage, and the incest TABOO; the imposition of culture on the continuum of NATURE. Keesing's comments regarding Lévi-Strauss's studies of myth can stand as a characterization of his entire program: ''Lévi-Strauss . . . is more concerned with 'Culture' than with 'a culture': he sees American Indian mythic structures as overlapping, interconnected patterns that transcend not only the cognitive organization of individual Bororo or Winnebago or Mandan actors, but in a sense transcend as well the boundaries of language and custom that divide different peoples'' (Keesing 1974:79).

Taking as its premise the organizing character of the human mind, structuralism investigates how the unconscious orders cultural phenomena by decoding the patterns of signification (recalling Saussure) inherent in cultural forms (see Rossi 1973). For Lévi-Strauss this is particularly evident in the cultural products of technologically simple societies. Thus tribal peoples

> build models of reality—of the natural world, of the self, of society. But they do so not as modern scientists do by integrating abstract propositions into a framework of formal theory . . . but by ordering perceived particulars into immediately intelligible wholes. The science of the concrete arranges directly sensed realities—the unmistakable differences between kangaroos and ostriches, the seasonal advance and retreat of flood waters, the progress of the sun or the phases of the moon. These become structural models representing the underlying order of reality as it were analogically. (Geertz 1973:352)

Lévi-Strauss has applied the structuralist program to such varied realms as myth, ritual, social structure, and native systems of knowledge, that is, ETHNOSCIENCE (see Lévi-Strauss 1966b).

A quite different view of the potential of structuralism is offered in the work of Louis Dumont. His study *Homo Hierarchicus: The Caste System and Its Implications* applied a structuralist perspective to the study of the Indian caste system, offering a contribution not only to ETHNOLOGY, but to comparative social theory (Dumont 1970). Dumont is concerned with elucidating the social logic underlying caste distinctions. He insists that the distinctive characteristics of caste groups not be considered in isolation but examined in relation to the total, hierarchical structure of Indian society. In his view, caste is predicated on a series of semiotic contrasts, manifesting through distinctions in diet, labor, and ritual a social hierarchy based on concepts of purity and pollution. By depicting caste as the product of a distinctive ideology, assuming the inevitability of social inequality, Dumont calls into question the universal relevance of much Western social thought, which for the most part manifests an implicit egalitarianism in its analysis of societies (see Barnett et al. 1976).

The assumptions of structuralism have to a degree become integrated with those of symbolic anthropology (see SYMBOLISM); structuralist perspectives have also been influential in the development of Marxist approaches in anthropology (see MODE OF PRODUCTION). Nonetheless, it is true that both the premises and methods of structuralism remain highly controversial among anthropologists (see Geertz 1973; Korn 1973; Kronenfeld and Decker 1979). Ironically, the work of Lévi-Strauss has received great acclaim in other fields, notably philosophy and literary criticism (see Sturrock 1979), reflecting the fact that structuralism has been perhaps the only theoretical tendency in postwar anthropology to remain grounded in fundamental issues regarding nature, culture, and mind—topics that should be of perennial concern for the anthropological tradition.

References

Barnett, Steve, et al. 1976. "Hierarchy Purified: Notes on Dumont and His Critics." *Journal of Asian Studies* 35:627–46. A useful discussion of Louis Dumont's structuralist program.

Bauman, Zygmunt. 1973. *Culture as Praxis*. Boston: Routledge & Kegan Paul.

Benveniste, Emile. 1971. "'Structure' in Linguistics." E. Benveniste, *Problems in General Linguistics*. M. E. Meek, trans. Coral Gables, Fla.: University of Miami Press.

Bouglé, Celestin. 1900. "Remarques sur le regime des castes." *L'année sociologique* 4:1–64. A work of the Durkheim school.

Caws, Peter. 1973. "Structuralism." *DHI* 4:322–30. A useful introduction.

Dumont, Louis. 1970. *Homo Hierarchicus: The Caste System and Its Implications*. Mark Sainsbury, trans. Chicago: University of Chicago Press.

Durkheim, Emile, and Marcel Mauss. 1903 [1963]. *Primitive Classification*. Rodney Needham, trans. Chicago: University of Chicago Press. Summarizes a perspective that strongly influenced anthropological structuralism.

Geertz, Clifford. 1973. "The Cerebral Savage: On the Work of Claude Lévi-Strauss." C. Geertz, *The Interpretation of Cultures*. New York: Basic Books.

Hubert, Henri, and Marcel Mauss. 1898 [1964]. *Sacrifice: Its Nature and Function*. Chicago: University of Chicago Press.

Ivic, Mikla. 1965. *Trends in Linguistics*. Muriel Heppell, trans. The Hague: Mouton.

Keesing, Roger. 1974. "Theories of Culture." *ARA* 3:73–97.

Korn, Francis. 1973. *Elementary Structures Reconsidered: Lévi-Strauss on Kinship*. Berkeley and Los Angeles: University of California Press. Highly critical.

Kronenfeld, David, and Henry W. Decker. 1979. "Structuralism." *ARA* 8:503–41. An important review, with extensive bibliography.

Lévi-Strauss, Claude. 1949 [1969]. *The Elementary Structures of Kinship*. Rev. ed. J. H. Bell et al., trans. Boston: Beacon Press. The first significant work of modern anthropological structuralism.

———. 1963. *Structural Anthropology*. Claire Jacobson and Brooke Schoepf, trans. New York: Basic Books. A useful collection of essays.

———. 1966a. "Introduction a l'oeuvre de Marcel Mauss." M. Mauss, *Sociologie et anthropologie*. Paris: Presses Universitaires de France.

———. 1966b. *The Savage Mind*. Chicago: University of Chicago Press.

Mauss, Marcel. 1925 [1967]. *The Gift: Forms and Functions of Exchange in Archaic Societies*. New York: Norton. A classic study, strongly influencing structuralism.

Radcliffe-Brown, A. R. 1935 [1952]. "On the Concept of Function in Social Science." A. R. Radcliffe-Brown, *Structure and Function in Primitive Society*. New York: Free Press.

Rossi, Ino. 1973. "The Unconscious in the Anthropology of Claude Lévi-Strauss." *AA* 75:20–48.

Saussure, Ferdinand de. 1915 [1959]. *Course in General Linguistics*. Charles Bally et al., eds. Wade Baskin, trans. New York: McGraw-Hill. The key work of structural linguistics.

Sturrock, John. 1979. "Introduction." J. Sturrock, ed., *Structuralism and Since: From Lévi-Strauss to Derrida*. Oxford: Oxford University Press.

Sources of Additional Information

In *Lévi-Strauss*, London: Fontana/Collins, 1970, Edmund Leach offers a readable, short introduction to Lévi-Strauss's work. A brief orientation is given by John von Sturmer, "Claude Lévi-Strauss," Diane J. Austin-Broos, ed., *Creating Culture*, Sydney: Allen & Unwin, 1987. For a readable study of the intellectual milieu of structuralism, see Simon Clarke, *The Foundations of Structuralism*, Sussex: Harvester Press, 1981. Jean Piaget, *Structuralism*, Chaninah Maschler, trans., New York: Harper & Row, 1970, also treats structuralism as a broad philosophical tendency, in a brief but technical presentation. For a critical review of structuralist and post-structuralist perspectives, see J. G. Merquior, *From Prague to Paris*, London: Verso, 1986.

SUPERORGANIC. CULTURE understood as a phenomenon sui generis, not to be explained in terms of psychological or other noncultural factors.

Proponents of a superorganic interpretation of culture oppose reductionism, the explanation of cultural phenomena in terms of an underlying noncultural factor, whether this be PERSONALITY, environment (see ADAPTATION), evolutionary biology (see SOCIOBIOLOGY), or RACE. In this view, the study of culture requires a distinctive science with unique methods and theories.

Debates of this type are not new. In the fourth century BC Aristotle discussed the classification of the various sciences, arguing that each must possess a distinctive subject matter (*Metaphysics* 997a). It was, however, nineteenth-century philosophers such as Comte and Spencer who offered a sustained argument for an autonomous science of social life. Auguste Comte (1798–1857), in his "positive philosophy," suggested a hierarchy of sciences from the most general to the most specialized, which he enumerated as mathematics (the most general science), astronomy, physics, chemistry, biology, and sociology (the most specialized). Comte emphasized the autonomy of each science and thus criticized the reduction involved, for example, in explaining sociological facts by questions of climate and race (Comte 1848:742, 748–49).

The term "superorganic" was introduced by Herbert Spencer (1820–1903). In his discussion of the principles of evolution he distinguished inorganic, organic, and "superorganic" realms, the superorganic involving the totality of effects of social interaction, results of "the actions of aggregated organic bodies on one another and on inorganic bodies" (Spencer 1867:316). Although he acknowledged that by this definition the superorganic designation could be applied to certain forms of animal social behavior, as a practical matter Spencer equated it with what today would be termed human culture (Spencer 1867:316–17).

The Superorganic in Anthropology

Alfred Kroeber (1876–1960) introduced Spencer's term into ANTHROPOLOGY in an influential 1917 article, "The Superorganic." His original argument was directed in particular against the correlation of race and culture, reflecting a then-prevalent assumption that differences in cultural achievement could be explained in terms of differences in "racial" capacity (see RACE; PSYCHIC UNITY). Kroeber insisted that differences between nations were in no sense "racially inherent" but rather reflected autonomous cultural developments (Kroeber 1917:181).

The main thrust of Kroeber's superorganic perspective lay, however, not with race but with an opposition between individual choice and cultural patterning. "Civilization, as such," he maintained, "begins only where the individual ends" (Kroeber 1917:193). Kroeber went to great lengths to demonstrate the seemingly autonomous nature of cultural cycles, whether manifested in periods of fluorescence and decline in philosophy, science, and the arts (Kroeber 1944), or in the hundred-year rise and fall of women's hemlines in the European fashion industry (Richardson and Kroeber 1940:369). Ultimately, for Kroeber, psychological or biological explanations of culture were spurious because—being scientific rather than historical in character—they could discern cause and process, but not the unique PATTERN and directionality of each CIVILIZATION (see HISTORICISM).

Leslie White's views were in many respects similar. Drawing on the work of Comte and Spencer, he argued the need for a distinct science of culturology, a term apparently coined by the chemist Wilhelm Ostwald (White 1949:56–60, 113–17). Culture, for White, "may be regarded as a thing *sui generis*, with a life of its own and its own laws" (White 1949:123). These laws (here White is very much in the tradition of Spencer) can best be understood as reflections of a long-term, global process of cultural EVOLUTION, a movement toward greater complexity based on the increasing utilization of energy (White 1959). Unlike Kroeber's historicist concern with the distinctive character of particular culture patterns—that which differentiates Yurok from Pomo, or Hindu from Sinhalese—White's MATERIALISM led to an emphasis on the broad stages of cultural evolution associated with shifts in ADAPTATION, as in the transformation of paleolithic to neolithic, or agrarian to industrial societies.

Within the sociological tradition, Emile Durkheim (1858–1917)—another scholar influenced by Comte and Spencer—offered a similar view (Durkheim 1895:18–20). Like Kroeber or White, Durkheim sought to build a distinct science, though one based on a concept of SOCIAL STRUCTURE rather than culture. The key for Durkheim lay in the idea of social facts (*faits sociaux*), "ways of acting, thinking, and feeling, external to the individual, and endowed with a power of coercion, by reason of which they control him" (Durkheim 1895:3). A pattern of KINSHIP, a mode of address, a religious RITUAL—all are examples of social facts, characteristic of a social order as a whole and not reducible to the psychological experience of one or another individual (see Lukes 1973:8–15). This concept was crucial for the development of British social anthropology, particular in the perspective of structural FUNCTIONALISM.

Critiques of the Superorganic

The heyday of the superorganic debate was the interwar period, when efforts to interpret culture through the idiom of personality were strongest. The superorganic argument was put forth as an alternative perspective. Particularly in its stronger versions (as in the work of Kroeber), the doctrine of the superorganic was framed in equally extreme terms, leaving little or no room for the effect of individual choice on the course of culture and history (Sapir 1917:441).

In an important critique, Edward Sapir emphasized that as all culture is transmitted and mediated by individuals, any simple dichotomy of culture and psychology, the collective and the individual, is untenable. He argued that "those of his [the individual's] thoughts, acts, dreams, and rebellions that somehow contribute in sensible degree to the modification or retention of the mass of typical reactions called culture we term social data; the rest . . . we term individual and pass by as of no historical or social moment" (Sapir 1917:442). The seemingly metaphysical implications of the superorganic concept were also widely criticized. As Franz Boas commented, in 1928, culture was not "a mystic entity that exists outside the society of its individual carriers, and that moves by its own force" (in Harris 1968:330).

In the postwar period the debate over the culture concept and the search for more adequate means of explaining culture patterns has changed the ground of debate and widened the range of theoretical alternatives. Disagreement over the relative value of psychological as opposed to sociocultural explanation has continued, in regard to WITCHCRAFT, for example (see Kennedy 1967). A parallel debate has centered on the significance of individual pragmatic choice, as opposed to collective sociocultural constraints, in shaping human action (see Barth 1966). To a large extent the issues raised over the superorganic have reappeared in the debate regarding the nature of cultural knowledge. Here a view of culture as an individual's authoritative, socially acquired knowledge, the perspective of ETHNOSCIENCE, stands opposed to that of culture as a collectively fashioned universe of meanings, generated in the interaction of social life, the perspective of symbolic anthropology (see SYMBOLISM; INTERPRETATION).

References

Barth, Fredrik. 1966 [1981]. "Models of Social Organization (I–III)." F. Barth, *Process and Form in Social Life*. London: Routledge & Kegan Paul.

Comte, Auguste. 1848 [1960]. "A General View of Positivism." Monroe C. Beardsley, ed., *The European Philosophers from Descartes to Nietzsche*. New York: Modern Library.

Durkheim, Emile. 1895 [1938]. *The Rules of Sociological Method*. Glencoe, Ill.: Free Press. A classic statement of the autonomy of the sociocultural realm.

Harris, Marvin. 1968. *The Rise of Anthropological Theory*. New York: Crowell.

Kennedy, John G. 1967. "Psychological and Social Explanations of Witchcraft." *Man* (n.s.) 2:216–25.

Kroeber, Alfred L. 1917. "The Superorganic." *AA* 19:163–213. An essential statement of the superorganic argument.

———. 1944. *Configurations of Culture Growth*. Berkeley and Los Angeles: University of California Press. An impressive yet essentially unsuccessful effort at implementing an extreme superorganic perspective, applied comparatively to major civilizations.

Lukes, Steven. 1973. *Emile Durkheim: His Life and Work*. Harmondsworth, England: Penguin.

Richardson, Jane, and Alfred Kroeber. 1940 [1952]. "Three Centuries of Women's Dress Fashions: A Quantitative Assessment." Alfred Kroeber, *The Nature of Culture*. Chicago: University of Chicago Press.

Sapir, Edward. 1917. "Do We Need a Superorganic?" *AA* 19:441–47. A reply to Kroeber.

Spencer, Herbert. 1867 [1958]. *First Principles*. New York: DeWitt Revolving Fund. A synopsis of Spencer's philosophical program.

White, Leslie. 1949. *The Science of Culture*. New York: Grove Press. Chapter 6 enunciates the "culturological" program.

———. 1959. *The Evolution of Culture*. New York: McGraw-Hill.

Sources of Additional Information

A useful introduction is provided by David Bidney, "On the Concept of Culture and Some Cultural Fallacies," *AA* 46:30–44, 1944. The appropriate relation of psychological and sociocultural explanations in anthropology is considered at length in Max Gluckman, ed., *Closed Systems and Open Minds*, Chicago: Aldine, 1964.

SURVIVAL. A practice or belief preserved from an earlier era, assumed to lack function or RATIONALITY in its contemporary setting.

The notion of survival implies the endurance of a CUSTOM or belief into a later age, where it remains an anomaly within the wider CULTURE. Conversely, survivals stand witness to an otherwise vanished cultural perspective. For example, various practices associated with sneezing are in this sense survivals. The exclamations "Gesundheit!," "God Bless You!," and the like advert to a once common belief in the association of a sneeze with the presence of an alien spirit, or the vulnerability of one's soul to malign influences (Tylor 1871:1:97–104). The practice remains, but the assumptions that gave it meaning have vanished.

Broadly synonymous with superstition (that which "stands over," from Latin *superstare*), the identification of survivals has a long pedigree. Cicero (d. 43 BC) commented on the empty formulae preserved in Roman auguries from an earlier era (*De divinatione* 2.33–34) and denounced superstition as the enemy of true religion. "Superstition [*superstitio*], which is widespread among the nations, has taken advantage of human weakness to cast its spell over the mind of almost every man" (Cicero, *De div.* 2.72).

The notions of survival and superstition are thus value-laden terms, reflecting a critique of inherited custom. Certain eras and intellectual movements have been more disposed than others to reject the beliefs of past generations, for what is welcomed in one period as the wisdom of TRADITION may be rejected in the next as a "mere" survival or a "base" superstition. The Enlightenment writers of the eighteenth century were self-nominated culture critics: "In proclaiming the omnipotence of criticism, the philosophes called, at the same time, for a disenchanted universe, an end to myth" (Gay 1966:145–46). Science was to be, in the phrase of Adam Smith, "the great antidote to the power of enthusiasm and superstition'' (*OED*). In this respect the evolutionists of the nineteenth century were true to the perspective of their Enlightenment predecessors.

Emergence of Survival in Anthropology

Among evolutionist writers (see EVOLUTION), interest in the concept of survival (though not use of the term itself) dates to the 1850s. John McLennan, writing in 1857, noted that "in Derbyshire and Cornwall, at one extreme, and in the Highlands and the Hebrides, at the other, . . . remains of pre-Christian customs and superstitions [endured]" (in Hodgen 1936:90). In *Primitive Marriage*, published in 1865, McLennan drew on the wide distribution of wife-capture in symbolic form, as well as the supposed prevalence of the practice in the Americas, Oceania, and other areas, to posit an early state of society in which obtaining wives by capture was the common and accepted procedure (McLennan 1865: chs. 2–4; see MARRIAGE). In what could serve as a general statement of the use of survivals in ETHNOLOGY, McLennan argued that "wherever we discover symbolical forms, we are justified in inferring that in the past life of the people employing them, there were corresponding realities" (McLennan 1865:7). In much the same vein, John Lubbock noted the significance of customs found "lingering on in civilised communities," which "tell a tale of former barbarism" (Lubbock 1870:341). Two decades later James Frazer took the concept of survival as one of the central ideas of his twelve-volume Victorian extravaganza, the *Golden Bough* (Frazer 1890).

The word survival was introduced to anthropology by Edward Tylor, in particular through his influential work *Primitive Culture* (Tylor 1871), substituting this more neutral term for the older, more invidious term "superstition" (Leopold 1980:52). In *Primitive Culture* he recorded numerous examples, among them the ascription of unexplained noises to spirits ("poltergeists"), the telling of fortune through palmistry, and the location of underground water through dowsing (Tylor 1871:1: ch. 4). Proverbs are a rich source of survivals. Today, Tylor noted, "to haul over the coals" implies chastisement. Originally, however, it signified an ordeal "of passing through a fire or leaping over burning brands" (Tylor 1871:1:85).

Tylor's reliance on the survival concept arose in the context of a debate between proponents of evolution, who assumed the progressive character of CULTURE CHANGE, and advocates of degeneration, who contended that human history involved a decline from a primordial high CIVILIZATION. For both parties, a central issue was the historical experience, and moral and intellectual character, of so-called PRIMITIVE peoples. Evolutionists perceived them as characterizing one or another of the original stages of human society, but capable, through the PSYCHIC UNITY of mankind, of unassisted improvement to a higher cultural level. Degenerationists, such as Archbishop Whately and the Duke of Argyll, explained primitive cultures as the irredeemable and degraded end product of higher social forms (Hodgen 1936: ch. 1).

The concept of survival assumed a major role in Tylor's defense of the doctrine of cultural evolution. As Margaret Hodgen has argued, "He [Tylor] alone seemed to realize that if . . . civilization was to be proved the product of orderly, slow, gradual, continuous, and progressive motion or change from an original state similar to that of contemporary savagery, the evidences of its lowly origin must be found in civilization itself'' (Hodgen 1936:34). Tylor defined survivals as ''processes, customs, opinions, and so forth, which have been carried on by force of habit into a new state of society different from that in which they had their original home,'' adding in reference to his controversy with the degenerationists, ''and they thus remain as proofs and examples of an older condition of culture out of which a newer has been evolved'' (Tylor 1871:1:16).

Critiques

R. R. Marett wrote, in 1918, that ''it would appear, inasmuch as survivals survive, that they are not quite dead after all—that in some humble or surreptitious way of their own, they help to constitute and condition the living present'' (Marett 1918:17–18). This was a telling criticism and one to be repeated and reinforced by later anthropologists. Ernest Crawley commented that ''the term is misused when it is implied that these are dead forms, surviving like fossil remains or rudimentary organs'' (Crawley 1927:4). Bronislaw Malinowski, speaking from the experience of prolonged participant-observation ETHNOGRAPHY, argued that ''the better a certain type of culture is known, the fewer survivals there appear to be in it'' (Malinowski 1931:624). Marett, among others, recognized that what had been treated by Tylor, Frazer, Lubbock, and McLennan as static survivals were in fact complex examples of culture change, whether this be a change in the meaning of a custom, or its social standing, or both. As he stated acutely, ''Origins are relative, and the regress of conditions is endless. . . . There never was a time, in short, when the interplay of old and new did not go on, exactly as it does now'' (Marett 1918:21).

The concept of survival belongs to the theoretical program of nineteenth-century evolutionism. It could not itself survive a transition to the methods, problems, and theories of twentieth-century ANTHROPOLOGY. By definition a survival is assumed to be without meaning or function in its contemporary setting. Yet whether one considers the HISTORICISM of American cultural anthropology, or the FUNCTIONALISM of British social anthropology, the need to analyze PATTERNS of belief and behavior in their total cultural context has been a primary axiom, reinforced by a tradition of intensive ethnographic research. Being incompatible with such developments, the notion of survival was relegated to the theoretical backwaters of FOLKLORE.

References

Crawley, Ernest. 1927 [1960]. *The Mystic Rose: A Study of Primitive Marriage and of Primitive Thought in Its Bearing on Marriage.* 2d ed., rev. and enl. Theodore Besterman, ed. New York: Meridian. A comparative, or cut-and-paste, treatment of the topic.

Frazer, James George. 1890 [1959]. *The New Golden Bough.* 1 vol., abr. Theodor H.

Gaster, ed. New York: Criterion. A useful one volume abridgement of Frazer's Victorian classic.

Gay, Peter. 1966. *The Enlightenment, an Interpretation: The Rise of Modern Paganism*. New York: Random House.

Hodgen, Margaret T. 1936. *The Doctrine of Survivals: A Chapter in the History of Scientific Method in the Study of Man*. London: Allenson. The key study of the concept of survival.

Leopold, Joan. 1980. *Culture in Comparative and Evolutionary Perspective: E. B. Tylor and the Making of* Primitive Culture. Berlin: Dietrich Reimer. A detailed study of the development of culture, survival, and related concepts in the work of Tylor.

Lubbock, John. 1870 [1978]. *The Origin of Civilization and the Primitive Condition of Man*. Peter Rivière, ed. Chicago: University of Chicago Press. An immensely popular work of evolutionist anthropology, illustrating all of the defects of that perspective.

McLennan, John F. 1865 [1970]. *Primitive Marriage*. Peter Rivière, ed. Chicago: University of Chicago Press.

Malinowski, Bronislaw. 1931. "Culture." *ESS* 4:621–46. A synoptic article by one of the masters of functionalism.

Marett, R. R. 1918. "The Transvaluation of Culture." *Folk-Lore* 29:15–33. An important critique of the concept of survival.

Tylor, Edward Burnett. 1871 [1958]. *Primitive Culture*. 2 vols. New York: Harper. & Brothers (Harper Tochbook). The most significant primary text on the topic of survivals.

Sources of Additional Information

For a brief introduction, see Ake Hultkrantz, *GEC*, s.v. "survival." For the intellectual background of survival and related concepts in evolutionist anthropology, see George W. Stocking, Jr., *Victorian Anthropology*, New York: Free Press, 1987, ch. 5.

SYMBOLISM. A relationship between two entities, abstract or concrete, in which one can represent the other by convention or through the recognition of common or analogous qualities.

"Symbol" is derived from the Latin *symbolum*, meaning a ticket or token. In this way symbol suggests a relationship of representation between two entities: the first tangible and discrete, the second (that which it signifies) often abstract. Thus a theater ticket represents the right to attend a performance on a particular date; a bus token represents the right to ride a stated distance. More characteristically, the Stars and Stripes may be said to symbolize the American nation, the Statue of Liberty to symbolize the ideal of freedom. For anthropological views on the nature of signification and the relation of symbols and signs, see SEMIOTICS; for views on the exegesis of symbolic forms, see INTERPRETATION.

The concept of symbolism has been of considerable importance in ANTHROPOLOGY, in particular as it figures in theories of CULTURE. It is an essential and distinctively human attribute to impose a web of meanings upon the world of NATURE—in short, to create a symbolic universe—which mediates both perception and action. The philosopher Ernst Cassirer has aptly stated that

> Physical reality seems to recede in proportion as man's symbolic activity advances. Instead of dealing with the things themselves man is in a sense constantly conversing with himself. He has so enveloped himself in linguistic forms, in artistic images, in mythical symbols or religious rites that he cannot see or know anything except by the interposition of this artificial medium. (Cassirer 1944:25)

Leslie White has argued similarly: "All human behavior consists of, or is dependent upon, the use of symbols. . . . The symbol is the universe of humanity" (White 1949:22).

Yet while symbolism is a constant of human experience, explicit recognition of symbolism is not. Certain tendencies in philosophy and the arts have encouraged an awareness and examination of symbolism, the romantic movement of the eighteenth and nineteenth centuries being a notable example. The concern with subjective over objective reality, emotional over intellectual understanding, the mysterious over the explicit and mundane—all these features made symbolism an attractive topic for the romantics. Thomas Carlyle (d. 1881) wrote, characteristically, that "in the Symbol proper . . . there is ever, more or less distinctly and directly, some embodiment and revelation of the Infinite" (in Symons 1899:2). Among the writers on symbolism of this era Johann Jacob Bachofen (1815–1887) has particular importance. His studies of classical mortuary symbolism offered significant insights into the nature and interpretation of symbolic forms, for example on the contrast of MYTH and symbol, and on the power of symbolism to combine a wide range of referents into a psychologically powerful unity (Bachofen 1859).

In the realm of the sciences rather than the arts, the psychoanalytic movement provided both recognition and theoretical justification for the study of symbolism, understood as a manifestation of unconscious mental processes. Here Sigmund Freud's *Interpretation of Dreams* (1900) was of decisive importance. By presenting detailed analyses of dream symbolism developed in the context of psychiatric practice, Freud demonstrated conclusively both the complexity of this symbolic process and the scientific significance of its study.

Within anthropology, in contrast, at least until the inter-war period, there were descriptions of symbolism but no theoretical perspective through which the topic of symbolism could be explored systematically. For example, Lewis Henry Morgan (in 1851) provided a detailed description of symbolism in the Iroquois White Dog ritual (see Firth 1973:106–7). Franz Boas noted that "the decorative designs used by primitive man do not serve purely esthetic ends. . . . they are not only decorations, but symbols of definite ideas" (Boas 1903:546). Boas also demonstrated the potential independence of form and meaning by comparing the interpretation of similar artistic motifs among different North American tribes (Boas 1903).

Symbolism in Anthropological Theory

As an explicit and theoretically grounded concept, symbolism has been treated in two quite different senses. Within the perspective of social anthropology, particularly in Britain, symbolism has been studied chiefly as an attribute of social action and, in this way, subsumed under the concept of RITUAL. Within the tradition of cultural anthropology, notably in the United States, symbolism has been posited as an attribute of culture generally, a perspective counterposed to that of cultural MATERIALISM. Thus for social anthropology symbolism is manifested through certain concrete objects and events, a view that serves to emphasize (or perhaps to reify) the discrete symbol as the constituent unit of symbolic action; for cultural anthropology, in contrast, all thought and behavior is symbolic insofar as it is cultural.

Social anthropology. Symbolism derived its importance from the Durkheimian tradition, as developed particularly in the FUNCTIONALISM of A. R. Radcliffe-Brown. Religious ritual, for Emile Durkheim, served to represent the unity of the social order (Durkheim 1915). Rituals of social interaction, for Radcliffe-Brown, expressed as well as reinforced sentiments essential to the maintenance of SOCIAL STRUCTURE (Radcliffe-Brown 1922). While still operating within this general framework, postwar studies have emphasized questions of meaning over function and thus have sought to understand symbols and rituals primarily through the indigenous interpretations of the society in question. Marcel Griaule's studies of the Dogon and Monica Wilson's of the Nyakyusa provide early examples (Griaule 1948; Wilson 1954). The work of Victor Turner has been particularly influential. Beginning with his 1958 paper "Symbols in Ndembu Ritual," Turner has developed a distinctive approach to ritual symbolism, drawing in part upon Sigmund Freud, C. G. Jung, and Edward Sapir, that has stimulated a host of other studies (see Turner 1967, 1975).

Cultural anthropology. To argue that all culture is symbolic is neither trivial nor tautological. Rather, it suggests a very different approach to organizing and explaining ethnographic data than that presumed by social anthropology. As Clifford Geertz has commented,

> Thinking consists not of "happenings in the head" . . . but of a traffic in what have been called, by G. H. Mead and others, significant symbols . . . [whatever] is disengaged from its mere actuality and used to impose meaning upon experience. . . . Undirected by culture patterns—organized systems of significant symbols—man's behavior would be virtually ungovernable, a mere chaos of pointless acts and exploding emotions. (Geertz 1973:45–46)

There are several important consequences of this viewpoint, the most significant being its implications for the nature of explanation in anthropology. Numerous writers—Karl Marx for one—have argued that cultural forms (e.g., LAW, art, RELIGION, FAMILY organization) are a reflection of more fundamental, precultural material conditions, centering on the organization of production (see MATERIALISM; MODE OF PRODUCTION). In contrast to this materialist perspective, from the standpoint of a symbolic anthropology there are no precultural constraints or adaptations, for all experience is necessarily symbolic and therefore culturally interpreted. As Marshall Sahlins has noted, "so-called material causes must be . . . the product of a symbolic system whose character it is our task to investigate; for without the mediation of this cultural scheme, no adequate relation between a given material condition and a specific cultural form can ever be specified'' (Sahlins 1976:57) The dialogue between these two views, between the primacy of ''culture'' (the symbolic) or ''practical reason'' (the material) as the prime determinant of social life, has been a long-term theme of anthropology (see Sahlins 1976).

References

Bachofen, J. J. 1859 [1967]. *Myth, Religion, and Mother Right: Selected Writings*. Ralph Manheim, trans. Princeton: Princeton University Press. An early example of the scholarly study of symbolism.

Boas, Franz. 1903 [1940] ''The Decorative Arts of the North American Indians.'' F. Boas, *Race, Language and Culture*. New York: Free Press.

Cassirer, Ernst. 1944. *An Essay on Man: An Introduction to a Philosophy of Human Culture*. New Haven, Conn.: Yale University Press. Symbolic expression was the focus of Cassirer's philosophical anthropology.

Durkheim, Emile. 1915 [1965]. *The Elementary Forms of the Religious Life*. Joseph W. Swain, trans. New York: Free Press.

Firth, Raymond. 1973. *Symbols: Public and Private*. Ithaca, N.Y.: Cornell University Press. A useful overview of the anthropological study of symbolism.

Freud, Sigmund. 1900 [1938]. *The Interpretation of Dreams*. A. A. Brill, ed., *The Basic Writings of Sigmund Freud*. New York: Modern Library. A major work illustrating the psychoanalytic approach to symbolism.

Geertz, Clifford. 1973. ''The Impact of the Concept of Culture on the Concept of Man.'' Clifford Geertz, *The Interpretation of Cultures: Selected Essays*. New York: Basic Books. One of a series of essays exploring the nature of symbolism in culture.

Griaule, Marcel. 1948 [1965]. *Conversations with Ogotemmeli: An Introduction to Dogon Religious Ideas*. London: Oxford University Press. A classic work on Dogon (West African) symbolism, myth, and ritual.

Radcliffe-Brown, A. R. 1922 [1964]. *The Andaman Islanders*. New York: Free Press.

Sahlins, Marshall. 1976. *Culture and Practical Reason*. Chicago: University of Chicago Press. Considers the debate between materialist and symbolic perspectives.

Symons, Arthur. 1899 [1958]. *The Symbolist Movement in Literature*. New York: Dutton.

Turner, Victor W. 1967. ''Symbols in Ndembu Ritual.'' Victor Turner, *The Forest of Symbols: Aspects of Ndembu Ritual*. Ithaca, N.Y.: Cornell University Press. Significant for the development of symbol theory in social anthropology.

————. 1975. ''Symbolic Studies.'' *ARA* 4:145–61. A useful review of research.

White, Leslie. 1949. ''The Symbol: The Origin and Basis of Human Behavior.'' Leslie White, *The Science of Culture: A Study of Man and Civilization*. New York: Grove Press. An influential statement relating symbolism and culture.

Wilson, Monica. 1954. ''Nyakyusa Ritual and Symbolism.'' *AA* 56:228–41. A summary of Nyakyusa rites of passage stressing the role of native interpretation.

Sources of Additional Information

A broad selection of readings on the topic of symbolism is provided in Janet Dolgin et al., eds., *Symbolic Anthropology*, New York: Columbia University Press, 1977. Mary Douglas, in *Natural Symbols*, New York: Pantheon, 1970, provides a series of imaginative essays on symbolism and ritual. Dan Sperber's *Rethinking Symbolism*, Alice L. Morton, trans., Cambridge: Cambridge University Press, 1975, is a provocative and witty analysis of symbolism and symbolic theory in anthropology. For an interesting reflection on the implications of symbolic anthropology, see James A. Boon, *Other Tribes, Other Scribes*, Cambridge: Cambridge University Press, 1982.

SYSTEM. A group of interrelated entities; more rigorously, a set of elements exhibiting wholeness, structure, hierarchy, and circular causation.

The idea of system implies a concern with interrelation, context, and holism. A systems perspective is thus congenial for ANTHROPOLOGY, implying an effort to understand social life not through the radical simplification and abstraction characteristic of classical physics, but by seeking the complex relationships that situate any element of human behavior in its cultural context.

In a more rigorous sense, to identify the elements and characteristics of a system is to create a model, a limited isomorphism that describes certain significant properties of a phenomenon. What anthropologists understand by the Omaha KINSHIP system, for example, is not an exhaustive description of all interactions between Omaha kin. Rather, it is a set of formal categories through which relationships can be classified, based upon patrilineal DESCENT and such variables as GENDER and generation, which is exemplified by the Omaha tribe but which models kin relationships in numerous societies. In varying degrees of formality and explicitness, such modeling is used throughout anthropology and in fact in all sciences (see Schneider 1965; Barth 1966). "System" can also be understood in a more specific, theoretically grounded sense, as developed in general systems theory (GST). This latter sense is treated below.

System and "Systems Theory"

General systems theory, also known as systems research or systems analysis, is a loose but ambitious conjunction of methods and disciplines aimed at modeling the broadest possible range of phenomena in systemic terms (i.e., as interrelated and bounded sets of variables). The field is eclectic in the extreme, drawing on cybernetics, information theory, game and decision theory, topology, set theory, and more broadly, on engineering, biology, and Gestalt psychology, among other fields (see Bertalanffy 1968). Given this foundation, it is not surprising that the concept of system is used with considerable looseness. By one definition,

> systems are sets of covariant entities, no subset of which is unrelated to any other subset. Systems analysis focuses on the meaningful interactions of the parts with one another and with the whole as they influence some process or outcome. No elemental part can be understood only in terms of itself; we must also study its interactions with the entire system, which is shaped by both internal and environmental processes and conditions over time. (Rodin et al. 1978:748)

Taking this statement as a starting point, three main characteristics of a general systems approach can be identified. These include a dynamic perspective; the properties of structure, wholeness, and hierarchy; and explanation in terms of circular causality (see Sengel 1979).

(1) A system is dynamic, modeling a process unfolding over time. Examples

include the EVOLUTION of TRIBES into STATES (Flannery 1972) and the interrelation of population density and social pathology (Sengel 1979). Stability over time is a possible but not inevitable outcome; there need be no assumption that the system as such is goal-directed toward its own perpetuation. In these respects, the systems perspective contrasts with the organismic analogy of classical FUNCTIONALISM.

(2) Systems exhibit structure, wholeness, and hierarchy. Structure is equivalent to the existence of constraint in behavior. A system is structured to the extent that the behavior of one element of a system affects the behavior of others. Thus a criminal trial exhibits greater structure than a cocktail party. Wholeness exists to the extent that structure is ramified throughout a set of elements, yielding a totality not reducible to the behavior of its parts. A High Mass manifests wholeness, as the participants through their respective roles jointly create that liturgical act; one hundred persons speaking and gesticulating randomly and independently (i.e., bedlam) do not. A system manifests hierarchy to the extent that it is partially decomposable into subsystems, loci of greater interaction. The distinction between system and subsystem is relative. Thus arteries, blood, nerves, and muscle are elements constituting the mammalian heart; the heart forms one element of a total organism; and the individual organism constitutes one element of a breeding population.

(3) Cause must be sought not in a single factor or prime mover but in the ensemble of mutual constraints constituting a system. In considering, for example, explanations for the evolution of CIVILIZATION, single-cause theories (e.g., the development of irrigation systems, or the increase of population) are less satisfactory in the systems perspective than theories that recognize "a whole series of important variables with complex interrelationships and feedback between them" (Flannery 1972:408). This reinterpretation of causality has broad implications. As Gregory Bateson has argued, "In no system which shows mental characteristics [i.e., which processes information] can any part have unilateral control over the whole. In other words, the mental characteristics of the system are immanent, not in some part, but in the system as a whole" (Bateson 1972:316).

Applications

Since the Second World War, systems analysis has had considerable success (or at least, considerable vogue) in management, engineering, and government policy, notably in U. S. Department of Defense procurement and strategy. Its policy uses have been extended to problem solving in the civilian sector, for example in crime control, health care, waste management, education, and urban development. Such applications have been widely criticized (see Hoos 1983), in part for their mechanical approach to understanding sociocultural systems: "The basic thought forms of system theory remain classical positivism and behaviorism . . . [and presume] mechanical models of thought and perception" (Lilienfeld 1978:250). Systems analysis and systems theory have nonetheless found numerous supporters in the social sciences, notably psychology, sociology, and political science (see Buckley 1968).

The development of the systems concept in anthropology has taken a rather different path, far from the assumptions of behaviorism. The systems paradigm has guided research in archaeology (Plog 1975), cultural evolution (Flannery 1972), CULTURAL ECOLOGY (Rappaport 1968; Dow 1976), and political ECONOMY (Nash 1981), among other fields. Perhaps more importantly, such ideas as wholeness, structure, and circular causation have inspired—particularly through the work of Gregory Bateson—a reconciliation of ecological and symbolic perspectives, which may permit anthropology to transcend the seemingly sterile argument between materialist and idealist approaches to cultural systems (see Bateson 1972; Rappaport 1979).

References

Barth, Fredrik. 1966 [1981]. "Models of Social Organization (I–III)." F. Barth, *Process and Form in Social Life*. London: Routledge & Kegan Paul.

Bateson, Gregory. 1972. *Steps to an Ecology of Mind*. New York: Ballentine Books. Intellectually rewarding, if idiosyncratic.

Bertalanffy, Ludwig von. 1968. "General System Theory—A Critical Review." Walter Buckley, ed., *Modern Systems Research for the Behavioral Scientist*. Chicago: Aldine. An overview by one of the originators of GST.

Buckley, Walter, ed. 1968. *Modern Systems Research for the Behavioral Scientist*. Chicago: Aldine.

Dow, James. 1976. "Systems Models of Cultural Ecology." *Social Science Information* 15:953–76.

Flannery, Kent V. 1972. "The Cultural Evolution of Civilizations." *Annual Review of Ecology and Systematics* 3:399–426. Flannery presents models from the systems perspective for the evolution of state societies.

Hoos, Ida R. 1983. *Systems Analysis in Public Policy: A Critique*. Rev. ed. Berkeley and Los Angeles: University of California Press. A broad attack on the failure of systems analysis in social programs and policy.

Lilienfeld, Robert. 1978. *The Rise of Systems Theory: An Ideological Analysis*. New York: Wiley. Another critique of systems analysis.

Nash, June. 1981. "Ethnographic Aspects of the World Capitalist System." *ARA* 10:393–423. An overview of anthropological studies derived from the world system model of I. Wallerstein.

Plog, Fred. 1975. "Systems Theory in Archaeological Research." *ARA* 4:207–24. A review.

Rappaport, Roy A. 1968. *Pigs for the Ancestors*. New Haven, Conn.: Yale University Press. A pathbreaking study of the interrelation of ecology and ritual in New Guinea, using a systems perspective.

———. 1979. *Ecology, Meaning, and Religion*. Richmond, Calif.: North Atlantic Books. Essays on symbolic and ecological themes, guided by a systems paradigm.

Rodin, Miriam, et al. 1978. "Systems Theory in Anthropology." *CA* 19:747–62. A useful review article, though abstract.

Schneider, David. 1965. "Some Muddles in the Models: or, How the System Really

Works.'' *The Relevance of Models for Social Anthropology*. A. S. A. Monographs, 1. New York: Praeger.

Sengel, Randal A. 1979. ''Further Comments on Systems Theory in Anthropology.'' *CA* 20:811–14. An attempt to define the systems perspective in brief compass.

Sources of Additional Information

A sense of the nature and variety of perspectives nestled within general systems theory is provided by F. E. Emery, ed., *Systems Thinking: Selected Readings*, Harmondsworth, England: Penguin, 1969.

T

TABOO. A ritual avoidance; an act that is culturally proscribed for symbolic rather than pragmatic reasons.

Taboo, a term native to Polynesia, was first described by explorers in the late eighteenth century. Shortly thereafter it passed into use both as a technical term of the anthropological vocabulary and as a word in common usage. The journals of the Polynesian expedition of Captain James Cook (1728–1779) were an influential source for interested Europeans. One passage (ca. 1780) described a request for land on which to create an observatory: "We fixed on a field of sweet potatoes . . . and the priests, to prevent the intrusion of the natives, immediately consecrated the place, by fixing their wands round the wall, by which it was enclosed. This sort of religious interdiction they call *taboo*" (in Steiner 1967:25).

A taboo, then, is a culturally stipulated prohibition. As with certain other anthropological concepts (e.g., SHAMANISM), the concept of taboo was first applied to a restricted CULTURE AREA and then gradually enlarged to embrace a much wider range of societies. This has resulted in considerable ambiguity. In Polynesia, land or crops could be tabooed by a chief, and life-crisis events for chiefly persons resulted in normal activities (cooking and eating, lighting fires, etc.) being tabooed throughout a village (Steiner 1967: ch. 3; Wagner 1987:233; see CHIEFDOM). In South Asia pollution taboos form a fundamental element of CASTE behavior, as seen in prohibitions against intercaste MARRIAGE, and against accepting food from someone of lower caste. For Judaism, the observance of numerous food taboos, based on biblical authority, remains a mark of orthodoxy (Lev. 11; see also Douglas 1970: ch. 3).

Margaret Mead may have been excessively restrictive in defining taboo as "a prohibition whose infringement results in an automatic penalty without human or supernatural mediation'' (Mead 1935:502; cf. Steiner 1967:143–46). None-theless, a taboo—whether observed or transgressed—is symbolically significant and emotionally charged. That which is taboo is forbidden, not merely by LAW but through TRADITION. In this respect RITUAL and taboo exhibit an interesting symmetry: from the perspective of a given CULTURE, both act and avoidance are transcendentally necessary.

Taboo and Victorian Anthropology

The topic of taboo exerted a fascination on the Victorian mind. The major step in integrating the discussion of taboo into anthropological theory came through the search for parallels to such Polynesian CUSTOMS in other societies, by means of the COMPARATIVE METHOD. One apparent parallel lay in the manifold prohibitions of ancient Judaism. In this fashion the issue of taboo was introduced into the debate over textual interpretation of the Bible—a major event in the intellectual landscape of the later nineteenth century—offering an opportunity to examine critically the cultural foundations of Judaism and thus of Christianity as well. Here the writings of the theologian and Semitic scholar W. Robertson Smith (1846–1894) were particularly important.

In *The Religion of the Semites* Smith sought to differentiate ''the old uncon-scious religious tradition'' of the Semitic peoples from Judaism's higher spiritual teaching, resulting from the acts of prophetic individuals (Smith 1889:1). From the perspective of cultural EVOLUTION, the former was PRIMITIVE and irrational, the latter ethical and progressive (see SURVIVAL). Taboo behavior seemed to epitomize this primitive stratum of human experience: ''The field covered by taboos among savage and half-savage races is very wide, for there is no part of life in which the savage does not feel himself to be surrounded by mysterious agencies and recognise the need of walking warily.'' Appropriately, the nu-merous rules regarding pollution observed by Arabs and Jews ''present the most startling agreement in point of detail with savage taboos.'' On the other hand, the prohibitions governing the holy (in sanctuaries, etc.) seemed to Smith to reflect the positive aspect of these religions and to contain ''germinant principles of social progress and moral order'' (Smith 1889:152–54; see also Steiner 1967: chs. 4–6).

Theories of Taboo

Scholars have sought in a variety of ways to integrate the category of taboo into a wider framework of anthropological theory. For the classicist James Frazer (1854–1941), taboo was the negative form of MAGIC: ''The aim of positive magic or sorcery is to produce a desired event; the aim of negative magic or taboo is to avoid an undesireable one.'' Both, for Frazer, were the result of a false association of ideas, ''mistaken notions of cause and effect'' (Frazer 1890:17; see RATIONALITY). For R. R. Marett, taboo was linked not with magic but with MANA, constituting a series of cautious injunctions protecting individuals from the dangers inherent in supernaturally powerful places, objects, and individuals (Marett 1914). Emile Durkheim saw in taboo a necessary element of RELIGION (the "negative cult"), prohibition of contact with the profane being in this view an essential precondition for contact with the sacred (Durkheim 1915:337–65). The phenomenon of taboo has also been frequently discussed in relation to TOTEMISM.

Most modern approaches to the analysis of taboo have been guided by the perspective of structural FUNCTIONALISM. A. R. Radcliffe-Brown insisted that taboos be interpreted in terms of the "ritual value" which they express and foster, such common values providing the basis for an orderly social life. Thus he interpreted the Andamanese taboo on naming individuals who are involved in RITES OF PASSAGE (e.g., ceremonies marking puberty, marriage, or death) as a symbolic expression of their abnormal or transitional status (Radcliffe-Brown 1939:139, 146–47; see also SYMBOLISM). Mary Douglas has extended this perspective, suggesting that any SOCIAL STRUCTURE exists in a complex dialectic with ideas of pollution, disorder, danger, and taboo (Douglas 1970; for a critique see Spiro 1968).

References

Douglas, Mary. 1970. *Purity and Danger: An Analysis of Concepts of Pollution and Taboo*. Harmondsworth, England: Penguin. An imaginative work combining symbolic and functionalist perspectives.
Durkheim, Emile. 1915 [1965]. *The Elementary Forms of the Religious Life*. Joseph Swain, trans. New York: Free Press.
Frazer, James G. 1890 [1959]. *The New Golden Bough*. 1 vol., abr. Theodor H. Gaster, ed. New York: Criterion. For Frazer's full treatment of taboo in this theoretically amorphous classic, see vol. 3 of the complete edition, *Taboo and the Perils of the Soul (in The Golden Bough*, 3d ed., New York: Macmillan, 1935).
Marett, R. R. 1914. *The Threshold of Religion*. 2d ed. New York: Macmillan. A classic discussion of taboo and mana.
Mead, Margaret. 1935. "Tabu." *ESS* 4:502–5.
Radcliffe-Brown, A. R. 1939 [1952]. "Taboo." A. R. Radcliffe-Brown, *Structure and Function in Primitive Society*. New York: Free Press.
Smith, W. Robertson. 1889 [1972]. *The Religion of the Semites: The Fundamental Institutions*. New York: Schocken. A significant work on the comparative study of taboo, and a theological cause célèbre.
Spiro, Melford. 1968. "Review of: Mary Douglas, *Purity and Danger*." *AA* 70:391–93. A critical evaluation.
Steiner, Franz. 1967. *Taboo*. Harmondsworth, England: Penguin. An indispensable guide to the topic.
Wagner, Roy. 1987. "Taboo." *Encyclopedia of Religion* 14:233–36.

Sources of Additional Information

Mary Douglas, "Pollution," *IESS* 12:336–42, 1968, offers an accessible if idiosyncratic introduction.

TOTEMISM. A system of culturally postulated correspondences between kin groups and entities (generally plant or animal species) that personify them; such systems often regulate exogamy.

Totemism involves a systematic identification between kin groups and natural phenomena, most commonly animal or plant species, in which the distinctive characteristics of the latter personify and legitimate social groupings. Totemism was originally studied primarily as a religious phenomenon, and in nineteenth century scholarship was often depicted as an identifiable stage in the EVOLUTION of RELIGION. Although earlier studies assumed that totemism possessed a conceptual unity, with certain unvarying characteristics, this view has been discredited.

The term derived from the North American Ojibwa word *ototeman*, signifying clan relations, that is, those sharing unilineal DESCENT from a common ancestor (Hartland 1921:393). The term was reported in 1791 by the Canadian trader J. Long, who erroneously defined the "totam" as a guardian spirit. More positively, Long did note the Ojibwa prohibition on killing the totem animal: "This totam they conceive assumes the shape of some beast or other, and therefore they never kill, hunt, or eat the animal whose form they think this totam bears" (in Hartland 1921:394). Such a TABOO was long considered a universal feature of totemism.

A more accurate account was provided by Peter Jones, an Ojibwa chief, who wrote (ca. 1856) that "their belief concerning their divisions into tribes [i.e., clans] is that many years ago the Great Spirit gave his red children their *toodaims* [totems], or tribes, in order that they might never forget that they were all related to each other." The Ojibwa totems, he noted, included Eagle, Reindeer, Otter, Bear, Buffalo, Beaver, and Catfish (in Hartland 1921:394). Parallels were soon drawn between the North American totem and similar beliefs on other continents. In 1841 Sir George Gray noted the similarity to Australian practices (Hartland 1921:394).

Totemism and Evolutionary Thought

John McLennan (1827–1881) had a major role in formulating the concept of totemism as an invariable complex and an evolutionary stage. In 1869 McLennan—who assumed the priority of matrilineal over patrilineal descent—argued that TRIBES at this stage of evolution understood themselves to be descended from, or akin to, a plant or animal species (their "symbol and emblem"), which was at the same time taboo to them. This identification between tribe and species was held to have engendered the principle of matriclan exogamy, or out-MARRIAGE (Stocking 1987:297). This theory was subsequently elaborated on by the theologian W. Robertson Smith (1846–1894), who introduced the idea that the totem animal, notwithstanding its normally tabooed status, was periodically consumed by the group "at an annual feast, with special and solemn ritual." Smith drew a parallel between ancient Semitic religions and the practices of "totem peoples," finding in the ethnographies of BAND and tribal societies a key to the communion RITUAL of Christian worship (Smith 1889:295).

Although totemism had first attracted attention as a North American phenom-

enon, interest shifted to the Australian data, in part because excellent ETHNOG-
RAPHY offered a wealth of detail (e.g., Spencer and Gillen 1899: chs. 4, 6).
The Australian example was also attractive because, from the distorted perspective of evolutionist thought, the Australian aborigines were held to be extremely PRIMITIVE, thus offering an unparalleled glimpse into the early history
of human society. In *The Elementary Forms of the Religious Life* (1915) Emile
Durkheim made Australian totemism the focus of analysis, this being "the most
primitive and simple religion which it is possible to find" (Durkheim 1915:115).
The "dubious and disputed" evidence (Evans-Pritchard 1965:52) for ritual consumption of the totem in Australia became a key element of Durkheim's argument
for the origins of religion (Durkheim 1915:366–92). In what can only be termed
an exercise in fantasy, Sigmund Freud in *Totem and Taboo* (1913) made of this
alleged totemic feast the expiation for a primeval act of parricide ("the totem
animal is in reality a substitute for the father"), as a result of which morality,
religion, and the family came into being (Freud 1913:141; cf. Kroeber 1920).

Critiques

For anthropologists of the Victorian era totemism was a unitary phenomenon,
reflecting in its global distribution the PSYCHIC UNITY of the human species. In
the early twentieth century this argument was strongly attacked by American
anthropologists, reflecting a greater emphasis on empirical research and a viewpoint dominated by HISTORICISM. Alexander Goldenweiser published a series of
studies, beginning in 1910, disproving the supposed unity of totemism. He
demonstrated that while certain totemic societies maintained a taboo on killing
the totem animal, others did not; while some had an ideology of descent from
the totem, others lacked this; and that a similar inconsistency obtained regarding
numerous other features, including the practice of naming the group after the
totem, or of holding rituals of increase for the totemic species (Goldenweiser
1931). As noted above, evidence for periodic sacrifice and communal consumption of the totem is weaker still. Thus "the features entering a totemic
complex are not inherently totemic but become such in the particular context"
(Goldenweiser 1931:378; see also Boas 1916).

Despite this critique of totemism as an evolutionary category, some ethnographic research on the topic has continued (e.g., Firth 1931; Brandenstein 1982).
From the perspective of STRUCTURALISM, Claude Lévi-Strauss has interpreted
totemism not as a unique phenomenon but as an example of a more general
human capacity for categorizing experience (Lévi-Strauss 1963, 1966; for a
critique see Worsley 1967).

References

Boas, Franz. 1916 [1966]. "The Origin of Totemism." F. Boas, *Race, Language and
    Culture*. New York: Free Press.
Brandenstein, C. G. von. 1982. *Names and Substance of the Australian Subsection System*.
    Chicago: University of Chicago Press.

Durkheim, Emile. 1915 [1965]. *The Elementary Forms of the Religious Life.* Joseph Swain, trans. New York: Free Press.

Evans-Pritchard, E. E. 1965. *Theories of Primitive Religion.* Oxford: Clarendon Press. An excellent treatment of the nineteenth century anthropology of religion.

Firth, Raymond. 1931 [1967]. "Totemism in Polynesia." R. Firth, *Tikopia Ritual and Belief.* Boston: Beacon Press.

Freud, Sigmund. 1913 [1950]. *Totem and Taboo: Some Points of Agreement Between the Mental Lives of Savages and Neurotics.* James Strachey, trans. New York: Norton.

Goldenweiser, Alexander. 1931. "Totemism: An Essay on Society and Religion." V. F. Calverton, ed., *The Making of Man: An Outline of Anthropology.* New York: Modern Library. A brief version of an influential critique.

Hartland, E. S. 1921. "Totemism." *ERE* 12:393–407.

Kroeber, Alfred. 1920 [1952]. "Totem and Taboo: An Ethnologic Psychoanalysis." A. Kroeber, *The Nature of Culture.* Chicago: University of Chicago Press. A critique of Freud.

Lévi-Strauss, Claude. 1963. *Totemism.* Rodney Needham, trans. Boston: Beacon Press.

———. 1966. *The Savage Mind.* Chicago: University of Chicago Press.

Smith, W. Robertson. 1889. [1972]. *The Religion of the Semites.* New York: Schocken. Of major importance in establishing totemism as an issue for evolutionary anthropology.

Spencer, Baldwin, and F. J. Gillen. 1899 [1968]. *The Native Tribes of Central Australia.* New York: Dover.

Stocking, George W., Jr. 1987. *Victorian Anthropology.* New York: Free Press.

Worsley, Peter. 1967. "Groote Eylandt Totemism and *Le totémisme aujourd'hui.*" Edmund Leach, ed., *The Structural Study of Myth and Totemism.* London: Tavistock.

Sources of Additional Information

Roy Wagner, in "Totemism," *Encyclopedia of Religion* 14:573–76, 1987, provides a useful overview, emphasizing structuralist issues. The significance of totemism for Victorian anthropology is described by Adam Kuper, *The Invention of Primitive Society*, London: Routledge, 1988, chs. 4–6. For a discussion of the North American data, see Ake Hultkrantz, *The Religions of the American Indians*, Monica Setterwall, trans., Berkeley and Los Angeles: University of California Press, 1979, ch. 5.

TRADITION. (1) An explicit cultural form transmitted through time, the perpetuation of which is itself a value. (2) A continuity of understanding relative to some activity, way of life, or mode of expression, which guides particular acts and beliefs.

Tradition, in its original sense, denoted the delivery or handing down of some instruction or doctrine, from the Latin *trado*, to hand over, to surrender. In modern usage, a tradition can involve either some relatively fixed cultural practice preserved over time (as in the tradition of monarchy in Great Britain), or more broadly, a continuity in aim, style, or understanding that guides particular acts (as in the gothic tradition in European architecture, or the baroque tradition in eighteenth-century music). In either case, the notion of tradition carries with it the idea that this act of cultural transmission is itself a value.

The European concept of tradition originated in theology. In early Christianity it denoted that continuity of apostolic teaching which guaranteed the authenticity of RITUAL and doctrine (2 Thess 2:15). Accordingly, for the church fathers any innovation in practice or belief had to be compatible with received teachings. In the dictum of Pope Stephen I (d. 257), "Let there be no innovation save through tradition" (*nihil innovetur nisi quod traditum est*: see Dölger 1929:1:79). Change, in short, must be guided by tradition.

In later European thought, the value of tradition was undermined in several ways. In philosophy, the writings of Descartes (d. 1650) propagated a new epistemology, in which certitude was to be found through the application of individual reason, not the authority of tradition (Descartes 1637). In aesthetics, with the advent of romanticism in the eighteenth and nineteenth centuries, tradition came to be perceived as an artifical constraint on an otherwise free and spontaneous human NATURE (see Rousseau 1754). In politics, tradition became a point of debate between conservative and radical. To the former, such as Edmund Burke (d. 1797), tradition constituted the prudent guide of social experience (see Burke 1790). To the latter, such as Karl Marx, it provided the justification for tyranny and oppression: "the tradition of all the dead generations weighs like a nightmare on the brain of the living" (Marx 1852:15).

Tradition, Myth, and Culture

In a number of nineteenth-century studies, tradition was used to refer to the collective body of MYTH or legend within a society. Thus regarding the supposed ritual slaying of kings in antiquity James Frazer wrote that "it is natural enough that reminiscences of it should survive in tradition long after the custom itself has been abolished" (Frazer 1890:237). Baldwin Spencer and F. J. Gillen, describing aboriginal Australian creation myths, noted that "the traditions of the tribe recognise four more or less distinct periods in the Alcheringa [Dream Time]" (Spencer and Gillen 1899:387).

Early twentieth-century anthropologists understood tradition far more broadly, as essentially synonymous with CULTURE. Alfred Kroeber, in arguing for the independence of culture from biology (see SUPERORGANIC), referred to tradition as "something superadded to the organisms that bear it, imposed upon them," and contrasted "the instinctive and traditional, the organic and the social" (Kroeber 1917:32). Robert Lowie (writing in 1934) defined culture simply as "the whole of social tradition," while in much the same vein, Ralph Linton (in 1936) equated culture with "social heredity" (in Kroeber and Kluckhohn 1952:90).

Tradition and Culture Change

As long as ETHNOGRAPHY was aimed primarily at capturing recollections of precontact culture PATTERNS, rather than documenting existing social life, there was little place in the technical vocabulary for a concept of tradition distinct from that of culture. It was, seemingly, the shift of anthropological concern to matters of ACCULTURATION, CULTURE CHANGE, and economic DEVELOPMENT which gave, by way of contrast, a more precise usage to tradition: as an explicit cultural form the transmission of which is itself a value. In this usage tradition was generally depicted as both static and irrational, necessarily in conflict with forces encouraging culture change.

As Franz Boas noted in *Anthropology and Modern Life*, "conflicts between the inertia of conservative tradition and the radicalism of rapid change are characteristic of our civilization" (Boas 1928:134). This view was reinforced by theorists in other disciplines, in particular by the sociologists Emile Durkheim (d. 1917) and Max Weber (d. 1920). Both Durkheim's contrast of mechanical and organic solidarity and Weber's contrast of traditional and rational action (see RATIONALITY) assumed the incompatibility of tradition and culture change (see Shanklin 1981).

The concept of tradition figured significantly in the work of Robert Redfield, who developed through his studies of peasant societies a distinction between the Great and Little Traditions. According to Redfield,

> In a civilization there is a great tradition of the reflective few, and there is a little tradition of the largely unreflective many. . . . The tradition of the philosopher, theologian, and literary man is a tradition consciously cultivated and handed down; that of the little people is for the most part taken for granted and not submitted to much scrutiny or considered refinement or improvement. (Redfield 1956:70)

In short, the Great Tradition is codified, literate, and linked with elites and a high CIVILIZATION; the Little Tradition is popular, unsystematic, generally nonliterate or at least nonliterary, and associated with peasant COMMUNITIES (see PEASANTRY; FOLK CULTURE). This distinction has been used in a number of studies of STATE-level societies, for example Melford Spiro's work on Buddhism in Burma and Milton Singer's on Hinduism in modern India (Spiro 1982; Singer 1972).

New Directions in the Study of Tradition

Since the 1960s the anthropological understanding of tradition has changed considerably. An earlier view of tradition as inflexible and irrational could not be reconciled either with newer ethnographic data concerning culture change or with world events. Postwar anthropological theory failed to predict the endurance and adaptability of political and religious traditions in the face of rapid technological change, as seen in the persistence of tribal solidarities in Africa, CASTE in India, or fundamentalist Islam in the Arab world (Levine 1968; see also DEVELOPMENT).

More recent culture theory recognizes tradition to be relatively fluid, capable of being invoked to justify or guide innovation, while conferring a sense of continuity with the past (Spicer 1971; Shanklin 1981; Winthrop 1985, 1990). The growth of anthropological theory in matters of SYMBOLISM and INTERPRETATION has provided a more sensitive grasp of the complex processes involved in learning, reinterpreting, and communicating the cultural principles that guide both dramatic ritual and everyday life. Based on these developments, it is more appropriate to understand by "tradition" not some fixed cultural content endlessly perpetuated, but a persisting pattern of understanding that allows continuity within change.

References

Boas, Franz. 1928. *Anthropology and Modern Life*. New York: Norton. Boas discusses the "stability of culture."

Burke, Edmund. 1790 [1968]. *Reflections on the Revolution in France*. Conor Cruise O'Brien, ed. Harmondsworth, England: Penguin. A classic statement of political conservatism.

Descartes, Rene. 1637 [1960]. "Discourse on Method." Monroe Beardsley, ed., *The European Philosophers from Descartes to Nietzsche*. New York: Modern Library. Argues against tradition as a source of reliable knowledge.

Dölger, Joseph. 1929. *Antike und Christentum*. Munster, Germany: Aschendorffsche Verlagsbuchhandlung.

Frazer, James George. 1890 [1959]. *The New Golden Bough*. 1 vol., abr. Theodor H. Gaster, ed. New York: Criterion Books. A nineteenth-century classic.

Kroeber, Alfred. 1917 [1952]. "The Superorganic." Alfred Kroeber, *The Nature of Culture*. Chicago: University of Chicago Press.

Kroeber, Alfred, and Clyde Kluckhohn. 1952. *Culture: A Critical Review of Concepts and Definitions*. New York: Random House/Vintage Books. A useful compendium.

Levine, Donald N. 1968. "The Flexibility of Traditional Culture." *Journal of Social Issues* 24 (4): 129–41. A strong critique of "modernization" theory, refuting the premise that tradition and change need be in conflict.

Marx, Karl. 1852 [1972]. *Die Achtzehnte Brumaire des Louis Bonaparte*. K. Marx and F. Engels, *Werke*, vol. 8. Berlin: Dietz Verlag.

Redfield, Robert. 1956. *Peasant Society and Culture: An Anthropological Approach to Civilization*. Chicago: University of Chicago Press. Redfield introduced in this work the concepts of Great and Little Traditions.

Rousseau, Jean-Jacques. 1754 [1967]. "Discourse on the Origin and Foundation of Inequality Among Mankind." J.-J. Rousseau, *The Social Contract and Discourse on the Origin of Inequality*. New York: Washington Square Press. Rousseau decries the "unnatural" constraints of civilization and its traditions.

Shanklin, Eugenia. 1981. "Two Meanings and Uses of Tradition." *Journal of Anthropological Research* 37:71–89. A useful review of the concept of tradition.

Singer, Milton. 1972. *When a Great Tradition Modernizes: An Anthropological Approach to Indian Civilization*. London: Pall Mall Press. Analyzes the Hindu "Great Tradition."

Spencer, Baldwin, and F. J. Gillen. 1899 [1968]. *The Native Tribes of Central Australia*. New York: Dover.

Spicer, Edward H. 1971. "Persistent Cultural Systems." *Science* 174:795–800. Analyses conditions that encourage the maintenance of traditions in cultural enclaves.

Spiro, Melford. 1982. *Buddhism and Society: A Great Tradition and Its Burmese Vicissitudes*. 2d ed. Berkeley and Los Angeles: University of California Press. On the Great/Little Tradition contrast in Theravada Buddhism.

Winthrop, Robert H. 1985. "Leadership and Tradition in the Regulation of Catholic

Monasticism.'' *Anthropological Quarterly* 58:30–38. An analysis of the interpretation of monastic tradition in situations of social change.

————. 1990. ''Persistent Peoples: Mechanisms of Cultural Survival in Southern Oregon and Northwestern California.'' Nan Hannon and Richard K. Olmo, eds., *Living with the Land: The Indians of Southwest Oregon.* Medford, Oreg.: Southern Oregon Historical Society.

Sources of Additional Information

In *Tradition*, Chicago: University of Chicago Press, 1981, Edward Shils offers a stimulating reflection on the phenomenon of tradition, from a sociological and historical perspective. T. S. Eliot's ''Tradition and the Individual Talent,'' in his *Selected Essays*, new ed., New York: Harcourt, Brace, 1950, is the classic statement on the role of tradition in artistic creativity. As a counterpoint to the above, Eric Hobsbawm and Terence Ranger provide an interesting set of essays under the title *The Invention of Tradition*, Cambridge: Cambridge University Press, 1983, arguing that what is taken for age-old tradition is often new practice crafted to appear continuous with the past.

TRANCE. A disruption of normal consciousness characterized by dissociation and altered motor behavior; in many societies such experiences are ritualized and subject to cultural interpretation (e.g., as possession or soul loss).

Trance (derived from the Latin *transire*, to pass over or cross) involves a psychological condition in which an individual passes from the normal, waking state to an altered state of consciousness. Trance thus constitutes a rupture in the normal functioning of PERSONALITY, ''a state of mental abstraction from external things; absorption, exhaltation, rapture, ecstasy'' (*OED*).

The phenomenon of trance is often considered in relation to individual psychopathology (e.g., hysteria or psychosis). ANTHROPOLOGY, however, is chiefly concerned with trance insofar as it involves ''institutionalized, culturally patterned altered states'' (Bourguignon 1973:9), typically in the context of RITUAL. Examples include the trance-based curing ceremonies of SHAMANISM and the divination accomplished through spirit mediumship. Such phenomena are actually quite common cross-culturally, as Bourguignon has noted: ''Of a sample of 488 societies, in all parts of the world . . . 437, or 90% are reported to have one or more institutionalized, culturally patterned forms of altered states of consciousness'' (Bourguignon 1973:11).

Trance is an etic concept, that is, a scientifically grounded category of observation, and should be contrasted with a series of emic, or culturally established, interpretations of trance phenomena, including possession, mediumship, and shamanism (see EMIC/ETIC). Spirit possession, to follow Raymond Firth, describes trance that is ''interpreted as evidence of a control of [a subject's] behaviour by a spirit normally external to him'' (in Beattie and Middleton 1969:xvii), although the cultural diagnosis of possession can also occur outside the trance state (Lewis 1971:45–46). Spirit mediumship, in contrast, is a form of possession ''in which the person is conceived as serving as an intermediary between spirits and men'' (Firth, in Beattie and Middleton 1969:xvii). The cultural assumptions underlying SHAMANISM are in a sense the reverse of those involved in possession. Rather than being controlled by spirits who descend into his body, the shaman masters the spirit world, undertaking cosmic flight with the aid of tutelary spirits so as to obtain the powers and knowledge to cure and prophesy.

Trance, Culture, and Psychopathology

The complexity of the trance concept stems in part from the existence of two potentially conflicting perspectives for its interpretation, one psychiatric, the other cultural. In the psychiatric view, trance behavior is a symptom of psychopathology, however exotic the social context in which it occurs. In this vein James Frazer (in 1913) characterized possessed individuals as "more or less crazed in their wits," noting that hysterics and epileptics "are for that very reason thought to be particularly favored by the spirits and are therefore consulted as oracles" (in Beattie and Middleton 1969:xxiv). George Devereux, taking a strongly Freudian perspective, argued similarly that "there is no reason and no excuse for not considering the shaman to be a severe neurotic or even a psychotic in a state of temporary remission" (Devereux 1956:14–15).

In contrast, many anthropologists have insisted that culturally validated trance behavior cannot be reduced to the categories of psychiatry (see Lewis 1971:182–83). As Jane Belo has commented regarding Bali, where numerous forms of possession and mediumship occur, "all the varieties of trance behavior are culturally stylized: they bear the imprint of cultural patterning" (Belo 1960:1). In a larger context, such culturally validated trance may be considered but one form of what Anthony Wallace has termed culturally enjoined "pseudo-illnesses," which would also include ritual intoxication (as with peyote) and self-mortification leading to hallucination (as in the vision quest) (Wallace 1970:227). While the physiological and psychological mechanisms involved may be the same as in classic psychopathologies, "the consequences of such experiences are vastly different, since a 'ceremonial' neurosis or psychosis, unlike the 'true' disease, is voluntarily initiated, is usually reversible, and leads neither the subject nor his associates to classify him as 'abnormal' and unworthy of complete social participation" (Wallace 1970:228).

Theoretical Approaches

Anthropologists have taken a wide range of approaches in analyzing trance phenomena. Numerous studies have examined the social and psychological functions of culturally patterned trance behavior. I. M. Lewis's important study *Ecstatic Religion* has emphasized the political dimensions of possession cults. In highly patriarchal societies, the cycle of spirit affliction and cure can provide women with "a means of insinuating their interests and demands in the face of male constraint" (Lewis 1971:79). In a study of the Umbanda spirit medium cults of urban Brazil, Esther Pressel has stressed the role of mediums not only in CURING but, through the guidance they provide the Umbanda adherents, in mediating the effects of industrialization and CULTURE CHANGE (Pressel 1973).

Virginia Hine (1973) has described glossolalia (the "speaking in tongues" interpreted as possession by the Holy Spirit) as an essential commitment mechanism within Pentecostalism, validating the Pentecostal ideology, reinforcing its distinctiveness, and aiding its growth as a SOCIAL MOVEMENT.

Other studies have analyzed the complex interaction of biological and cultural processes involved in such phenomena. In a study of the South African Nguni, Judith Gussler has identified stress and pellagra as factors precipitating trance experience: "Ecological change, subsistence practices, and traditional social patterns have combined to produce certain nutritional deficiencies that in turn produce some of the physical, physiological, and behavioral changes associated with ukuthwasa [possession illness]" (Gussler 1973:115). Calcium deficiency has also been suggested as a factor in trance behavior (Kehoe and Gileti 1981; for a critique see Bourguignon et al. 1983). Finally, studies of the neurobiology of trance phenomena—including the range of cultural practices used to induce such states—suggest that, rather than being the domain of a minority of pathological individuals, the capacity for such experience is universal (Lex 1979:118).

References

Beattie, John, and John Middleton. 1969. "Introduction." J. Beattie and J. Middleton, eds., *Spirit Mediumship and Society in Africa*. New York: Africana Publishing.

Belo, Jane. 1960 [1977]. *Trance in Bali*. Westport, Conn.: Greenwood Press. Based on research in the 1930s, a pioneering and meticulous study.

Bourguignon, Erika. 1973. "Introduction: A Framework for the Comparative Study of Altered States of Consciousness." E. Bourguignon, ed., *Religion, Altered States of Consciousness, and Social Change*. Columbus: Ohio State University Press.

Bourguignon, Erika, et al. 1983. "Women, Possession Trance Cults, and the Extended Nutrient-Deficiency Hypothesis." *AA* 85:413–16.

Devereux, George. 1956 [1980]. "Normal and Abnormal." G. Devereux, *Basic Problems of Ethnopsychiatry*. Basia M. Gulati and George Devereux, trans. Chicago: University of Chicago Press. A strongly psychoanalytic view.

Gussler, Judith. 1973. "Social Change, Ecology, and Spirit Possession among the South African Nguni." E. Bourguignon, ed., *Religion, Altered States of Consciousness, and Social Change*. Columbus: Ohio State University Press.

Hine, Virginia H. 1973. "Pentecostal Glossolalia—Toward a Functional Interpretation." Benjamin Beit-Hallahmi, ed., *Research in Religious Behavior: Selected Readings*. Monterey, Calif.: Brooks/Cole Publishing.

Kehoe, Alice B., and Dody H. Gileti. 1981. "Women's Preponderance in Possession Cults: The Calcium-Deficiency Hypothesis Extended." *AA* 83:549–61.

Lewis, I. M. 1971. *Ecstatic Religion: An Anthropological Study of Spirit Possession and Shamanism*. Harmondsworth, England: Penguin. An essential synthesis, emphasizing a broadly functionalist viewpoint.

Lex, Barbara W. 1979. "The Neurobiology of Ritual Trance." Eugene G. d'Aquili et al., eds., *The Spectrum of Ritual: A Biogenetic Structural Analysis*. New York: Columbia University Press.

Pressel, Esther. 1973. "Umbanda in Sao Paulo: Religious Innovation in a Developing

Society." E. Bourguignon, ed., *Religion, Altered States of Consciousness, and Social Change*. Columbus: Ohio State University Press.

Wallace, Anthony F. C. 1970. *Culture and Personality*. 2d ed. New York: Random House.

Sources of Additional Information

Erika Bourguignon, *Possession*, San Francisco: Chandler & Sharp, 1976, offers a brief introduction. A readable history of the interdisciplinary study of trance is provided by Brian Inglis, *Trance: A Natural History of Altered States of Mind*, London: Grafton Books, 1989. Two ethnographic accounts are Michael Lambek, *Human Spirits: A Cultural Account of Trance in Mayotte*, Cambridge: Cambridge University Press, 1981; and Jay D. Dobbins, *The Jombee Dance of Montserrat: A Study of Trance Ritual in the West Indies*, Columbus: Ohio State University Press, 1986.

TRIBE. A culturally homogeneous, nonstratified society possessing a common territory, without centralized political or legal institutions, whose members are linked by extended KINSHIP ties, RITUAL obligations, and mutual responsibility for the resolution of disputes.

The concept of tribe is fundamentally a category of political organization and as such is frequently contrasted with other political forms, in particular with the BAND and the STATE. Like the band, the tribe is a kin-based society. Typically, however, tribes are situated in richer environments or utilize more productive modes of ADAPTATION (for example, horticulture or pastoralism), allowing an ECONOMY with significant surplus. This in turn makes possible more elaborate patterns of economic exchange than occur in band societies, joining much larger populations into a common political framework.

Unlike the state, the political functioning of a tribe depends not upon distinct, centralized political institutions, but develops out of the ongoing social life of kin-based groups. As Ronald Berndt has noted, "The term 'tribe' should be applied only in situations where there is no centralization of authority mediated through formally differentiated political and administrative structures" (Berndt 1959:82). In this way, the concept of tribe implies a distinctive SOCIAL STRUCTURE (see also CHIEFDOM). Furthermore, tribe carries with it a sense of ethnic or cultural unity (see ETHNICITY). In John Honigmann's phrase, a tribe possesses "a common territory, a common language, and a common culture" (Honigmann 1964).

The word tribe is derived from the Latin *tribus*, signifying the three divisions of the Roman people, a word later used in the Vulgate Bible (sixth century) to describe the DESCENT groups of the ancient Israelites (Gen. 49:28). The term appears with this sense in English from the thirteenth century. By the late sixteenth century, tribe had acquired a broader (and loosely ethnological) sense of a distinct people, for example in *Othello* (3.3.175): "The souls of all my tribe defend from jealousy!" (*OED*). "Tribe" appeared in a specifically ethnographic context from the early nineteenth century, though it was usually applied rather vaguely, particularly in Africanist studies. In nineteenth-century American anthropology, in contrast, the term was originally used to denote a grouping of lineages, a clan (see DESCENT). By the late nineteenth century (e.g., in Lewis Henry Morgan's *Ancient Society* [1877]) it took approximately its present meaning: a nonstratified, culturally distinctive, kin-based society.

Defining Tribe

Various definitions of tribe have been advanced, reflecting the considerable ambiguity surrounding the concept (Fried 1968:5). For A. R. Radcliffe-Brown (writing in 1913), "the tribe is distinguished from its neighbours by possession of a name, a language, and a defined territory" (in Berndt 1959:81). "In its simplest form," observed Ralph Linton (1936:231), "the tribe is a group of bands occupying contiguous territories and having a feeling of unity deriving from numerous similarities in culture, frequent friendly contacts, and a certain community of interest." According to Aidan Southall, the tribe is commonly defined as "a whole society, with a high degree of self-sufficiency at a near subsistence level, based on a relatively simple technology without writing or literature, politically autonomous and with its own distinctive language, culture and sense of identity, tribal religion being also coterminous with tribal society" (Southall 1970:28). However, tribe is often used more narrowly to refer to the largest politically independent unit within a tribally organized people (Evans-Pritchard 1940:117–22).

In reality, the range of meanings attaching to tribe is wider than these definitions suggest, for the term is commonly used in at least four quite different contexts. (1) Tribe is understood as an objective ethnological category, relevant to the practical problem of classifying social groups, distinguishing Klamath from Modoc, Pathan from Baluch (see ETHNOLOGY). (2) Tribe figures as one stage in an evolutionary sequence (e.g., band, tribe, chiefdom, state), stressing the historical transformation of certain features of politics, economy, and social organization (Godelier 1977; see EVOLUTION). (3) Tribe serves as an expression of social identity and distinctiveness among the descendants of aboriginal social groups now threatened by assimilation or destruction at the hands of encroaching states. The concept of tribe in jurisprudence (e.g., in federal law in the United States) closely follows this usage (see Weatherhead 1980). (4) Within certain intellectual traditions the distinction of tribe and state takes the character of a total, qualitative assessment of two patterns of existence. In part, this reflects certain objective contrasts: in scale, degree of technological complexity, or extent of social INEQUALITY. Yet the distinction goes beyond differences in social or economic form, to subsume a complex philosophical or moral judgment of considerable importance in Western thought: that between so-called PRIMITIVE and civilized societies (see CIVILIZATION).

Tribe and Kinship

The members of a tribe share the bonds engendered by common kinship and residence (see FAMILY). Ties of common descent (manifested in particular by membership in clans and lineages) are particularly important in organizing tribal societies. A wide variety of descent structures can provide a basis for tribal social and political organization. In the case of dispersed clans, characteristic of many Native American societies, members of the various clans are distributed throughout tribal territory. Clan membership creates "not a group but an uncoordinated category of people" (Sahlins 1968:53), crosscutting other affiliations. Because such clans are exogamous (outmarrying) groups, clan membership also regulates MARRIAGE. Territorial clans, in contrast, are geographically localized groups. In the New Guinea Highlands, for example, "the clan claims and defends a definite territory, within which most adult men of the group reside" (Sahlins 1968:52).

Other structures include the highly egalitarian and decentralized segmentary lineage systems, characteristic of a number of African pastoralist tribes, and cognatic descent groups, based on affiliation through either the mother's or father's line, common among American Indian tribes of the Northwest Coast (see DESCENT). Systems utilizing conical clans (as in Polynesia), in which clans are hierarchically ordered by genealogical distance from a real or mythical founder, provide a basis for distinctions of social rank, characteristic of chiefdoms (see Sahlins 1968: ch. 4). Regardless of the particular pattern involved, the creation of a social order on the basis of kinship and marriage distinguishes the tribe from the autonomous political order characteristic of the state, a fact recognized by Lewis Henry Morgan more than a century ago (Morgan 1877:61).

Tribe and Economy

Tribal economies are relatively small in scale, exhibiting simplicity and self-sufficiency, and functioning with limited surplus. Tribal societies exhibit a wide range of subsistence adaptations, including pastoralism, hunting and gathering, fishing, and agriculture. These differences notwithstanding, in all tribes the organization of production is carried out through broader ("functionally generalized") social relationships, based fundamentally upon kinship, which also provide a foundation for political alignments and ritual obligations. The family is crucial to tribal production: "The first characteristic common to all 'tribal' societies . . . is the fact that all elementary social units are multifamilial groups which collectively exploit an area of common resources and form a residential unit the whole year round, or the major part of it" (Godelier 1977:80). In this way, the structure of the family or multifamily group provides the common framework for production, distribution, and consumption within the tribe (see ECONOMY).

Certain patterns of economic organization are conventionally assumed to characterize tribal as opposed to state societies (see MODE OF PRODUCTION). It may be more useful, however, to see the economic differences between tribes and states as relative, not absolute. In India, for example, recognized tribal groups constitute a small proportion of the population, while the cultural heterogeneity implied by the system of CASTE permits the gradual absorption of many tribes into a Hindu frame of reference. In the Indian case, at least, F. G. Bailey has argued that tribe and state constitute not antitheses but ends of a continuum, the crucial variable involving the ownership of resources, specifically "the proportion of a given society which has direct access to the land" (Bailey 1961:14).

Ethnological Problems of Tribe

At least three questions arise in trying to apply the concept of tribe to ethnographic data. First, is it correct to assume the equivalence of language, culture, and self-identity as ethnological markers of a tribe? Second, should a tribe be defined by common ethnological traits (culture, language, etc.), or by the limits of effective political organization? Third, should the definition of tribe be flexible enough to accommodate the fact of culture change?

(1) The ethnological assumption of one tribe—one language is of dubious validity. As Dell Hymes (1968) has demonstrated, there are numerous ethnographic examples that elude the mapping of tribe to language, variously because of a lack of identity between group boundaries, communication boundaries, and linguistic boundaries (e.g., Nuba, Chinook, or Siane), or because of the non-correspondence of lexicon, phonology, and syntax (e.g., Hupa/Yurok), or because of other confounding factors.

Similarly, discovery of an unambiguous tribal identity is frequently impossible. Edmund Leach's study of shifting Kachin identity and politics in highland Burma (Leach 1954) offers a classic example; similar arguments have been advanced by others (Southall 1970; Sturtevant 1983; cf. Moerman 1965). Thus the naming and bounding of tribal units can be an arbitrary process, often reflecting more the misunderstanding of the observer than the ethnographic reality. This problem has been discussed for the ethnology of the Great Basin by Julian Steward (1938:263–265), for that of Australia by Ronald Berndt (1959), and for that of Africa by Aidan Southall (1970).

(2) As indicated above, even where the boundaries of language, culture, and identity coincide, these need not correspond to the limits of effective political organization. As Alfred Kroeber has commented, the idea of tribe implies co-ordinated action, common identity, and control of a distinct territory. Yet he noted, speaking of the Pomo of aboriginal California, that "these traits attached to the Masut Pomo, again to the Elem Pomo, to the Yokaia Pomo, and to the 30 other Pomo tribelets. They did not attach to the Pomo as a whole, because the Pomo as a whole did not act or govern themselves, or hold land as a unit" (in Bean 1978:673). Under the impetus of FUNCTIONALISM, in British anthropology in particular, tribe has come to be defined in political terms, leaving unsettled the problem of how to describe this wider cultural/ethnic unity. To quote I. M. Lewis, tribe signifies "the widest territorially defined, politically independent unit in a tribal society" (Lewis 1968:149). This usage is increasingly common, but not universal.

(3) In the classical view, tribes are nonliterate, culturally uniform, religiously cohesive, technologically simple, economically self-sufficient, and politically autonomous. This may have characterized the groups encountered by Europeans in the sixteenth through eighteenth centuries; it does not characterize them today. Conquest, educational programs, missionization and revitalistic movements,

market economies, massive demographic change, and the dominance of industrial states have all had their effect. Yet in most areas of the world there are organized descendants of such aboriginal peoples who insist, for a variety of reasons (cultural, religious, legal, ideological), on the continuing validity of the designation "tribe" for themselves and for similar groups.

Such contemporary "tribes" manifest intricate patterns of persisting TRADITION in combination with ACCULTURATION and CULTURE CHANGE (see Gulliver 1969; Castile and Kushner 1981; Winthrop 1990). In many societies (the United States, for example), government policy regarding aboriginal peoples is predicated upon the continuing relevance of the tribe concept (see Weatherhead 1980; Sturtevant 1983). Under these circumstances, the question of how appropriately to define and apply the concept of tribe in the modern world must be seen not only as an analytic issue, but also as a political and ethical problem.

References

Bailey, F. G. 1961. "'Tribe' and 'Caste' in India." *Contributions to Indian Sociology* 5:7–19. Argues that the degree of autonomous access to resources is the major differentiating factor between tribe and state.

Bean, Lowell John. 1978. "Social Organization." Robert F. Heizer, ed., *Handbook of North American Indians*, vol. 8, *California*. Washington, D.C.: Smithsonian Institution. A summary of aboriginal California social organization.

Berndt, Ronald M. 1959. "The Concept of 'the Tribe' in the Western Desert of Australia." *Oceania* 30:81–107. Discusses problems of identifying tribal, cultural, and linguistic units in aboriginal Australia.

Castile, George P., and Gilbert Kushner, eds. 1981. *Persistent Peoples: Cultural Enclaves in Perspective*. Tucson: University of Arizona Press. Seeks a theoretical basis for cultural (notably tribal) stability within states.

Evans-Pritchard, E. E. 1940. *The Nuer*. Oxford: Clarendon Press. A classic ethnography of a tribal society.

Fried, Morton. 1968. "On the Concepts of 'Tribe' and 'Tribal Society.' " June Helm, ed., *Essays on the Problem of Tribe*. American Ethnological Society, *Proceedings (1967)*:3–20. Fried argues that tribal organization reflects a reaction to the intrusion of state societies.

Godelier, Maurice. 1977. "The Concept of the 'Tribe': A Crisis Involving Merely a Concept or the Empirical Foundations of Anthropology Itself?" M. Godelier, *Perspectives in Marxist Anthropology*. Cambridge: Cambridge University Press. A complex Marxist critique of the concepts of tribe and cultural evolution.

Gulliver, P. H., ed. 1969. *Tradition and Transition in East Africa: Studies in the Tribal Element in the Modern Era*. Berkeley and Los Angeles: University of California Press. Emphasizes the transformations of tribal structures and sentiments.

Honigmann, John J. 1964. "Tribe." Julius Gould and William L. Kolb, eds., *A Dictionary of the Social Sciences*. New York: Free Press.

Hymes, Dell. 1968. "Linguistic Problems in Defining the Concept of 'Tribe.' " June Helm, ed., *Essays on the Problem of Tribe*. American Ethnological Society, *Proceedings (1967)*:23–48. Demonstrates the fallacy of equating territorial, cultural, and linguistic units in tribal societies.

Leach, E. R. 1954 [1965]. *Political Systems of Highland Burma: A Study of Kachin*

Social Structure. Boston: Beacon Press. The classic study on shifts in identity and social organization in a tribal society.

Lewis, I. M. 1968. "Tribal Society." *IESS* 16:147–50.

Linton, Ralph. 1936. *The Study of Man: An Introduction*. N.p.: Appleton-Century-Crofts.

Moerman, Michael. 1965. "Ethnic Identification in a Complex Civilization: Who are the Lue?" *AA* 67:1215–30. Suggests ethnic self-identity as a guide to tribal boundaries.

Morgan, Lewis Henry. 1877 [1963]. *Ancient Society*. Eleanor Leacock, ed. New York: World Publishing.

Sahlins, Marshall. 1968. *Tribesmen*. Englewood Cliffs, N.J.: Prentice-Hall. An excellent overview.

Southall, Aidan W. 1970. "The Illusion of Tribe." *Journal of Asian and African Studies* 5:28–50. Southall considers sources of error and misinterpretation inherent in the process of identifying tribal groupings.

Steward, Julian H. 1938. *Basin-Plateau Aboriginal Sociopolitical Groups*. Bureau of American Ethnology, *Bulletin* 120. Washington, D.C.: Smithsonian Institution.

Sturtevant, William C. 1983. "Tribe and State in Sixteenth and Twentieth Centuries." E. Tooker, ed., *The Development of Political Organization in Native North America*. American Ethnological Society, *Proceedings (1979)*. Sturtevant discusses the effect of state societies on tribal organization and identity.

Weatherhead, L. R. 1980. "What is an 'Indian Tribe'?—The Question of Tribal Existence." *American Indian Law Review* 8:1–47. Weatherhead reviews material from U.S. treaties, statutes, case law, and federal regulations.

Winthrop, Robert H. 1990. "Persistent Peoples: Mechanisms of Cultural Survival in Southern Oregon and Northwestern California." Nan Hannon and Richard K. Olmo, eds., *Living With the Land: The Indians of Southwest Oregon*. Medford, Oreg.: Southern Oregon Historical Society.

Sources of Additional Information

Previous attempts to formulate adequate criteria for identifying tribal groupings are reviewed in Raoul Naroll, "On Ethnic Unit Classification," *CA* 5:283–312, 1964; the author's suggested alternative concept, the "cultunit," has not been widely accepted. Access to the enormous literature on tribal societies can be obtained in several ways. George Peter Murdock's *Atlas of World Cultures*, Pittsburgh, Pa.: University of Pittsburgh Press, 1981, provides initial bibliographic references for several hundred tribal societies. Numerous ethnographic handbooks, anthologies, and bibliographic surveys exist for major culture areas. See Timothy J. O'Leary, "Ethnographic Bibliographies," Raoul Naroll and Ronald Cohen, eds., *A Handbook of Method in Cultural Anthropology*, New York: Columbia University Press, 1970, chap. 7.

U

URBANISM. The existence of large, densely populated settlements within a society, creating a concentration of trade, wealth, and bureaucratic power.

Urban settlements have formed a significant element of human societies for the past five thousand years. Ancient Mesopotamia, Egypt, China, the Indus Valley, and, in the New World, Mesoamerica were all early sites of urbanism. The major factors characterizing the STATE—institutionalized authority, literacy, specialization of labor, economic stratification, and centralized control of surplus—have likewise been essential characteristics of urbanism (see INEQUALITY). From a culture-historical perspective, the city has been an essential element in the development of CIVILIZATION (see Mumford 1961). Both terms have a common origin in the Latin *civis*, citizen.

In a classic paper, the sociologist Louis Wirth defined the city as "a relatively large, dense, and permanent settlement of socially heterogeneous individuals" (Wirth 1938:13). However, the phenomenon of urbanism should not be equated merely with the existence of cities, considered in isolation, but with the manner in which urban settlement structures patterns of trade, transportation, social organization, and cultural transmission in an entire society. As Anthony Leeds has noted, "Any society which has in it what we commonly call 'towns' or 'cities' is in all aspects an 'urban' society, including its agricultural and extractive domains" (Leeds 1980:6).

Development of Urban Anthropology

The interest of cultural anthropologists in urban societies has been sporadic. Questions of the emergence of urban civilizations bulked large in nineteenth-century evolutionary theory, as in Lewis Henry Morgan's proposed sequence of savagery, barbarism, and civilization (see EVOLUTION). However, until the 1950s most cultural anthropologists ignored urban field settings to concentrate on ETH-NOGRAPHY among TRIBES and PEASANTRY.

Much sociological theory—which has had considerable influence on this sub-field of ANTHROPOLOGY—has taken a highly critical view of urban life, charac-terizing it as impersonal, culturally heterogeneous, and destructive of the intimate groups within which a moral, orderly social life can prevail. Thus for Wirth, ur-banism involves "the weakening of bonds of kinship, and the declining social significance of the family, the disappearance of the neighborhood, and the under-mining of the traditional basis of social solidarity" (Wirth 1938:22; see also Uz-zell and Provencher 1976: ch. 1). The anthropologist Robert Redfield drew on these assumptions in his contrast of the harmonious rural peasant COMMUNITY, guided by TRADITION and communal RITUAL, and the fragmented and secularized city. Redfield's research in the 1920s and 1930s, comparing communities in Yu-catán, Mexico, ranging from a small village to a city, provided an important model of comparative research (see Redfield 1953; FOLK CULTURE).

Most urban ethnographic studies in the United States have had little influence within the wider field of anthropology. Both the early participant-observation study of Muncie, Indiana, titled *Middletown* (Lynd and Lynd 1929), and the studies of Newburyport, Massachusetts, begun by W. Lloyd Warner in 1930, published under the pseudonym *Yankee City* (Warner et al. 1963), received far more attention from sociologists (see Gulick 1973:980–81). In contrast Oscar Lewis's research on the culture of poverty has been unusually influential, if controversial. Based on the study of the urban poor in Puerto Rico, Mexico City, and New York, Lewis sketched an image of social disorganization attributed not to urbanism per se but to a self-perpetuating lower-class WORLD VIEW (Lewis 1970; for a critique, see Uzzell and Provencher 1976:48–50).

Recent Directions

According to earlier theories of CULTURE CHANGE, MIGRATION from tribes or peasant communities to towns and cities necessarily involves a disorienting loss of kin ties and customary behavior, in short, ACCULTURATION to an urban, nontraditional environment. Subsequent research, for example in sub-Saharan Africa and South Asia, has contradicted this view. In fact, ties between rural and urban areas often remain strong, an original tribal or ethnic affiliation may remain socially relevant, and in many cases various quarters within a city may be predominantly settled from particular villages or rural regions (Mitchell 1966:51–56; Rowe 1973). Much urban research has replaced the conventional ethnographic concern over corporate DESCENT groups with the study of NET-WORKS and voluntary ASSOCIATIONS, generally of far greater importance in towns and cities.

Urban settlement is a pervasive aspect not only of industrial societies, but of most Third World societies as well. Perhaps for this very reason the aims and unifying theoretical assumptions of an urban anthropology remain unclear. As Clifford Geertz has remarked, "The locus of study is not the object of study. Anthropologists don't study villages . . . They study *in* villages" (Geertz

1973:22). The same may be said of towns and cities. Furthermore, an older rationale, by which a local community was studied (in Warner's phrase) "as a convenient microcosm" to reveal economic and social conditions at a national level, no longer appears tenable (Warner et al. 1963:xiii; cf. Geertz 1973).

In short, the relation between the microscopic and macroscopic perspectives, between the local urban community and the total society, remains problematic. In various ways, a number of urban anthropologists advocate research that bridges these levels. Thus Anthony Leeds (1980) advocates study of the structured interrelations, both political and economic, of urban centers and rural periphery, and Jack Rollwagen (1980) would extend this to encompass the contraints imposed by a global political economy (the "world-systems" perspective; see DEVELOPMENT). Whether such research can develop in a direction that is distinctly anthropological and ethnographic remains to be seen.

References

Geertz, Clifford. 1973. "Thick Description: Toward an Interpretive Theory of Culture." C. Geertz, *The Interpretation of Cultures*. New York: Basic Books.

Gulick, John. 1973. "Urban Anthropology." John J. Honigmann, ed., *Handbook of Social and Cultural Anthropology*. Chicago: Rand McNally. A useful introduction.

Leeds, Anthony. 1980. "Towns and Villages in Society: Hierarchies in Order and Cause." Thomas W. Collins, ed., *Cities in a Larger Context*. Southern Anthropological Society, *Proceedings*, 14.

Lewis, Oscar. 1970. "The Culture of Poverty." Oscar Lewis, *Anthropological Essays*. New York: Random House.

Lynd, Robert S., and Helen M. Lynd. 1929 [1956]. *Middletown*. New York: Harcourt Brace Jovanovich.

Mitchell, J. Clyde. 1966. "Theoretical Orientations in African Urban Studies." Michael Banton, ed., *The Social Anthropology of Complex Societies*. London: Tavistock. Has an extensive bibliography.

Mumford, Lewis. 1961. *The City in History*. New York: Harcourt, Brace & World.

Redfield, Robert. 1953. *The Primitive World and Its Transformations*. Ithaca, N.Y.: Cornell University Press.

Rollwagen, Jack. 1980. "New Directions in Urban Anthropology: Building an Ethnography and an Ethnology of the World System." George Gmelch and Walter P. Zenner, eds., *Urban Life: Readings in Urban Anthropology*. New York: St. Martin's Press.

Rowe, William L. 1973. "Caste, Kinship, and Association in Urban India." Aidan Southall, ed., *Urban Anthropology: Cross-Cultural Studies of Urbanization*. New York: Oxford University Press.

Uzzell, J. Douglas, and Ronald Provencher. 1976. *Urban Anthropology*. Dubuque, Iowa: W. C. Brown. A brief, informal introduction.

Warner, W. Lloyd, et al. 1963. *Yankee City*. 1 vol., abr. New Haven, Conn.: Yale University Press. Originally published in five volumes between 1941 and 1959.

Wirth, Lewis. 1938 [1980]. "Urbanism as a Way of Life." George Gmelch and Walter P. Zenner, eds., *Urban Life: Readings in Urban Anthropology*. New York: St. Martin's Press. A classic sociological perspective.

Sources of Additional Information

An extensive bibliography is provided in Peter C. W. Gutkind, "Bibliography on Urban Anthropology," Aidan Southall, ed., *Urban Anthropology: Cross-Cultural Studies of Urbanization*, New York: Oxford University Press, 1973. An intriguing review of the development of urban anthropology is provided in Ulf Hannerz, *Exploring the City: Inquiries Toward an Urban Anthropology*, New York: Columbia University Press, 1980. A broad range of papers are included in the following anthologies: Irwin Press and M. Estellie Smith, eds., *Urban Place and Process*, New York: Macmillan, 1980; Ghaus Ansari and Peter J. M. Nas, eds., *Town-Talk: The Dynamics of Urban Anthropology*, Leiden, the Netherlands: Brill, 1983; and Leith Mullings, ed., *Cities of the United States: Studies in Urban Anthropology*, New York: Columbia University Press, 1987. See also the journal *Urban Anthropology* (1972–).

W

WAR. Organized violence between politically constituted, autonomous groups.

Modern history, from one perspective, is a chronicle of war conducted on an ever larger and more lethal scale. The Second World War, for example, caused close to thirty-five million deaths and sixty million total casualties, while the potentially universal destruction afforded by thermonuclear war has become a macabre symbol of late twentieth century life. Under these circumstances, the cross-cultural study of war has an importance far beyond narrowly ethnological issues. ANTHROPOLOGY has the potential to clarify the relation between war and biologically patterned aggression; the place of war in cultural EVOLUTION; the contrasting character of war in BANDS, TRIBES, and STATES; the relation of war and feud to other forms of dispute settlement; the conditions under which war forms part of stable as opposed to unstable and self-destructive social systems; and most significantly, the possibility of peace as a general characteristic of future societies.

The term war is derived from the Old High German *werra*, signifying confusion, discord, or strife (*OED*). War has been defined by Alvin Johnson as "armed conflict between population groups conceived of as organic unities, such as races or tribes, states or lesser geographic units, religious or political parties, economic classes" (Johnson 1934:331). Similarly, Bronislaw Malinowski described war as "an armed contest between two independent political units, by means of organized military force, in the pursuit of a tribal or national policy" (Malinowski 1941:523). In short, war involves organized violence between politically constituted, essentially autonomous entities.

War should be distinguished from warfare. While warfare refers specifically to the process of battle, war refers more broadly to the entire SYSTEM, not only military but also political, economic, and social, through which hostilities are sustained.

War and Feud

Violence between individuals occurs in all societies. In state-level societies such individual violence commonly constitutes a crime (e.g., assault or homicide), with formal mechanisms for redress and punishment imposed by LAW. Kin-based societies commonly lack such autonomous legal institutions to resolve conflict and punish offenders; hence, violence between individuals easily escalates to conflict between their respective kin. This is feud, derived from the Old High German *fehida*, enmity (*OED*). Such intergroup violence involves feud rather than war because the groups involved exist within some wider sociopolitical organization. In E. E. Evans-Pritchard's usage, feud is "lengthy mutual hostility between local communities within a tribe" (Evans-Pritchard 1940:150). More formally, Leopold Pospisil defines feud as violence "committed by members of two groups related to each other by superimposed political-structural features . . . and acting on the basis of group solidarity" (in Otterbein 1973:924).

War and Western Thought

European thought betrays a deep ambivalence regarding the ethical value of war and conflict, deriving in part from early Christian TRADITION. Recall that Jesus praised reconciliation ("Blessed are the peacemakers: for they shall be called the children of God" [Matt. 5:9]), yet defended zealotry in defense of his cause ("I came not to send peace, but a sword" [Matt. 10:34]). While there was a significant pacifist dimension to the teachings of the early church fathers, the Christian Church soon compromised this view, as in the doctrine of the just war. In assuming the role of the established religion of the empire, the Church inherited and accepted the doctrine of a *Pax Romana*, of "civil peace secured under a strong central authority" (Flower 1973:441).

Yet the peace bestowed by the strong state is paradoxical, for it comes about not through the abolition of violence, but through its monopolistic control, exerted by police, magistrates, and a standing army. In CIVILIZATION, in short, only government has recourse to legitimate force. It was in this special sense that Thomas Hobbes (1588–1679) could contrast the "peace" maintained by the state with the "war" that prevailed in the state of NATURE, that is, in the kin-based societies of band and tribe: "During the time men live without a common Power to keep them all in awe, they are in that condition which is called Warre; and such a warre, as is of every man, against every man" (Hobbes, in Slotkin 1965:160). Ironically, the economic and political power of the state makes possible a level of violence unattainable in so-called PRIMITIVE societies. As Hobbes's contemporary Hugo Grotius (1583–1645) noted, "Throughout the Christian world I observed a lack of restraint in relation to war, such as even barbarous races should be ashamed of" (Grotius, in Slotkin 1965:147). This convergence of increasingly powerful and centralized state authority with increasingly lethal military technology remains one of the key dilemmas of cultural evolution.

The Ethnography of War

Contrasting the anthropological treatment of law and war, the two dimensions of social conflict, Paul Bohannon has commented that "with some noteworthy exceptions, the ethnography on [war] is of poorer quality than that on law, and the theoretical and comparative essays are comparatively rare" (Bohannon 1967:xiii). This situation may be explained both by the ambivalence regarding war in European intellectual tradition and by the strong preference for models emphasizing harmony and stability rather than conflict and change in anthropological theory (see FUNCTIONALISM). Nonetheless, the anthropological literature on war has become extensive, though highly diverse in the level of analysis and theoretical orientation. Ferguson and Farragher's bibliography—a compilation not intended to be exhaustive—includes approximately 1,800 citations, an impressive figure even if a certain proportion is by other social scientists treating characteristically "anthropological" issues of tribal or premodern war (Ferguson and Farragher 1988).

Examples of the ETHNOGRAPHY of war in the first half of this century include Rafael Karsten's study of the Jibaro of Ecuador, Reo Fortune's of the Arapesh of New Guinea, and E. E. Evans-Pritchard's of the Nuer of the Sudan. Karsten provided both detailed descriptions of techniques of Jibaro warfare and analysis of the systems of belief underlying particular practices such as head-hunting (Karsten 1923). Fortune's treatment stressed the social organization of Arapesh war, that is, the relations of clans and sovereign localities in the undertaking of war, as well as the distinctive role of wife stealing in the generation of hostilities (Fortune 1939). Evans-Pritchard's study analyzed Nuer war and feud as part of a more comprehensive treatment of ecology, politics, and social organization. He demonstrated the key role of "segmentary opposition" as an organizational principle allowing groups to combine on the basis of unilineal kin ties for purposes of war or defense, without encumbering themselves with permanent rulers (Evans-Pritchard 1940; see DESCENT). In the same period, H. H. Turney-High published one of the few comprehensive anthropological studies, *Primitive War: Its Practice and Concepts*, a work notable for its detailed treatment of comparative tactics and military organization (Turney-High 1949).

Anthropological Theories of War

In the postwar period a variety of anthropological approaches have been applied to the cross-cultural study of war. Among these are theories that derive war from biologically grounded aggression, which explain it as part of an adaptive, functionally related complex of cultural practices, and which interpret it as a key factor in cultural evolution.

War and aggression. The relation between cultural expression and the human genotype ("instinct," "nature," etc.) has been a long-standing problem in anthropology (see SUPERORGANIC). One version of this debate—advocated chiefly by certain biologists and their amateur followers—has taken the form of explaining warfare as the direct expression of human aggression and territoriality.

The playwright Robert Ardrey has popularized a sweeping version of this argument: "If we defend the title to our land or the sovereignty of our country, we do it for reasons no different, no less innate, no less ineradicable, than do the lower animals" (in Montagu 1973:125; see also Ardrey 1961). The anthropological reaction to this highly reductionist argument has been, on the whole, strongly negative (see Montagu 1973). As Marshall Sahlins has aptly commented, "The reasons people fight are not the reasons wars take place" (Sahlins 1976:8; see also SOCIOBIOLOGY).

War and adaptation. War does not occur in isolation, but necessarily forms part of a complex cultural system, serving as both cause and consequence of other cultural features. A number of theories emphasize such functional relationships, interpreting war as part of an adaptive culture complex (see FUNCTIONALISM; ADAPTATION). Thus Napoleon Chagnon (1968) has explained chronic warfare and an ideology of male ferocity among the Yanomamo of Venezuela as serving to maintain village autonomy and maximize control of women in the context of intervillage hostility, fragile alliances, shifting settlements, and a slash-and-burn horticulture. William Divale and Marvin Harris (1976) have interpreted war in band- and tribal-level societies as a self-perpetuating system, functionally associated with polygyny, male dominance, and population control through preferential female infanticide. Functionalist interpretations of warfare have also been strongly criticized (see Hallpike 1973).

War and evolution. Herbert Spencer (1820–1903) argued that war was a key factor in sociocultural evolution. Specifically, the requirements of waging war gradually reshaped SOCIAL STRUCTURE and the political order: "A society's power of self-preservation will be great in proportion as, besides the direct aid of all who can fight, there is given the indirect aid of all who cannot fight" (Spencer 1876:189). Robert Carneiro (1970) has developed this perspective in explaining the evolution of the state through war conducted by environmentally circumscribed societies (i.e., those with a sharply delimited resource base). A broader effort at explaining war in evolutionary terms has been undertaken by Keith Otterbein (1985).

References

Ardrey, Robert. 1961. *African Genesis*. New York: Dell. An influential if dubious statement of the biological roots of war.

Bohannon, Paul. 1967. "Introduction." Paul Bohannon, ed., *Law and Warfare: Studies in the Anthropology of Conflict*. Garden City, N.Y.: Natural History Press

Carneiro, Robert L. 1970. "A Theory of the Origin of the State." *Science* 169:733–38.

Chagnon, Napoleon A. 1968. "Yanomamo Social Organization and Warfare." Morton Fried et al., eds., *War: The Anthropology of Armed Conflict and Aggression*. Garden City, N.Y.: Natural History Press.

Divale, William T., and Marvin Harris. 1976. "Population, Warfare, and the Male Supremacist Complex." *AA* 78:521–38.

Evans-Pritchard, E. E. 1940. *The Nuer*. New York: Oxford University Press. A classic work linking social structure, ecology, and cultural norms favoring warfare.

Ferguson, R. Brian, and Leslie E. Farragher. 1988. *The Anthropology of War: A Bibliography*. Occasional Papers of the Harry Frank Guggenheim Foundation (New York), no. 1. A major (361 pages) bibliographic source.

Flower, Elizabeth. 1973. "Ethics of Peace." *DHI* 3:440–47.

Fortune, Reo. 1939. "Arapesh Warfare." *AA* 41:22–41.

Hallpike, C. R. 1973. "Functionalist Interpretations of Primitive Warfare." *Man* (n.s.) 8:451–70. A strong critique of functionalist analyses.

Johnson, Alvin. 1934. "War." *ESS* 15:331–42. A useful survey from a broad social science perspective.

Karsten, Rafael. 1923 [1967]. "Blood Revenge and War among the Jibaro Indians of Eastern Ecuador." Paul Bohannon, ed., *Law and Warfare*. Garden City, N.Y.: Natural History Press [extract].

Malinowski, Bronislaw. 1941. "An Anthropological Analysis of War." *American Journal of Sociology* 46:521–50.

Montagu, Ashley, ed. 1973. *Man and Aggression*. 2d ed. New York: Oxford University Press. A strong critique of biological determinist theories of war.

Otterbein, Keith F. 1973. "The Anthropology of War." John J. Honigmann, ed., *Handbook of Social and Cultural Anthropology*. Chicago: Rand McNally. A useful overview of anthropological theories of war.

———. 1985. *The Evolution of War: A Cross-Cultural Study*. New Haven, Conn.: HRAF Press. An evolutionary study based on cross-cultural survey data.

Sahlins, Marshall D. 1976. *The Use and Abuse of Biology*. Ann Arbor: University of Michigan Press. A critique of sociobiology.

Slotkin, J. S. 1965. *Readings in Early Anthropology*. Viking Fund Publications in Anthropology, 40. New York: Wenner-Gren Foundation.

Spencer, Herbert. 1876 [1972]. *On Social Evolution: Selected Writings*. J. D. Y. Peel, ed. Chicago: University of Chicago Press.

Turney-High, Harry H. 1949. *Primitive War: Its Practice and Concepts*. Columbia: University of South Carolina Press. An excellent survey, emphasizing military organization.

Sources of Additional Information

Jeffrey P. Blick, "Genocidal Warfare in Tribal Societies as a Result of European-Induced Culture Conflict," *Man* (n.s.) 23:654–70, 1988, argues for the effects of European culture-contact on war in tribal societies. Marshall D. Sahlins, *Tribesmen*, Englewood Cliffs, N.J.: Prentice-Hall, 1968, ch. 1, contains a useful discussion of war and peace in state and tribal societies.

WITCHCRAFT. A system of belief postulating the exertion of malign supernatural influence, not through the use of specific techniques (as in magic), but by virtue of certain indwelling powers or cooperating spirits.

Witchcraft, the powers or practices of witches, has its root in the Old English *wicca*, a sorcerer, from which "wicked" also derives. Anthropologists have applied the term to patterns of belief in a wide range of CULTURES. Because the concept of the witch is so strongly polarized in European tradition, there is a danger that specifically Western assumptions will distort the analysis of non-Western realities. At least in anthropological usage, a distinction is generally drawn between witchcraft and sorcery, witchcraft being believed to operate through an indwelling power of the witch, or of spirit familiars, sorcery through the performance of MAGIC, which will be effective for anyone possessing the proper spell (see Lieban 1967). Thus, "a witch performs no rite, utters no spell, and possesses no medicines. An act of witchcraft is a psychic act" (Evans-Pritchard 1937:21).

Western Conceptions of Witchcraft

The perspective of ancient Judaism toward magic and related arts appears to have been similar to that of many tribal cultures described by anthropologists. Diviners, sorcerers and the like were regarded with fear and suspicion, being associated with the supposedly idolatrous enemies of Israel (Deut. 18:10); their powers could, however, be harnessed to useful ends, as Saul found in consulting the Witch of Endor (1 Sam. 28). In contrast, the WORLD VIEW of later post-exilic Judaism (after perhaps 200 BC) was marked by a complex demonology, which assumed the active involvement of hosts of demons spreading evil throughout the world. This perspective, possibly the result of Iranian influences on Judaism, was formative for early Christianity (Cohn 1970).

The Western association of witchcraft with satanic worship was largely a late medieval creation of the Inquisition, which linked an existing demonology to the alleged actions of human collaborators. Witchcraft was perceived to be wholly malign, "a form of magic whereby with the help of a demon one man does an injury to another" (Guazzo 1608:163). Magical practices, which as an element of European FOLK CULTURE had coexisted with Christianity for centuries, were transformed in the European imagination into a collage of witches' sabbaths, devil worship, and cannibalistic feasts, resulting in the terrible witch trials of the sixteenth and seventeenth centuries, in which hundreds of thousands perished (Cohn 1970:7–12).

Witchcraft in Tribal Societies

The conception of witchcraft that has emerged from the ethnographic literature is altogether different. Although historians' accounts of European witchcraft trials suggest an unusual and disruptive phenomenon, witchcraft in tribal societies commonly forms part of a stable system of belief and social control through which misfortune is explained, deviance categorized, and social friction diagnosed and treated. In this context witchcraft scarcely pertains to overt behavior at all. Rather, it explains adverse events—sickness, blighted crops, a collapsing granary—by attributing them to an individual's malign influence, the result of an inner psychic capacity, often exerted unconsciously.

Most anthropological studies of witchcraft have been based on the perspective of FUNCTIONALISM, emphasizing the adaptive character of the witchcraft complex, either at a psychological or social level of explanation. One of the pioneering studies in this field, Clyde Kluckhohn's *Navaho Witchcraft*, stressed the important functions of witchcraft accusations in socializing the young, releasing aggression, and allaying anxiety (Kluckhohn 1944:95–111; see also PER-

SONALITY). Equally, witchcraft can serve as an economic leveling mechanism: "A rich man knows that if he is stingy with his relatives or fails to dispense generous hospitality . . . he is likely to be spoken of as a witch" (Kluckhohn 1944:111). In the fine-grained studies of social relations common in modern ETHNOGRAPHY, accusations of witchcraft (and sorcery) are commonly analyzed as extensions of existing rivalries (Marwick 1967:125–126; Epstein 1967).

An alternative approach to the ANTHROPOLOGY of witchcraft was provided by E. E. Evans-Pritchard's highly influential study *Witchcraft, Oracles and Magic among the Azande*. Evans-Pritchard's major concern involved the sociology of knowledge, depicting an alien system of thought so as to expose its underlying RATIONALITY (see Douglas 1970). Although his study also employed functionalist assumptions, its strength and originality lay in demonstrating that Azande belief in witchcraft, witch doctors (who identify witches), oracles, and TABOO collectively created a closed and consistent cultural system through which misfortune could be explained and ideological contradictions resolved (Evans-Pritchard 1937). More recently, the influential distinction that Evans-Pritchard formulated between witchcraft and sorcery has been criticized as arbitrary and alien to indigenous conceptions (Turner 1967). In a similar vein, I. M. Lewis has argued that witchcraft should not be studied as an isolated phenomenon but considered in relation to such patterns of belief as spirit possession and SHAMANISM (Lewis 1986: ch. 3).

References

Cohn, Norman. 1970. "The Myth of Satan and His Human Servants." Mary Douglas, ed., *Witchcraft Confessions and Accusations*. London: Tavistock. A historian's analysis of the origins of medieval witchcraft beliefs.

Douglas, Mary. 1970. "Introduction: Thirty Years after *Witchcraft, Oracles and Magic*." Mary Douglas, ed., *Witchcraft Confessions and Accusations*. London: Tavistock.

Epstein, Scarlett. 1967. "A Sociological Analysis of Witch Beliefs in a Mysore Village." John Middleton, ed., *Magic, Witchcraft, and Curing*. Garden City, N.Y.: Natural History Press. On witchcraft in south India.

Evans-Pritchard, E. E. 1937. *Witchcraft, Oracles and Magic among the Azande*. Oxford: Clarendon Press. The classic study.

Guazzo, Francesco. 1608 [1970]. *Compendium Maleficarum*. Montague Summers, ed. E. A. Ashwin, trans. New York: Barnes & Noble.

Kluckhohn, Clyde. 1944 [1967]. *Navaho Witchcraft*. Boston: Beacon Press. An influential work, drawing on functionalism and psychological anthropology.

Lewis, I. M. 1986. *Religion in Context: Cults and Charisma*. Cambridge: Cambridge University Press. Recommended.

Lieban, Richard W. 1967. *Cebuano Sorcery: Malign Magic in the Philippines*. Berkeley and Los Angeles: University of California Press.

Marwick, M. G. 1967. "The Sociology of Sorcery in a Central African Tribe." John Middleton, ed., *Magic, Witchcraft, and Curing*. Garden City, N.Y.: Natural History Press.

Turner, Victor. 1967. "Witchcraft and Sorcery: Taxonomy versus Dynamics." V. Turner,

The Forest of Symbols: Aspects of Ndembu Ritual. Ithaca, N.Y.: Cornell University Press. Opposes the witchcraft/sorcery distinction.

Sources of Additional Information

For the European perspective see Alan C. Kors and Edward Peters, *Witchcraft in Europe, 1100–1700: A Documentary History*, Philadelphia: University of Pennsylvania Press, 1972. A highly readable ethnography is provided by William S. Simmons, *Eyes of the Night: Witchcraft among a Senegalese People*, Boston: Little, Brown, 1971.

WORLD VIEW. The underlying logic and guiding assumptions of a culture, regarding such categories of experience as time, causality, nature, society, and the self.

World view originally appeared in English as a translation of the German *Weltanschauung*. In the work of the philosopher Wilhelm Dilthey (1833–1911), "a *Weltanschauung* . . . is an overall perspective on life, which encompasses the way a person perceives the world, evaluates and responds to it" (Makkreel 1975:346). The connotations of *Weltanschauung* are quite broad: *Welt* signifies not only world but earth, people, society, humanity, and even the universe generally, while *Anschauung* involves not merely a view, but an act of contemplation (New Cassell's Dictionary). Thus "world view," at least in its anthropological use, has a broad, philosophical, and abstract character. For the anthropologist Robert Redfield (1897–1958) a world view encompassed "that outlook upon the universe that is characteristic of a people . . . the picture the members of a society have of the properties and characters upon their stage of action" (Redfield 1952:270).

The concept of world view is exemplified in the work of a number of European culture historians. In the writings of Wilhelm Dilthey world view offered an important tool of historical and aesthetic analysis (see HISTORICISM). The study of Renaissance Italy by the Swiss historian Jacob Burckhardt (1818–1897) considered not only political history, but sketched the emergence of a distinctly Renaissance understanding of the individual, the state, and the value of classical antiquity (Burckhardt 1860). Oswald Spengler (1880–1936), in his widely read *Decline of the West*, presented the history of CIVILIZATIONS as a sequence of radically incompatible world views. Among these he included the Apollinian (Apollonian) of classical antiquity, with its emphasis on sensuous form, balance, and repose, exhibited alike in Euclidian geometry and classical sculpture; and the Faustian of post-medieval Europe, concerned with movement and limitless perspective, seen for example in Gothic architecture and romantic music (Spengler 1928:97–100). For Spengler, "every Culture possesses a wholly individual way of looking at and comprehending the world-as-Nature" (Spengler 1928:78).

Anthropological Studies

An anthropological interest in world view is apparently a twentieth-century phenomenon, at least in the English-speaking world. Such studies implied a recognition of the intellectual validity and importance of non-Western patterns of thought and value, particularly those of smaller, technologically simple societies (see RATIONALITY; PRIMITIVE).

Working from the perspective of the diffusionist *Kulturkreislehre* (see DIFFUSION), Leo Frobenius (1873–1938) included an extensive discussion of style, world view, and MYTH in his synoptic study of African cultures (Frobenius 1933). Within French ANTHROPOLOGY, a uniquely detailed and sympathetic account of a tribal philosophy and world view—that of the African Dogon— was provided by Marcel Griaule and colleagues (Griaule and Dieterlen 1954). In her studies of contrasting world views, Dorothy Lee has stressed the culture-bound character of many fundamental Western assumptions, for example, notions of time and causality. Thus in contrast to a Western ideal of historical progress, "to the Trobriander, climax in history is abominable, a denial of all good, since it would imply not only the presence of change, but also that change increases the good. . . . What is good in life is exact identity with all past Trobriand experience, and all mythical experience" (Lee 1950:117).

A number of anthropologists have utilized world view as a means of analyzing the distinctive character of PEASANTRY. Redfield approached this through his concept of FOLK CULTURE, characterized by stability, social homogeneity, and pervasive RITUAL, with a strong sense of group identity and the obligatory character of TRADITION—all standing in strong contrast to the perspective of URBANISM. George Foster has presented a quite different sense of the peasant world view, characterized by what he termed the "image of limited good." For Foster,

> peasants view their social, economic, and natural universes—their total environment—as one in which all of the desired things in life such as land, wealth, health, friendship and love, manliness and honor, respect and status, power and influence, security and safety, exist in finite quantity and are always in short supply. . . . It follows that an individual or a family can improve a position only at the expense of others. (Foster 1965:296–97)

This thesis has been controversial (see Gregory 1975).

World View and Cultural Knowledge

Although the concept of world view is intended to synthesize the subjective aspects of CULTURE, the phrase nonetheless suggests (at least in English) a restriction of cultural knowledge to the domain of explicit propositions. It is a people's "picture of the way things in sheer actuality are, their concept of nature, of self, of society" (Geertz 1973:127). However, much that is essential to the cultural mediation of experience—questions of underlying motive, style, and value—cannot be effectively verbalized. As Edward Sapir noted, "Relations between the elements of experience which serve to give them their form and significance are more powerfully 'felt' or 'intuited' than consciously perceived" (Sapir 1927:548). We act, as Sapir said, regarding the interpretation of gesture, "in accordance with an elaborate and secret code that is written nowhere, known by none, and understood by all" (Sapir 1927:556).

For some authors, this suggests a need for paired concepts, an explicit and rational world view complemented by an implicitly grasped ethos. Thus for Gregory Bateson, ethos involved "a culturally standardised system of organisation of the instincts and emotions" (Bateson 1936:118). Geertz, similarly, has described a people's ethos as "the tone, character, and quality of their life, its moral and aesthetic style and mood" (Geertz 1973:127). Clyde Kluckhohn's contrast of overt culture and covert culture expressed a similar insight (Kluckhohn 1943). Such distinctions have not, however, been consistently observed. It may be more satisfactory simply to acknowledge the complex character of world view or *Weltanschauung* and to insist that a rendering of cultural knowledge not be artificially limited—as is true in ETHNOSCIENCE—to the domain of language and the process of classification (see Kearney 1975:247–48). In the postwar period the various modalities of cultural knowledge have also been explored through the study of SYMBOLISM

References

Bateson, Gregory. 1936 [1958]. *Naven*. 2d ed. Stanford, Calif.: Stanford University Press.
Burckhardt, Jacob. 1860 [1958]. *The Civilization of the Renaissance in Italy*. 2 vols. S. G. C. Middlemore, trans. New York: Harper & Brothers. An early analysis of cultural distinctiveness and world view.
Foster, G. M. 1965. "Peasant Society and the Image of Limited Good." *AA* 67:293–315. An influential thesis regarding the effect of world view on peasant life.
Frobenius, Leo. 1933 [1954]. *Kulturgeschichte Afrikas*. Zurich: Phaidon.
Geertz, Clifford. 1973. "Ethos, World View, and the Analysis of Sacred Symbols." C. Geertz, *The Interpretation of Cultures*. New York: Basic Books.
Gregory, James R. 1975. "Image of Limited Good, or Expectation of Reciprocity?" *CA* 16:73–92. A discussion of Foster's thesis.
Griaule, Marcel, and Germaine Dieterlen. 1954. "The Dogon of the French Sudan." Daryll Forde, ed., *African Worlds*. London: Oxford University Press.
Kearney, Michael. 1975. "World View Theory and Study." *ARA* 4:247–70. A useful review with extensive references.
Kluckhohn, Clyde. 1943. "Covert Culture and Administrative Problems." *AA* 45:213–27.
Lee, Dorothy. 1950 [1959]. "Codifications of Reality: Lineal and Nonlineal." D. Lee, *Freedom and Culture*. N.p.: Prentice-Hall. Lee stresses the arbitrary character of the Euro-American world view.
Makkreel, Rudolf A. 1975. *Dilthey: Philosopher of the Human Studies*. Princeton, N.J.: Princeton University Press.
Redfield, Robert. 1952 [1962]. "The Primitive World View." R. Redfield, *Human Nature and the Study of Society*. [Papers, vol. 1.] Margaret P. Redfield, ed. Chicago: University of Chicago Press.
Sapir, Edward. 1927 [1949]. "The Unconscious Patterning of Behavior in Society." David G. Mandelbaum, ed., *Selected Writings of Edward Sapir in Language, Culture and Personality*. Berkeley and Los Angeles: University of California Press.

Spengler, Oswald. 1928 [1962]. *The Decline of the West*. 1 vol., abr. Charles F. Atkinson, trans. New York: Modern Library.

Sources of Additional Information

Walter J. Ong, "World as View and World as Event," *AA* 71:634–47, 1969, offers an interesting critique, arguing that the concept of world view may itself be culture-bound. A variety of world views are presented in Stanley Diamond, ed., *Primitive Views of the World*, New York: Columbia University Press, 1960. A critical review of the concept and pertinent anthropological research is provided in Michael Kearney, *World View*, Novato, Calif.: Chandler & Sharp, 1984.

Name Index

Ackerknecht, Erwin, 67
Acosta, Joseph de, 101
Adelung, Johann Christoph, 53, 62
Allen, Elizabeth, 270
Allport, Gordon, 214
American Ethnological Society, 102
Anthropological Society of London, 13, 102
Aquinas, Saint Thomas, 88
Ardener, Edwin, 135
Ardrey, Robert, 320
Arensberg, Conrad, 41
Argyll, George J. D. Campbell, 8th Duke of, 284
Aristotle, 40; class, 143; concept of the state, 273; economics of, 88; language, 157; myth, 193
Arnold, Matthew, 51
Augustine, Saint, 146

Bachofen, Johann, 76, 134, 287
Bailey, F. G., 309
Bandelier, Adolph, 67
Barlett, Peggy, 212
Barth, Fredrik: caste, 29; ethnicity, 96; generative models, 265; social change, 65; transactional perspective, 56
Bartholomaeus Anglicus, 214
Barton, R. F., 165

Bascom, William, 125
Bastian, Adolph, 61, 223
Bateson, Gregory, 209, 291-92, 326
Bayle, Pierre, 194
Beals, Alan, 42
Beattie, John, 245
Belo, Jane, 305
Bender, Donald, 117
Benedict, Ruth: configurationism, 215; culture pattern, 208; historicism, 54; relativism, 237; ritual, 245
Berlin, Brent, 105
Berndt, Ronald, 307, 310
Bernier, Francois, 227
Berreman, Gerald, 106
Beuchat, Henri, 24
Blumenbach, Johann Friedrich, 228, 229
Blundell, V., 271
Boas, Franz: acculturation, 4; comparative method, 45, 111; critique of superorganic, 282; culture, 53-54; culture history, 103; culture pattern, 208; diffusion, 83, 84; historicism, 140; influence of Dilthey, 208; Kwakiutl ethnography, 99; linguistic relativity, 160; native view, 91; phonology, 159; plasticity of human types, 230; race and intellect, 230; rejection of materialism, 183; relativism, 236, 237; ritual,

247; symbolism, 287; tradition and
change, 302
Bock, Kenneth, 271
Boemus, Johann, 71, 101, 176
Bohannon, Paul, 117, 319
Boissevain, Jeremy, 202
Bouglé, Celestin, 28
Bourdieu, Pierre, 58
Bourguignon, Erika, 304
Bowrey, Thomas, 71
Brinton, Daniel, 158
Broca, Paul, 229
Brodie, B. C., 16
Bruno, Giordano, 167
Buckle, Henry, 34
Burckhardt, Jacob, 324
Bureau of American Ethnology, 17, 99
Bureau of Indian Affairs, 17
Burke, Edmund, 143, 301

Caamano, Jacinto, 31
Carlyle, Thomas, 287
Carneiro, Robert, 273, 320
Cassirer, Ernst, 287
Ch'ien, Ssu-ma, 255
Chagnon, Napoleon, 320
Chambers, Robert, 182
Chardin, John, 7
Chateaubriand, Francois René, Vicomte
de, 236
Chayanov, A. V., 211, 212
Childe, V. Gordon, 35
Chirino, Pedro, 23
Chomsky, Noam, 38, 56
Cicero, Marcus Tullius, 51, 127, 283
Clement of Alexandria, 218
Clements, Forrest, 67
Clifford, James, 58
Cobbett, William, 258
Codrington, R. H., 171
Cohen, Gary, 96
Cohen, Yehudi, 56
Comte, Auguste, 280
Condorcet, Marie Jean A. N. de Caritat,
Marquis de, 24, 108, 240
Conklin, Harold, 48
Cook, James, 295

Crawley, Ernest, 233, 285
Cushing, Frank, 99

Darwin, Charles: cultural evolution, 109;
influence on materialism, 182; natural
selection, 7-8, 268; primitive society,
23-24
Davies, John, 71
De Heusch, Luc, 256
De Vos, George, 96
Degérando, J. M., 88, 98
Democritus of Abdera, 181
Descartes, René, 301
Devereux, George, 305
Diamond, Stanley, 220
Diderot, Denis, 182, 220
Dilthey, Wilhelm, 140, 147-48, 207, 324
Divale, William, 320
Dobzhansky, Theodosius, 230
Dogbe, Korsi, 42
Douglas, Mary, 244, 297
Dow, James, 257
DuBois, Cora, 216
Dubois, J. A., 28
Dumont, Louis, 35, 145, 178-79, 278
Dundes, Alan, 124
Durkheim, Emile: analysis of symbolism,
288; collective representations, 236;
cultural classification, 105; defines reli-
gion, 239; folk/urban contrast, 121;
foundations of structuralism, 276;
functionalism, 54; magic and religion,
169; religion and social structure, 241;
ritual and the sacred, 248; social facts,
262, 281; social theory, 129; taboo and
the sacred, 296, 297; totemism, 299;
tradition and change, 302

Eggan, Fred, 45
Eliade, Mircea, 256, 257
Ellen, Roy, 62
Engels, Friedrich, 145, 183, 258
Epstein, A. L., 203
Errington, Frederick, 136
Ethnological Society of London, 102
Evans-Pritchard, E. E.: anthropology of
religion, 240; Azande witchcraft, 67,
91, 234, 323; cultural ecology, 47;

Subject Index

Note: *Italicized* page numbers refer to main entries.

About the Author

ROBERT H. WINTHROP is the principal of Winthrop Associates Cultural Research and an Adjunct Professor at Southern Oregon State College. He edited the 1990 book *Culture and the Anthropological Tradition* and contributed a chapter to *Living with the Land* and has published in *Anthropology Quarterly*.